INUYASHA

VOL. 4

Action Edition

STORY AND ART BY
RUMIKO TAKAHASHI

CONTENTS

Long ago, in the "Warring States" era of Japan's Muromachi period (Sengoku-jidai, approximately 1467-1568 CE), a legendary doglike half-demon called "Inu-Yasha" attempted to steal the Shikon Jewel, or "Jewel of Four Souls," from a village, but was stopped by the enchanted arrow of the village priestess, Kikyo. Inu-Yasha fell into a deep sleep, pinned to a tree by Kikyo's arrow, while the mortally wounded Kikyo took the Shikon Jewel with her into the fires of her funeral pyre. Years passed.

Fast forward to the present day. Kagome, a Japanese high school girl, is pulled into a well one day by a mysterious centipede monster, and finds herself transported into the past, only to come face to face with the trapped Inu-Yasha. She frees him, and Inu-Yasha easily defeats the centipede monster.

The residents of the village, now fifty years older, readily accept Kagome as the reincarnation of their deceased priestess Kikyo, a claim supported by the fact that the Shikon Jewel emerges from a cut on Kagome's body. Unfortunately, the jewel's rediscovery means that the village is soon under attack by a variety of demons in search of this treasure. Then, the jewel is accidentally shattered into many shards, each of which may have the fearsome power of the entire jewel.

Although Inu-Yasha says he hates Kagome because of her resemblance to Kikyo, the woman who "killed" him, he is forced to team up with her when Kaede, the village leader, binds him to Kagome with a powerful spell. Now the two grudging companions must fight to reclaim and reassemble the shattered shards of the Shikon Jewel before they fall into the wrong hands.

THIS VOLUME Two demons with the power of thunder and lightning, a new traveling companion, and a tragic young ghost.

INU-YASHA

A half-human, half-demon hybrid, Inu-Yasha has doglike ears, a thick mane of white hair, and demonic strength. Hoping to increase his demonic powers, he once stole the Shikon Jewel from a village, but was cast into a fifty-year sleep by the arrow of the village priestess, Kikyo, who died as a result of the battle. Now, he assists Kagome in her search for the shards of the Jewel, mostly because he has no choice in the matter—a charmed necklace allows Kagome to restrain him with a single word.

KAGOME

A Japanese schoolgirl from the modern day who is also the reincarnation of Kikyo, the priestess who imprisoned Inu-Yasha for fifty years with her enchanted arrow. As Kikyo's reincarnation, Kagome has the power to see the Shikon Jewel shards, even ones hidden within a demon's body.

MYOGA

Servant to Inu-Yasha, this flea-demon often offers sage advice, but he is also the first to flee when a situation turns dangerous. His powers are unknown, but his flealike blood-sucking seems to have the ability to weaken certain spells.

SHIPPO

A young fox-demon, orphaned by two other demons whose powers had been boosted by the Shikon Jewel, the mischievous Shippo enjoys goading Inu-Yasha and playing tricks with his shape-changing abilities.

SCROLL ONE

THE THUNDER BROTHERS

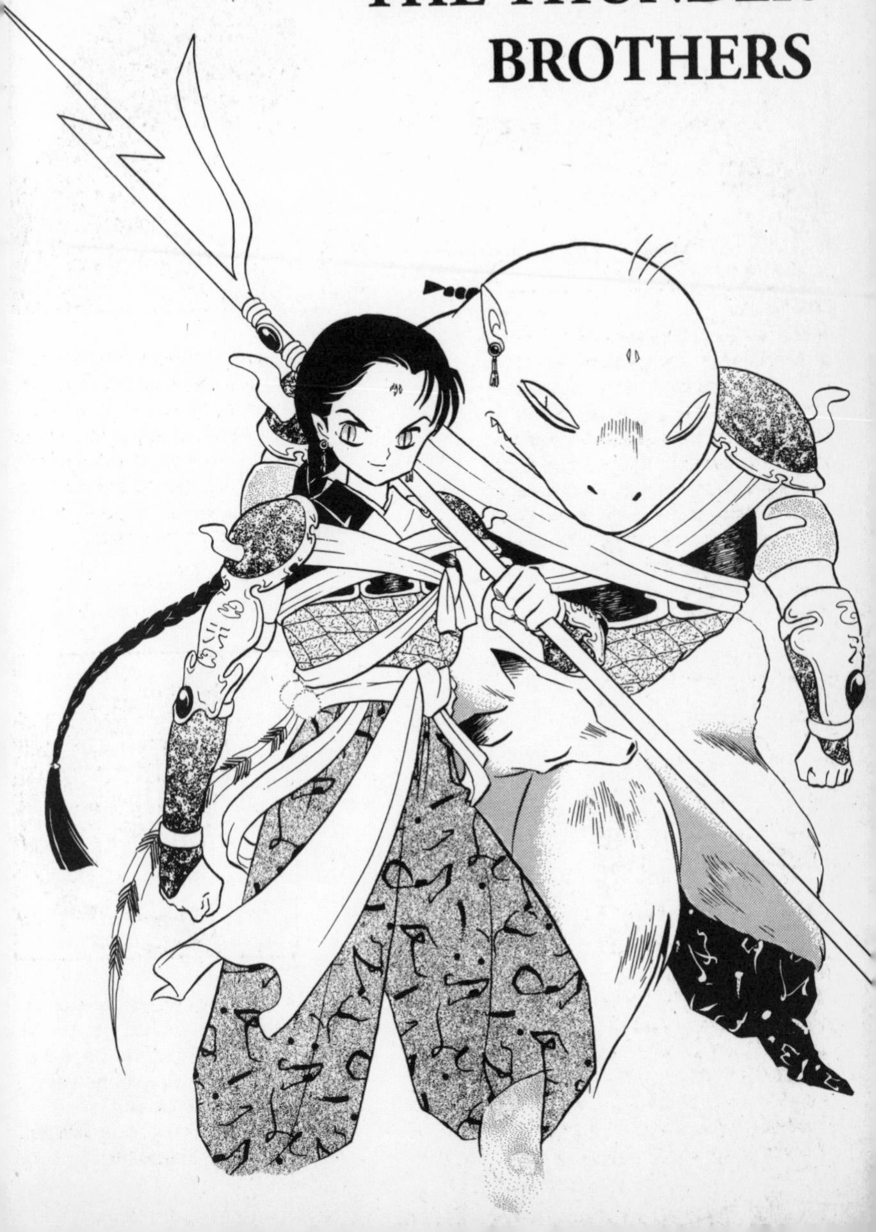

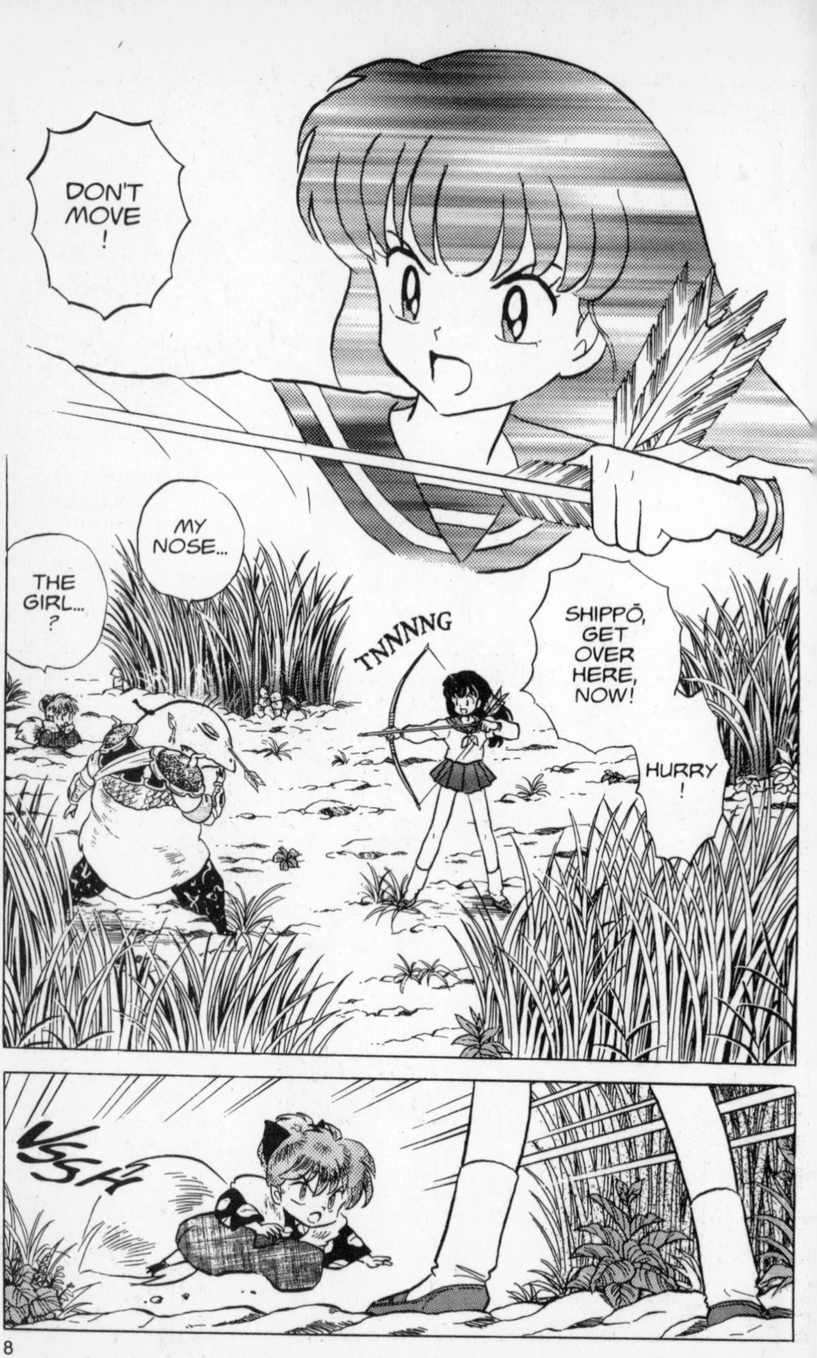

DON'T MOVE !
THE GIRL... ?
MY NOSE...
TNNNNG
SHIPPŌ, GET OVER HERE, NOW!
HURRY !
VSSH

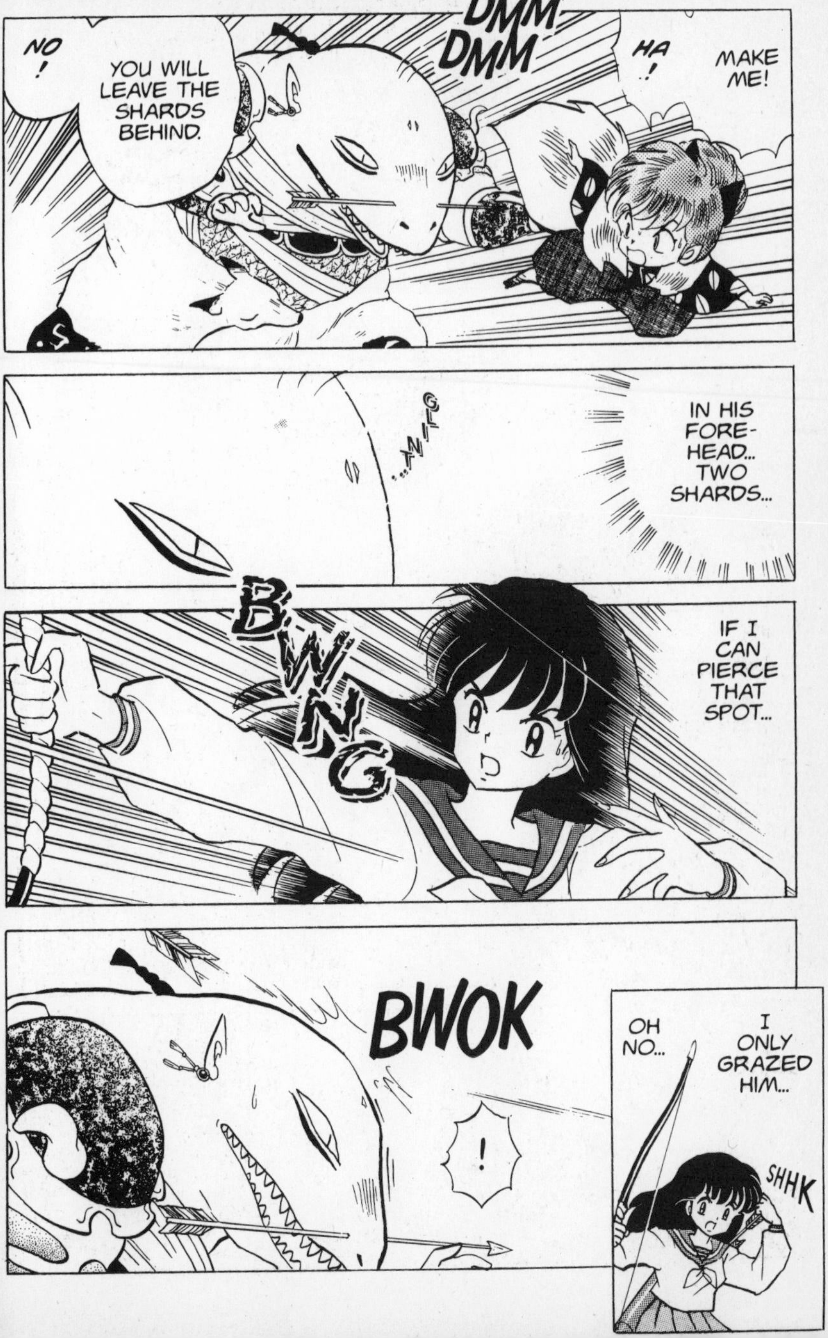

NO!
YOU WILL LEAVE THE SHARDS BEHIND.
DMM DMM
HA!
MAKE ME!
GLINT...
IN HIS FORE-HEAD... TWO SHARDS...
BWNG
IF I CAN PIERCE THAT SPOT...
BWOK
!
OH NO...
I ONLY GRAZED HIM...
SHHK

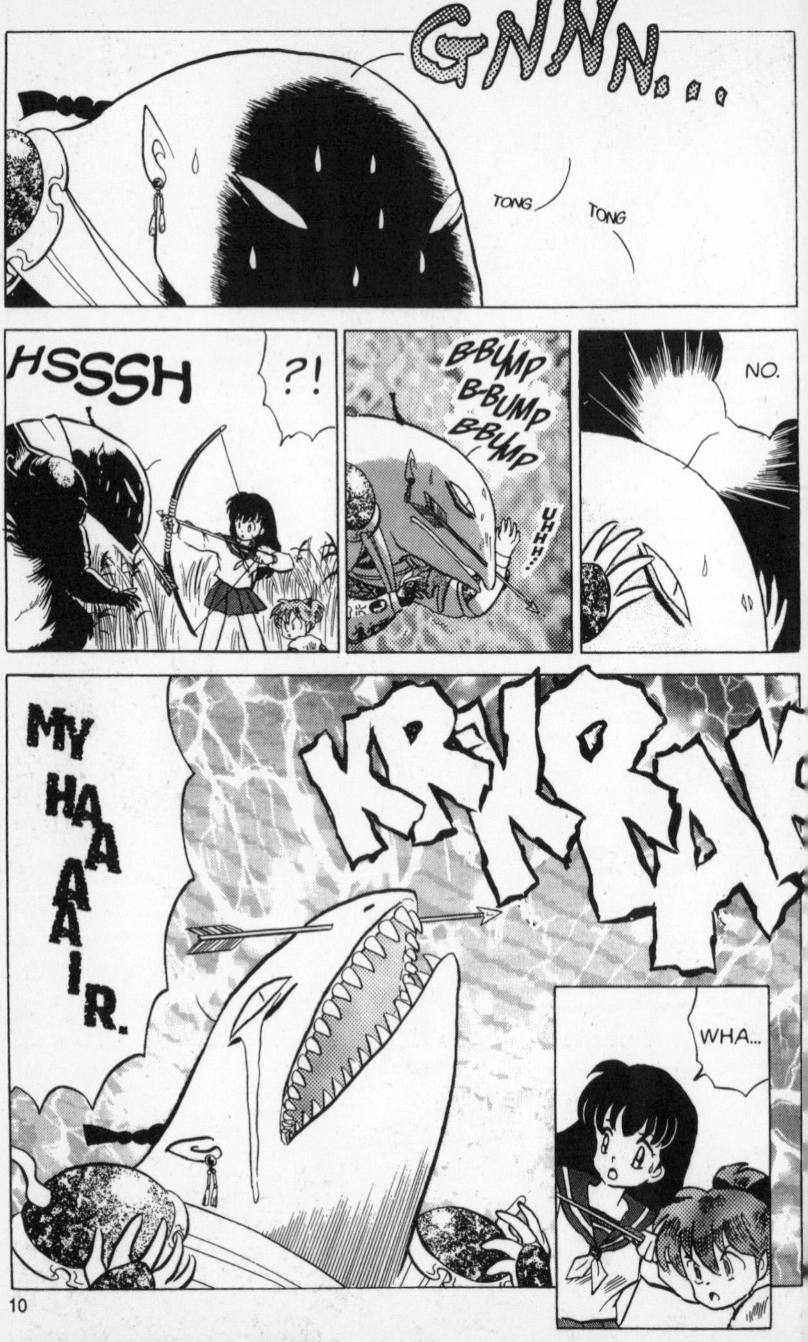

GNNN...
TONG
TONG
HSSSH
?!
B-BUMP
B-BUMP
B-BUMP
UHHH...
NO.
MY HAAAAIR.
KRKRAK
WHA...

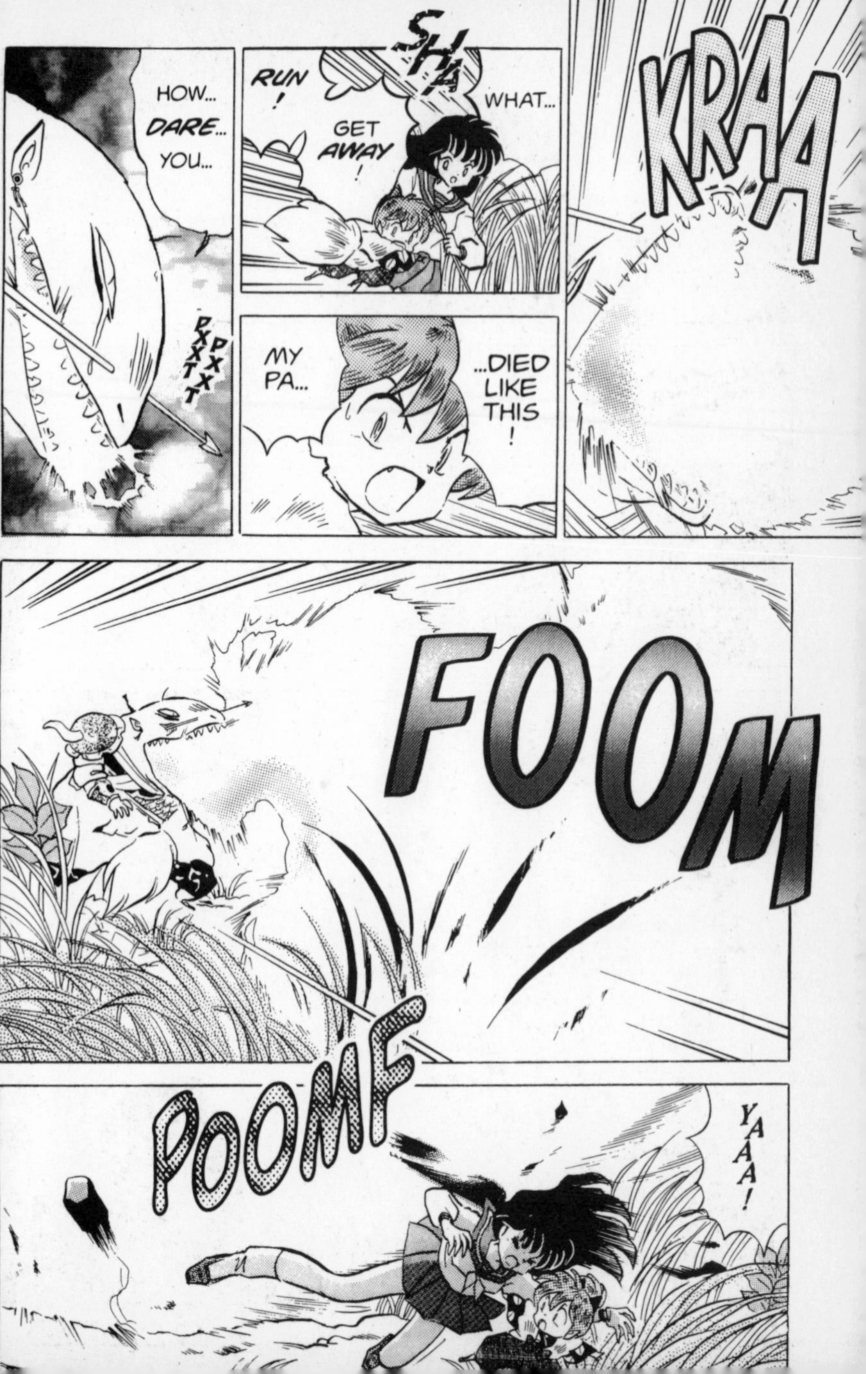
HOW... DARE... YOU...
PXXT
PXXT
SHA
RUN!
GET AWAY!
WHAT...
MY PA...
...DIED LIKE THIS!
KRAA
FOOM
POOMF
YAAA!

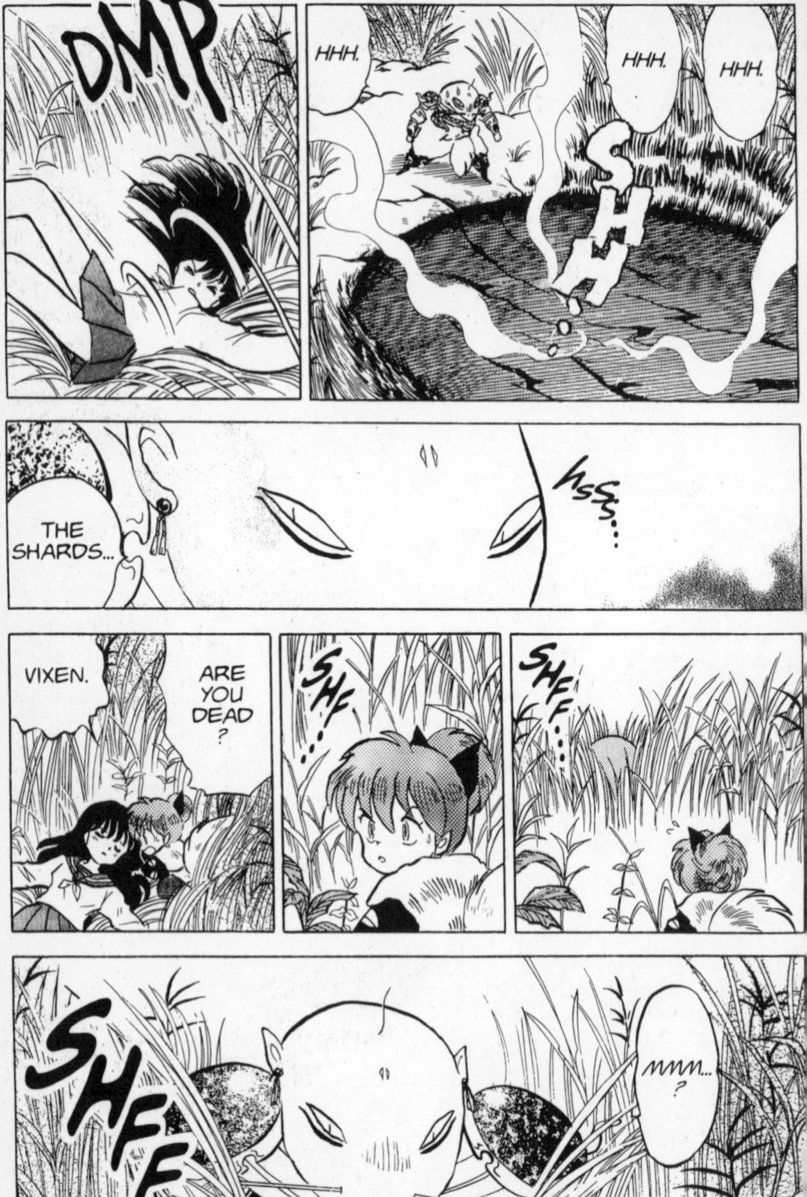
DMP
HHH.
HHH.
HHH.
SHH
THE SHARDS...
HSSS...
VIXEN.
ARE YOU DEAD?
SHF...
SHFF...
SHFF
MMM...?

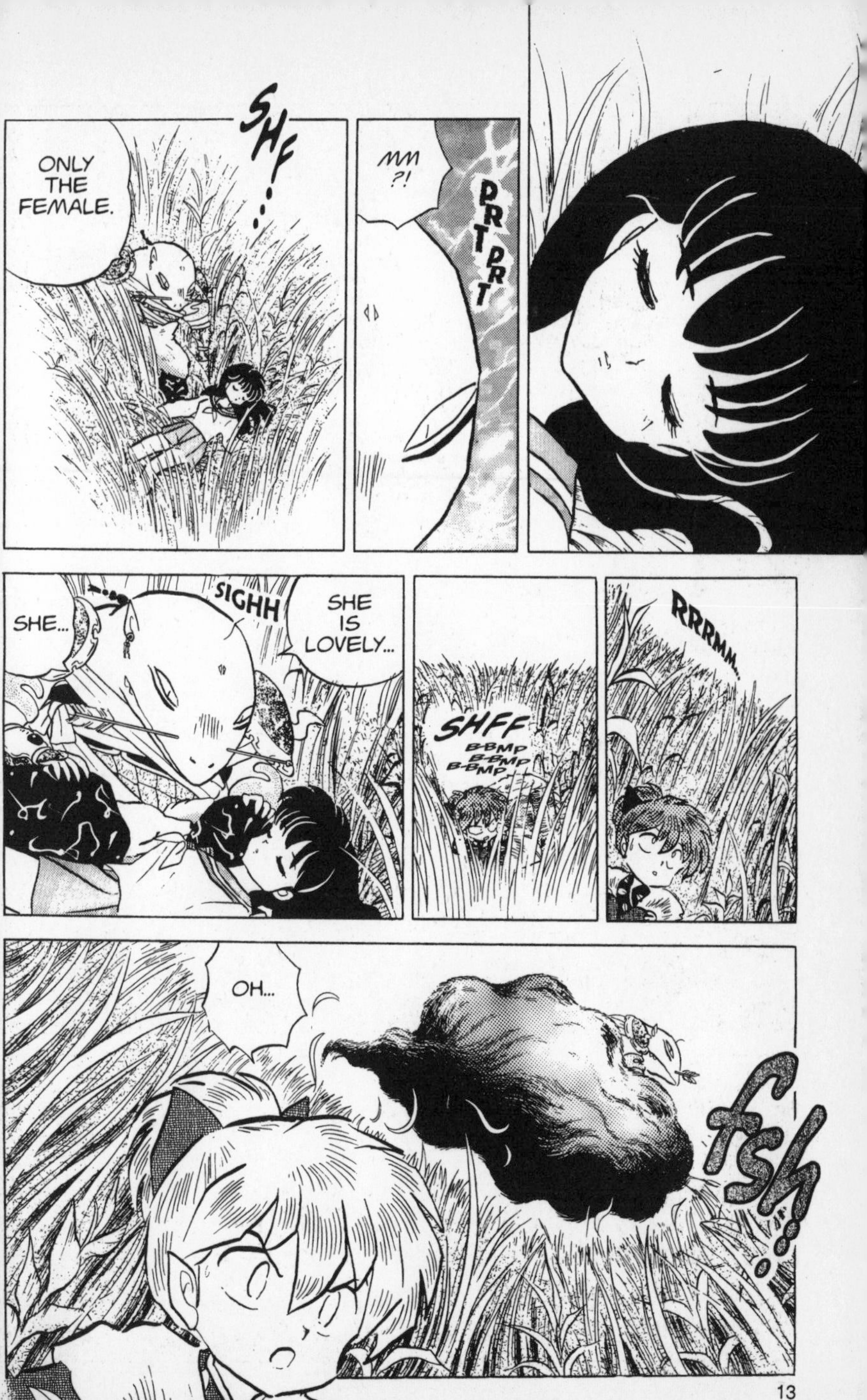
ONLY THE FEMALE.
SHF...
MM ?!
PRT PRT PRT
SHE...
SIGHH
SHE IS LOVELY...
SHFF
B-BMP B-BMP B-BMP
RRRMM...
OH...
fsh

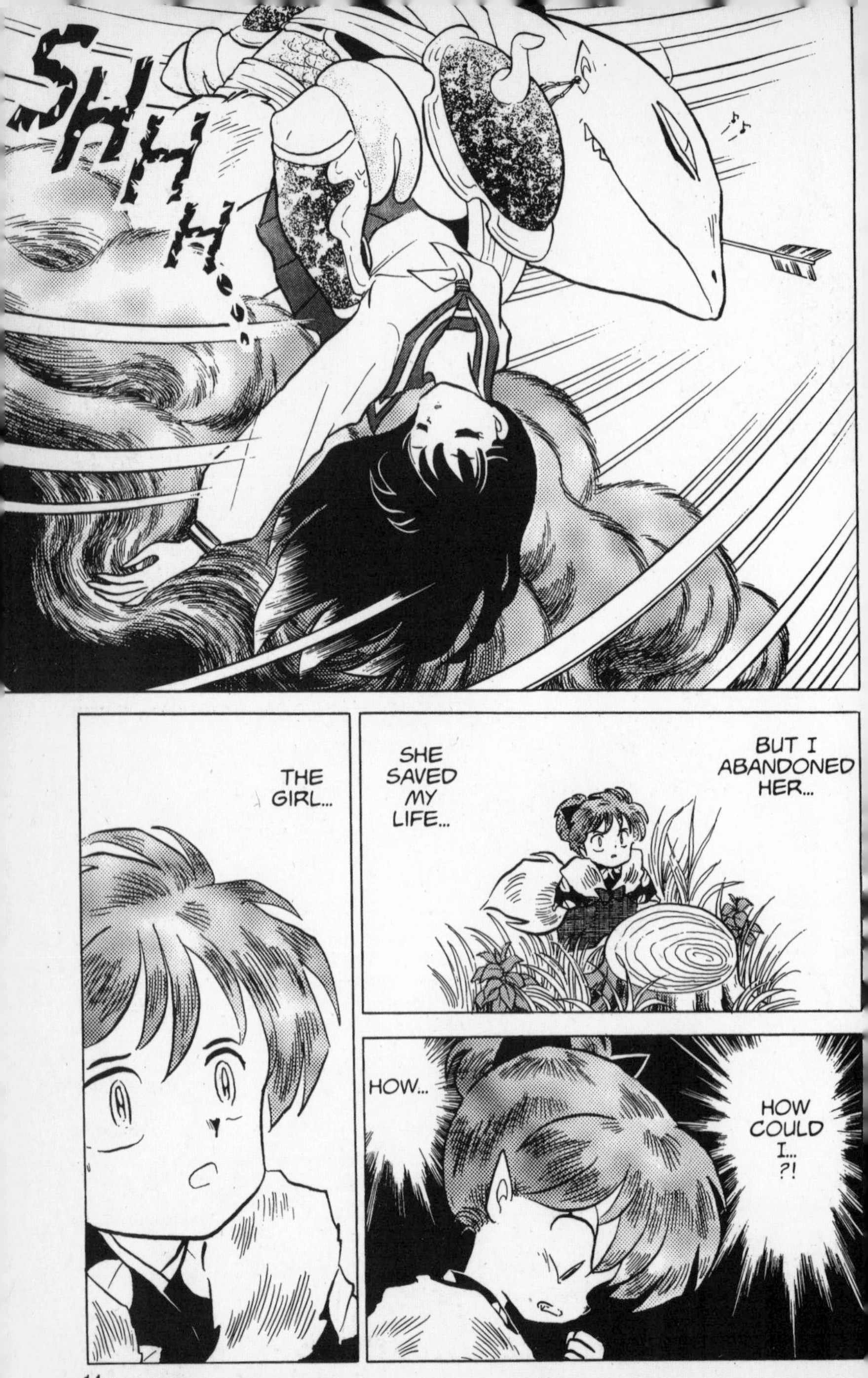
SHHH...
THE GIRL...
SHE SAVED MY LIFE...
BUT I ABANDONED HER...
HOW...
HOW COULD I... ?!

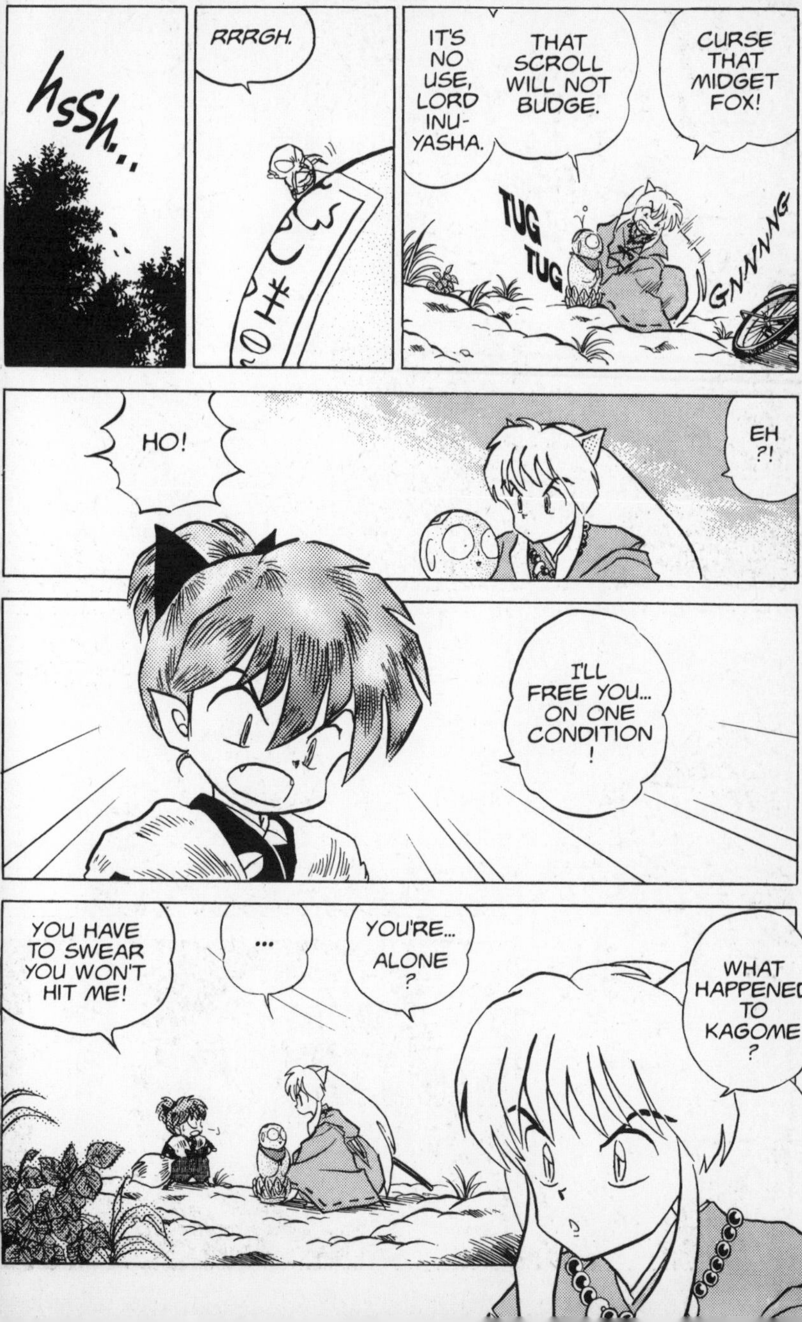
hssh...
RRRGH.
IT'S NO USE, LORD INU-YASHA.
THAT SCROLL WILL NOT BUDGE.
CURSE THAT MIDGET FOX!
TUG TUG
GNNNNG
HO!
EH ?!
I'LL FREE YOU... ON ONE CONDITION !
YOU HAVE TO SWEAR YOU WON'T HIT ME!
...
YOU'RE... ALONE ?
WHAT HAPPENED TO KAGOME ?

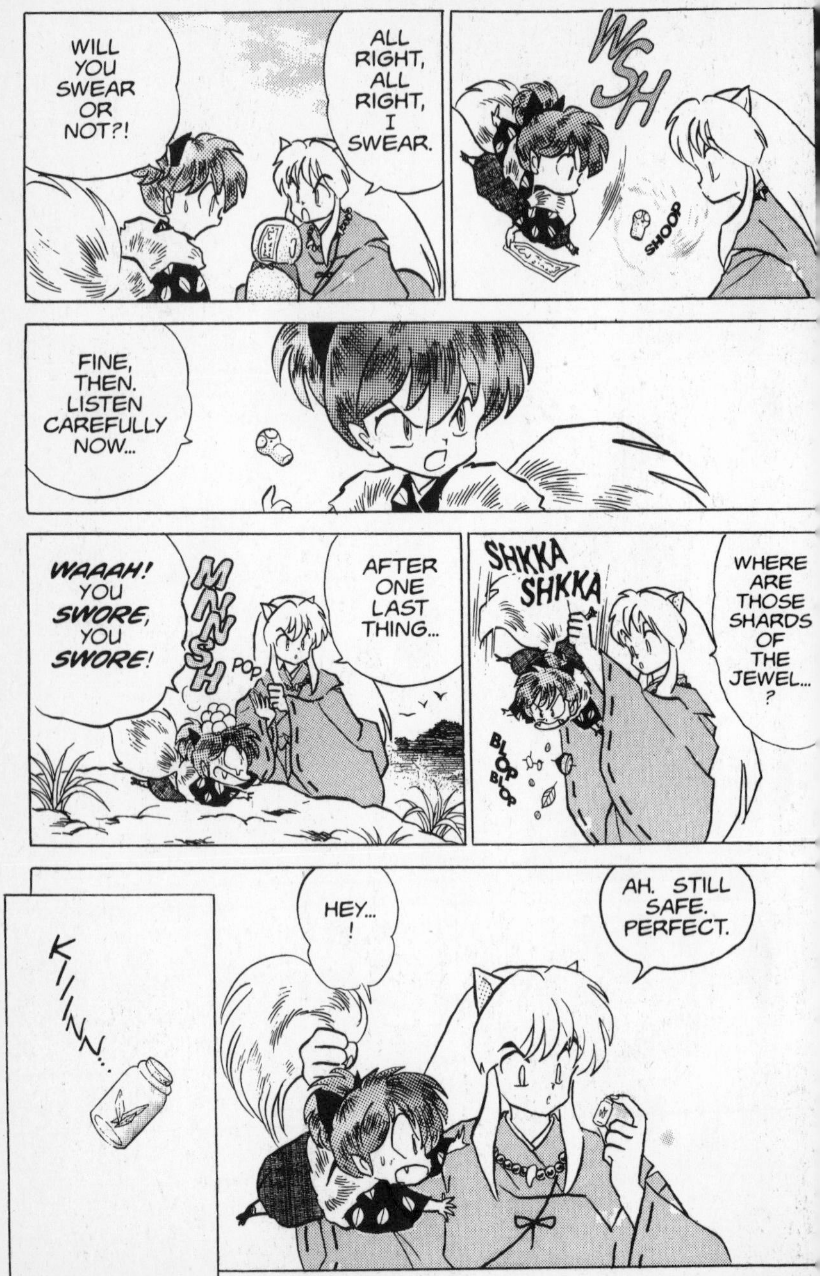
WILL YOU SWEAR OR NOT?!
ALL RIGHT, ALL RIGHT, I SWEAR.
WSH
SHOOP
FINE, THEN. LISTEN CAREFULLY NOW...
WAAAH! YOU *SWORE*, YOU *SWORE*!
MNNSH
POP
AFTER ONE LAST THING...
SHKKA SHKKA
WHERE ARE THOSE SHARDS OF THE JEWEL...?
BLOP BLOP
KIIINN...
HEY...!
AH. STILL SAFE. PERFECT.

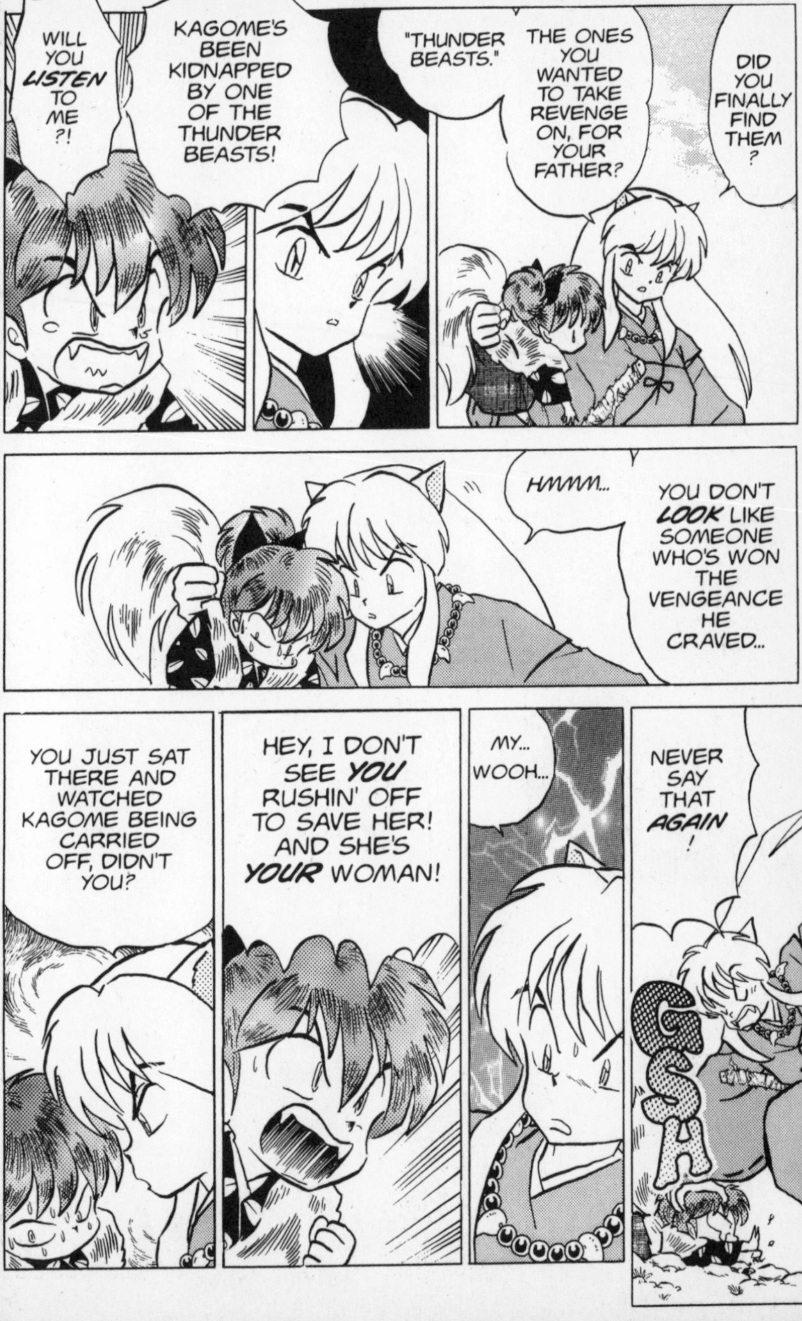
WILL YOU LISTEN TO ME?!
KAGOME'S BEEN KIDNAPPED BY ONE OF THE THUNDER BEASTS!
"THUNDER BEASTS."
THE ONES YOU WANTED TO TAKE REVENGE ON, FOR YOUR FATHER?
DID YOU FINALLY FIND THEM?
HMMM...
YOU DON'T LOOK LIKE SOMEONE WHO'S WON THE VENGEANCE HE CRAVED...
YOU JUST SAT THERE AND WATCHED KAGOME BEING CARRIED OFF, DIDN'T YOU?
HEY, I DON'T SEE YOU RUSHIN' OFF TO SAVE HER! AND SHE'S YOUR WOMAN!
MY... WOOH...
NEVER SAY THAT AGAIN!

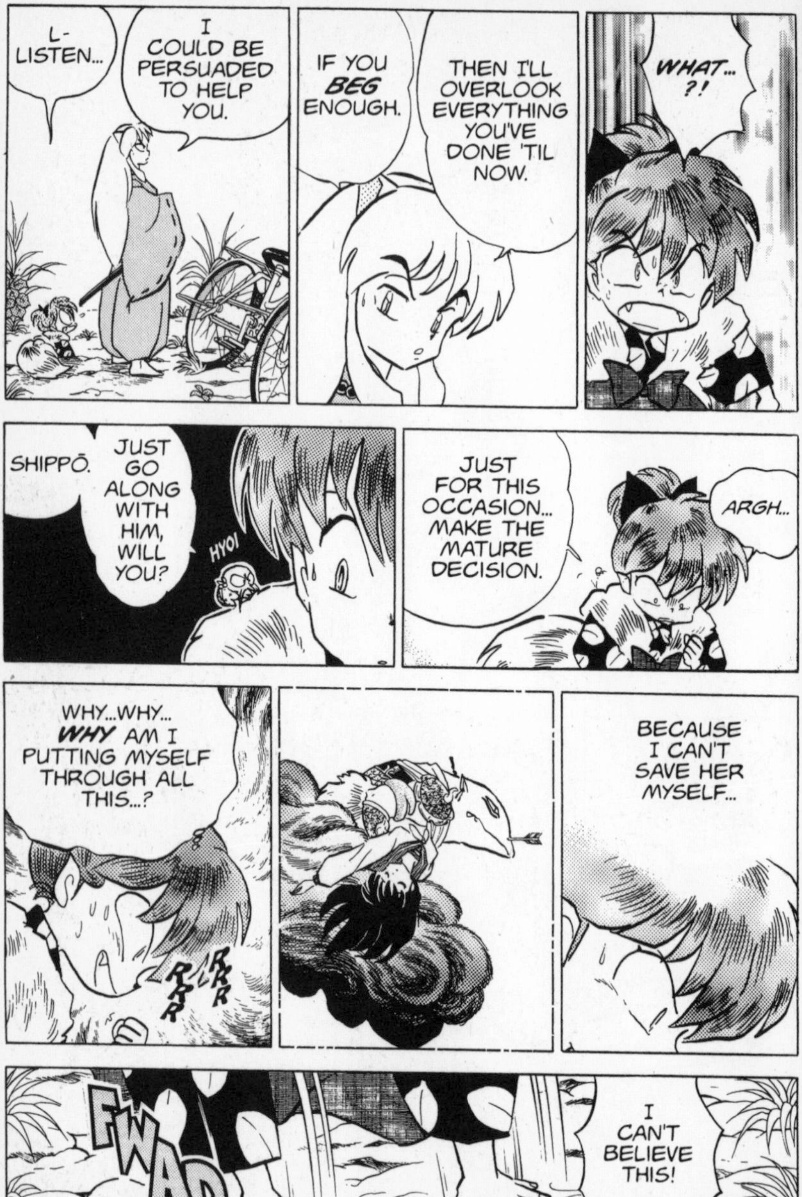
L-
LISTEN...
I COULD BE PERSUADED TO HELP YOU.
IF YOU BEG ENOUGH.
THEN I'LL OVERLOOK EVERYTHING YOU'VE DONE 'TIL NOW.
WHAT... ?!
SHIPPŌ.
JUST GO ALONG WITH HIM, WILL YOU?
HYOI
JUST FOR THIS OCCASION... MAKE THE MATURE DECISION.
ARGH...
WHY...WHY... WHY AM I PUTTING MYSELF THROUGH ALL THIS...?
RRR
RRR
BECAUSE I CAN'T SAVE HER MYSELF...
FWAP
I CAN'T BELIEVE THIS!

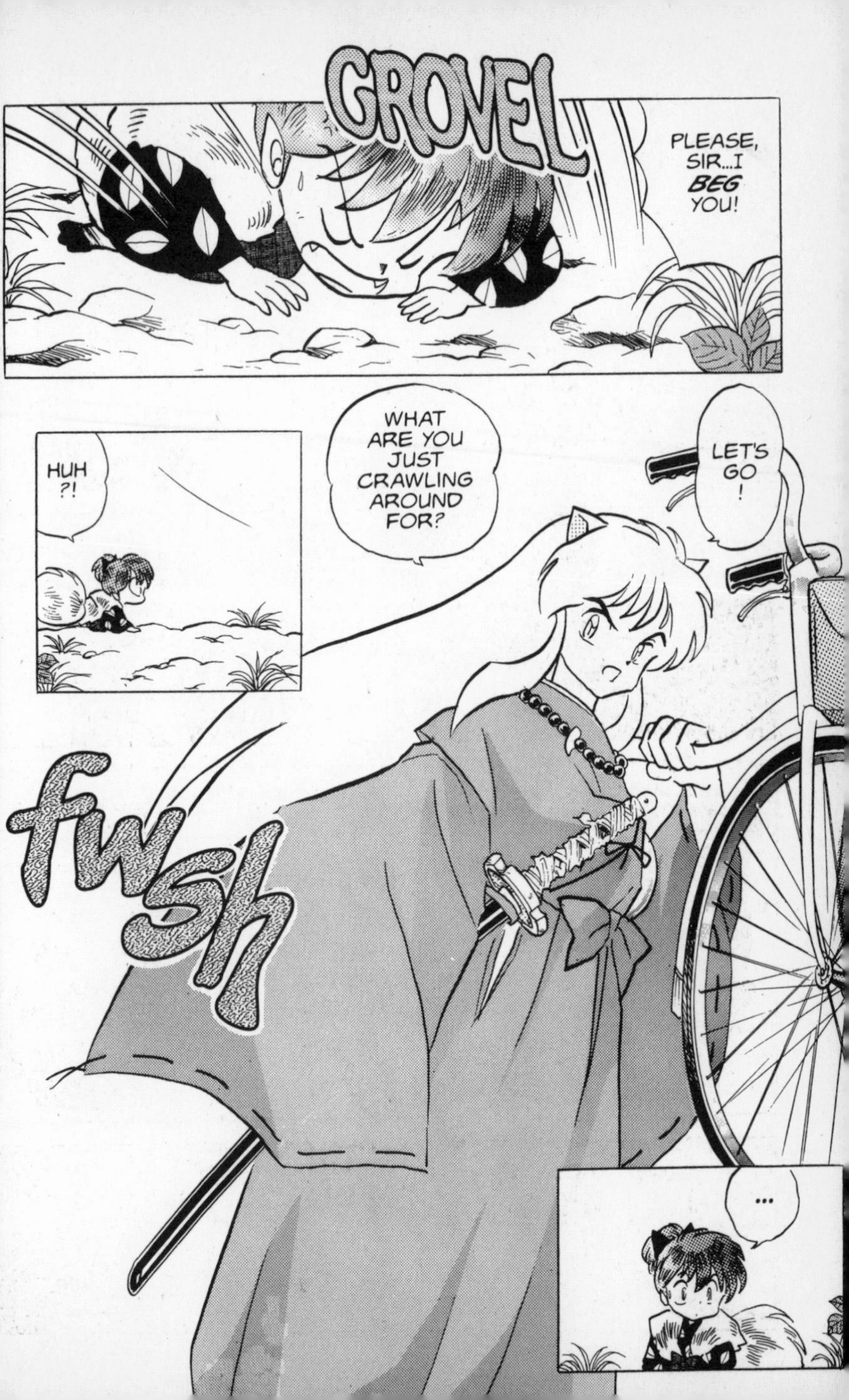
GROVEL
PLEASE, SIR...I BEG YOU!
HUH ?!
WHAT ARE YOU JUST CRAWLING AROUND FOR?
LET'S GO !
fwsh
...

GORORORO...

KA-RAKK

N...

HUH...
?

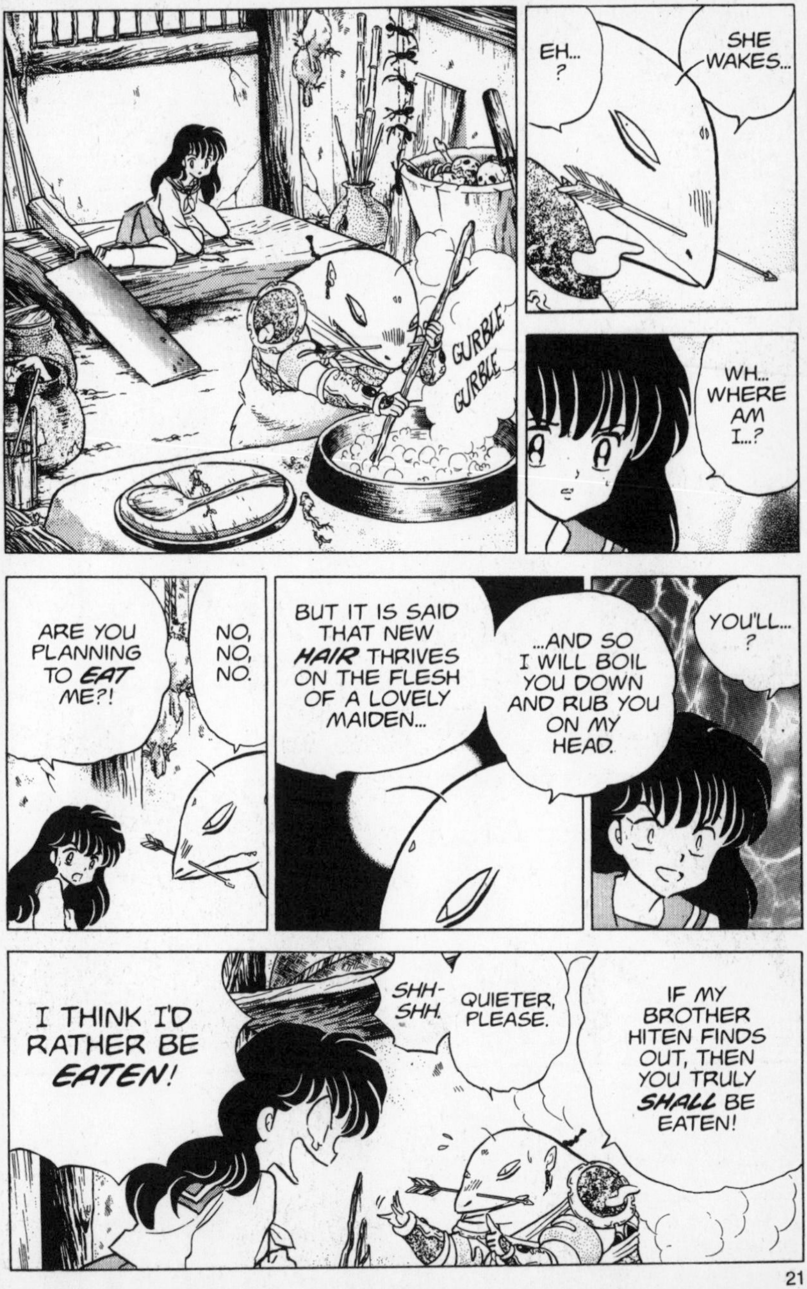
GURBLE GURBLE
EH... ?
SHE WAKES...
WH... WHERE AM I...?
ARE YOU PLANNING TO EAT ME?!
NO, NO, NO.
BUT IT IS SAID THAT NEW HAIR THRIVES ON THE FLESH OF A LOVELY MAIDEN...
...AND SO I WILL BOIL YOU DOWN AND RUB YOU ON MY HEAD.
YOU'LL... ?
I THINK I'D RATHER BE EATEN!
SHH-SHH.
QUIETER, PLEASE.
IF MY BROTHER HITEN FINDS OUT, THEN YOU TRULY SHALL BE EATEN!

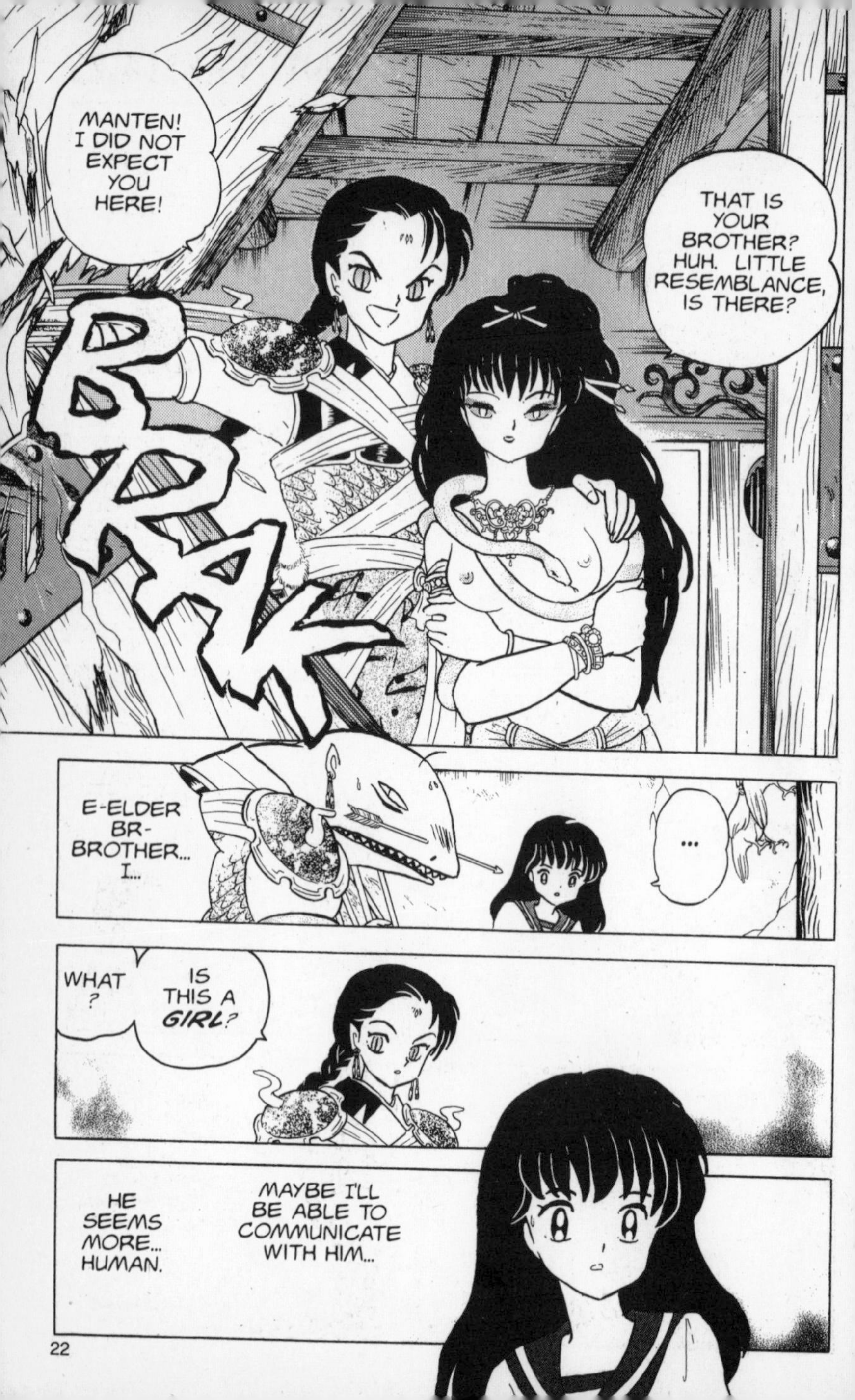
MANTEN! I DID NOT EXPECT YOU HERE!
BRAK
THAT IS YOUR BROTHER? HUH. LITTLE RESEMBLANCE, IS THERE?
E-ELDER BR-BROTHER... I...
...
WHAT?
IS THIS A *GIRL*?
HE SEEMS MORE... HUMAN.
MAYBE I'LL BE ABLE TO COMMUNICATE WITH HIM...

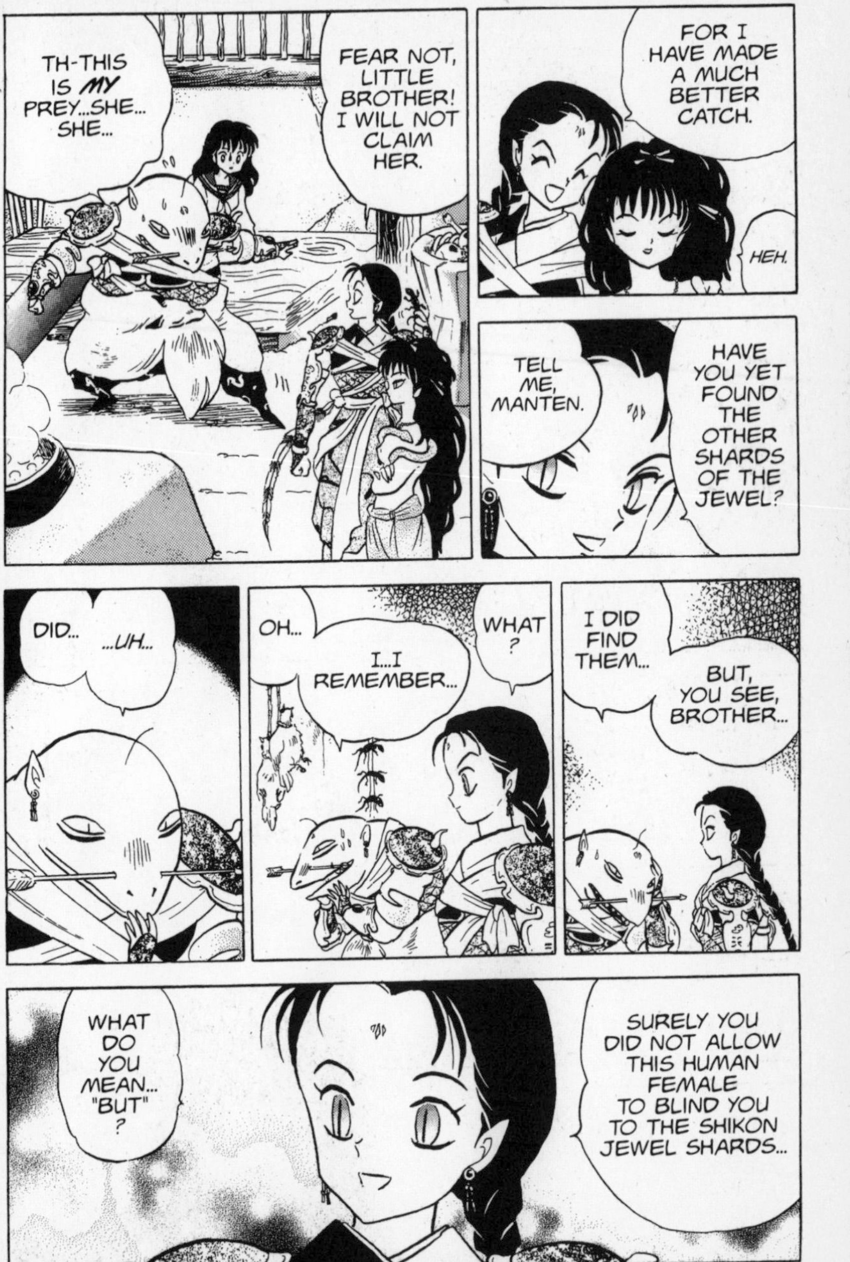
TH-THIS IS *MY* PREY...SHE... SHE...
FEAR NOT, LITTLE BROTHER! I WILL NOT CLAIM HER.
FOR I HAVE MADE A MUCH BETTER CATCH.
HEH.
TELL ME, MANTEN.
HAVE YOU YET FOUND THE OTHER SHARDS OF THE JEWEL?
DID...
...UH...
OH...
WHAT?
I...I REMEMBER...
I DID FIND THEM...
BUT, YOU SEE, BROTHER...
WHAT DO YOU MEAN... "BUT"?
SURELY YOU DID NOT ALLOW THIS HUMAN FEMALE TO BLIND YOU TO THE SHIKON JEWEL SHARDS...

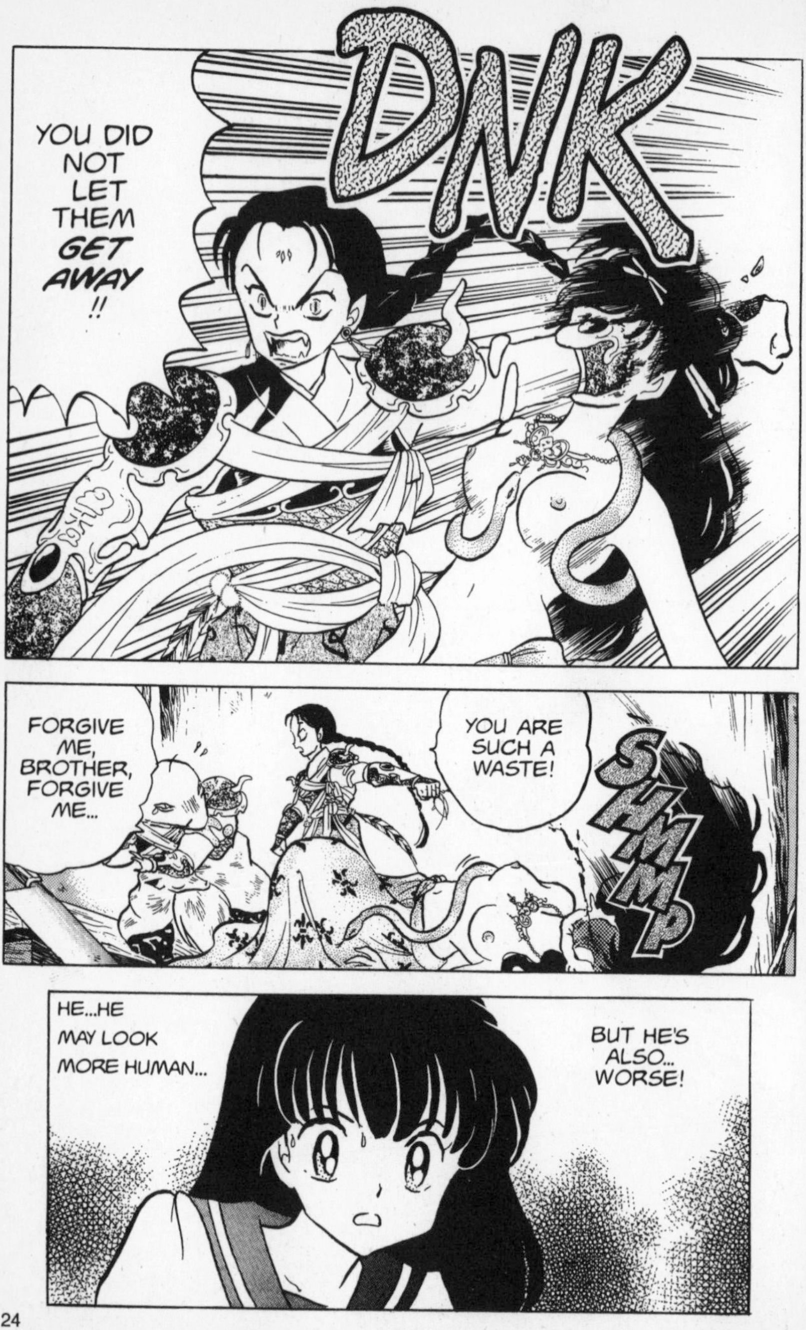
DNK
YOU DID NOT LET THEM GET AWAY!!
FORGIVE ME, BROTHER, FORGIVE ME...
YOU ARE SUCH A WASTE!
SHMMP
HE...HE MAY LOOK MORE HUMAN...
BUT HE'S ALSO... WORSE!

SCROLL TWO

THE CRUSH

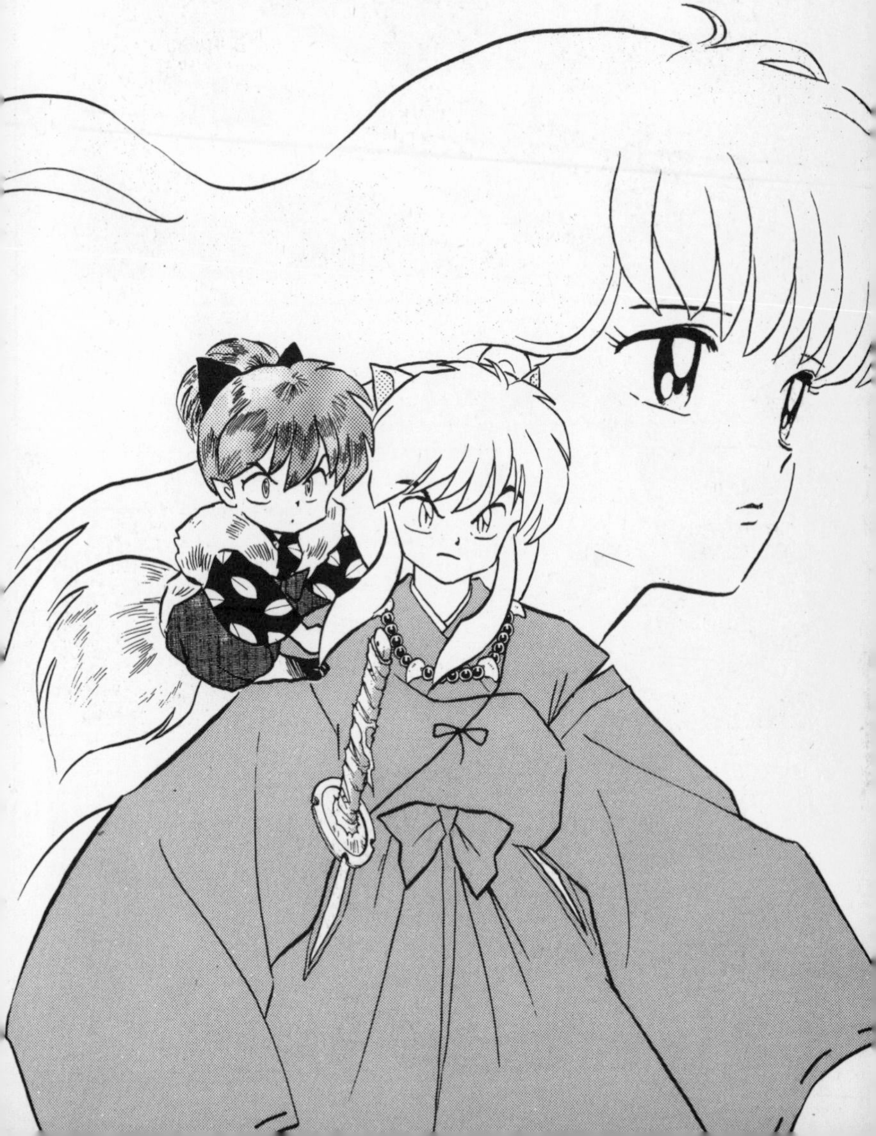

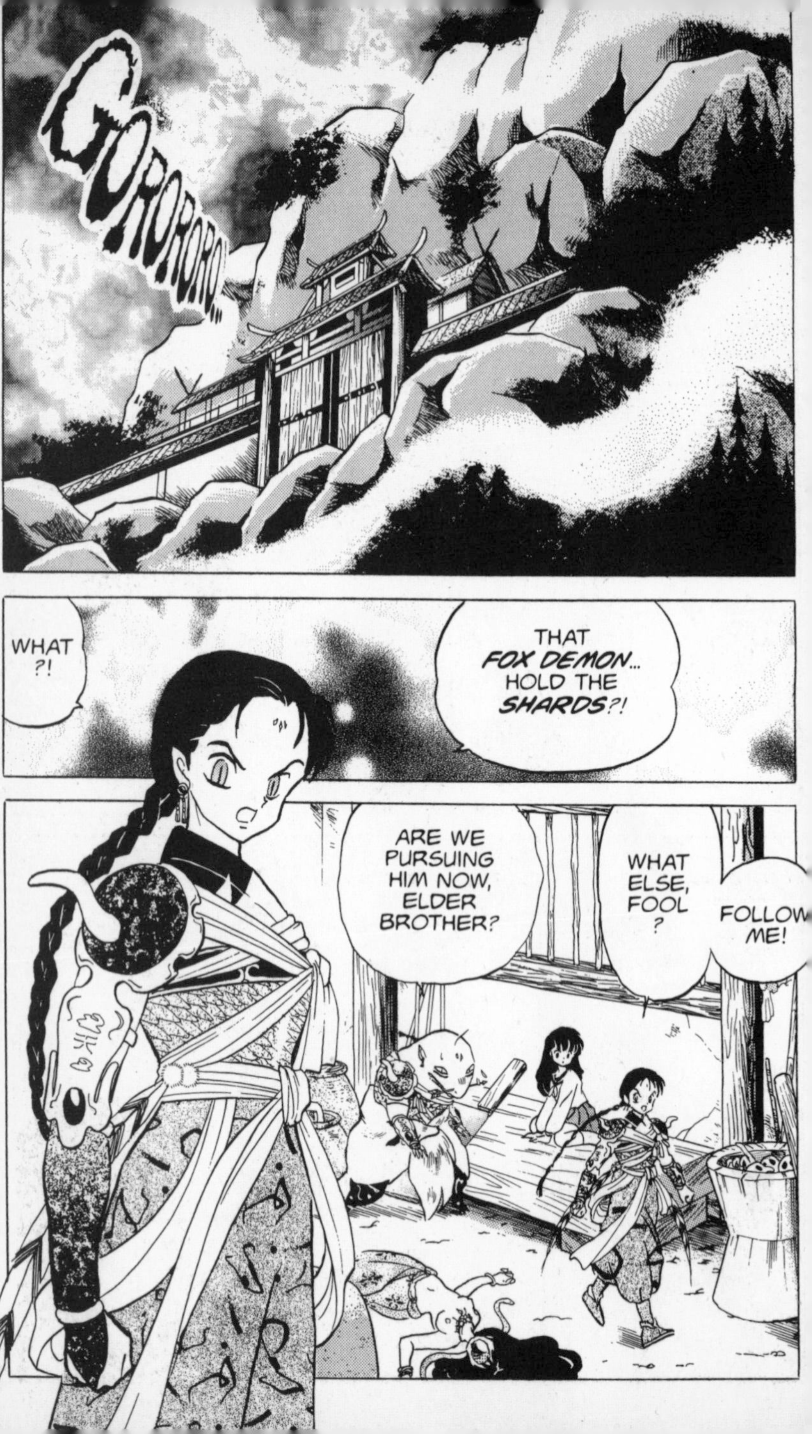
GOROROROㅡ...
WHAT ?!
THAT FOX DEMON... HOLD THE SHARDS?!
ARE WE PURSUING HIM NOW, ELDER BROTHER?
WHAT ELSE, FOOL ?
FOLLOW ME!

A CHANCE TO ESCAPE... !

OH... HITEN. ONE MOMENT.

EEEEK!

WHAT'S THE BIG IDEA?!

"THE BIG IDEA"...?

WHY, I AM KILLING YOU SO THAT YOU CANNOT FLEE.

I MUST HAVE MY HAIR POTION, YOU SEE.

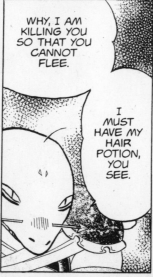

B-BUT WAIT... IF YOU KILL ME...

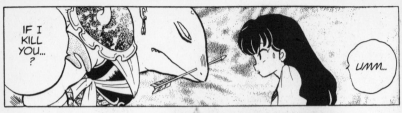

IF I KILL YOU...?

UMM...

THAT'S IT!

YOU NEVER FIND THE SHARDS OF THE JEWEL!

WHAT--?

HAVE YOU HEARD OF INU-YASHA?

HE'S A POWERFUL DEMON...

POWERFUL?

HE IS ONLY HALF A DEMON.

BUT HE *IS* POWERFUL.

BECAUSE HE'S ALREADY GATHERED MOST OF THE SHIKON SHARDS TOGETHER FOR *HIMSELF!*

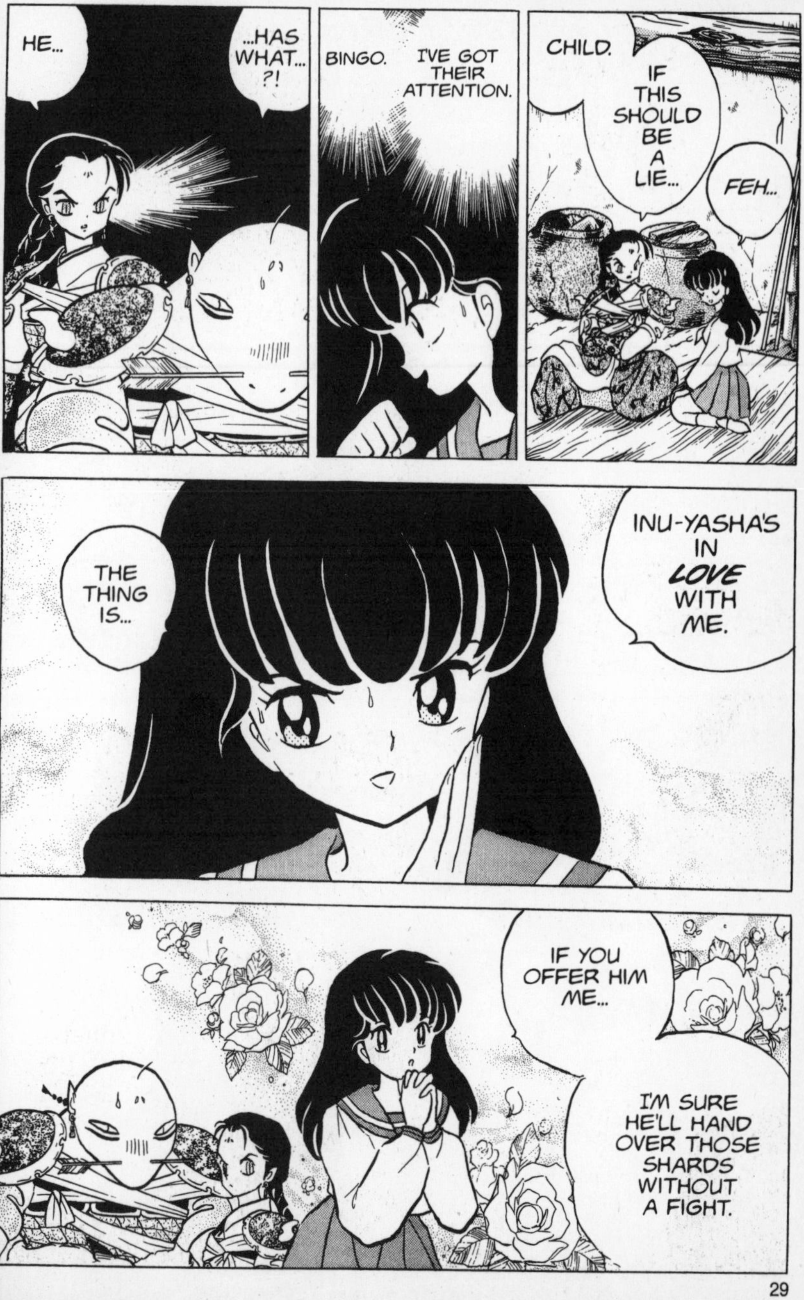
HE...
...HAS WHAT... ?!
BINGO.
I'VE GOT THEIR ATTENTION.
CHILD.
IF THIS SHOULD BE A LIE...
FEH...
THE THING IS...
INU-YASHA'S IN LOVE WITH ME.
IF YOU OFFER HIM ME...
I'M SURE HE'LL HAND OVER THOSE SHARDS WITHOUT A FIGHT.

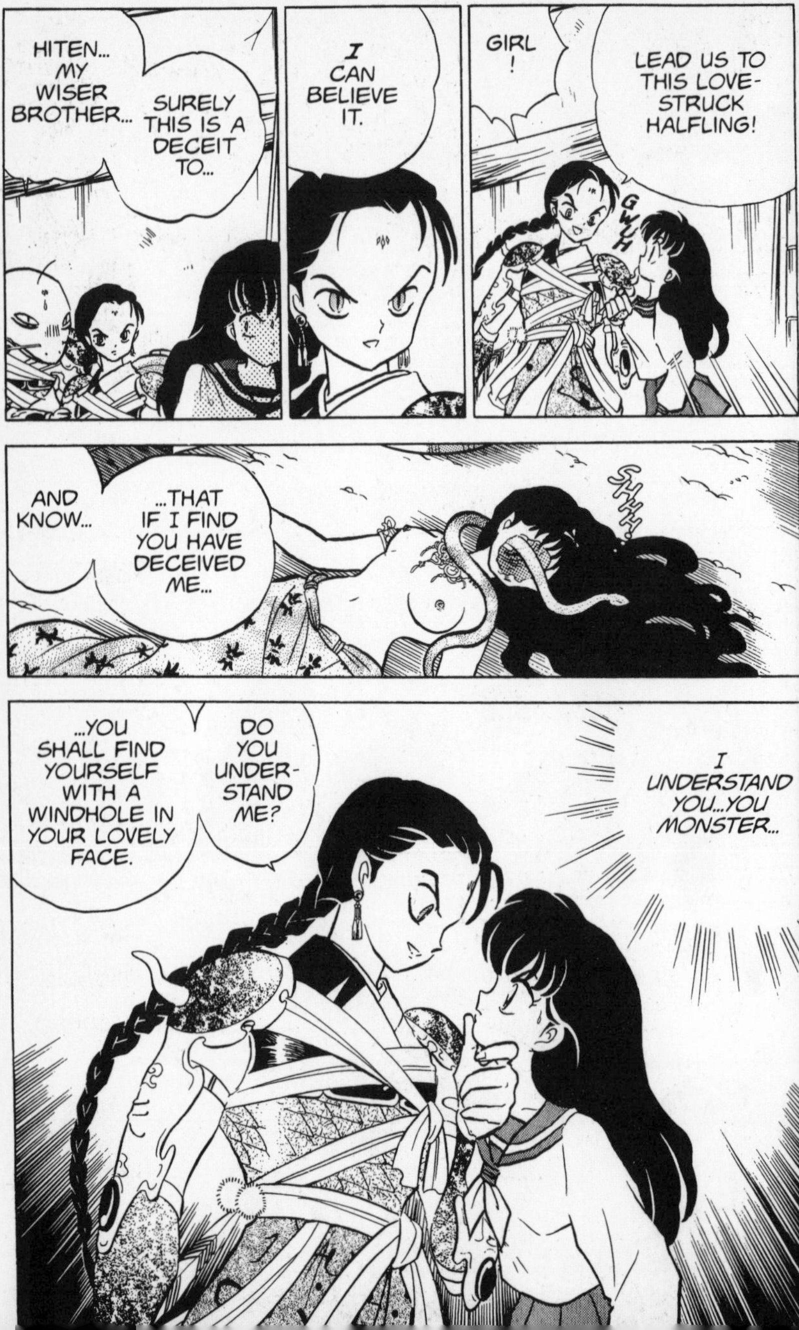
HITEN... MY WISER BROTHER...
SURELY THIS IS A DECEIT TO...
I CAN BELIEVE IT.
GIRL!
LEAD US TO THIS LOVE-STRUCK HALFLING!
GWUH
AND KNOW...
...THAT IF I FIND YOU HAVE DECEIVED ME...
SHHH
...YOU SHALL FIND YOURSELF WITH A WINDHOLE IN YOUR LOVELY FACE.
DO YOU UNDER-STAND ME?
I UNDERSTAND YOU...YOU MONSTER...

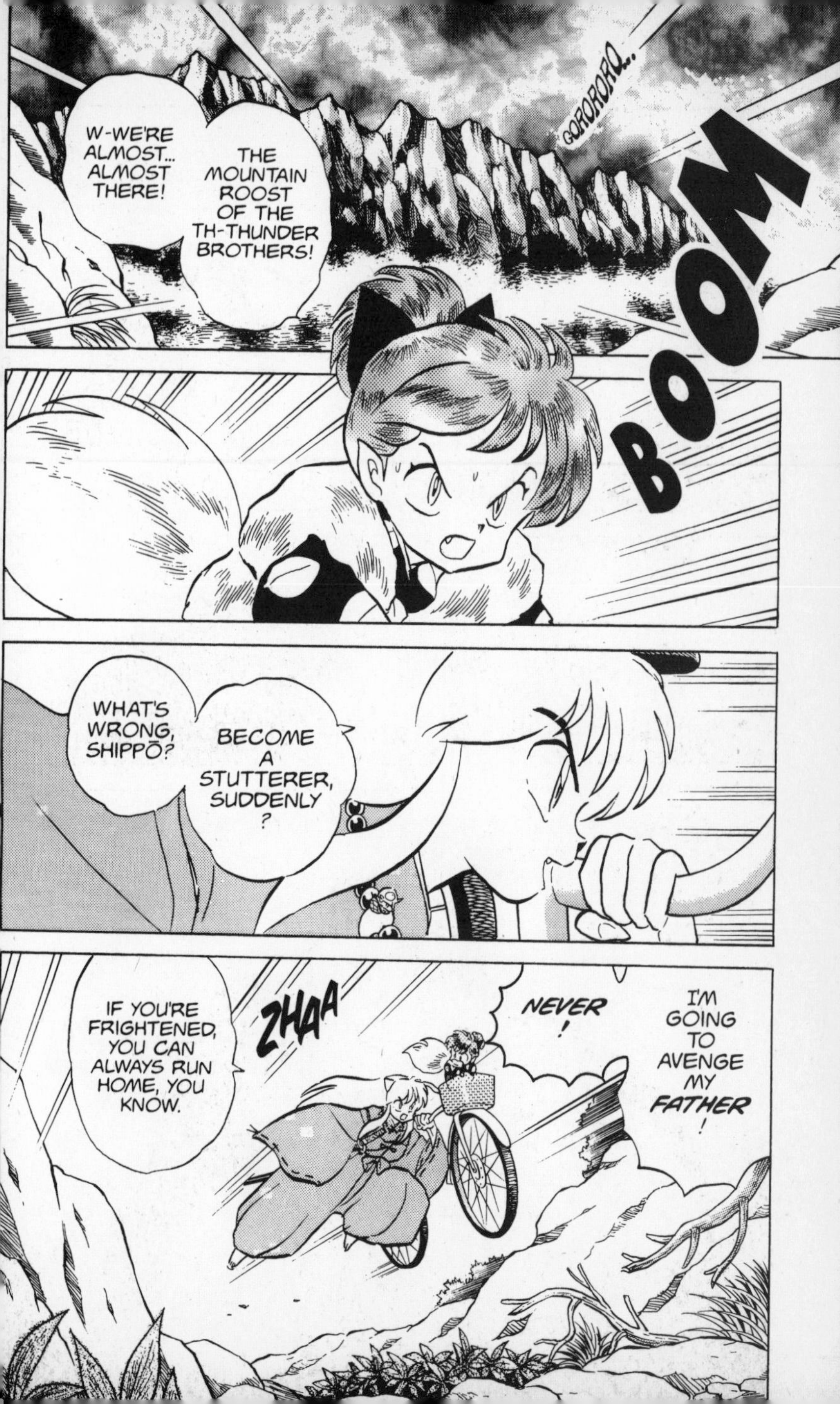
W-WE'RE ALMOST... ALMOST THERE!
THE MOUNTAIN ROOST OF THE TH-THUNDER BROTHERS!
GOROROROO...
BOOM
WHAT'S WRONG, SHIPPŌ?
BECOME A STUTTERER, SUDDENLY?
IF YOU'RE FRIGHTENED, YOU CAN ALWAYS RUN HOME, YOU KNOW.
ZHAA
NEVER!
I'M GOING TO AVENGE MY FATHER!

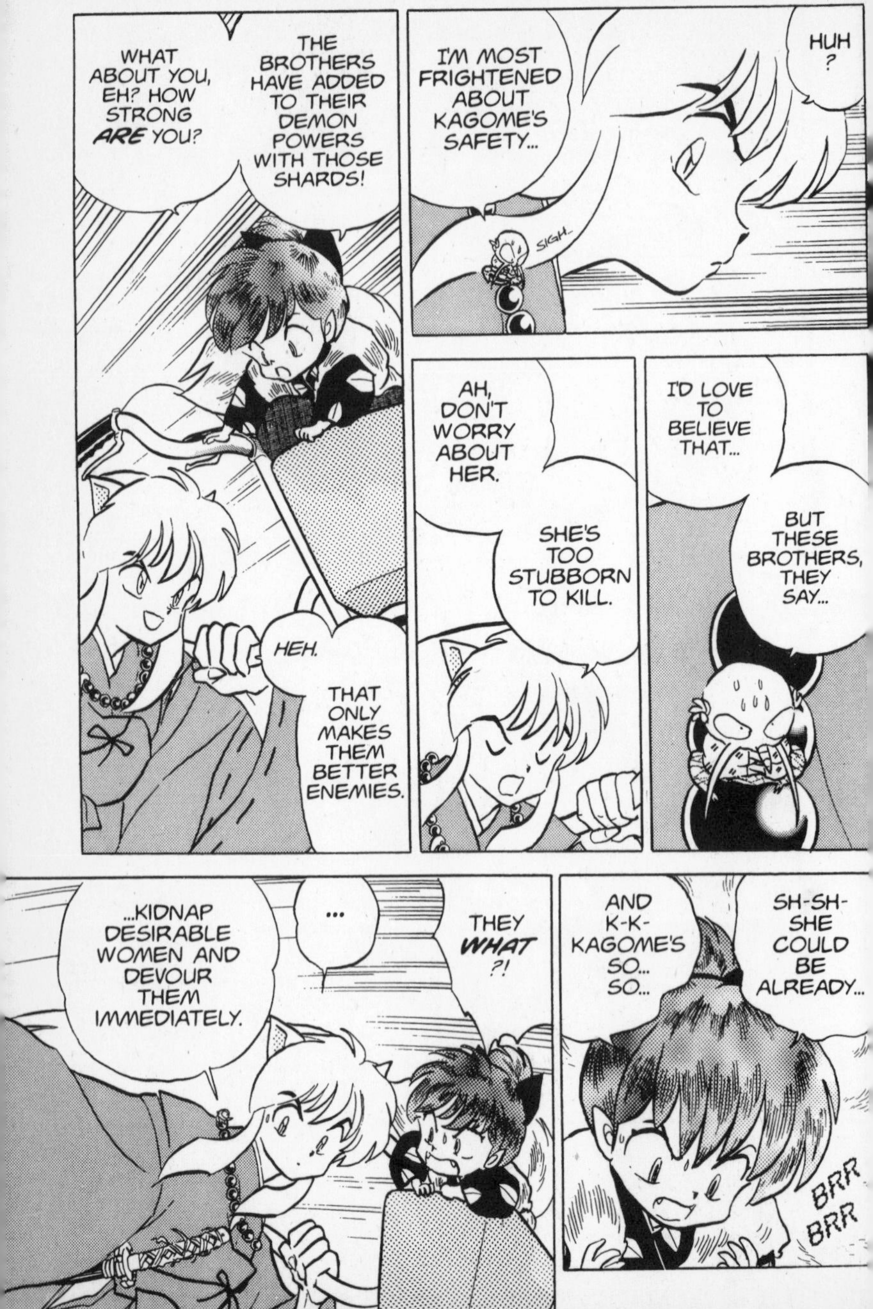

WHAT ABOUT YOU, EH? HOW STRONG ARE YOU?
THE BROTHERS HAVE ADDED TO THEIR DEMON POWERS WITH THOSE SHARDS!
HEH.
THAT ONLY MAKES THEM BETTER ENEMIES.
I'M MOST FRIGHTENED ABOUT KAGOME'S SAFETY...
SIGH...
HUH?
AH, DON'T WORRY ABOUT HER.
SHE'S TOO STUBBORN TO KILL.
I'D LOVE TO BELIEVE THAT...
BUT THESE BROTHERS, THEY SAY...
...KIDNAP DESIRABLE WOMEN AND DEVOUR THEM IMMEDIATELY.
...
THEY WHAT?!
AND K-K-KAGOME'S SO... SO...
SH-SH-SHE COULD BE ALREADY...
BRR BRR

IDIOT. WHY SHOULD KAGOME WORRY-- IF THEY EAT *DESIRABLE* WOMEN?!

WHAT?! DO YOU HAVE *HOLES* FOR EYES?!

OH, YES. "DESIRABLE." THAT'S WHAT I'D CALL *HER*.

WAAAH!!

THEY'RE PICKING HER FROM THEIR TEETH ALREADY!

AND IT'S ALL MY FAULT!!

WILL YOU *SHUT UP*, FOOL!

K-BLLAAANG

GORORORO...

VRAK

WHAT?!

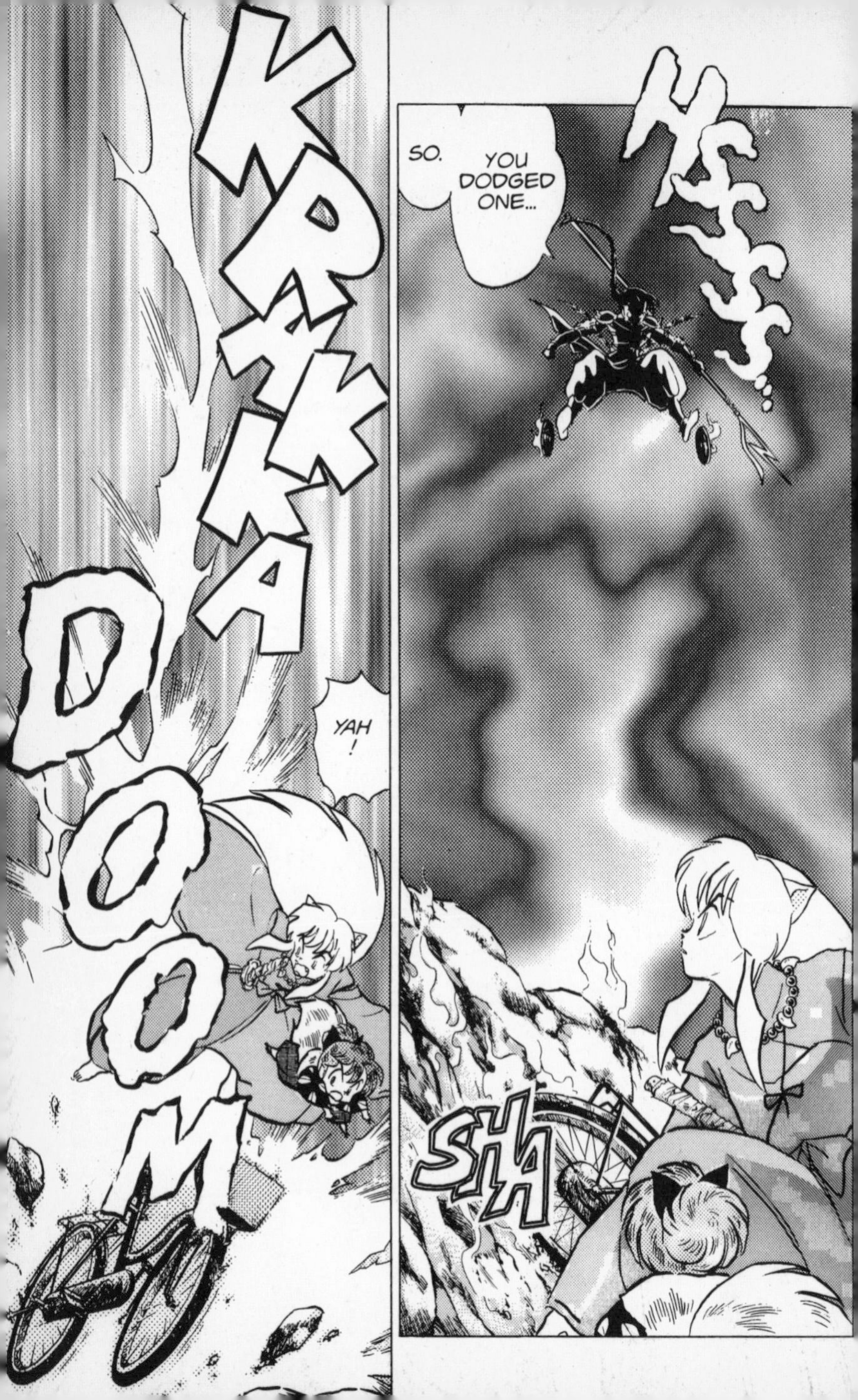
KRAKA
DOOM
YAH!
SO.
YOU DODGED ONE...
HSSSS...
SHA

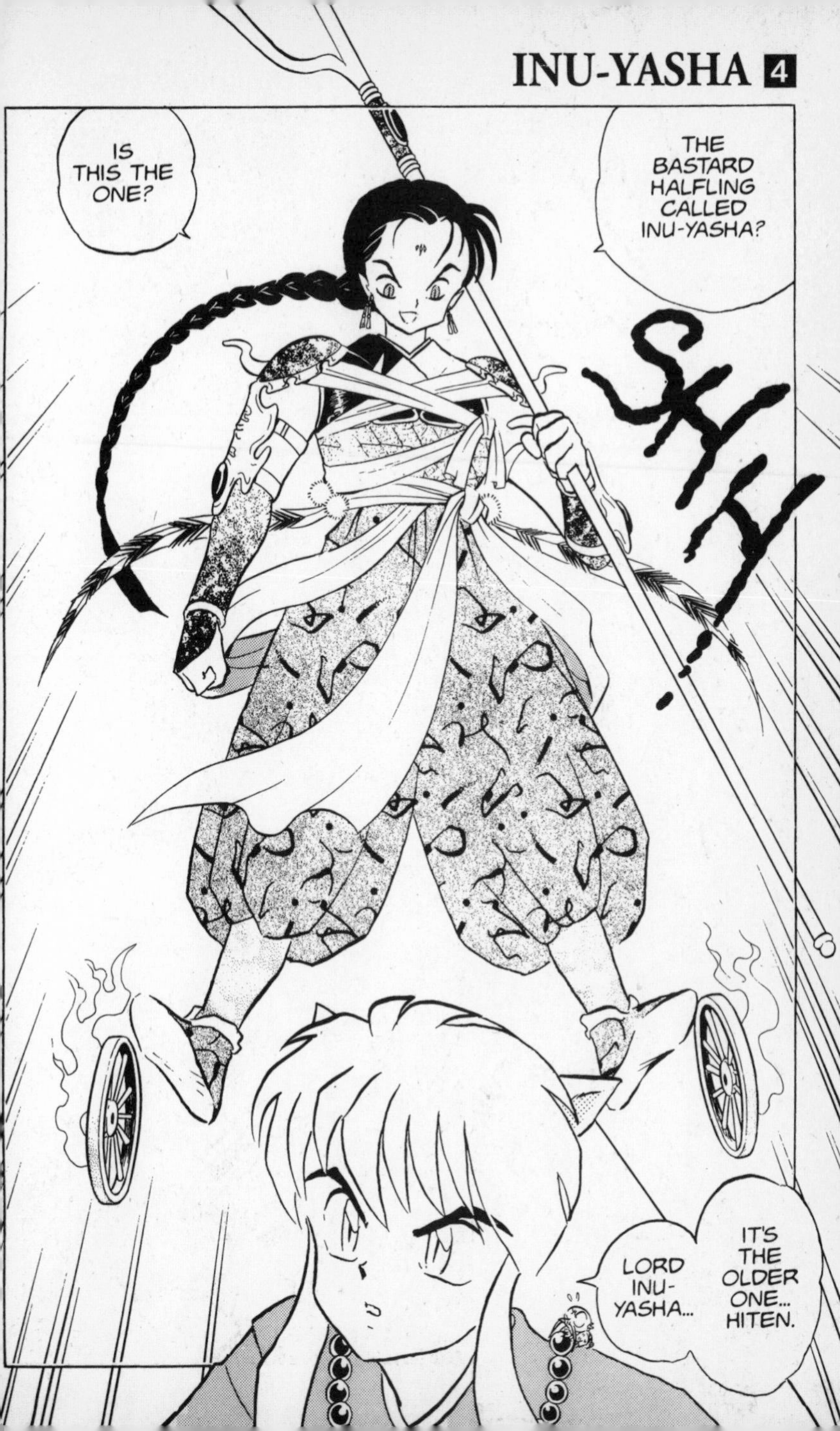
IS THIS THE ONE?
THE BASTARD HALFLING CALLED INU-YASHA?
SHH!
LORD INU-YASHA...
IT'S THE OLDER ONE... HITEN.

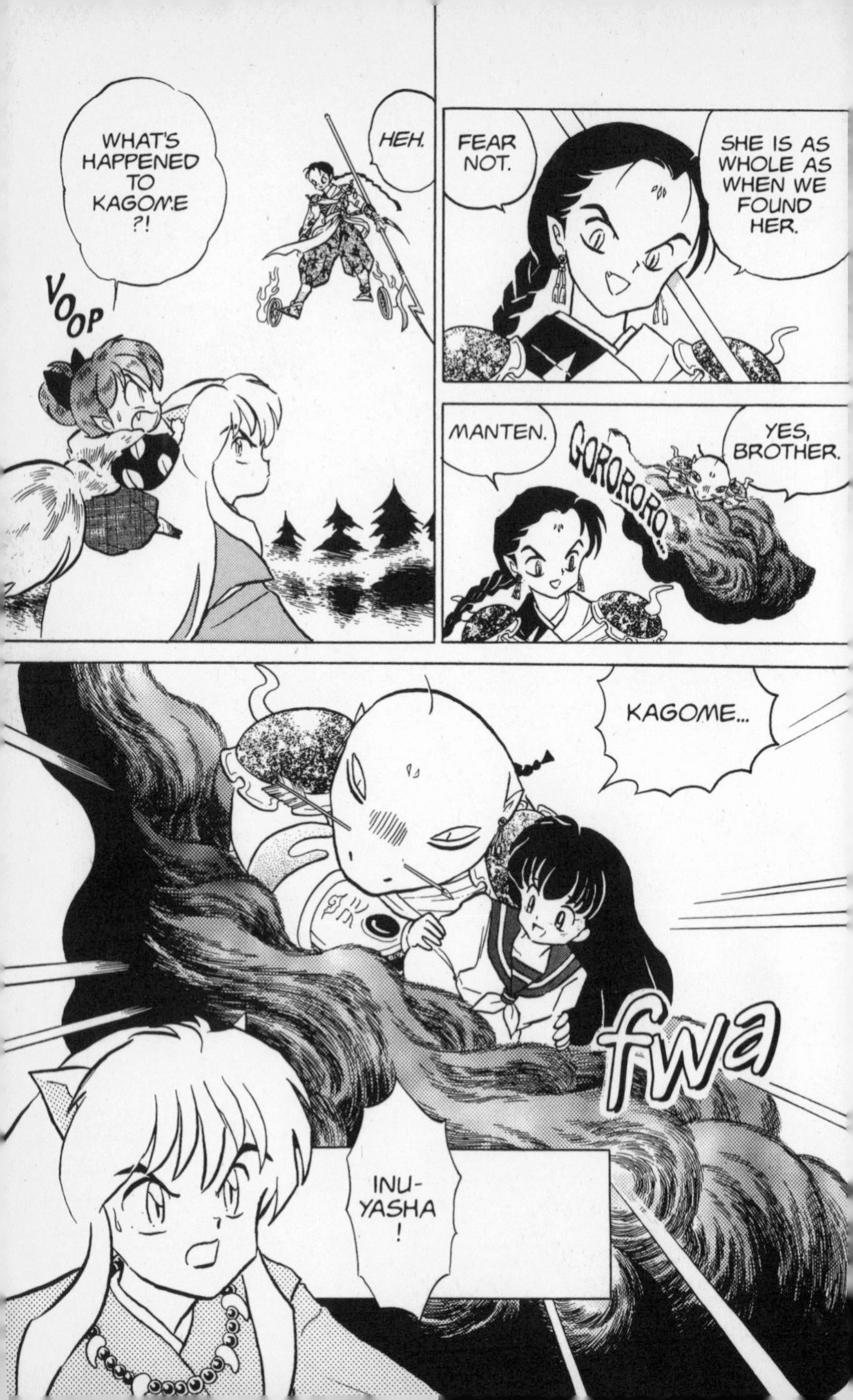
WHAT'S HAPPENED TO KAGOME ?!
HEH.
VOOP
FEAR NOT.
SHE IS AS WHOLE AS WHEN WE FOUND HER.
MANTEN.
GORORORO...
YES, BROTHER.
KAGOME...
fwa
INU-YASHA !

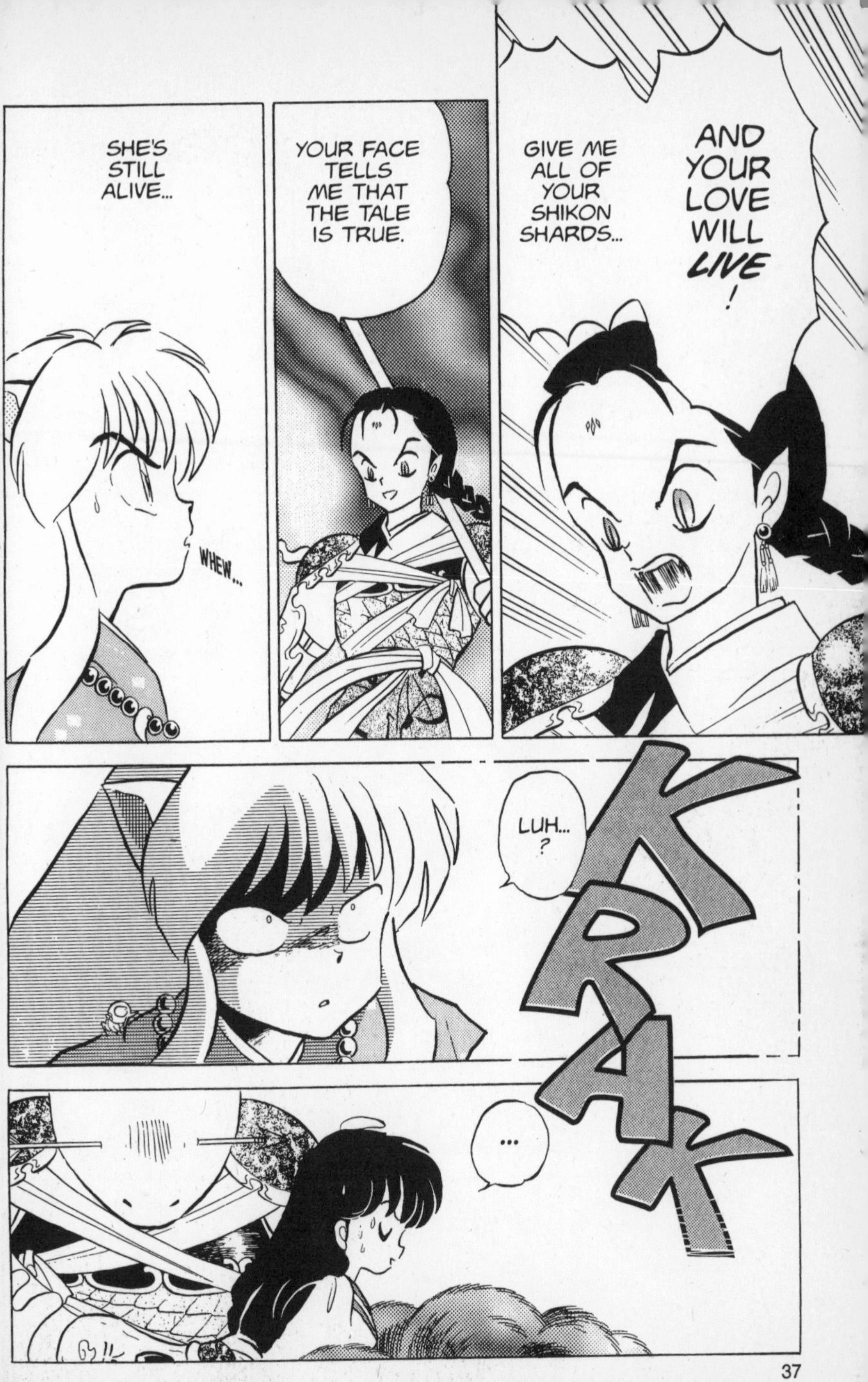
SHE'S STILL ALIVE...
WHEW...
YOUR FACE TELLS ME THAT THE TALE IS TRUE.
GIVE ME ALL OF YOUR SHIKON SHARDS...
AND YOUR LOVE WILL LIVE!
LUH...?
KRAK
...

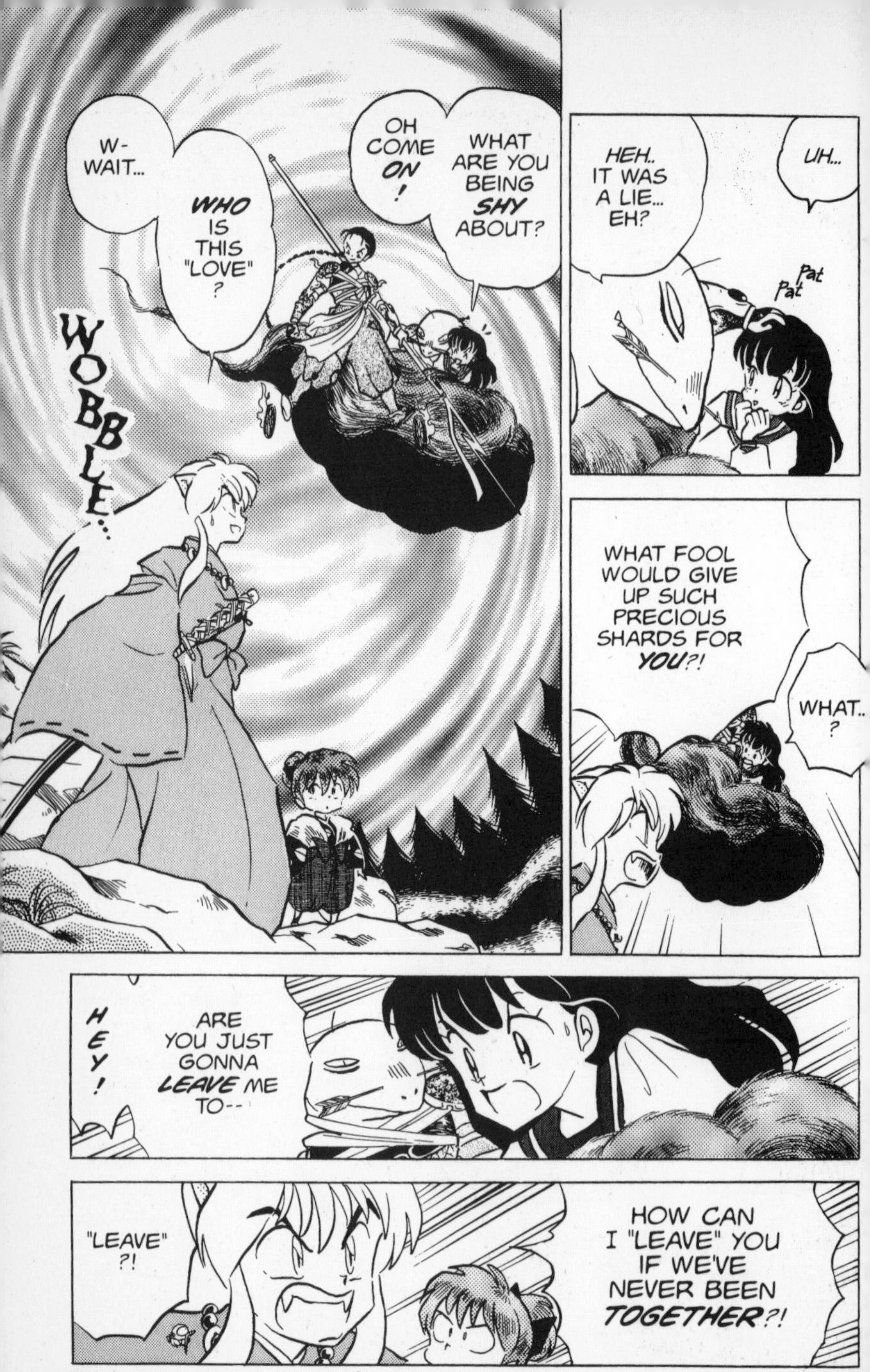
W- WAIT...
WHO IS THIS "LOVE"?
OH COME ON!
WHAT ARE YOU BEING SHY ABOUT?
WOBBLE...
HEH.. IT WAS A LIE... EH?
UH...
Pat Pat
WHAT FOOL WOULD GIVE UP SUCH PRECIOUS SHARDS FOR YOU?!
WHAT..?
HEY!
ARE YOU JUST GONNA LEAVE ME TO--
"LEAVE"?!
HOW CAN I "LEAVE" YOU IF WE'VE NEVER BEEN TOGETHER?!

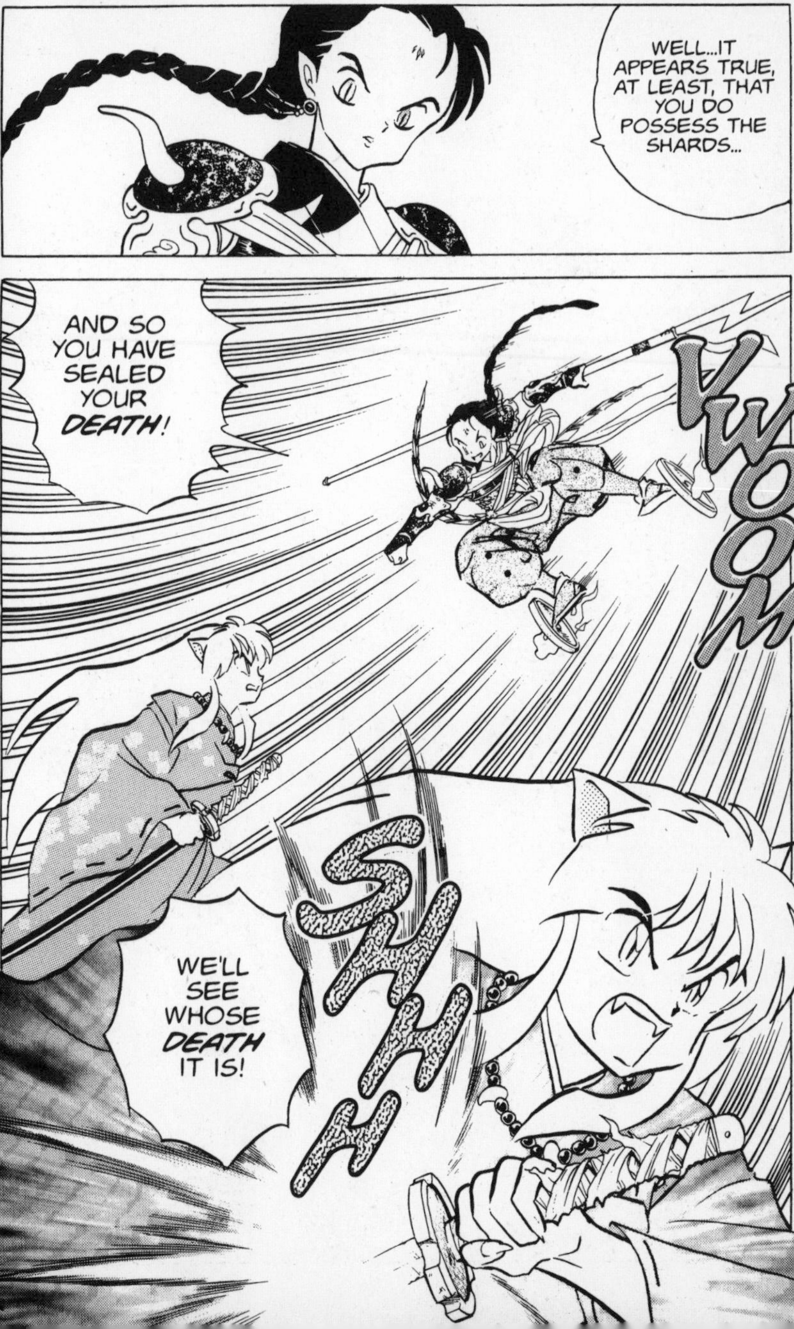
WELL...IT APPEARS TRUE, AT LEAST, THAT YOU DO POSSESS THE SHARDS...
AND SO YOU HAVE SEALED YOUR *DEATH*!
VWOOM
WE'LL SEE WHOSE *DEATH* IT IS!
SHH

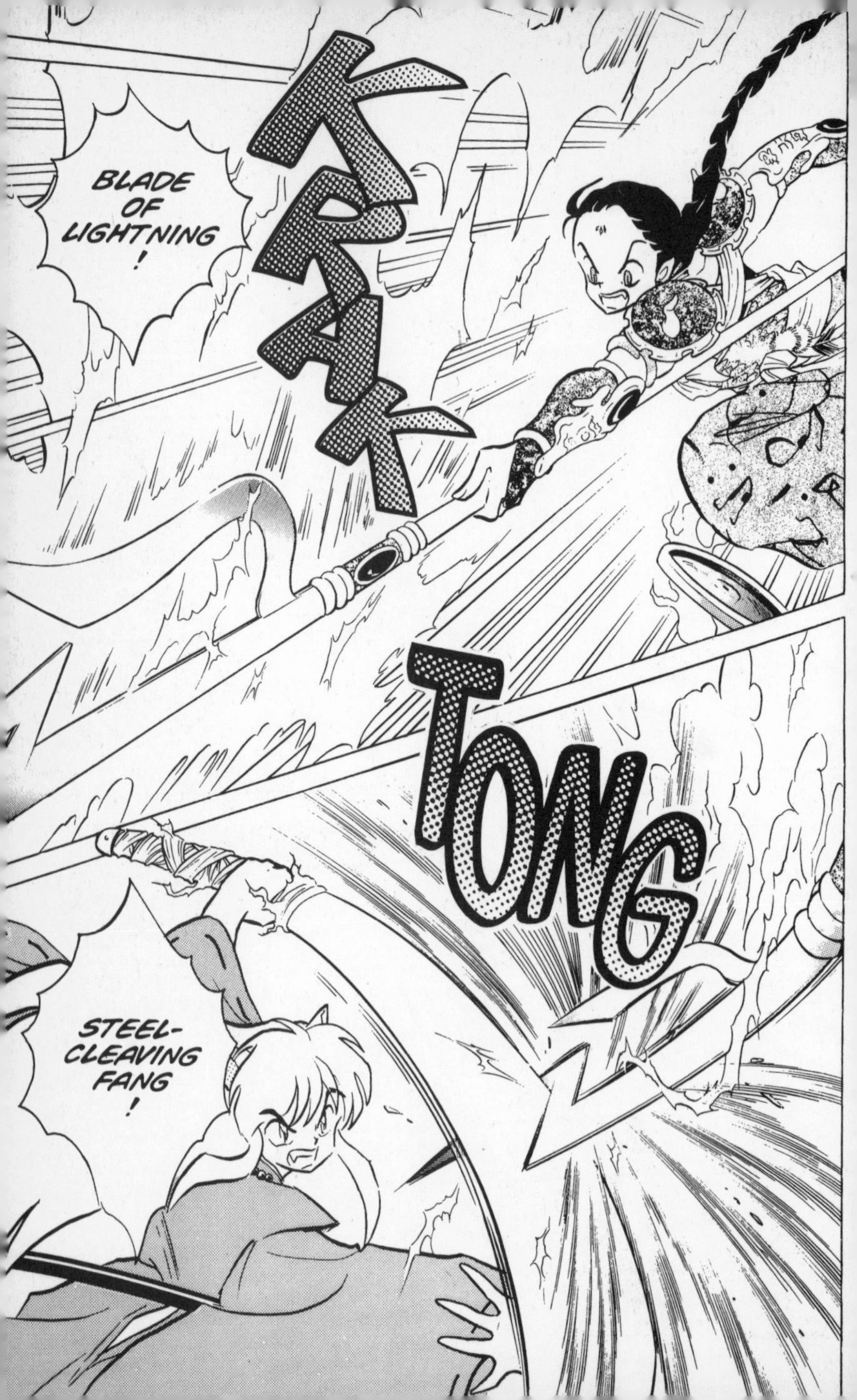
BLADE OF LIGHTNING!
KRAK
TONG
STEEL-CLEAVING FANG!

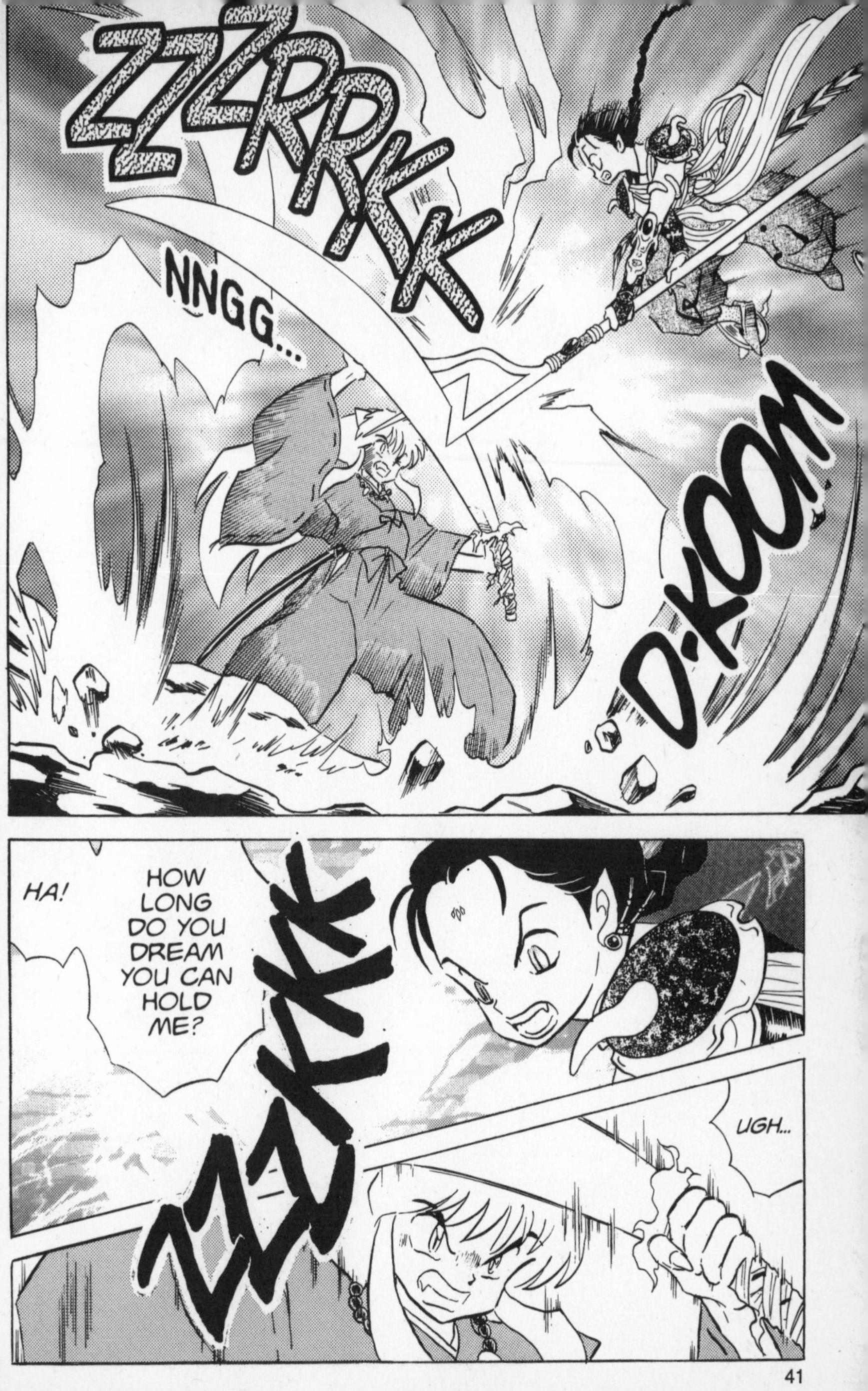
ZZRRKK
NNGG...
D-KOOM
HA!
HOW LONG DO YOU DREAM YOU CAN HOLD ME?
ZZSKK
UGH...

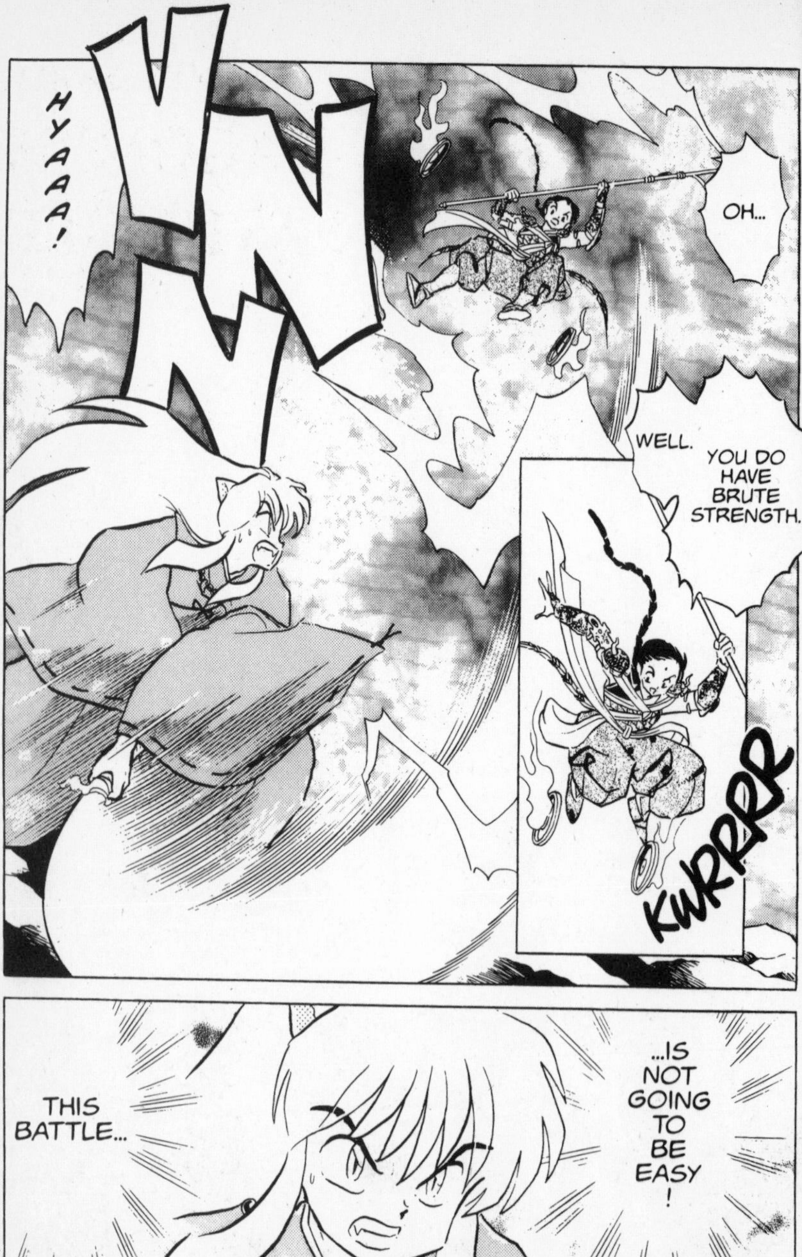
HYAAAA!
OH...
WELL.
YOU DO HAVE BRUTE STRENGTH.
KWRRRR
THIS BATTLE...
...IS NOT GOING TO BE EASY!

SCROLL THREE

KAGOME'S LAST HOPE

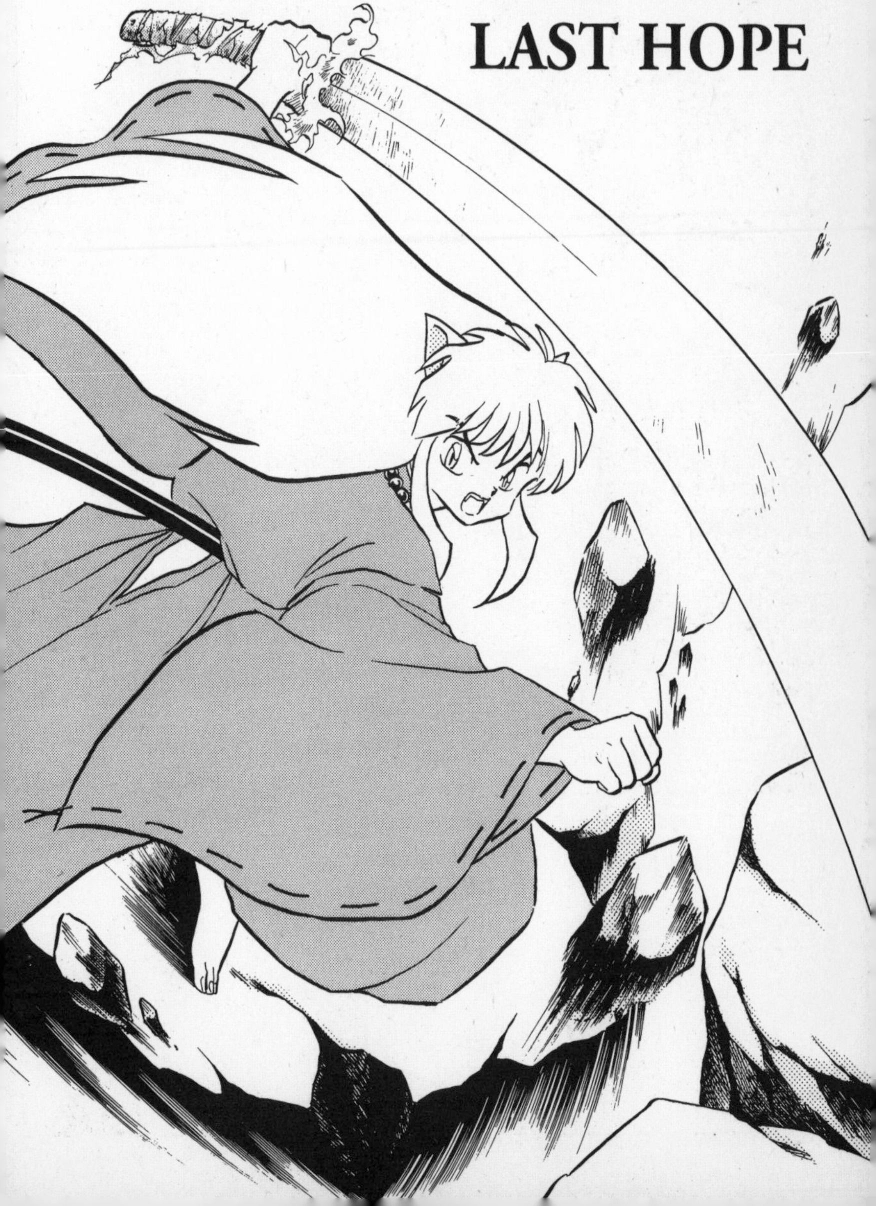

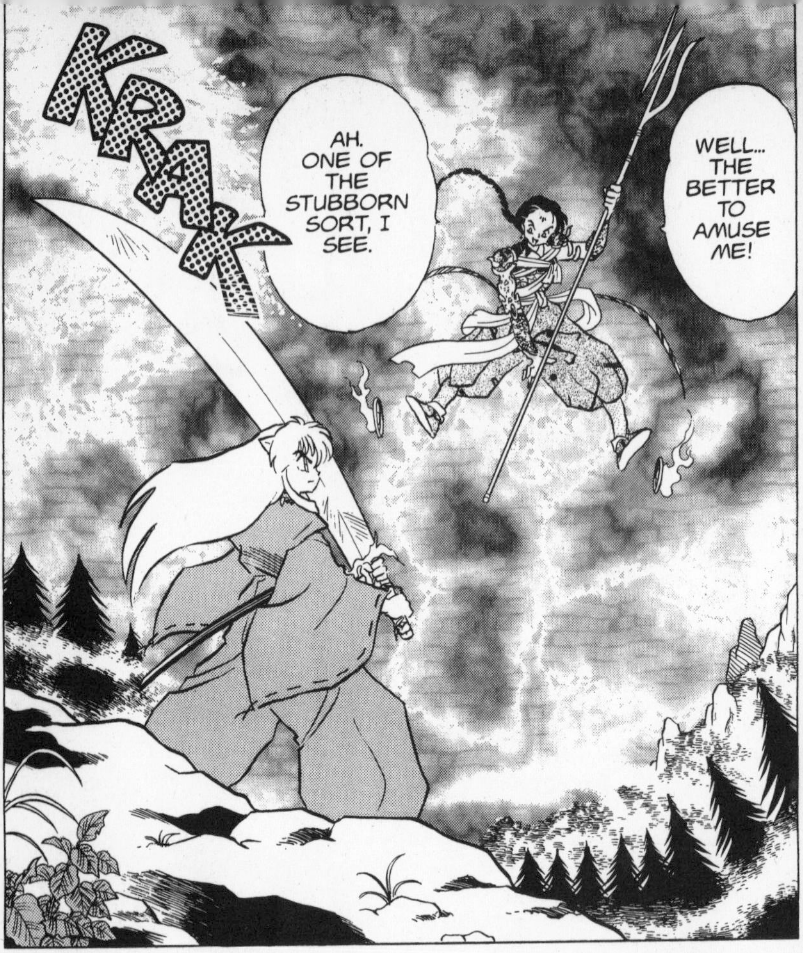
KRAKK
AH. ONE OF THE STUBBORN SORT, I SEE.
WELL... THE BETTER TO AMUSE ME!

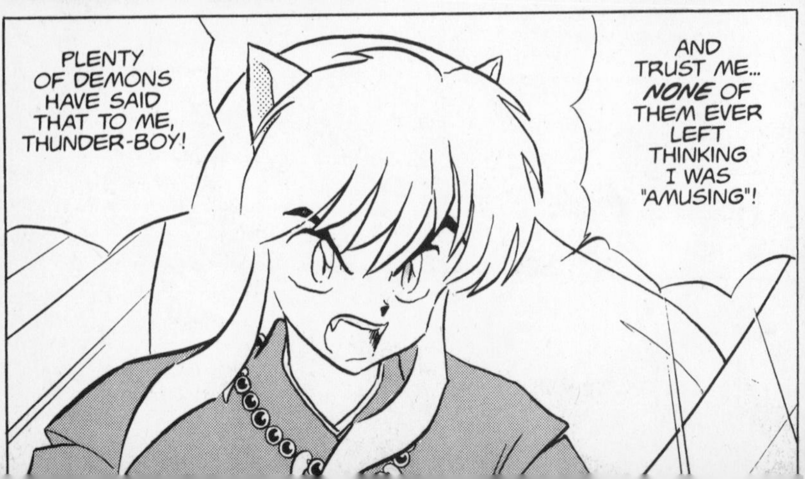
PLENTY OF DEMONS HAVE SAID THAT TO ME, THUNDER-BOY!
AND TRUST ME... *NONE* OF THEM EVER LEFT THINKING I WAS "AMUSING"!

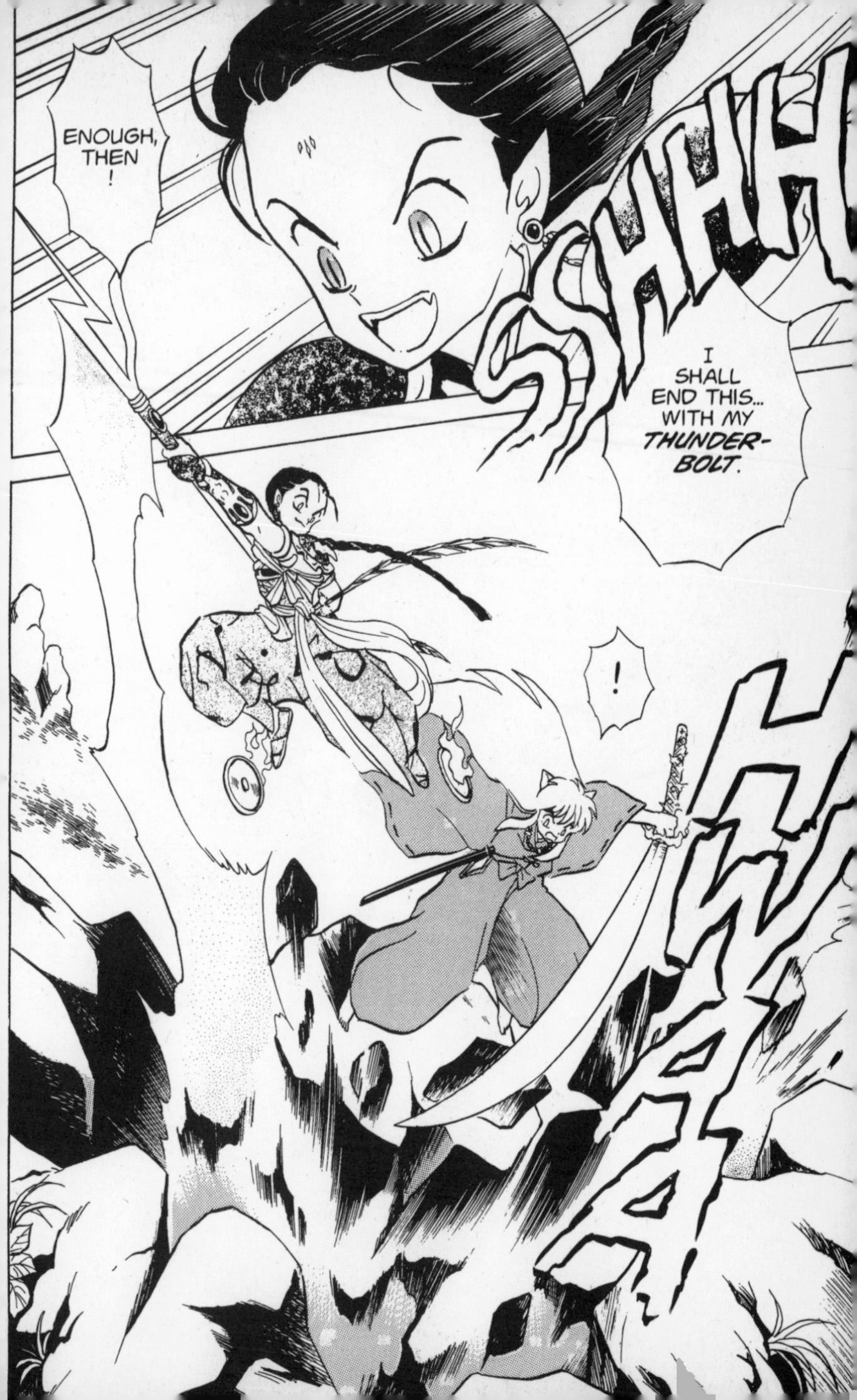
ENOUGH, THEN !
SHHH
I SHALL END THIS... WITH MY *THUNDER-BOLT*.
!

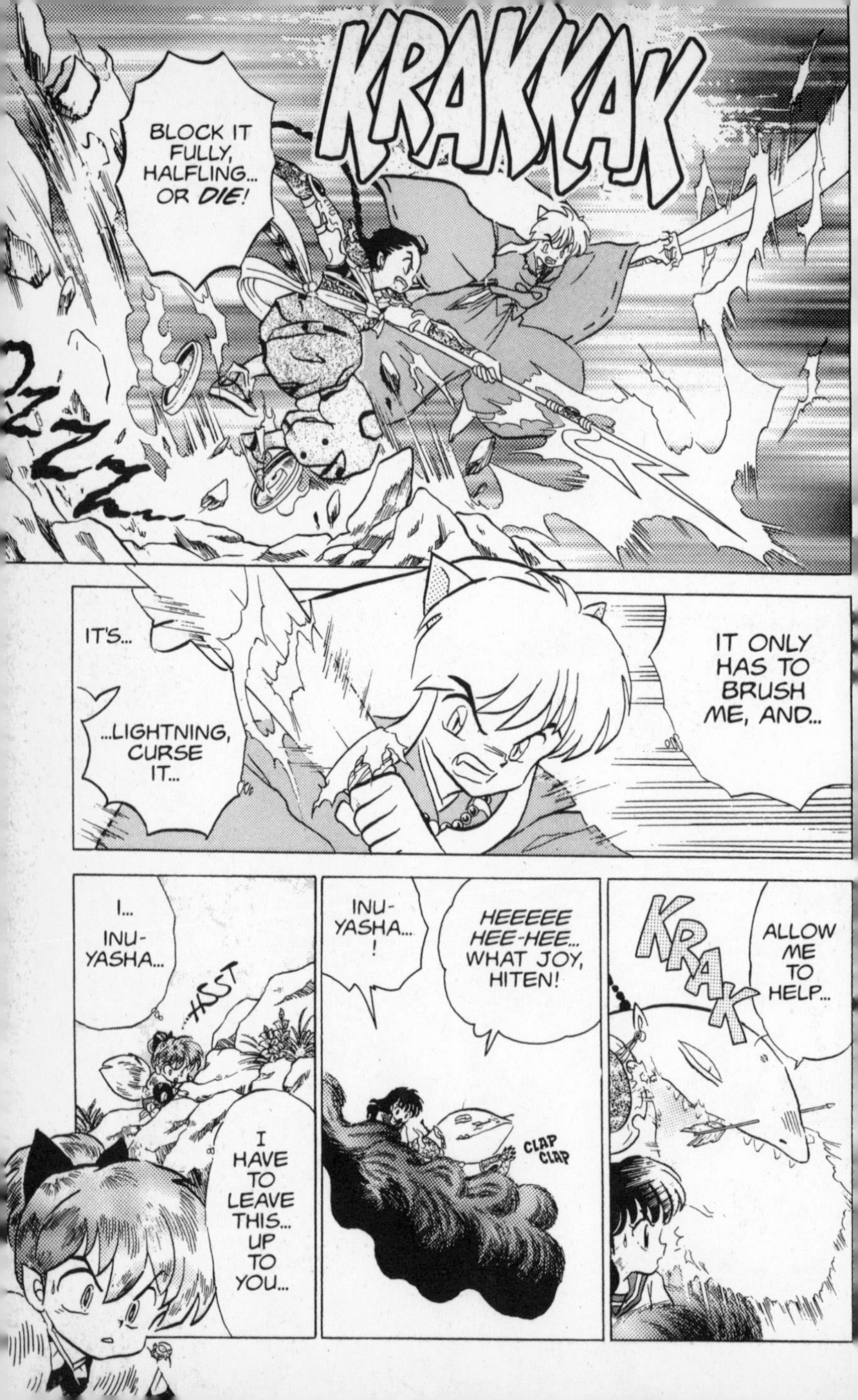
KRAKKAK
BLOCK IT FULLY, HALFLING... OR DIE!
IT ONLY HAS TO BRUSH ME, AND...
IT'S...
...LIGHTNING, CURSE IT...
KRAK
ALLOW ME TO HELP...
HEEEEE HEE-HEE... WHAT JOY, HITEN!
INU-YASHA... !
CLAP CLAP
I... INU-YASHA...
HSST
I HAVE TO LEAVE THIS... UP TO YOU...

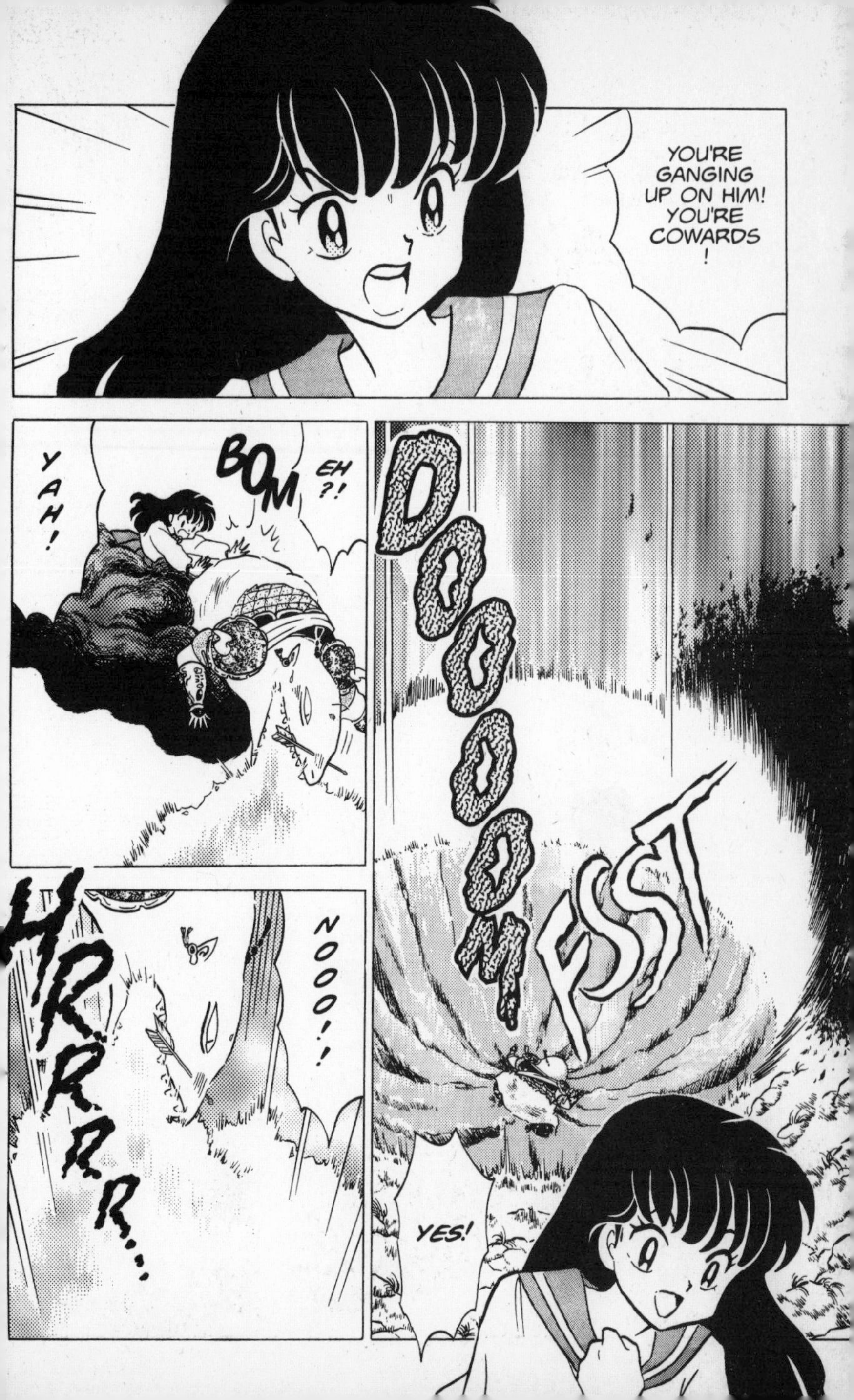
YOU'RE GANGING UP ON HIM! YOU'RE COWARDS!
YAH!
BOM
EH?!
HRRRRR...
NOOOO!!
DOOOOM
FSST
YES!

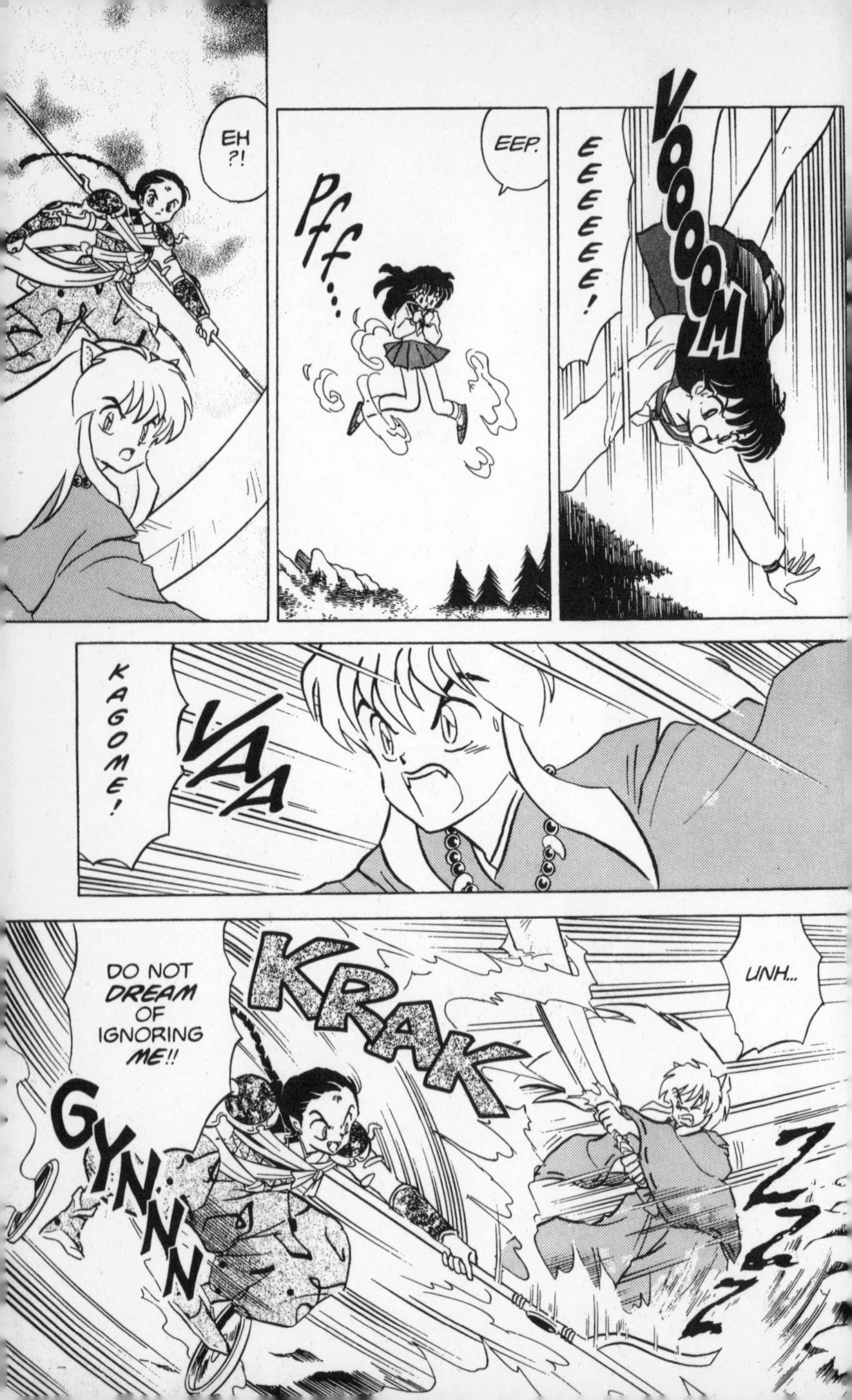
EH ?!
EEP.
Pff...
EEEEEEE!
VOOOOM
KAGOME!
VAA
DO NOT DREAM OF IGNORING ME!!
KRAK
UNH...
GYNNN
ZZZZ

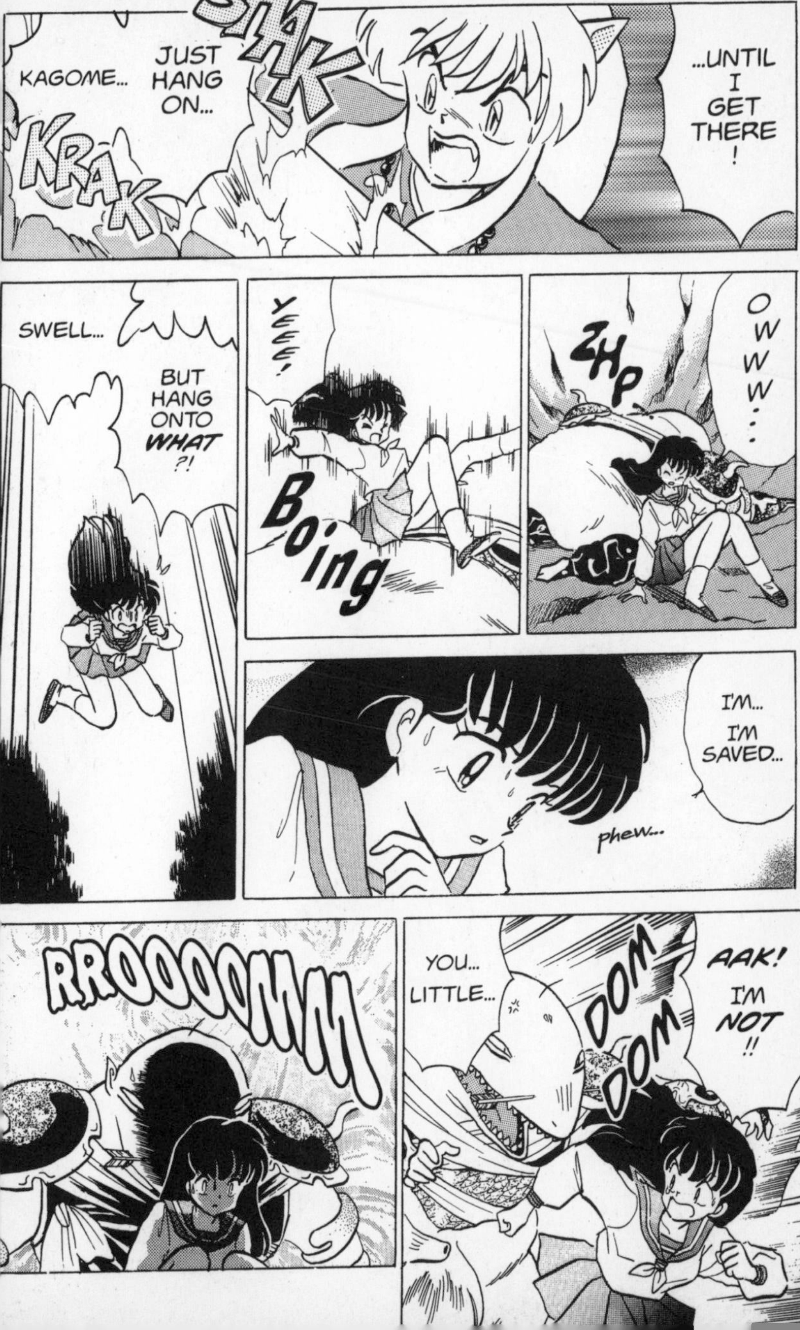
SHAK
KRAK
KAGOME...
JUST HANG ON...
...UNTIL I GET THERE!
SWELL...
BUT HANG ONTO WHAT?!
YEEE!
Boing
ZHP
OWWW...
I'M... I'M SAVED...
phew...
RROOOOMM
YOU... LITTLE...
DOOM DOOM
AAK! I'M NOT!!

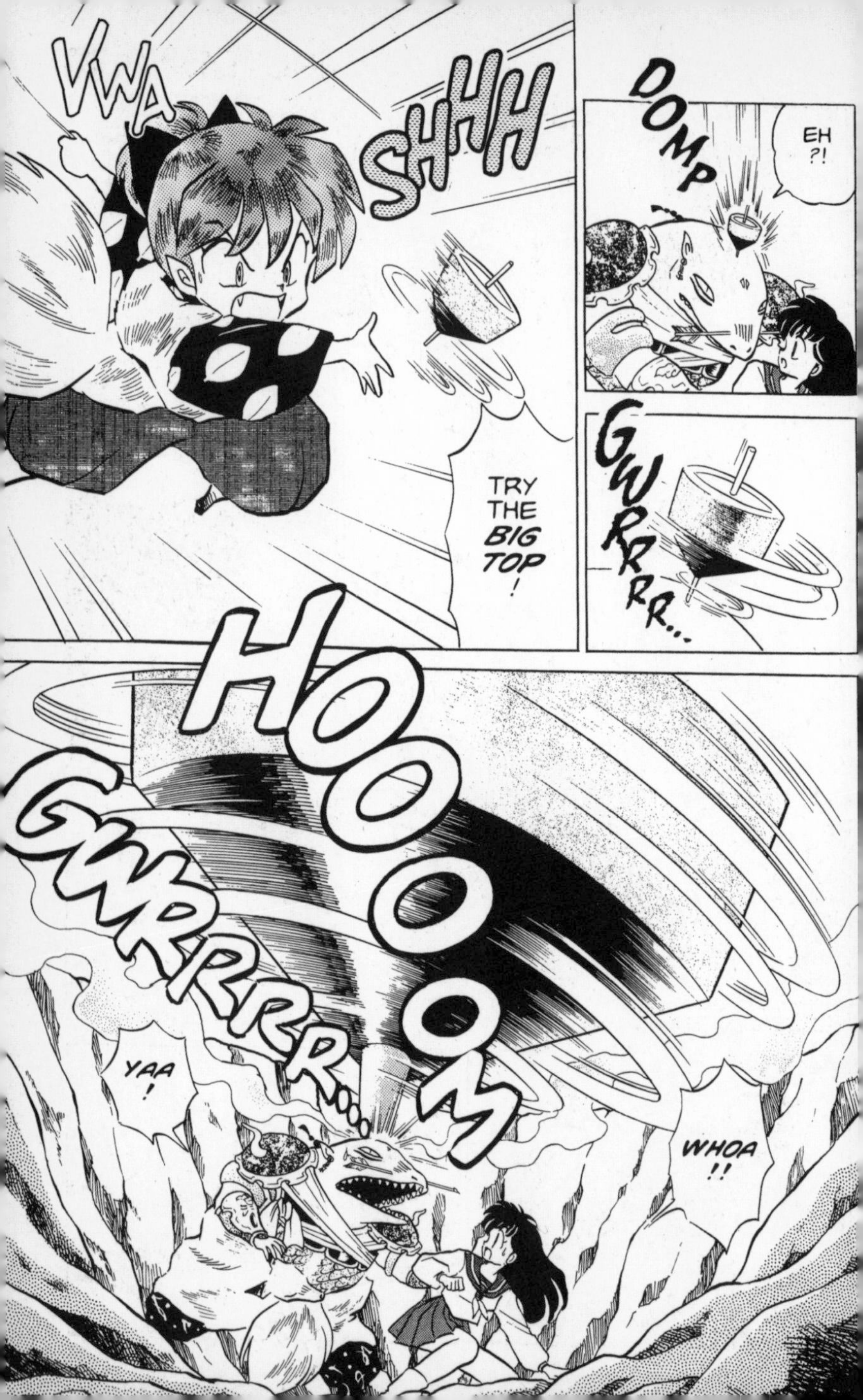

VWA
SHHH
TRY THE BIG TOP!
DOMP
EH ?!
GWRRRRR...
HOOOOOM
GWRRRRR...
YAA!
WHOA!!

OVER HERE, KAGOME! HURRY!

SHIPPŌ-CHAN!

MAN, TALK ABOUT BEING THE *TOP DOG*...!

AH, IT WAS NOTHIN'.

PINNNG

DO NOT RELAX YOUR GUARD YET.

FOX SORCERY IS, AFTER ALL, ONLY DECEPTION.

YOU... YOU MEAN, THAT'S...

MERELY AN ILLUSION.

GRNG GRNG

OW OW OW OW...

KRRRRRORO...

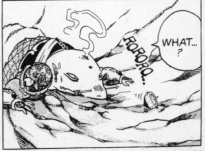

ROROR...

WHAT...?

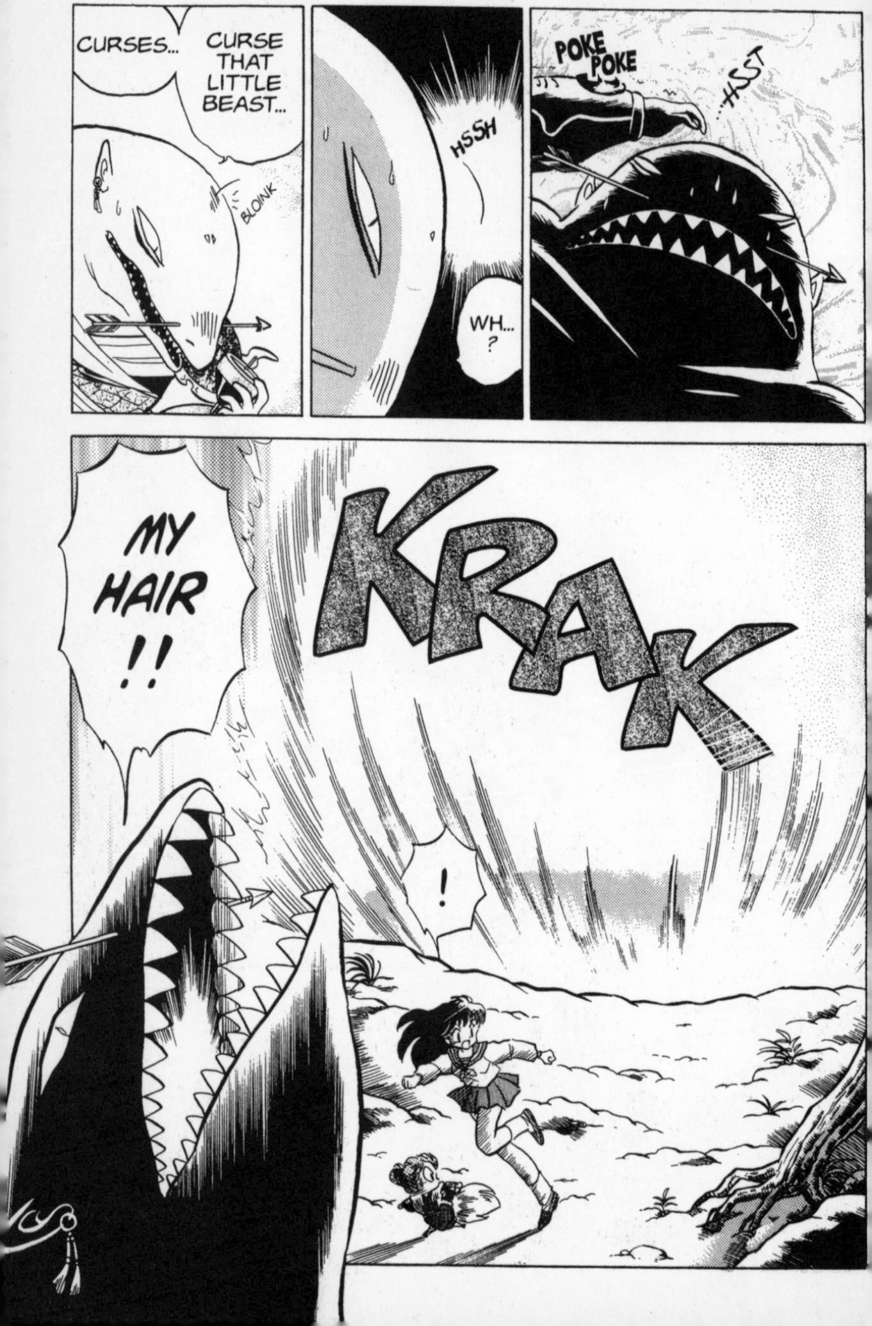
CURSES...
CURSE THAT LITTLE BEAST...
BLOINK
HSSH
WH... ?
POKE POKE
HSST
MY HAIR !!
KRAK
!

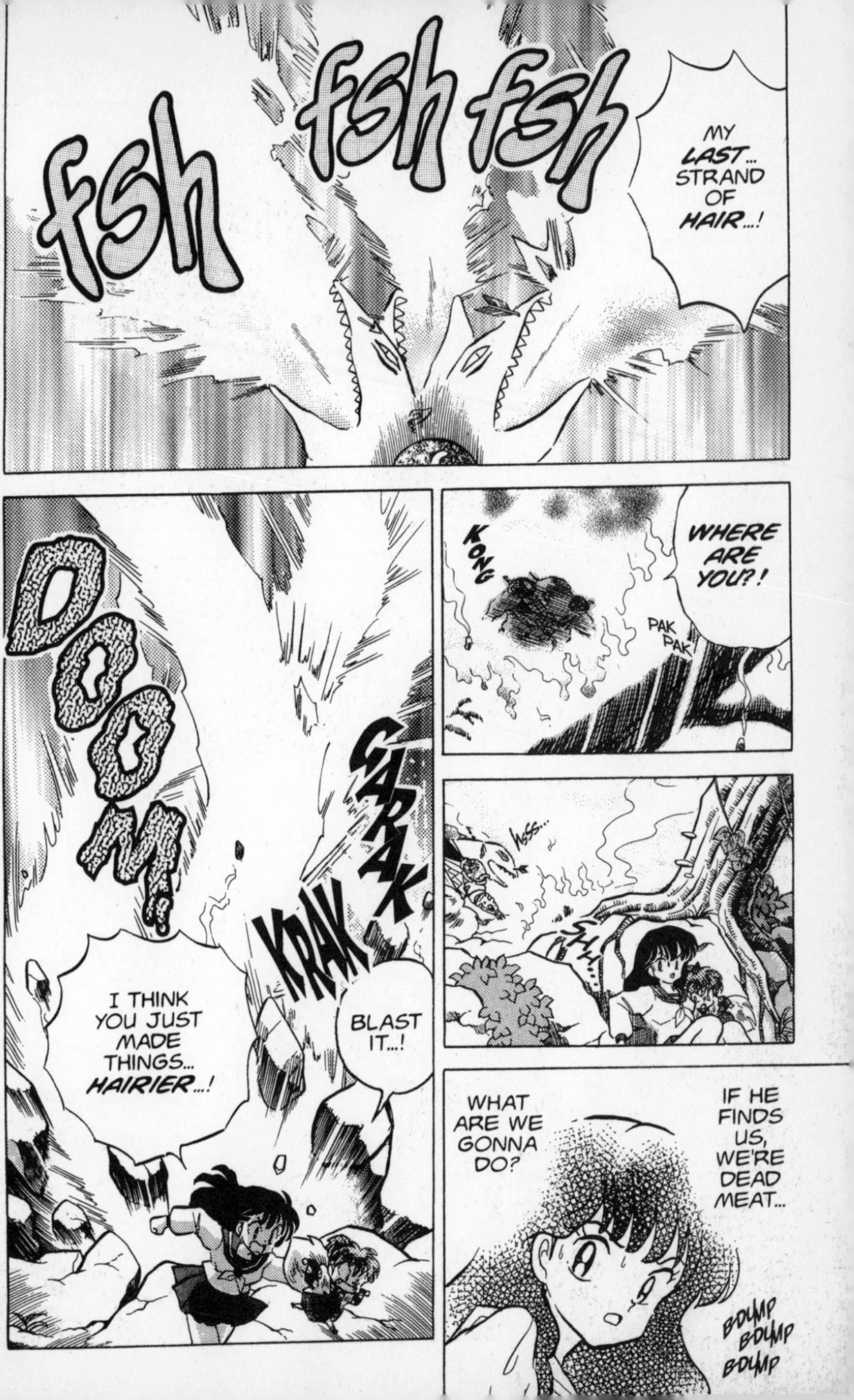
fsh fsh fsh
MY LAST... STRAND OF HAIR...!
DOOM
GARAK
KRAK
I THINK YOU JUST MADE THINGS... HAIRIER...!
BLAST IT...!
KONG
WHERE ARE YOU?!
PAK PAK
WSS...
SHH...
WHAT ARE WE GONNA DO?
IF HE FINDS US, WE'RE DEAD MEAT...
B-DUMP B-DUMP B-DUMP

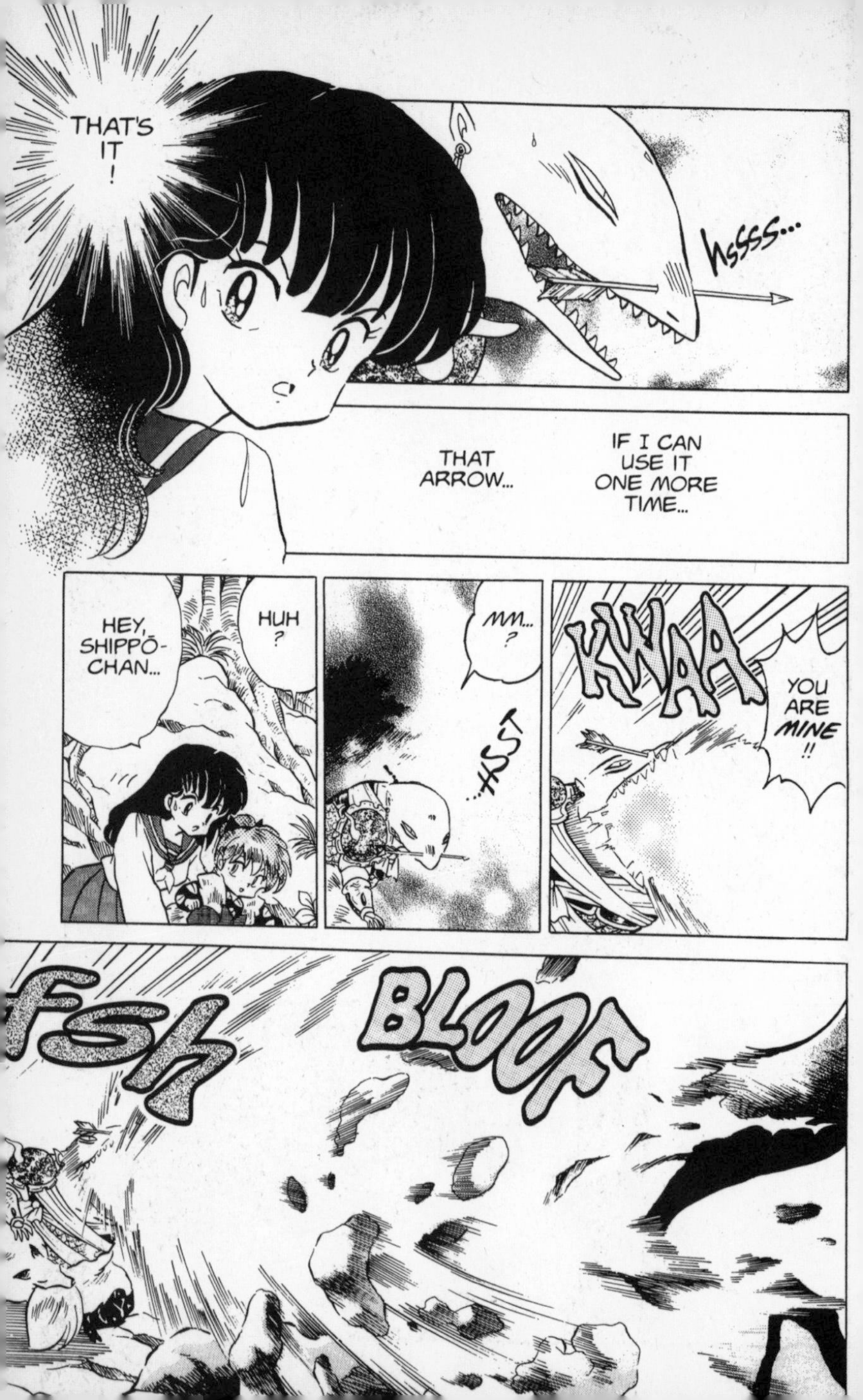
THAT'S IT !
hssss...
THAT ARROW...
IF I CAN USE IT ONE MORE TIME...
HEY, SHIPPŌ-CHAN...
HUH ?
MM... ?
...HSST
KWAA
YOU ARE MINE !!
FSH
BLOOF

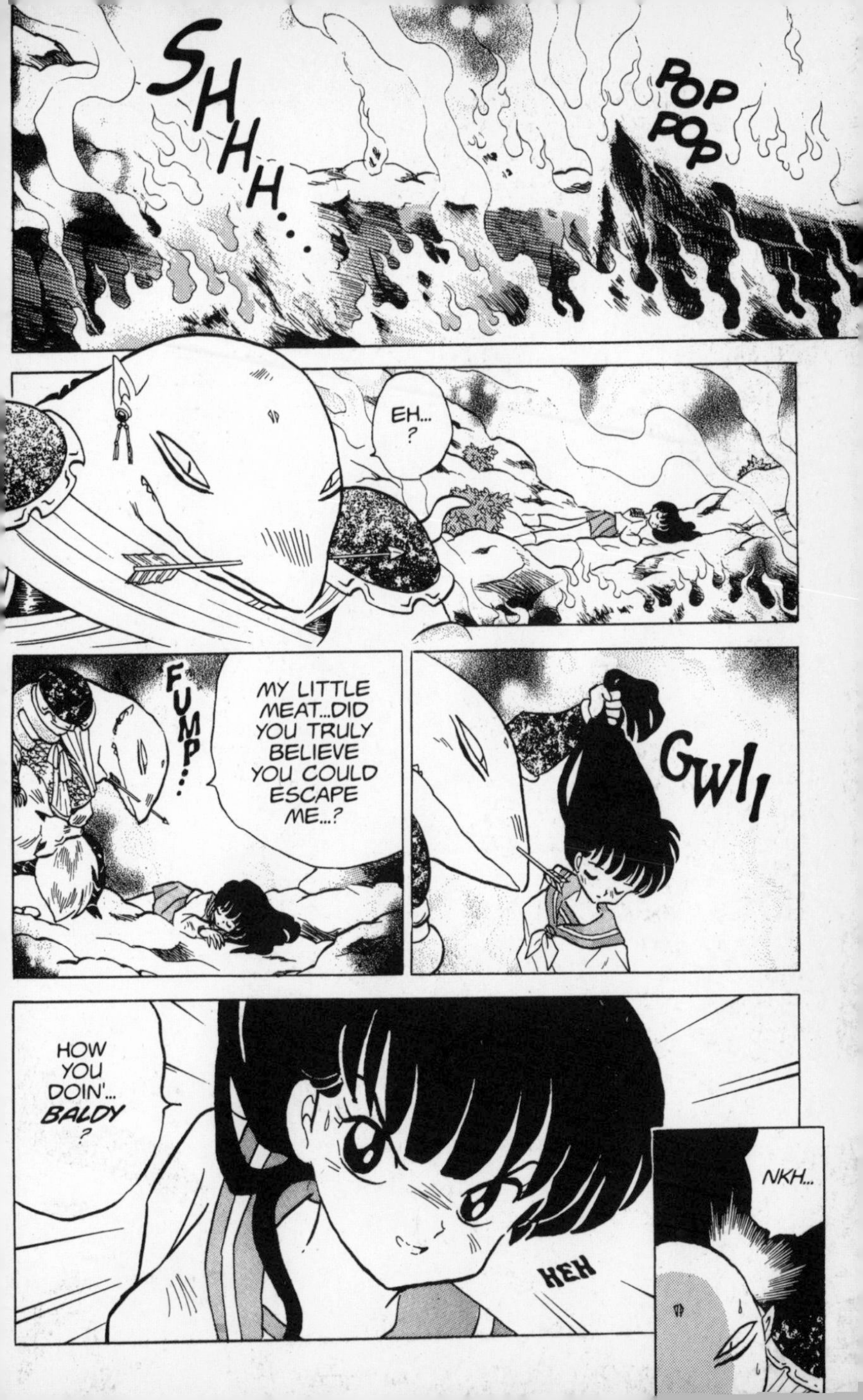
SHHH...
POP POP
EH... ?
FUMP...
MY LITTLE MEAT...DID YOU TRULY BELIEVE YOU COULD ESCAPE ME...?
GWII
HOW YOU DOIN'... BALDY ?
HEH
NKH...

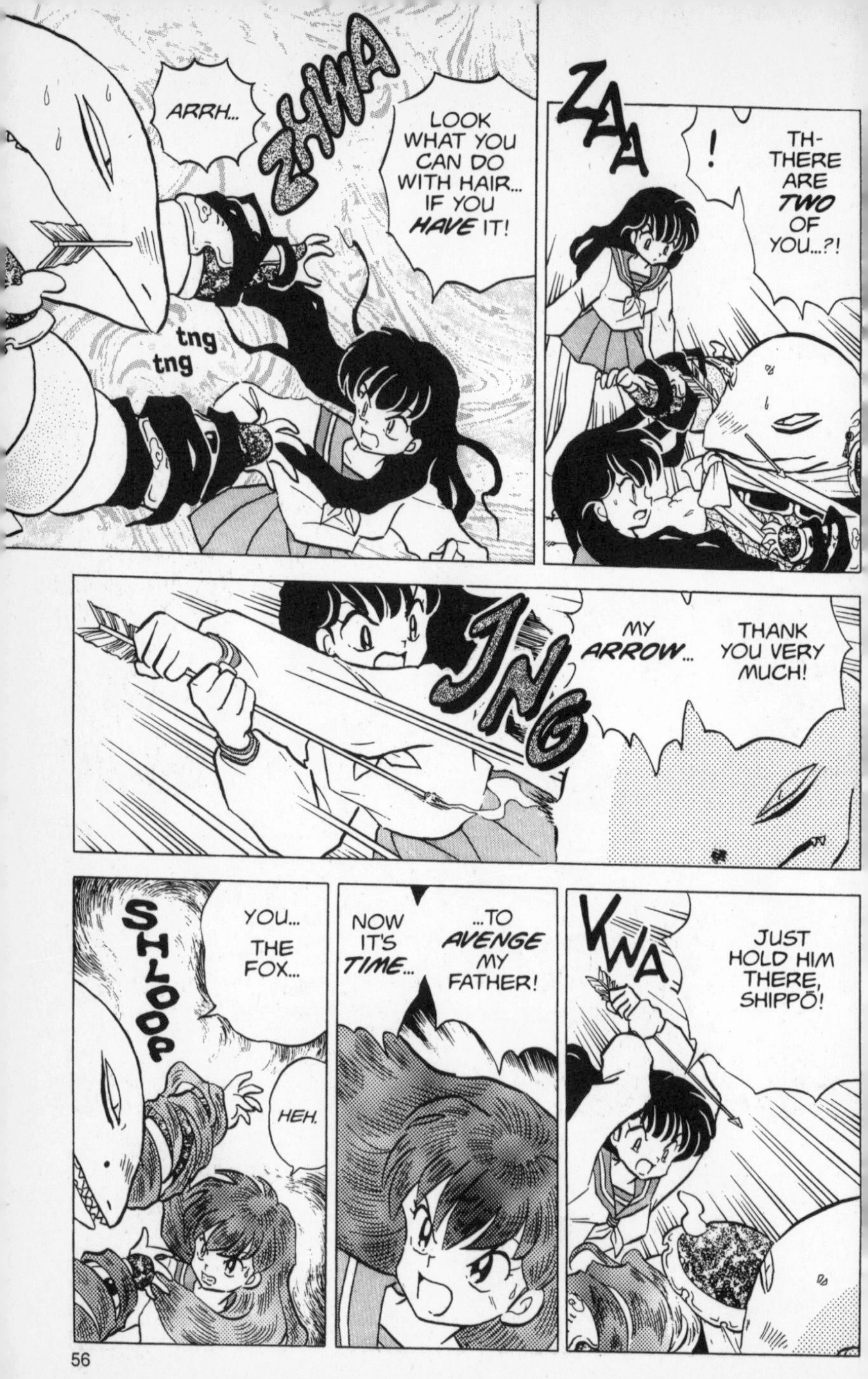
ARRH...
ZHWA
LOOK WHAT YOU CAN DO WITH HAIR... IF YOU HAVE IT!
tng tng
ZAAA
!
TH-THERE ARE TWO OF YOU...?!
JNG
MY ARROW...
THANK YOU VERY MUCH!
SHLOOP
YOU... THE FOX...
HEH.
NOW IT'S TIME...
...TO AVENGE MY FATHER!
KWA
JUST HOLD HIM THERE, SHIPPŌ!

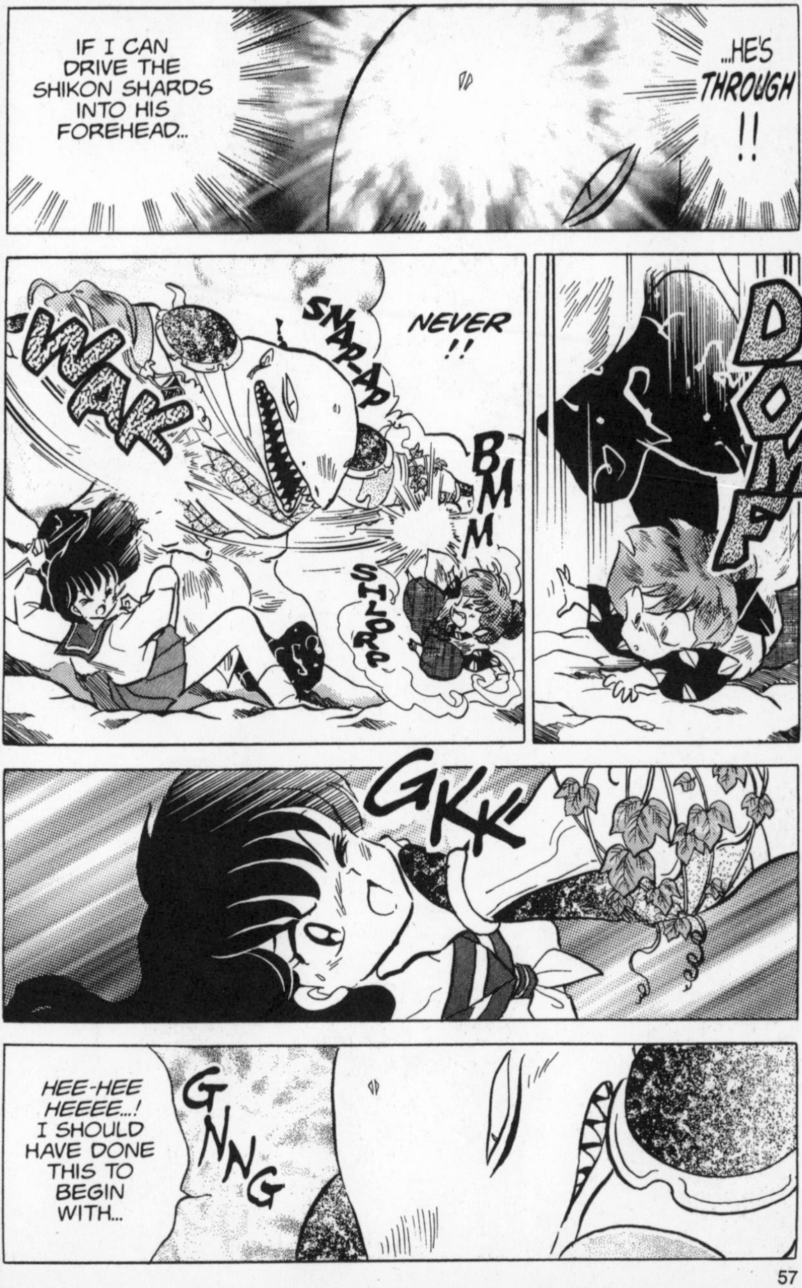
IF I CAN DRIVE THE SHIKON SHARDS INTO HIS FOREHEAD...
...HE'S THROUGH !!
WHAK
SNAP-AP
NEVER !!
BMMM
SHLORP
DOMPF
GKK
HEE-HEE HEEEE...! I SHOULD HAVE DONE THIS TO BEGIN WITH...
GNNG

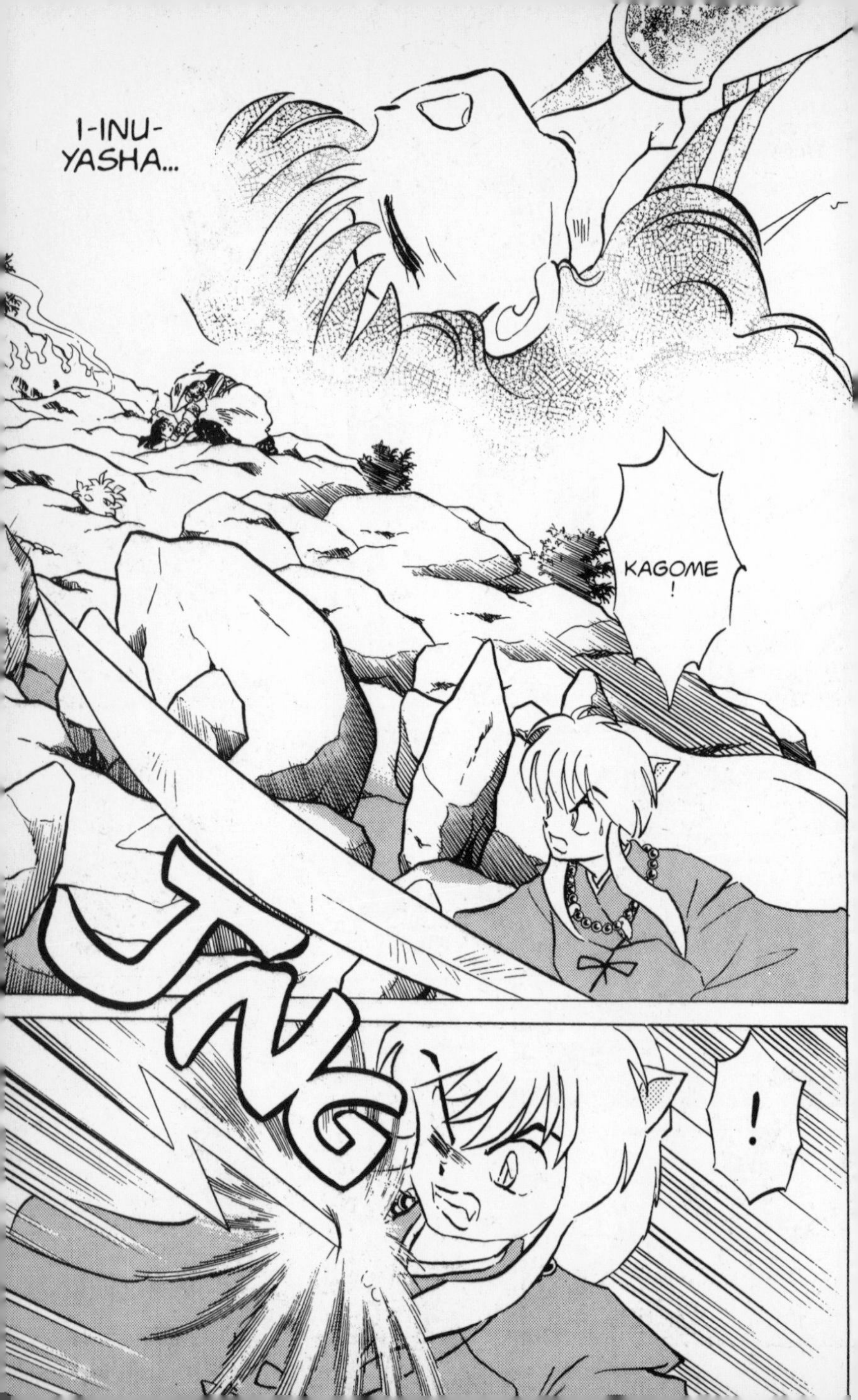
I-INU-
YASHA...
KAGOME
!
JING
!

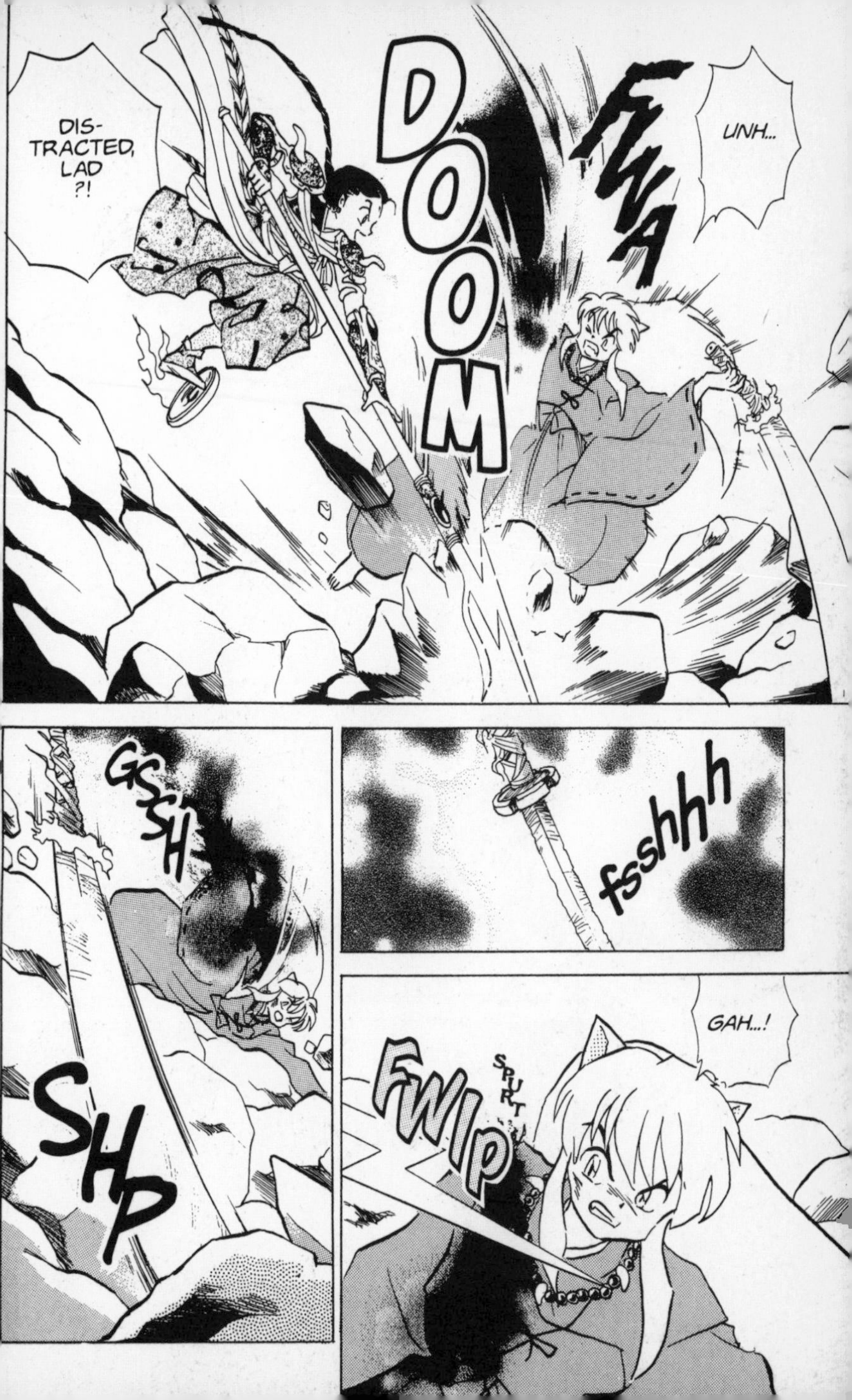
DIS-TRACTED, LAD ?!
DOOM
FWA
UNH...
GSSH
SHP
fsshhh
FWIP
SPURT
GAH...!

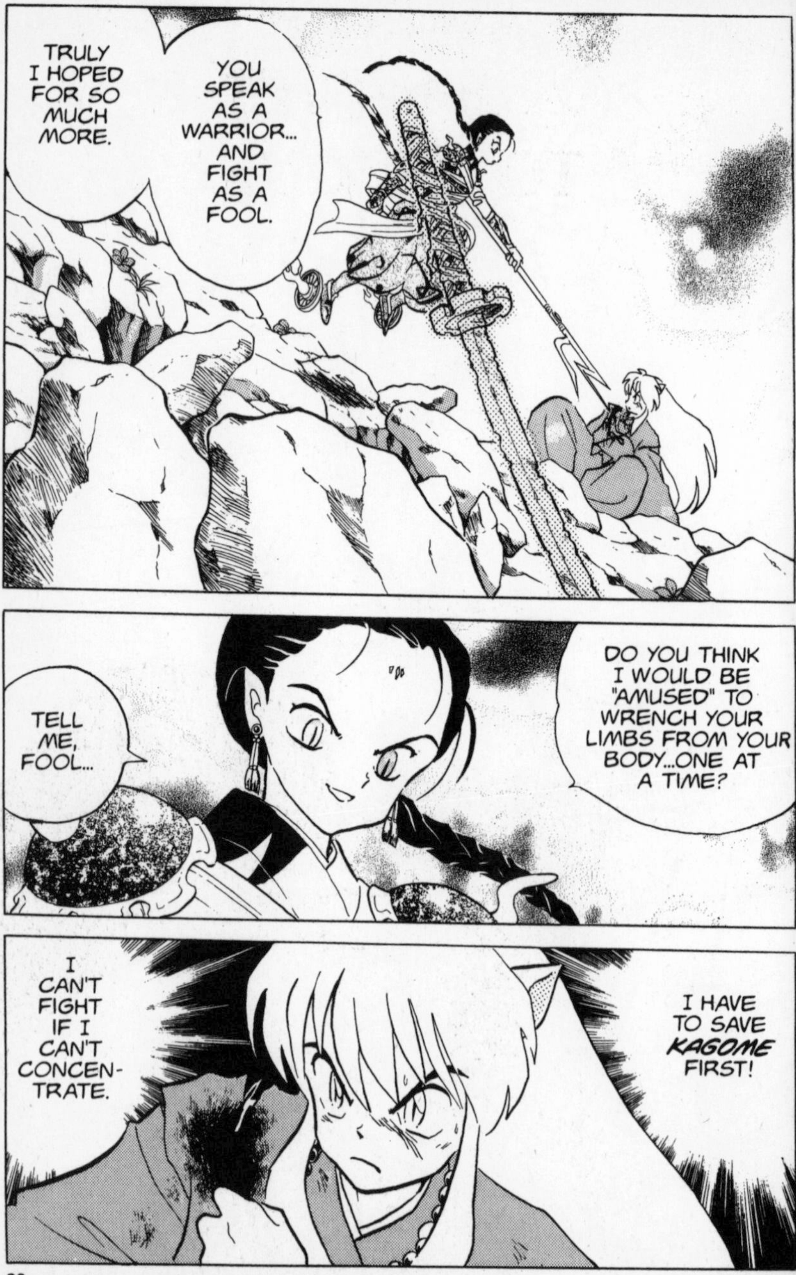
TRULY I HOPED FOR SO MUCH MORE.
YOU SPEAK AS A WARRIOR... AND FIGHT AS A FOOL.
TELL ME, FOOL...
DO YOU THINK I WOULD BE "AMUSED" TO WRENCH YOUR LIMBS FROM YOUR BODY...ONE AT A TIME?
I CAN'T FIGHT IF I CAN'T CONCENTRATE.
I HAVE TO SAVE *KAGOME* FIRST!

SCROLL FOUR

THE POWER TO DEVOUR

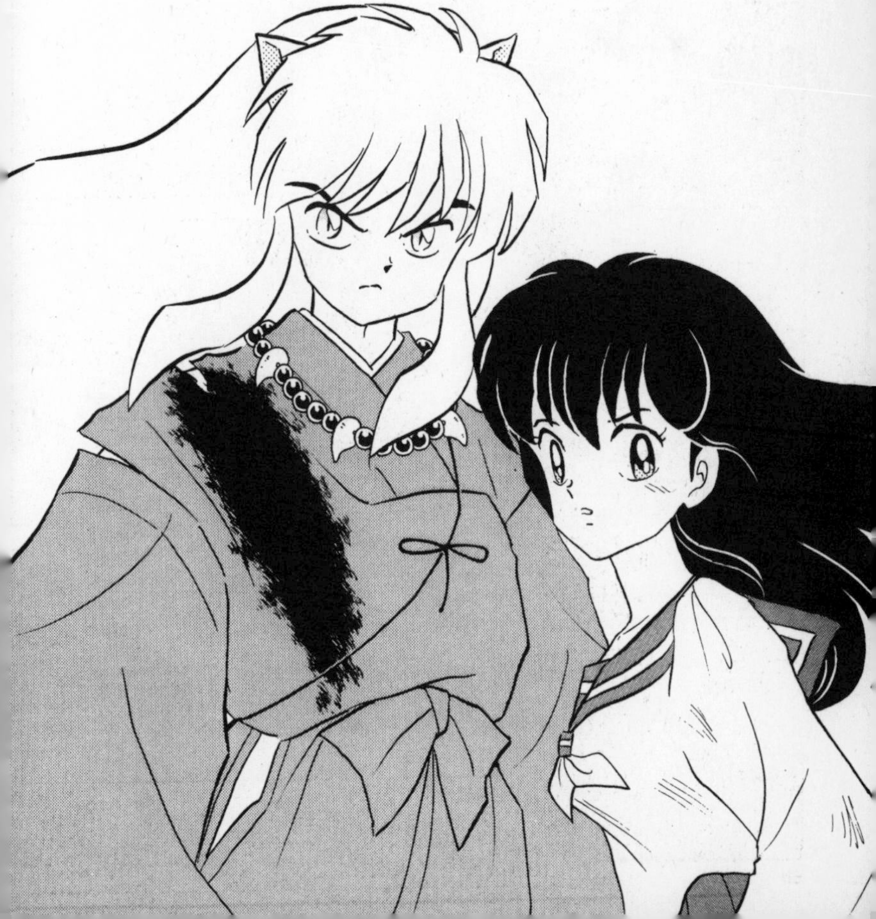

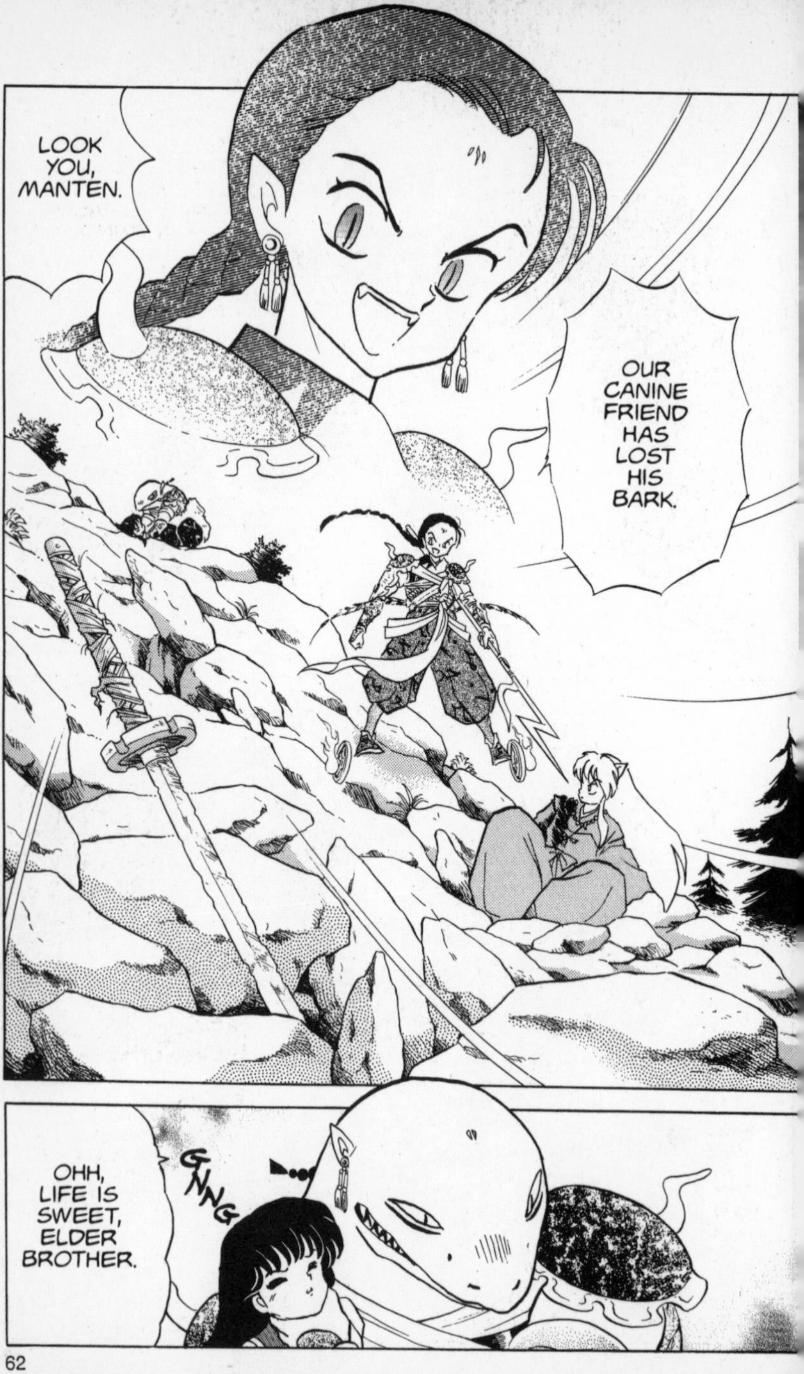
LOOK YOU, MANTEN.
OUR CANINE FRIEND HAS LOST HIS BARK.
OHH, LIFE IS SWEET, ELDER BROTHER.
GNNG

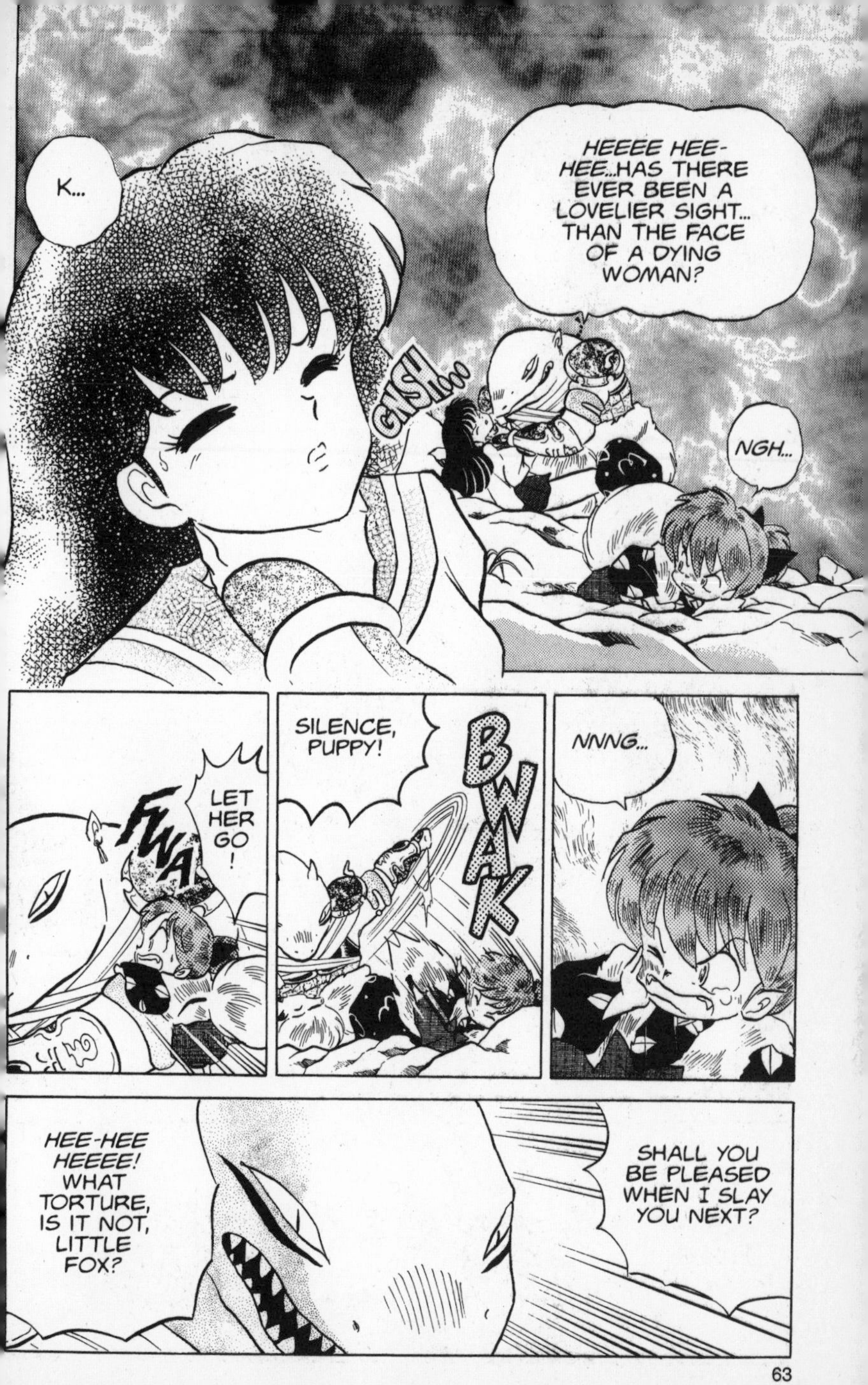
K...
HEEEE HEE-HEE...HAS THERE EVER BEEN A LOVELIER SIGHT... THAN THE FACE OF A DYING WOMAN?
GISH...
NGH...
FWA
LET HER GO!
SILENCE, PUPPY!
BWAK
NNNG...
HEE-HEE HEEEE! WHAT TORTURE, IS IT NOT, LITTLE FOX?
SHALL YOU BE PLEASED WHEN I SLAY YOU NEXT?

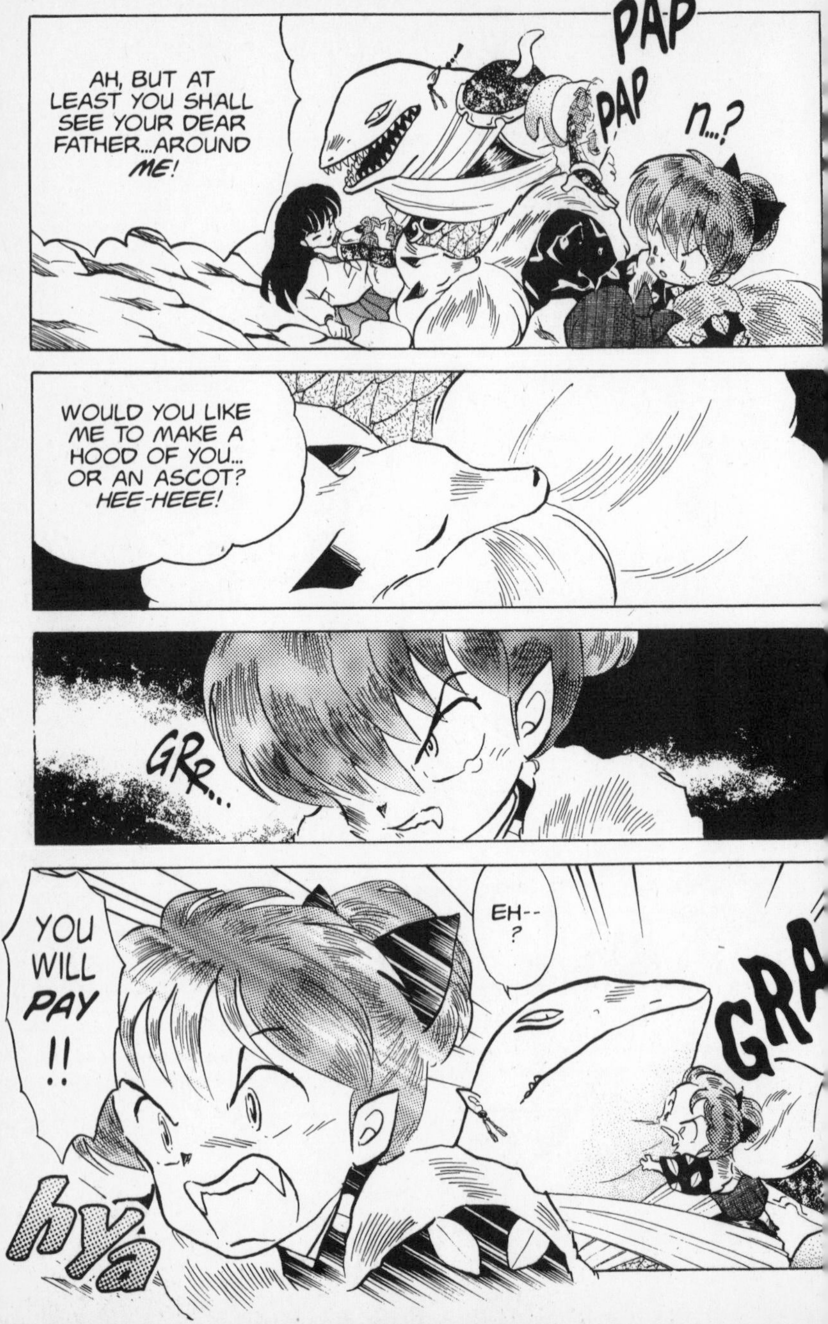
AH, BUT AT LEAST YOU SHALL SEE YOUR DEAR FATHER...AROUND ME!
PAP PAP
PAP
n...?
WOULD YOU LIKE ME TO MAKE A HOOD OF YOU... OR AN ASCOT? HEE-HEEE!
GRR...
YOU WILL PAY !!
EH-- ?
GRA
hya

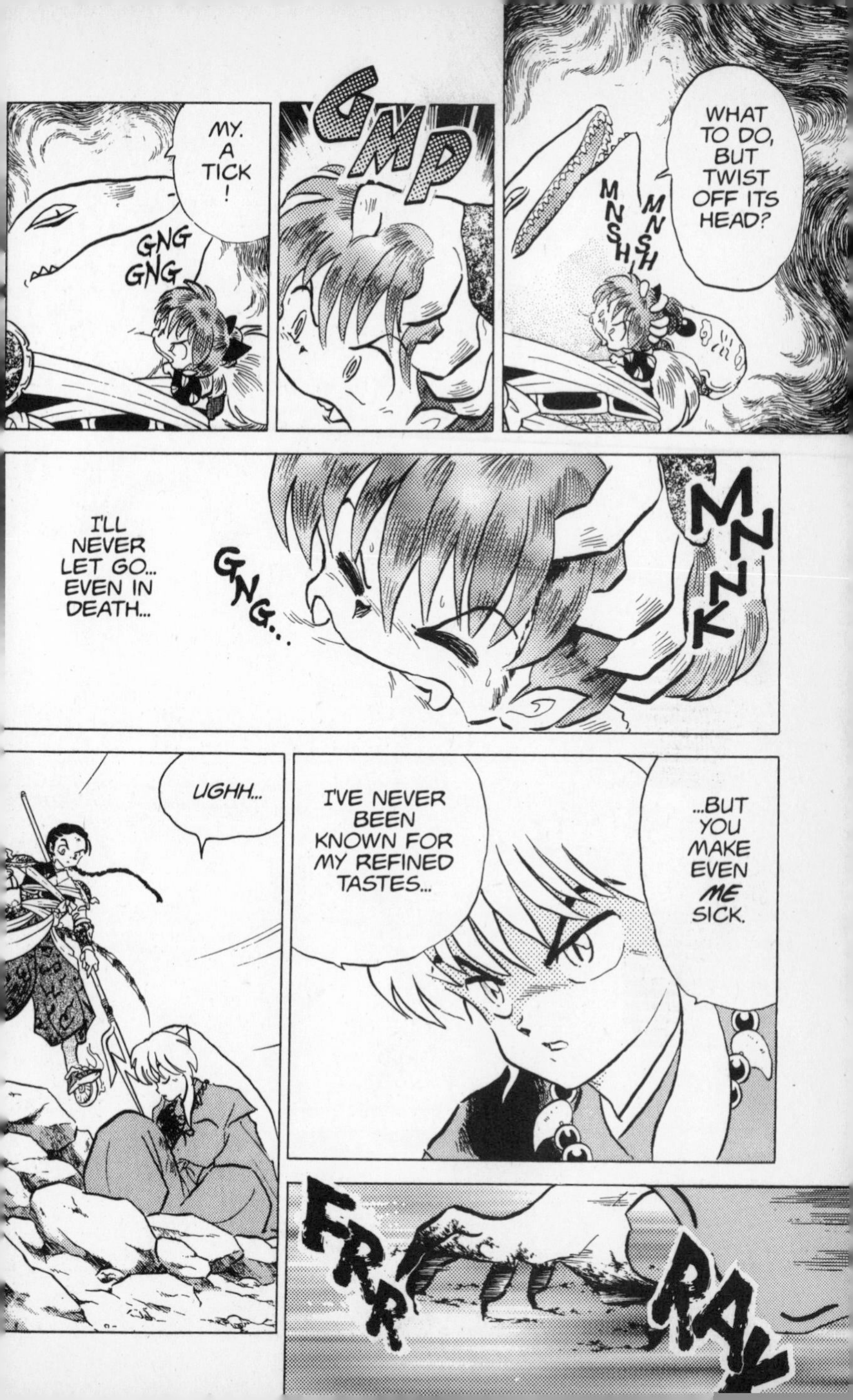
MY. A TICK!
GNG GNG
GMP
MNSH MNSH
WHAT TO DO, BUT TWIST OFF ITS HEAD?
I'LL NEVER LET GO... EVEN IN DEATH...
GNG...
MNNK
UGHH...
I'VE NEVER BEEN KNOWN FOR MY REFINED TASTES...
...BUT YOU MAKE EVEN ME SICK.
FRR
PAK

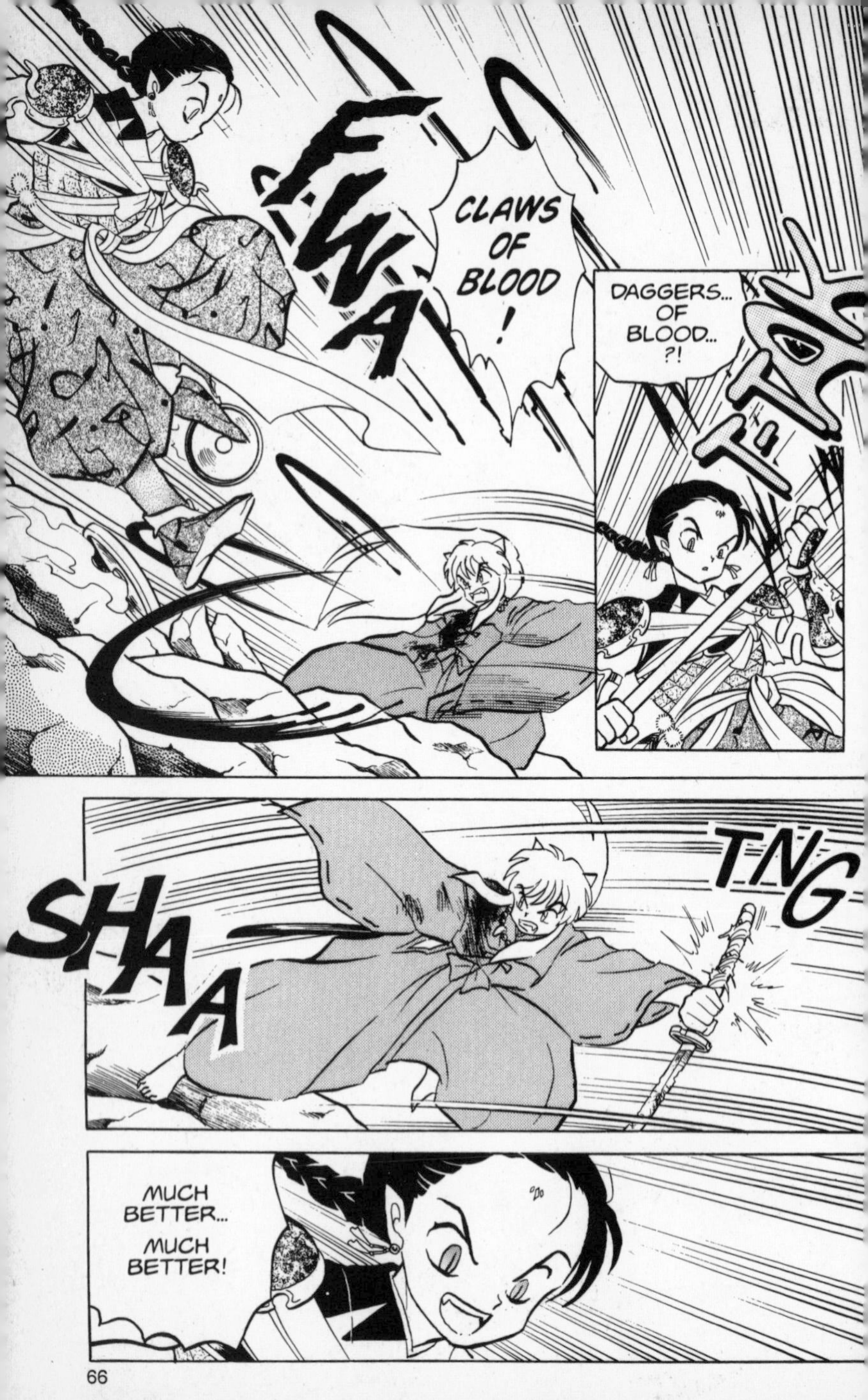
FWA
CLAWS OF BLOOD!
DAGGERS... OF BLOOD...?!
SHAA
TNG
MUCH BETTER... MUCH BETTER!

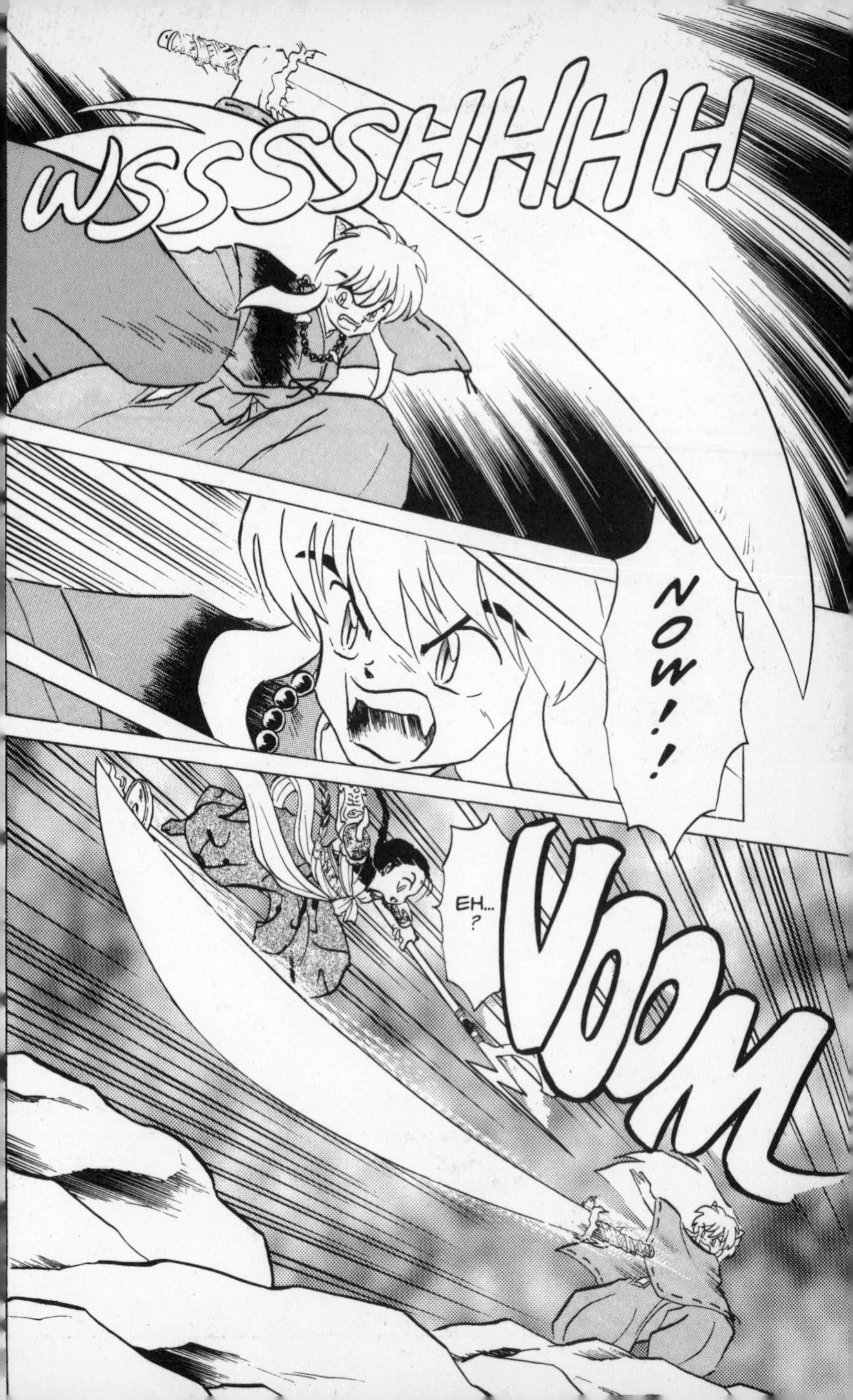
WSSSSHHHH
NOW!!
EH...?
VOOM

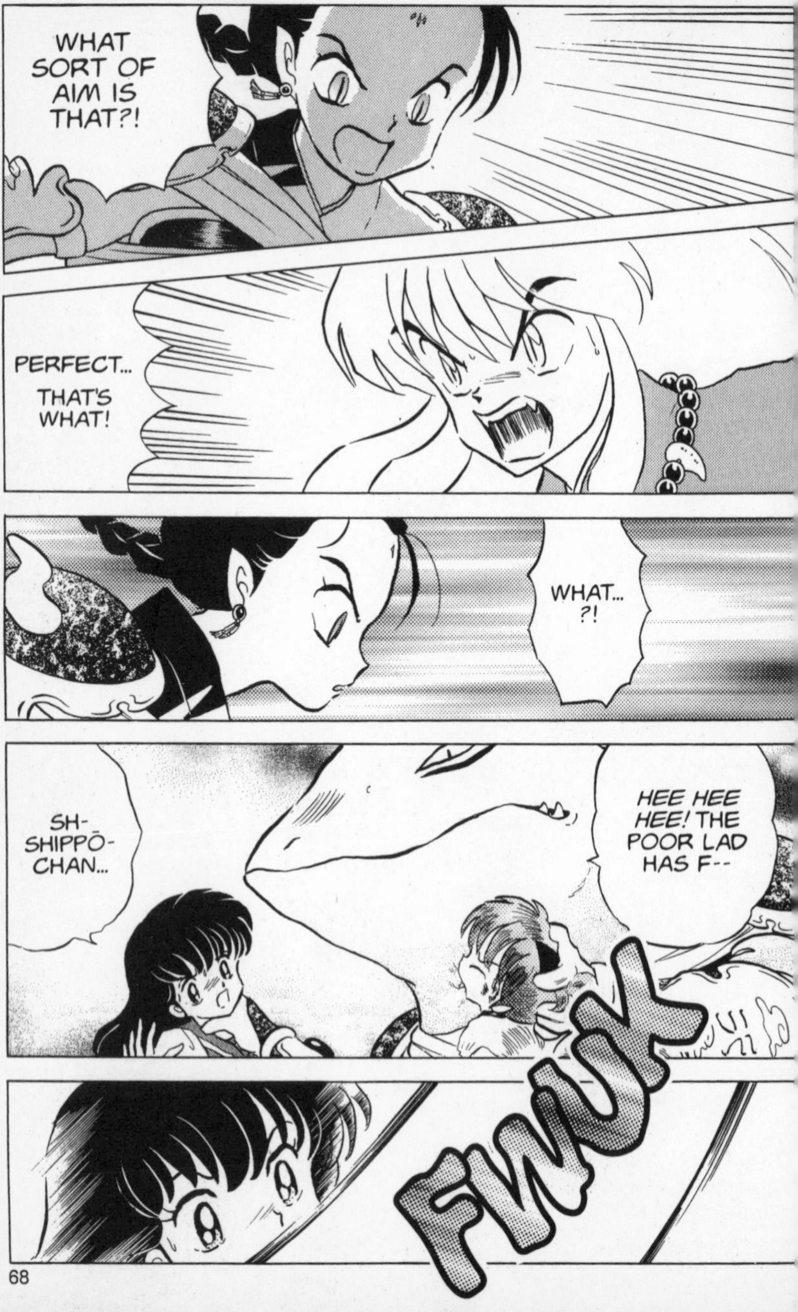
WHAT SORT OF AIM IS THAT?!
PERFECT... THAT'S WHAT!
WHAT... ?!
SH- SHIPPŌ- CHAN...
HEE HEE HEE! THE POOR LAD HAS F--
FWUK

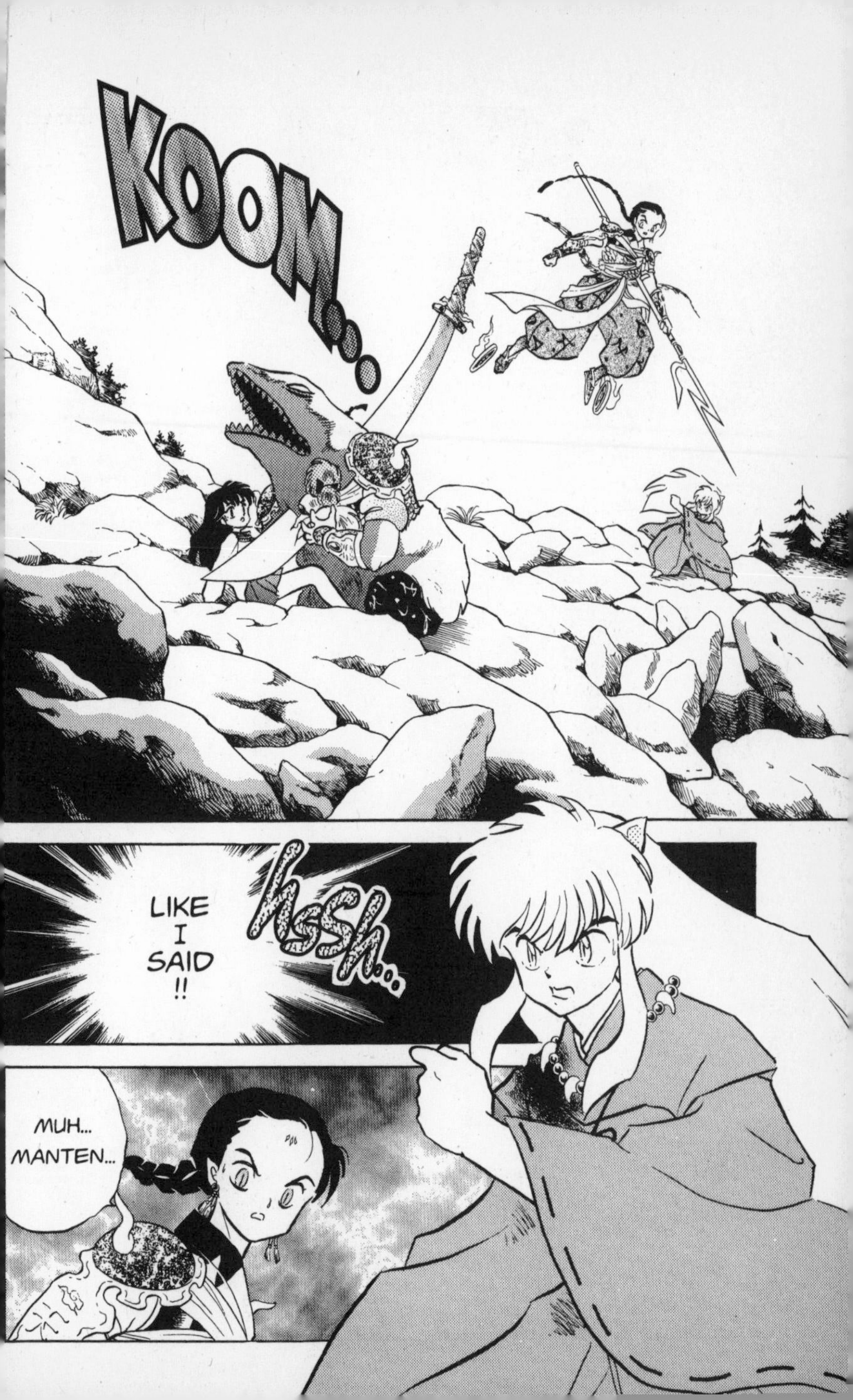
KOOM...
LIKE I SAID !!
hssh...
MUH... MANTEN...

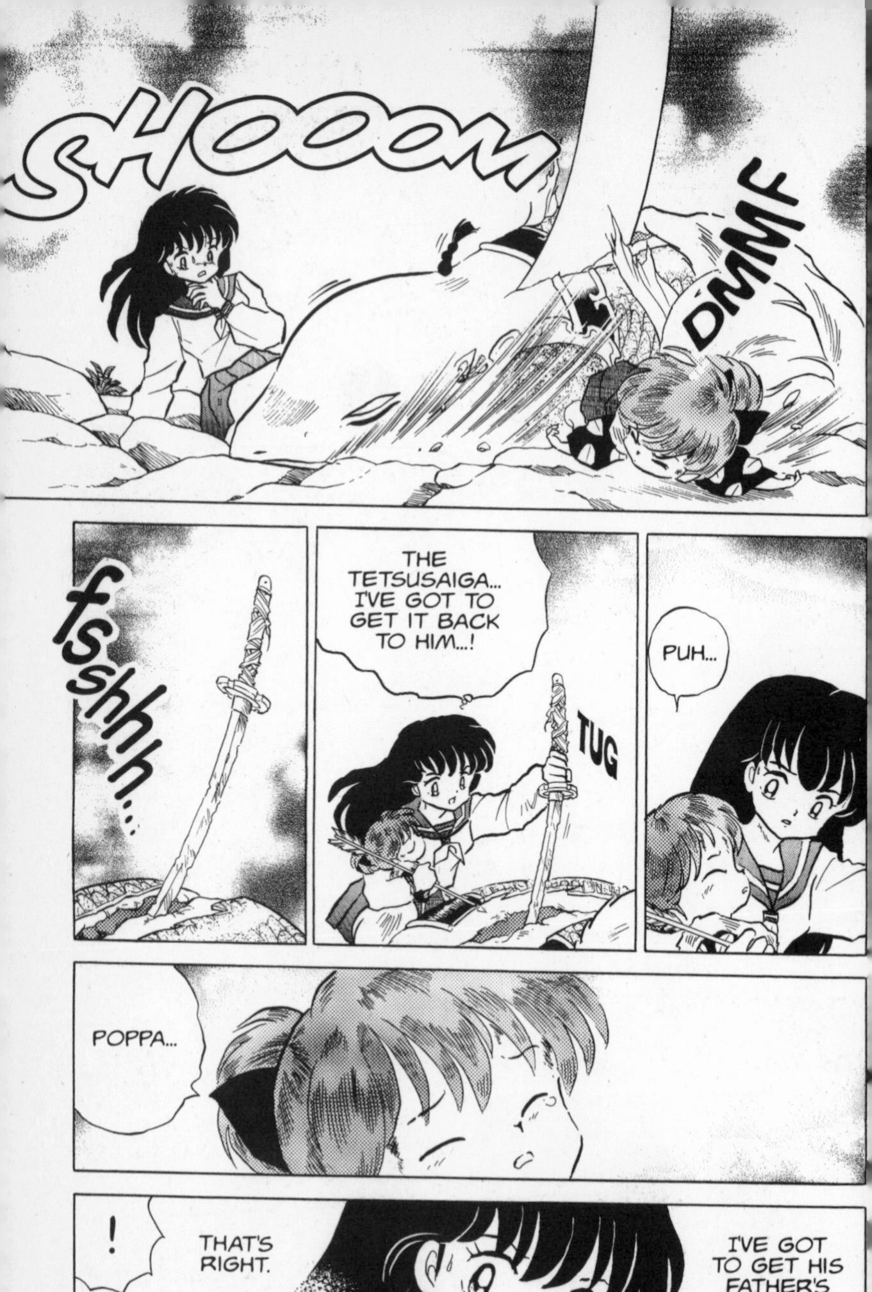
SHOOOM
DMMF
fsshhh...
THE TETSUSAIGA... I'VE GOT TO GET IT BACK TO HIM...!
TUG
PUH...
POPPA...
!
THAT'S RIGHT.
I'VE GOT TO GET HIS FATHER'S PELT, TOO...

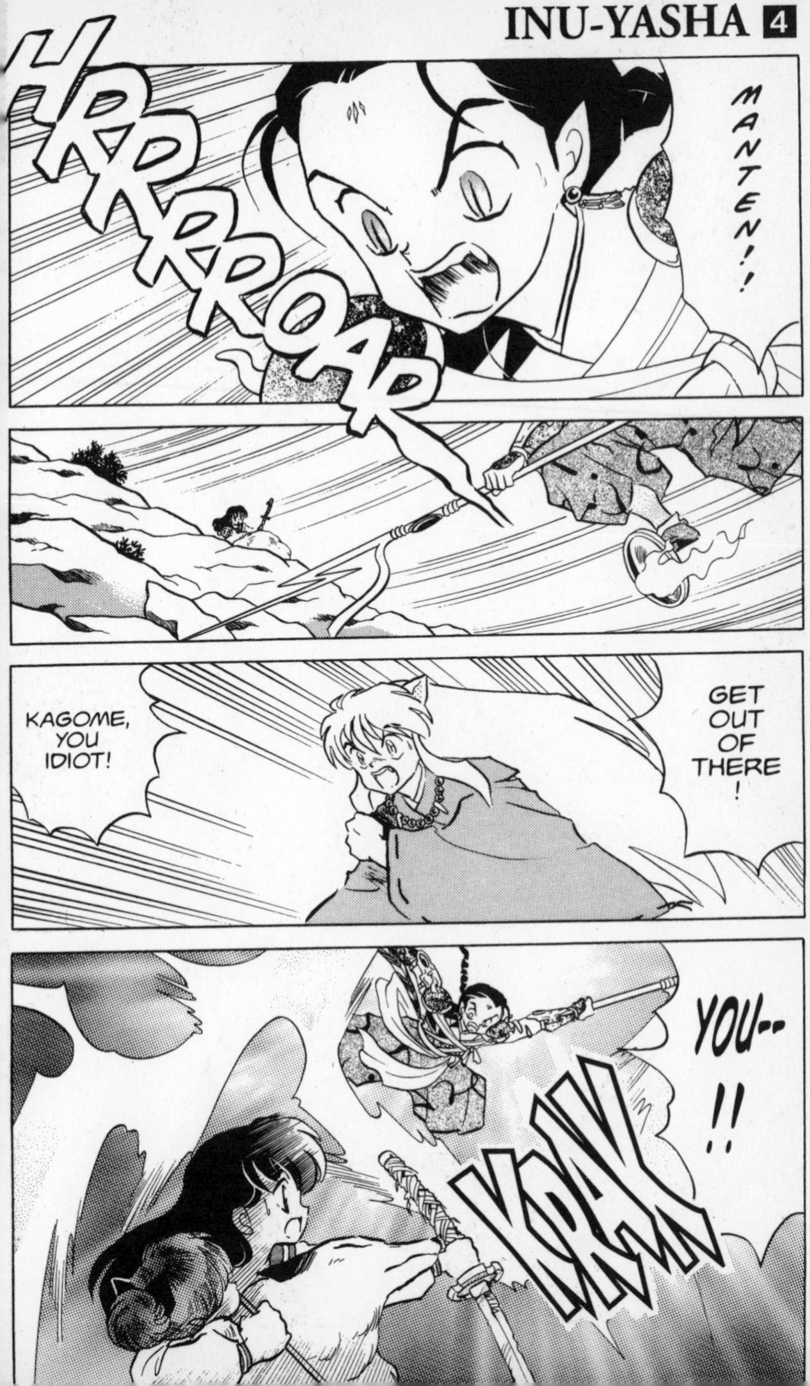
HRRROAR
MANTEN!!
KAGOME, YOU IDIOT!
GET OUT OF THERE!
YOU-- !!
KRAK

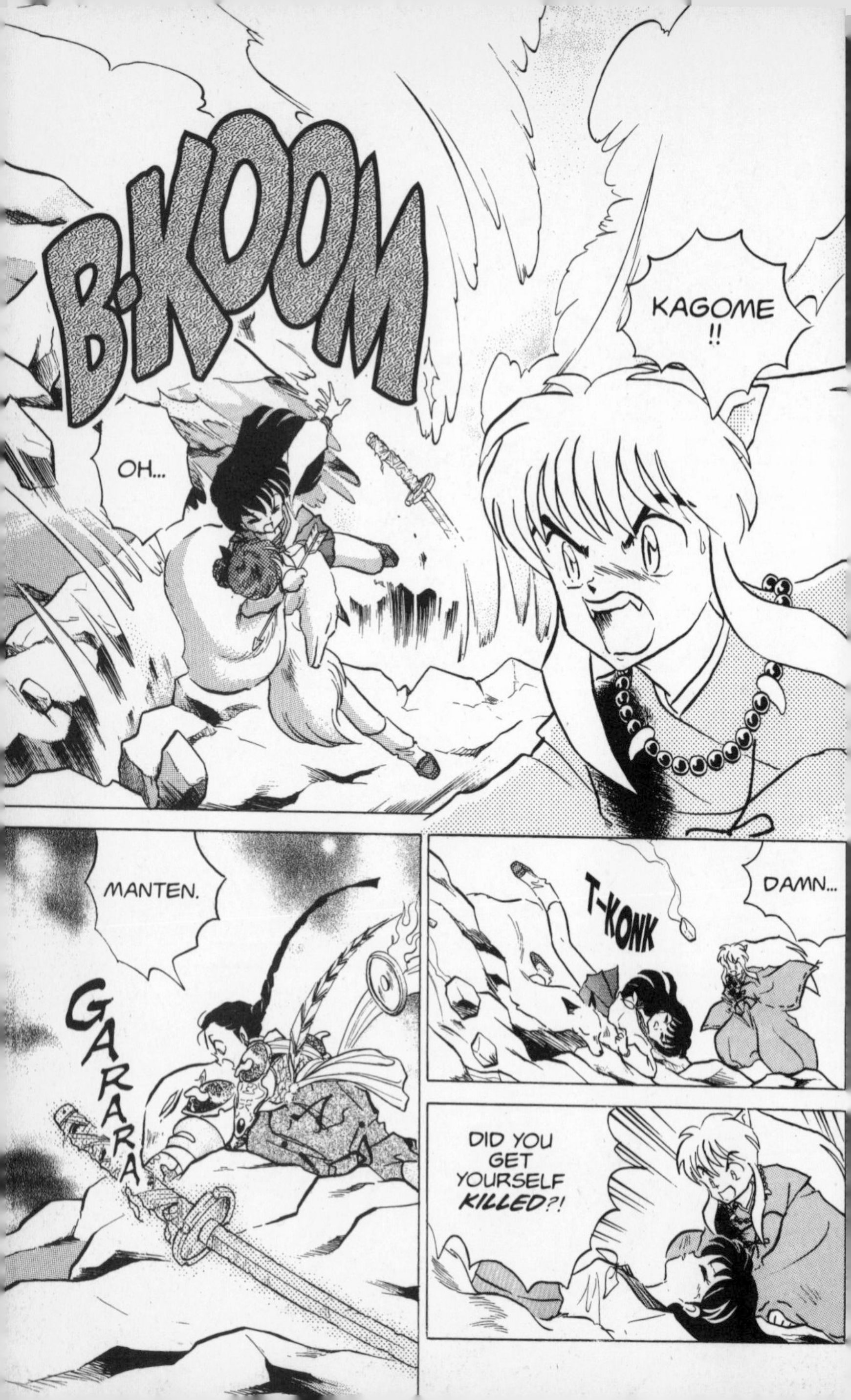
B-KOOM
KAGOME !!
OH...
MANTEN.
GARARA
T-KONK
DAMN...
DID YOU GET YOURSELF KILLED?!

 INU... YASHA... I'M SORRY...

 UH?

 THE SWORD...I... COULDN'T GET IT...

THAT'S WHY SHE DAWDLED SO LONG...?

 YOU SAVED ME...

BUT I COULDN'T DO ANYTHING...

 ARGH! STOP BABBLING, WILL YOU?!

I DON'T NEED A WEAPON TO...

 RRRRRRRR...

MANTEN...

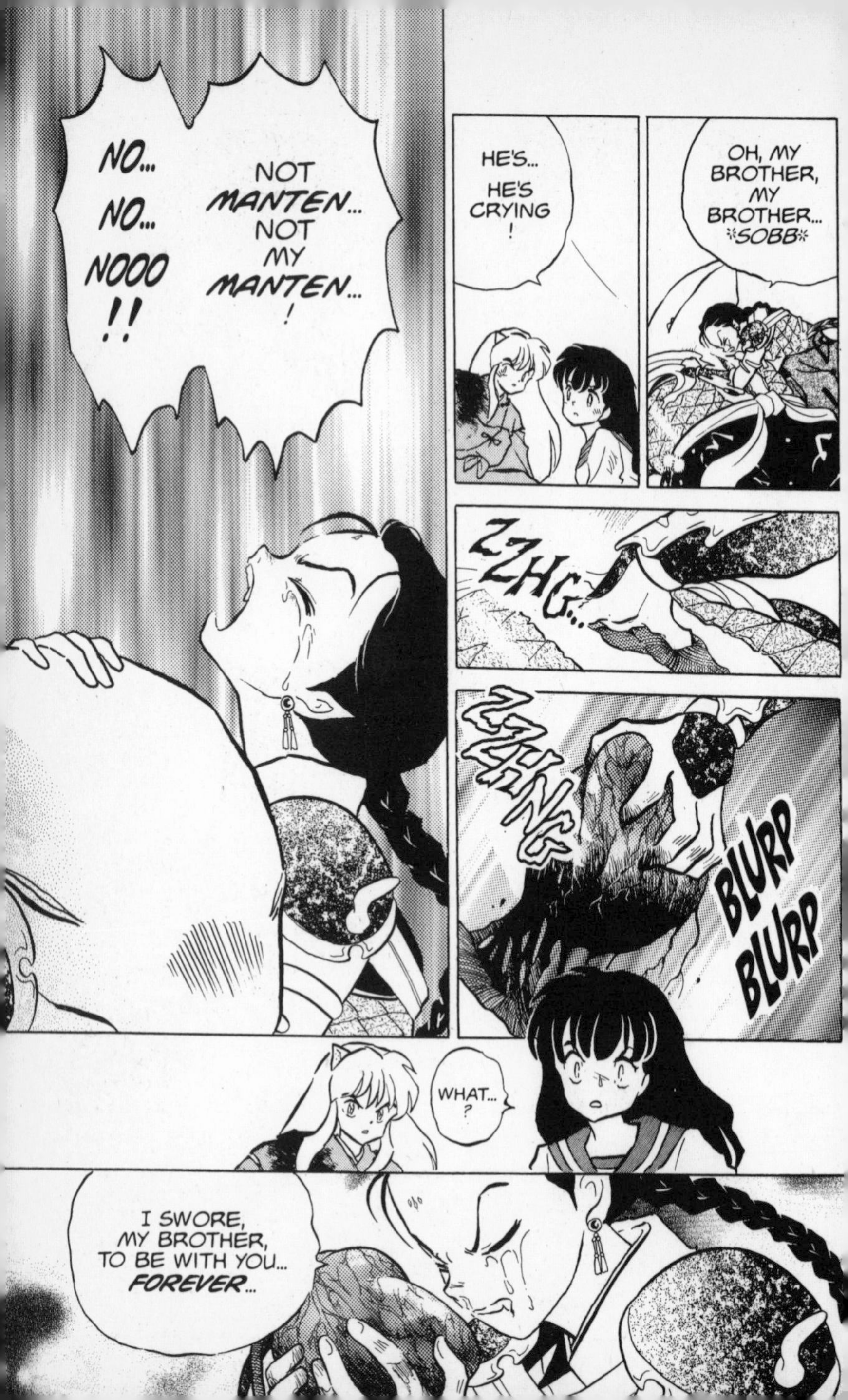
NO... NO... NOOO !!
NOT MANTEN... NOT MY MANTEN... !
HE'S... HE'S CRYING !
OH, MY BROTHER, MY BROTHER... *SOBB*
ZZHG...
ZZHNG
BLURP BLURP
WHAT... ?
I SWORE, MY BROTHER, TO BE WITH YOU... FOREVER...

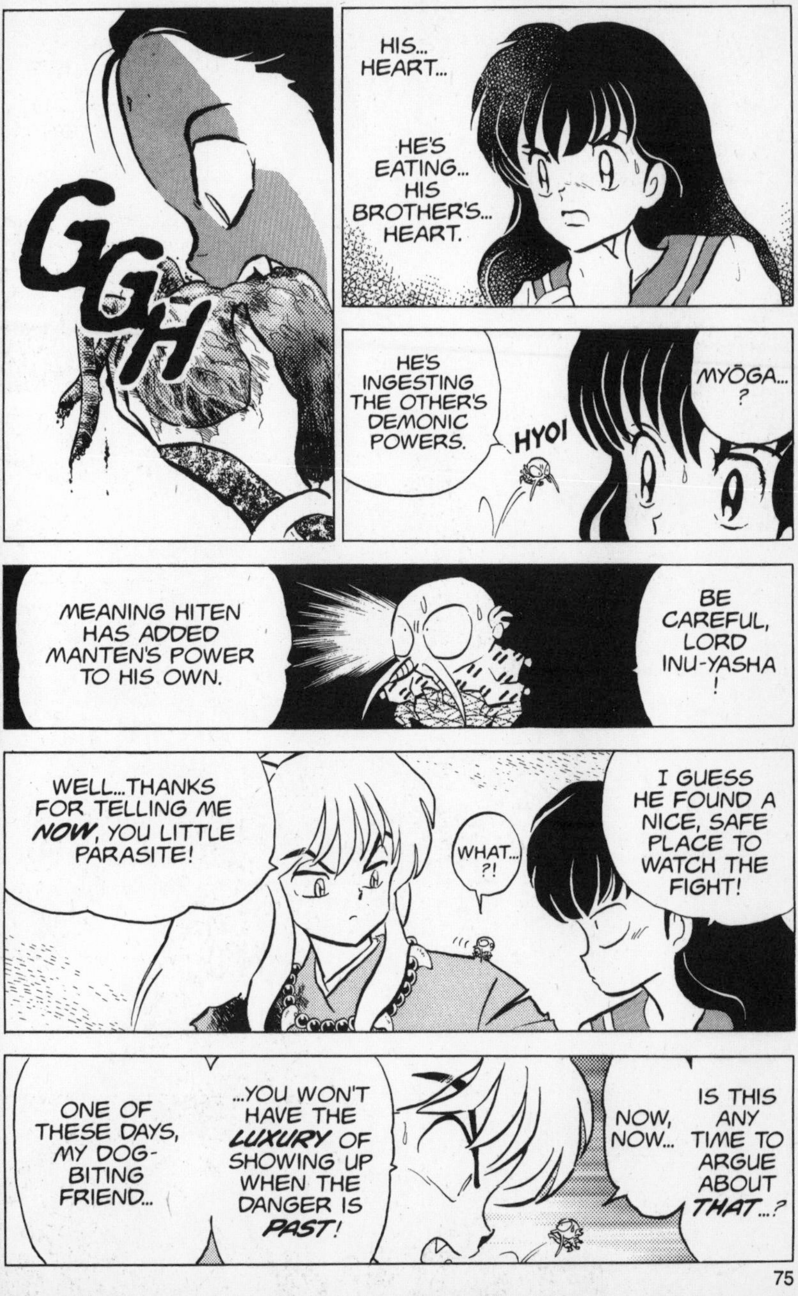
GGH
HIS... HEART...
HE'S EATING... HIS BROTHER'S... HEART.
HE'S INGESTING THE OTHER'S DEMONIC POWERS.
HYOI
MYŌGA...?
MEANING HITEN HAS ADDED MANTEN'S POWER TO HIS OWN.
BE CAREFUL, LORD INU-YASHA!
WELL...THANKS FOR TELLING ME *NOW*, YOU LITTLE PARASITE!
WHAT...?!
I GUESS HE FOUND A NICE, SAFE PLACE TO WATCH THE FIGHT!
ONE OF THESE DAYS, MY DOG-BITING FRIEND...
...YOU WON'T HAVE THE *LUXURY* OF SHOWING UP WHEN THE DANGER IS *PAST*!
NOW, NOW...
IS THIS ANY TIME TO ARGUE ABOUT *THAT*...?

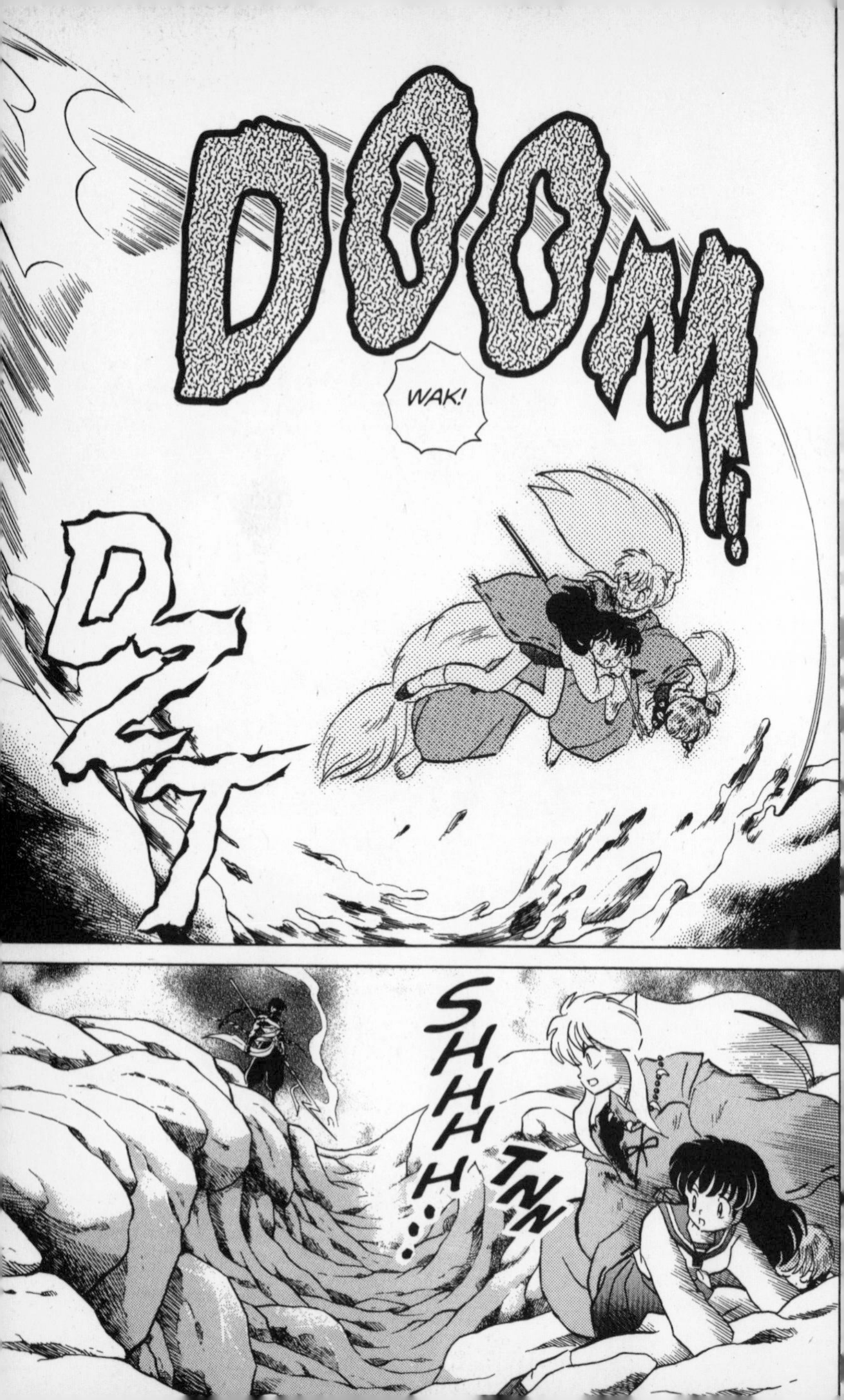
DOOM!
WAK!
SHHHH...
TNN

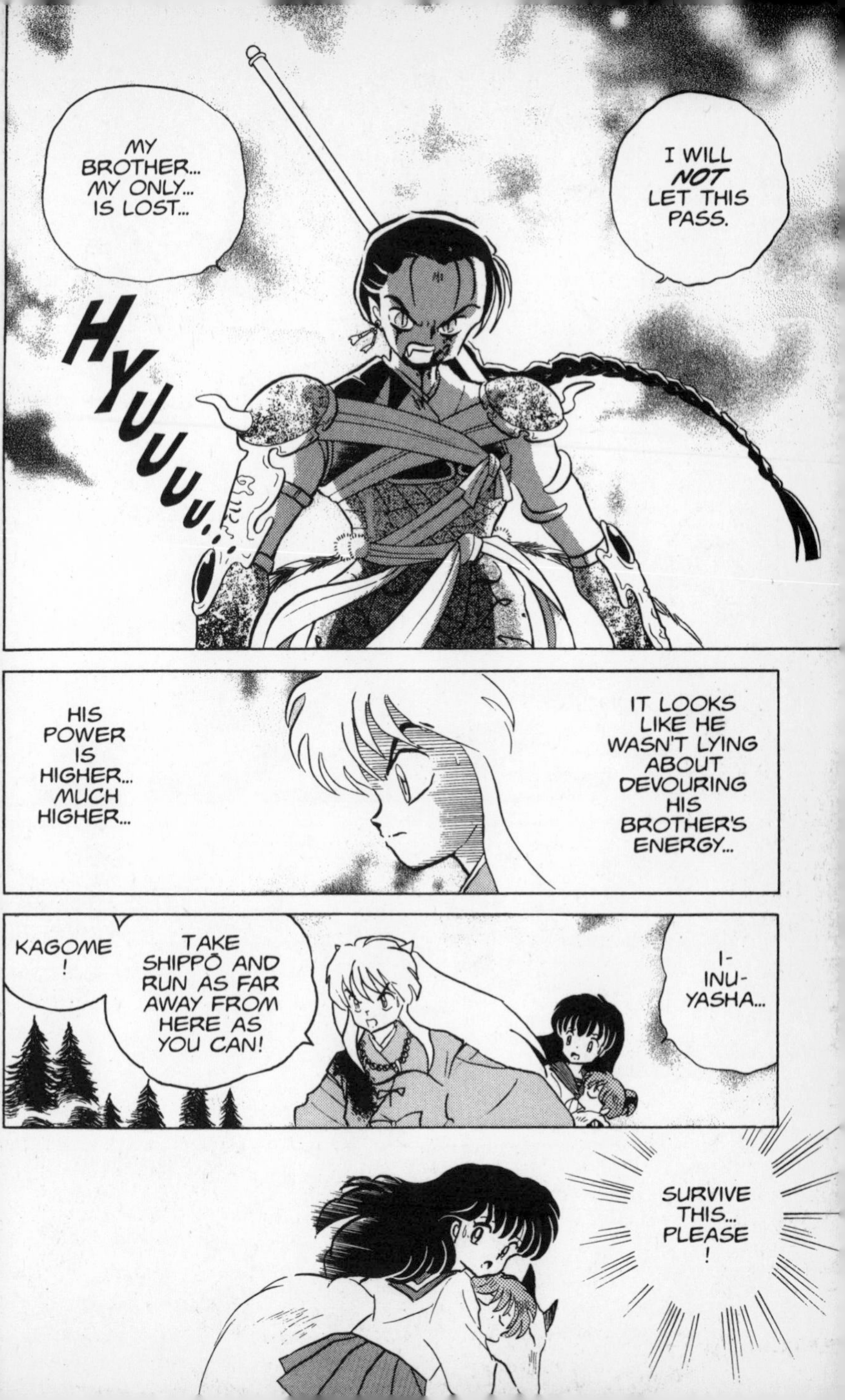
MY BROTHER... MY ONLY... IS LOST...
I WILL NOT LET THIS PASS.
HYUUUU...
HIS POWER IS HIGHER... MUCH HIGHER...
IT LOOKS LIKE HE WASN'T LYING ABOUT DEVOURING HIS BROTHER'S ENERGY...
KAGOME!
TAKE SHIPPŌ AND RUN AS FAR AWAY FROM HERE AS YOU CAN!
I- INU-YASHA...
SURVIVE THIS... PLEASE!

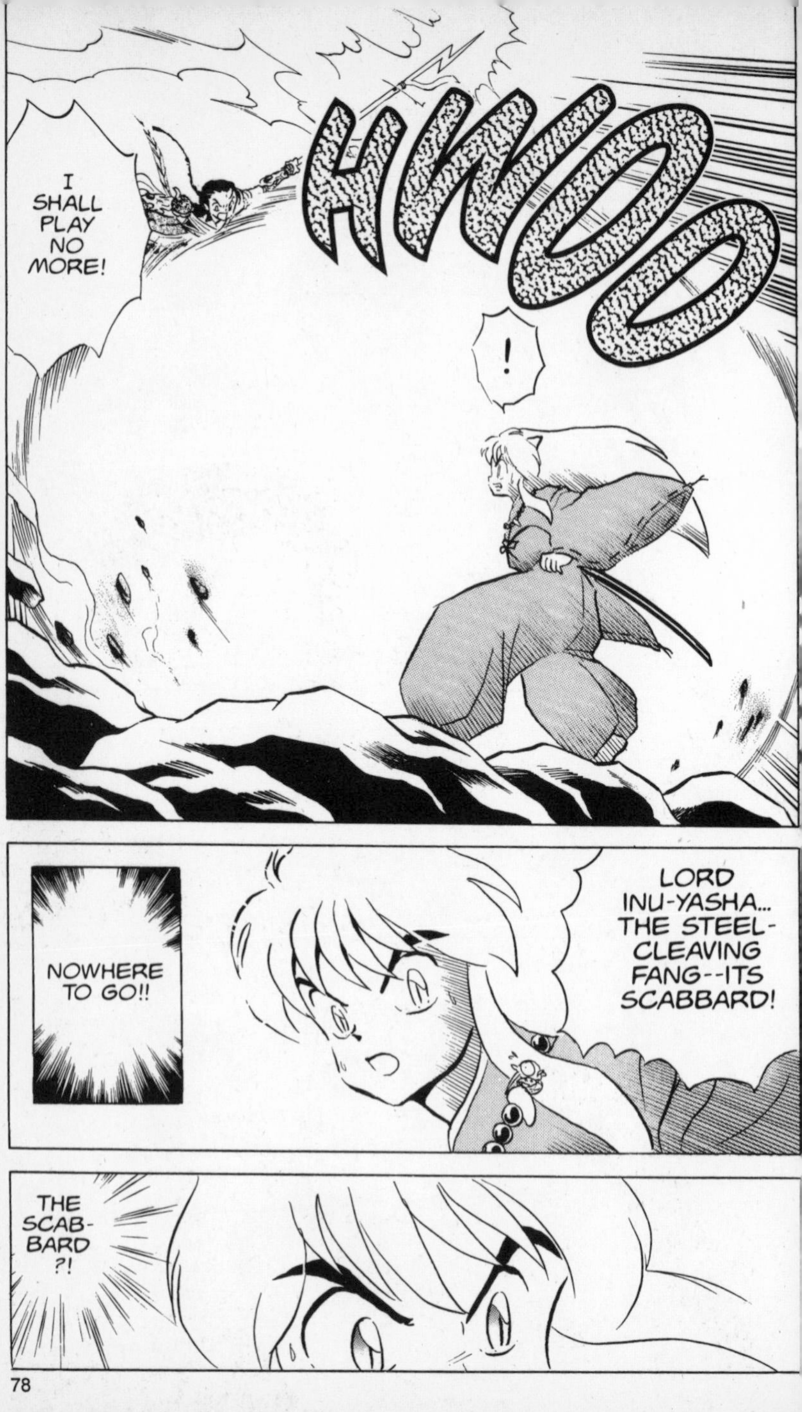
I SHALL PLAY NO MORE!
HWOO
!
NOWHERE TO GO!!
LORD INU-YASHA... THE STEEL-CLEAVING FANG--ITS SCABBARD!
THE SCAB-BARD ?!

SCROLL FIVE
WITH ONLY A SCABBARD...

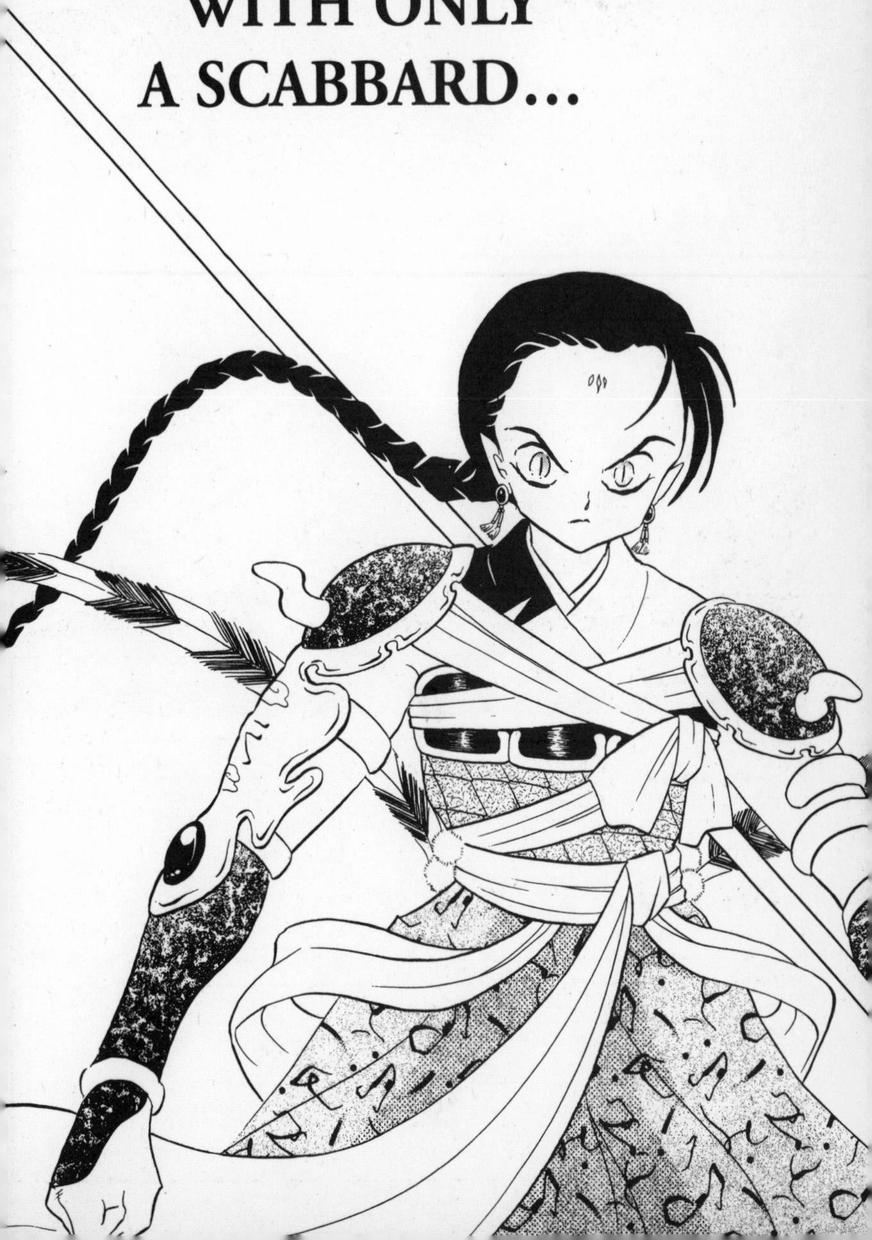

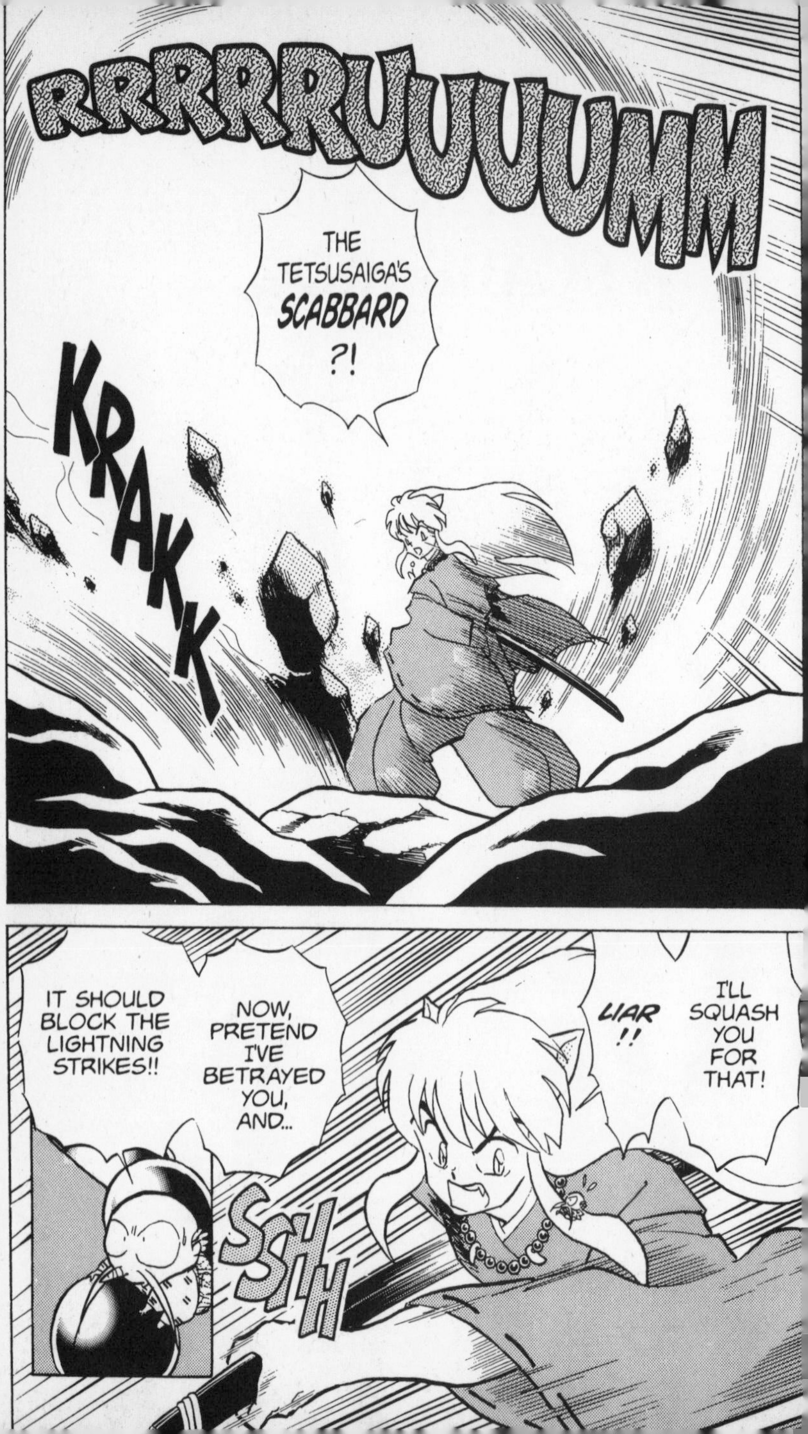
RRRRRRUUUUMM
THE TETSUSAIGA'S SCABBARD ?!
KRAKK
IT SHOULD BLOCK THE LIGHTNING STRIKES!!
NOW, PRETEND I'VE BETRAYED YOU, AND...
LIAR !!
I'LL SQUASH YOU FOR THAT!
SSHH

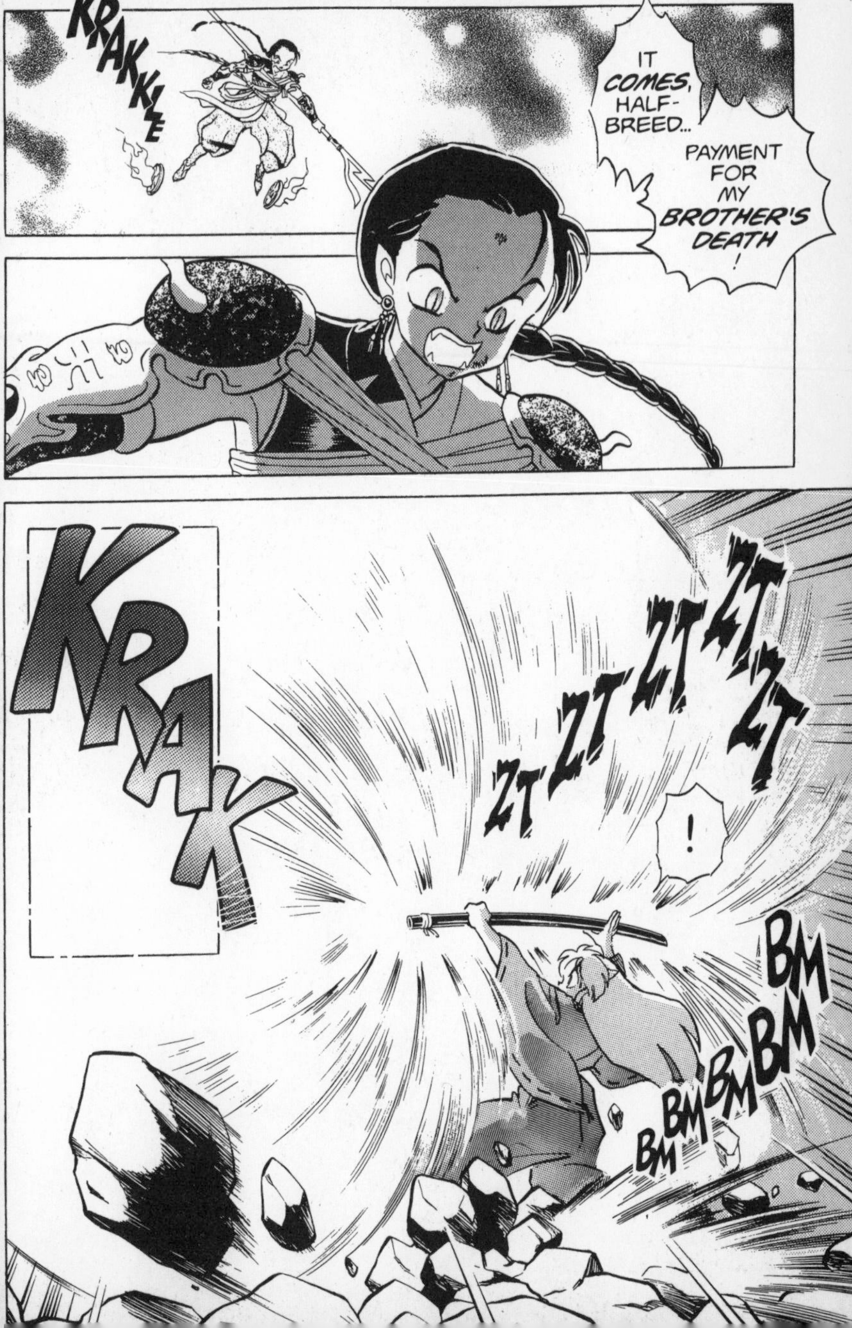
KRAKKLE
IT COMES, HALF-BREED...
PAYMENT FOR MY BROTHER'S DEATH!
KRAK
ZT ZT ZT ZT ZT ZT ZT
!
BM BM BM BM BM BM

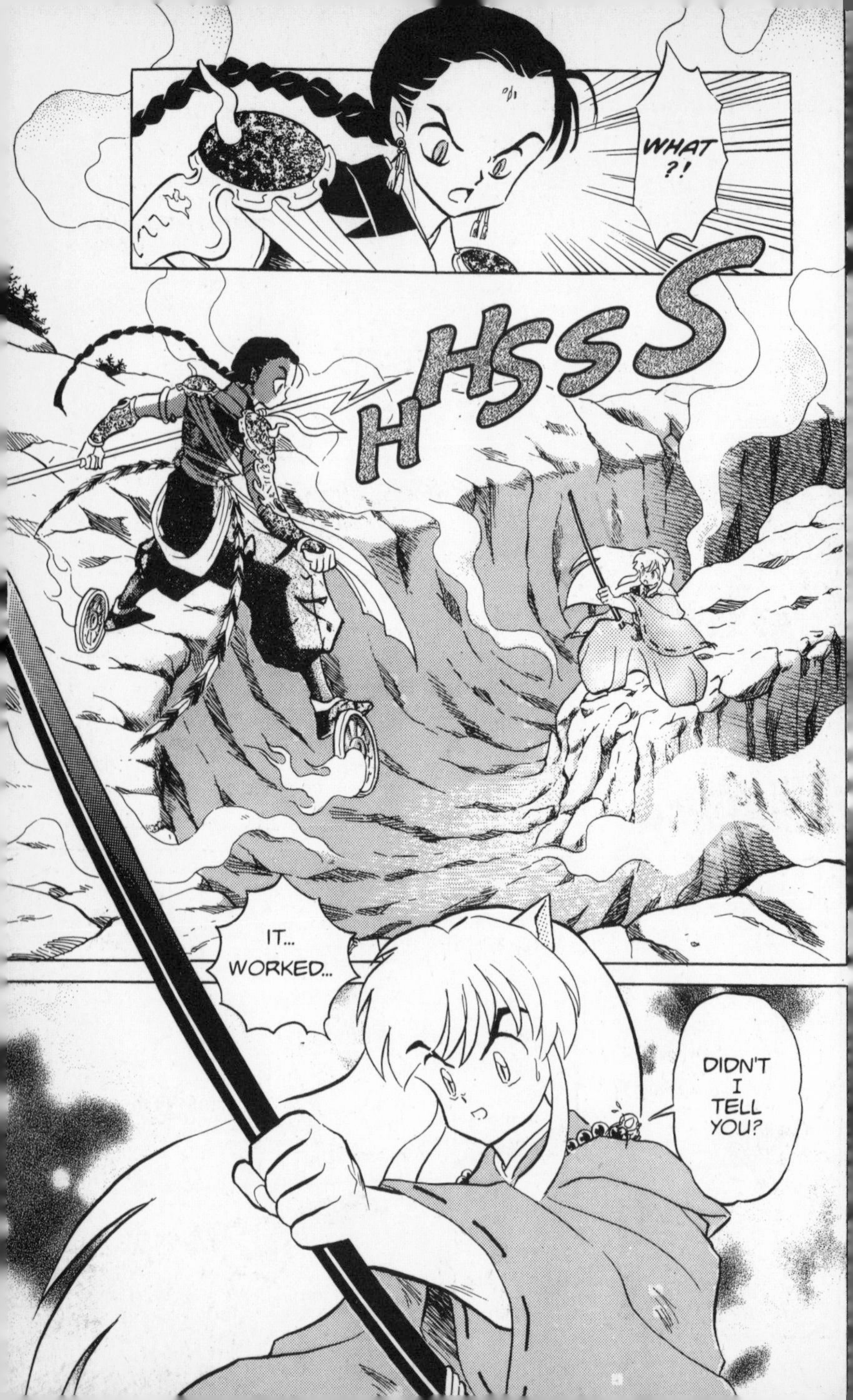
WHAT ?!
HHSSS
IT... WORKED...
DIDN'T I TELL YOU?

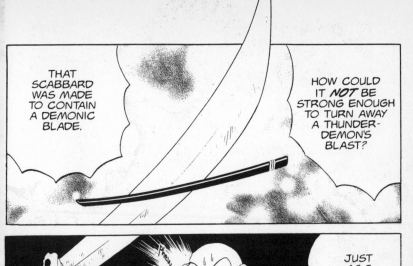

THAT SCABBARD WAS MADE TO CONTAIN A DEMONIC BLADE.

HOW COULD IT *NOT* BE STRONG ENOUGH TO TURN AWAY A THUNDER-DEMON'S BLAST?

JUST AS I GUESSED...

"YOU... GUESSED..." ?!

YOU DIDN'T *KNOW* ?!

WHO SAYS I DIDN'T ?

IN ANY CASE, NOW THAT YOU'VE SURVIVED...

...SHOULDN'T WE BE RUNNING?!

RUNNING *WHERE* ?!

I CAN *USE* THIS !

EEP.

FWA

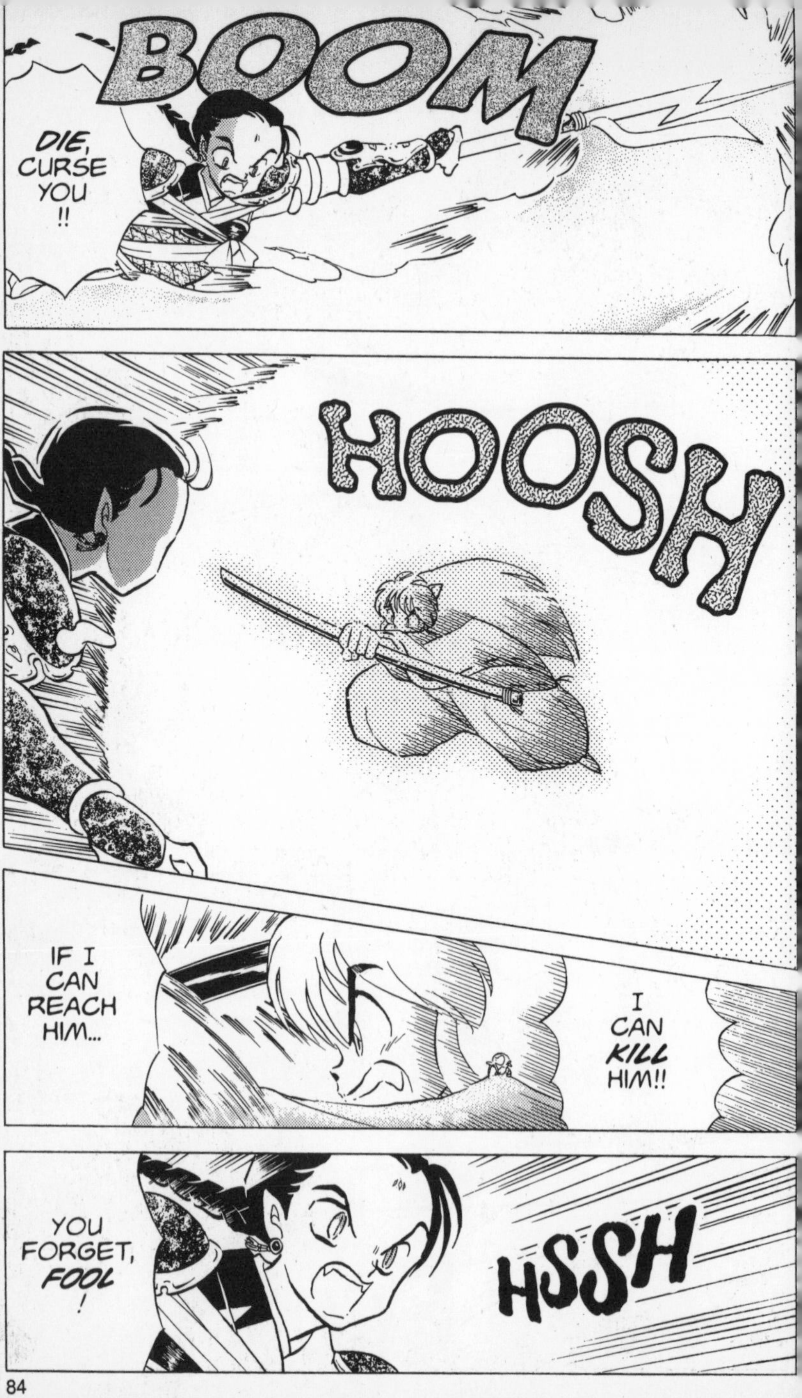
BOOM
DIE, CURSE YOU !!
HOOSH
IF I CAN REACH HIM...
I CAN KILL HIM!!
YOU FORGET, FOOL !
HSSH

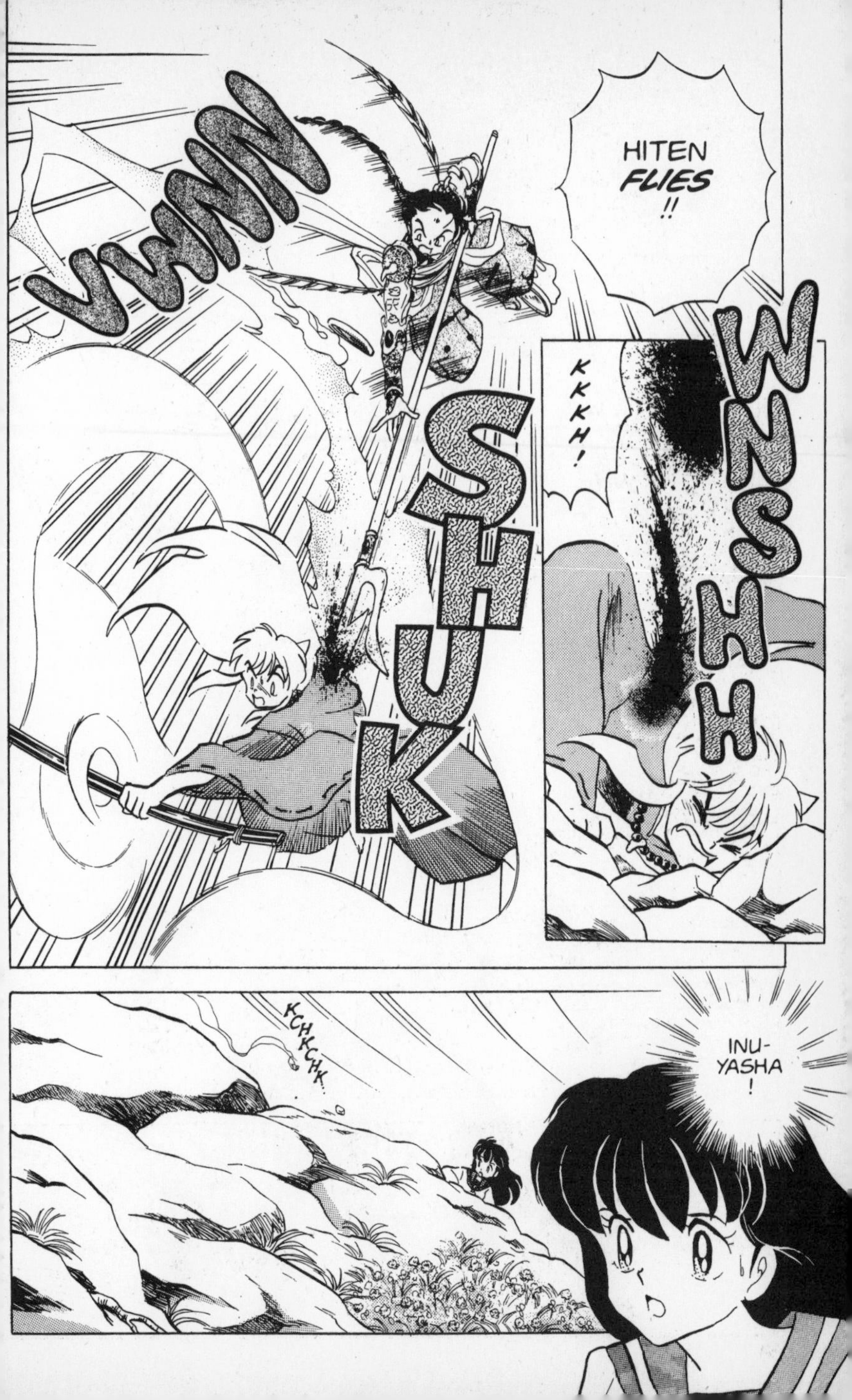

VVWNN
HITEN FLIES!!
SHUK
KKKH!
WNSHHH
KCHKCHK...
INU-YASHA!

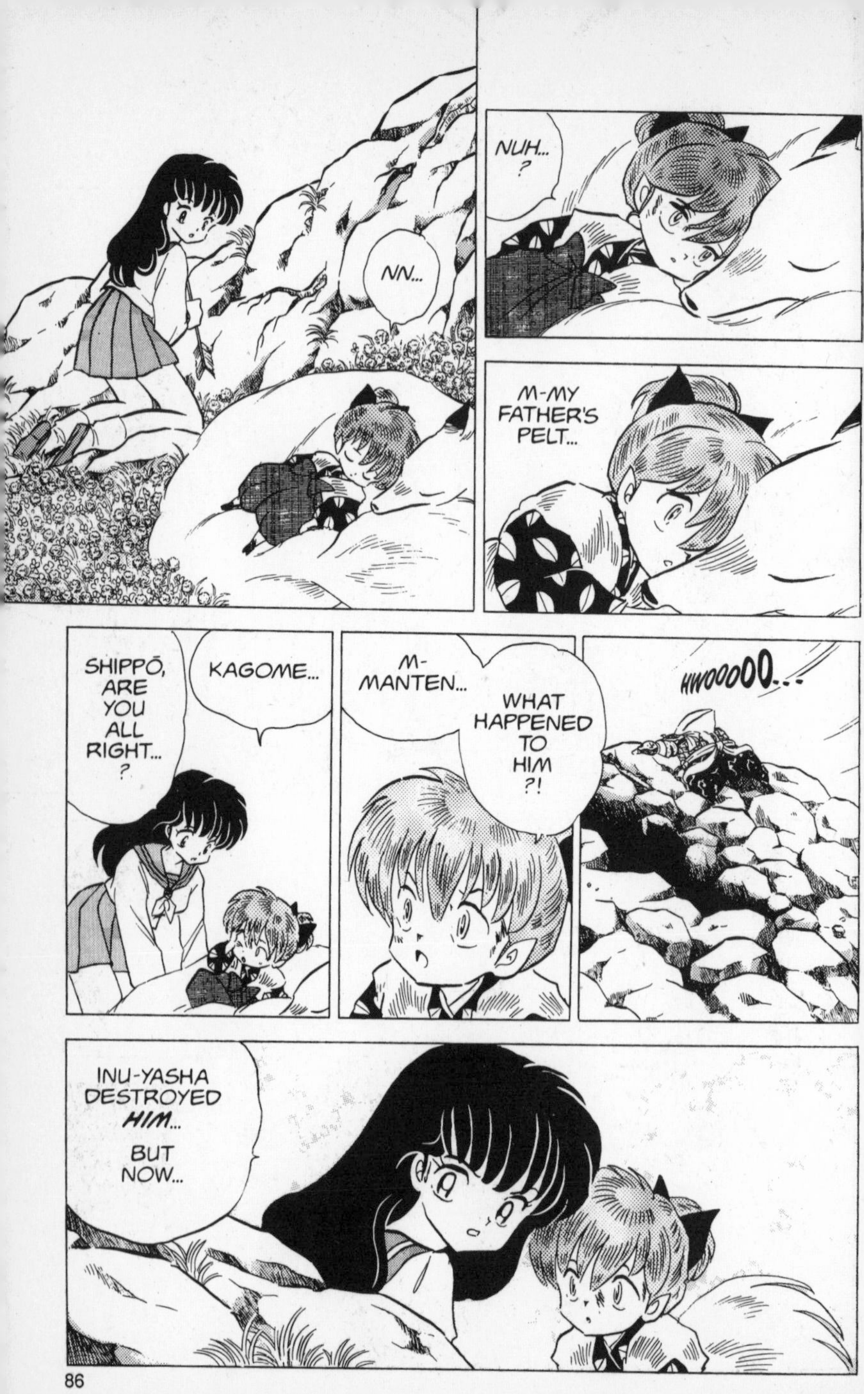
NN...
NUH...?
M-MY FATHER'S PELT...
SHIPPŌ, ARE YOU ALL RIGHT...?
KAGOME...
M-MANTEN...
WHAT HAPPENED TO HIM?!
HWOOOOO...
INU-YASHA DESTROYED *HIM*...
BUT NOW...

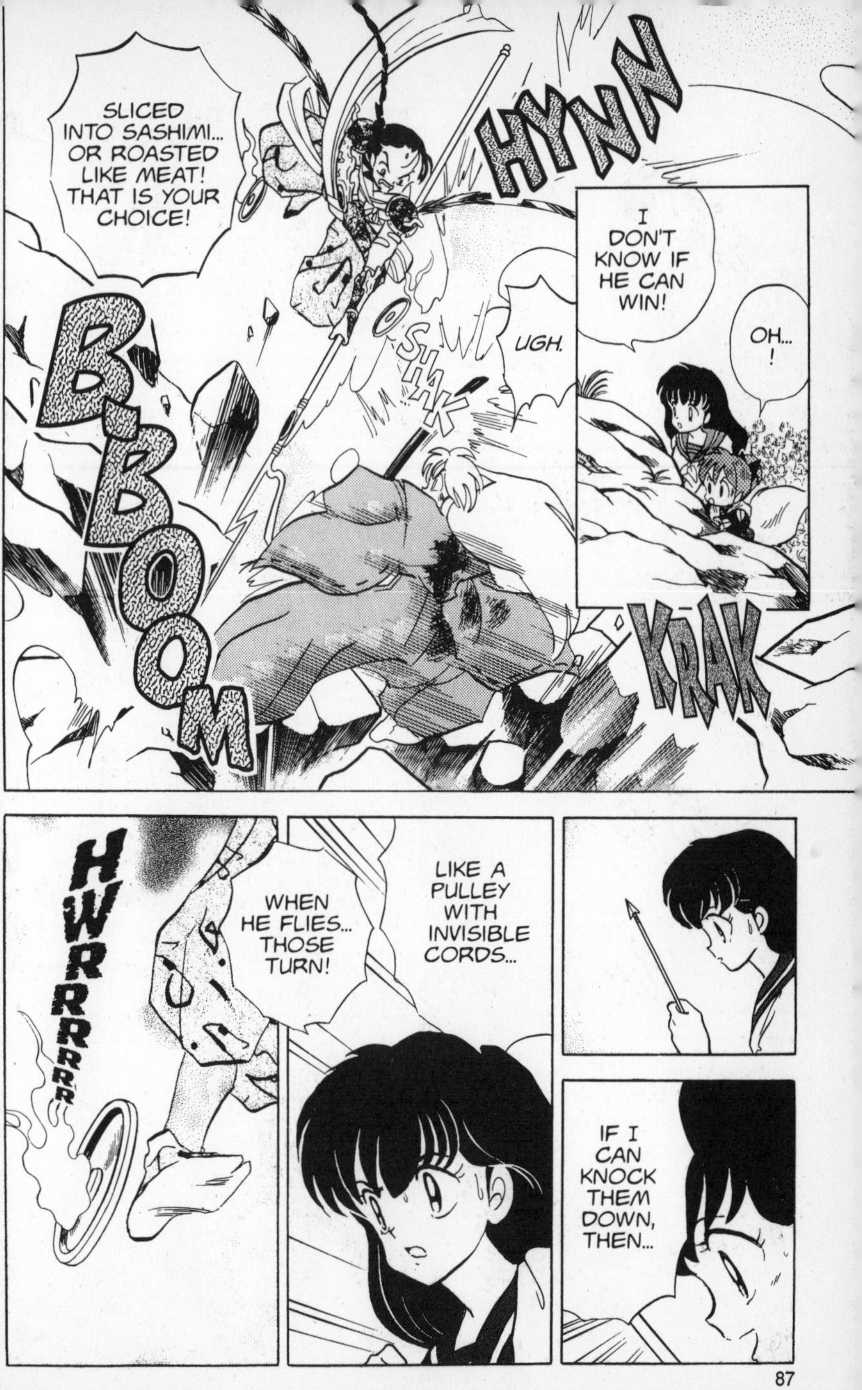
SLICED INTO SASHIMI... OR ROASTED LIKE MEAT! THAT IS YOUR CHOICE!
HYNN
B-BOOM
SHAK
UGH.
I DON'T KNOW IF HE CAN WIN!
OH...!
KRAK
HWRRRRRR
WHEN HE FLIES... THOSE TURN!
LIKE A PULLEY WITH INVISIBLE CORDS...
IF I CAN KNOCK THEM DOWN, THEN...

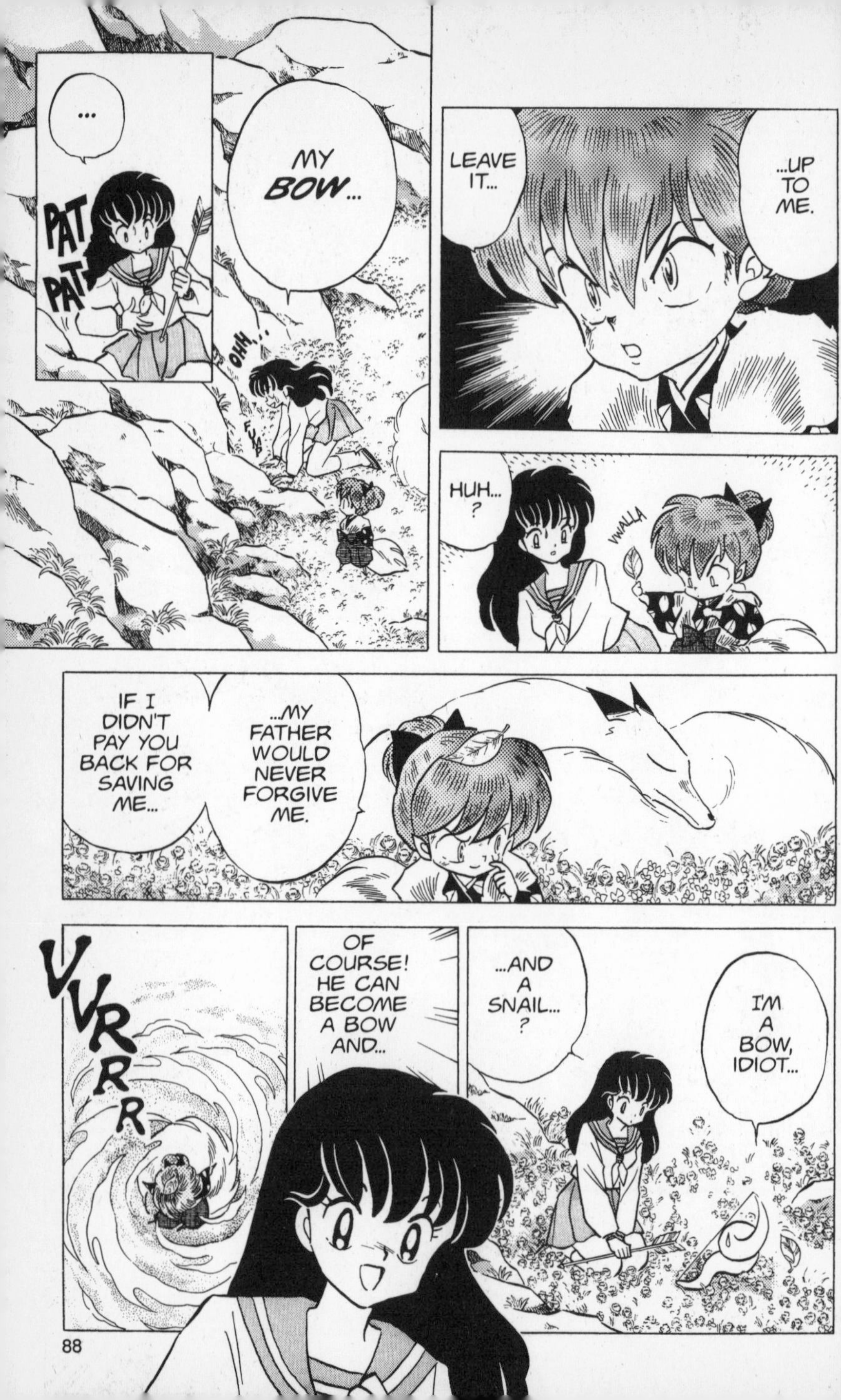
...
PAT PAT
MY BOW...
OHH...
FUMP
LEAVE IT...
...UP TO ME.
HUH...?
VWALLA
IF I DIDN'T PAY YOU BACK FOR SAVING ME...
...MY FATHER WOULD NEVER FORGIVE ME.
VVRRR
OF COURSE! HE CAN BECOME A BOW AND...
...AND A SNAIL...?
I'M A BOW, IDIOT...

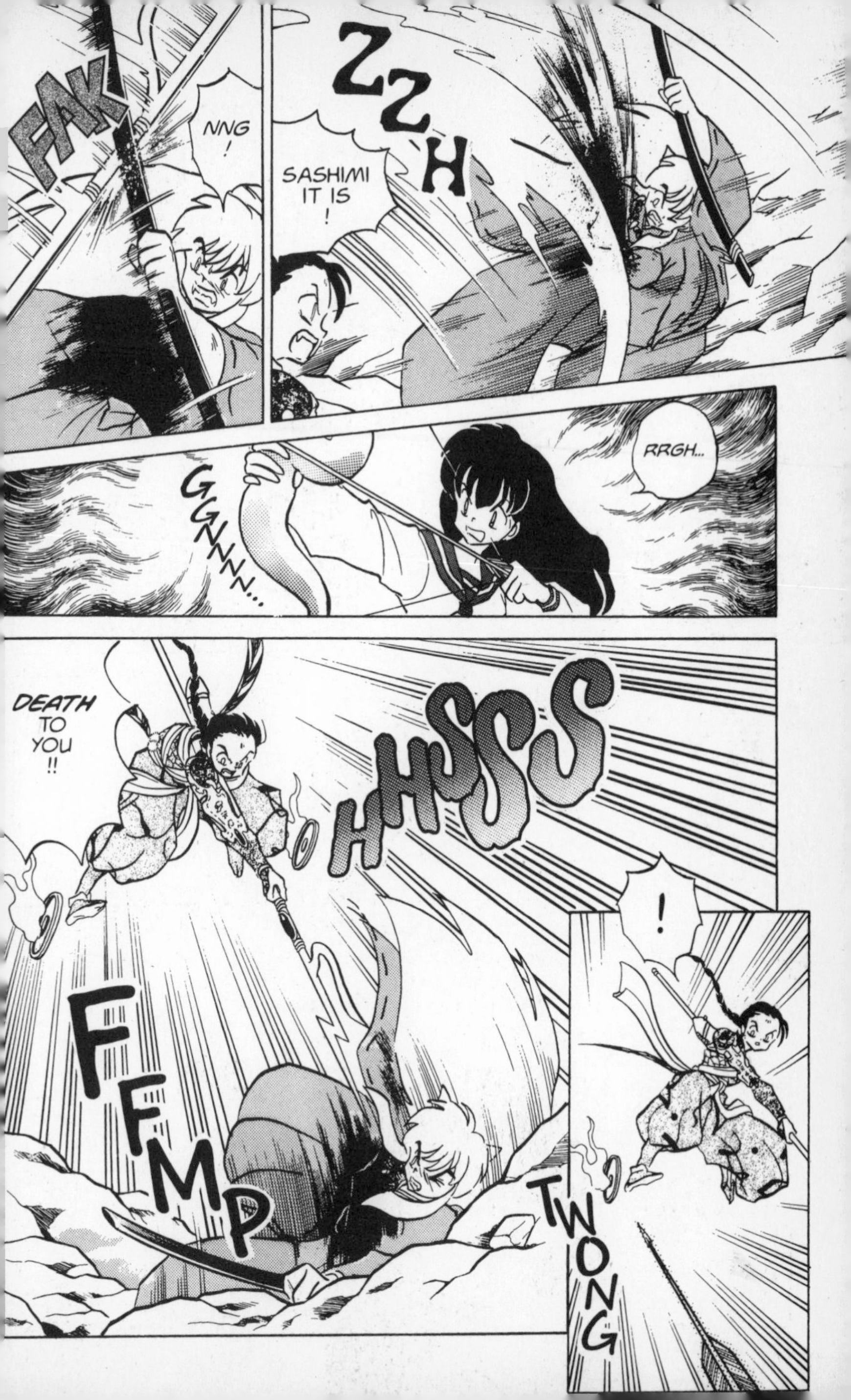
FAK
NNG!
ZZZH
SASHIMI IT IS!
GGNNNN...
RRGH...
DEATH TO YOU!!
HHSSS
FFFMP
!
TWONG

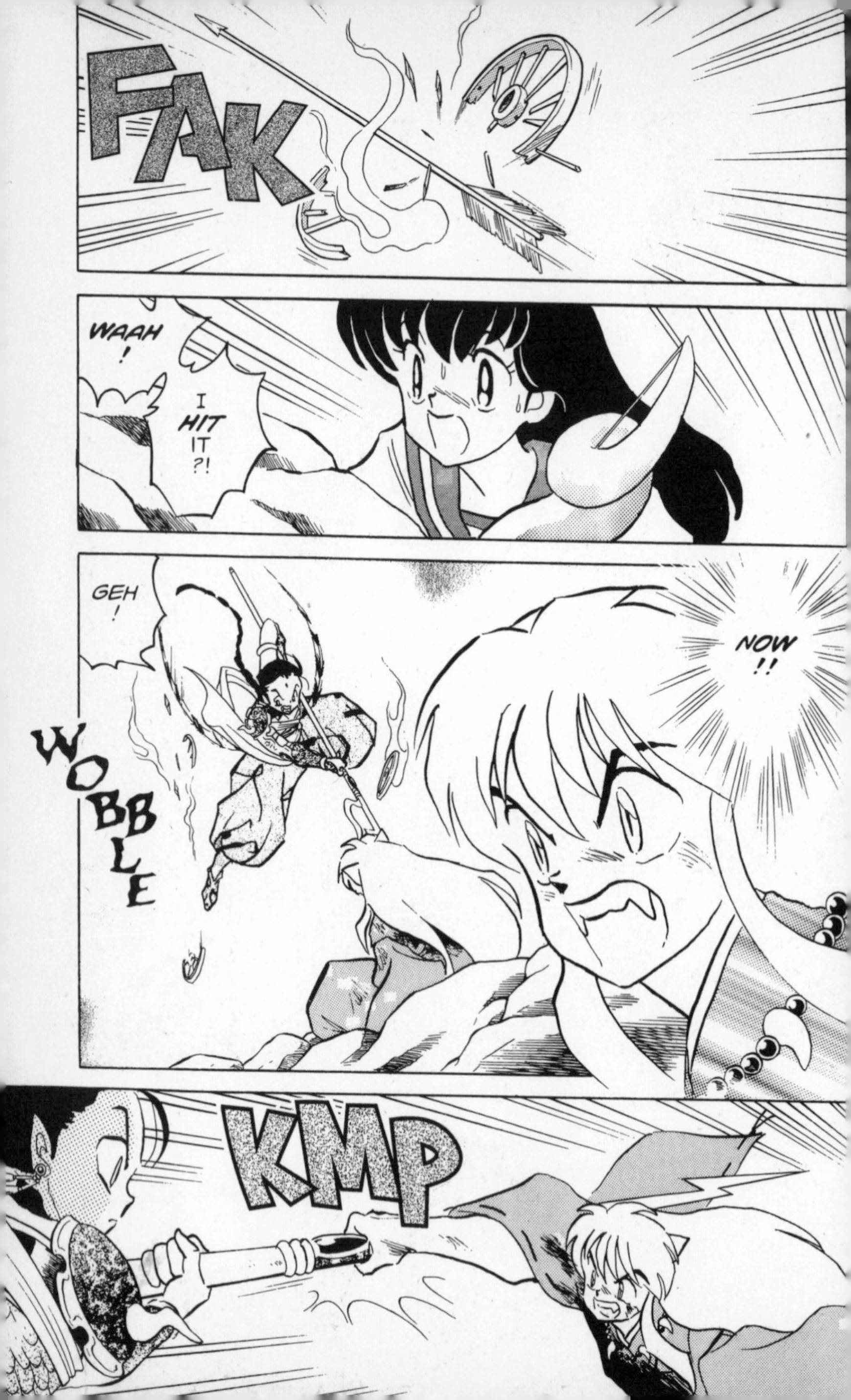
FAK
WAAH!
I HIT IT?!
GEH!
WOBBLE
NOW!!
KMP

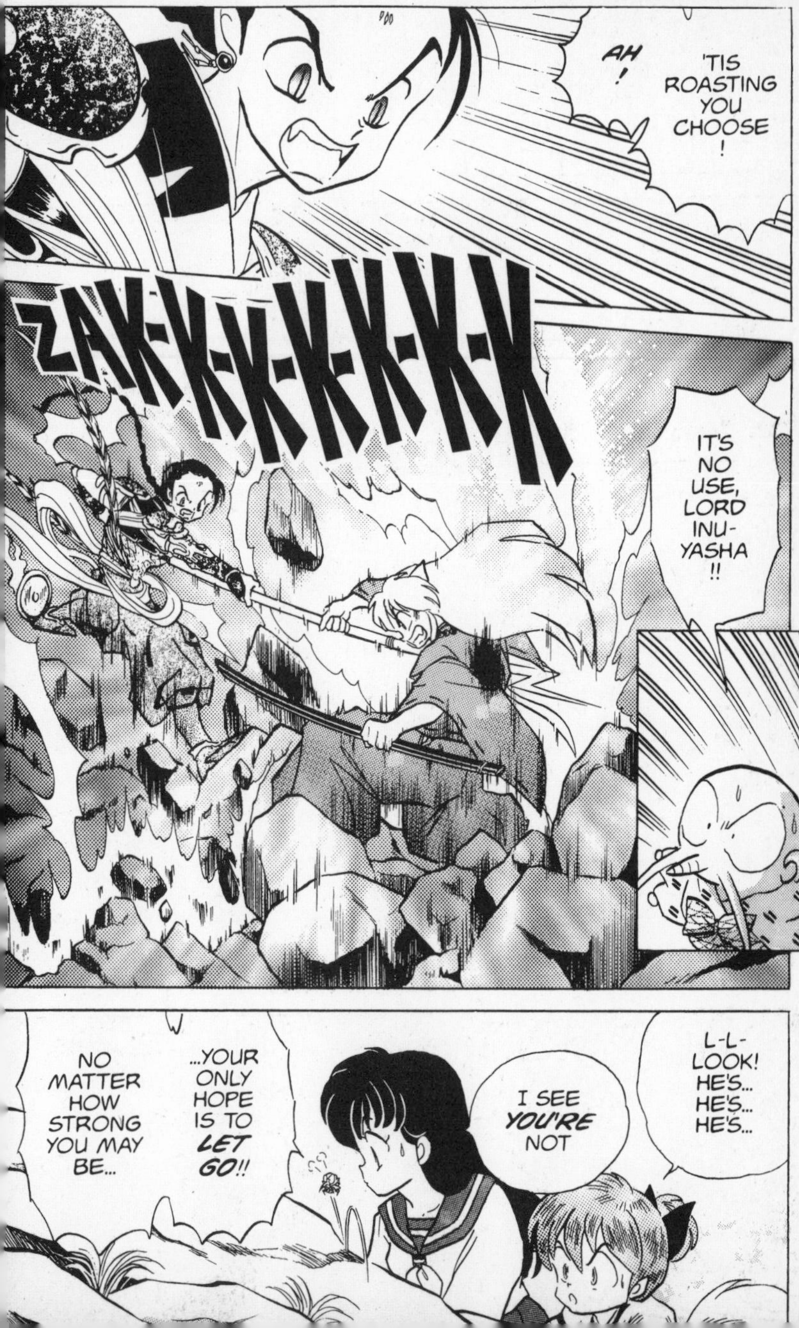
AH!
'TIS ROASTING YOU CHOOSE!
ZAK-K-K-K-K-K-K
IT'S NO USE, LORD INU-YASHA!!
NO MATTER HOW STRONG YOU MAY BE...
...YOUR ONLY HOPE IS TO LET GO!!
I SEE YOU'RE NOT
L-L-LOOK! HE'S... HE'S... HE'S...

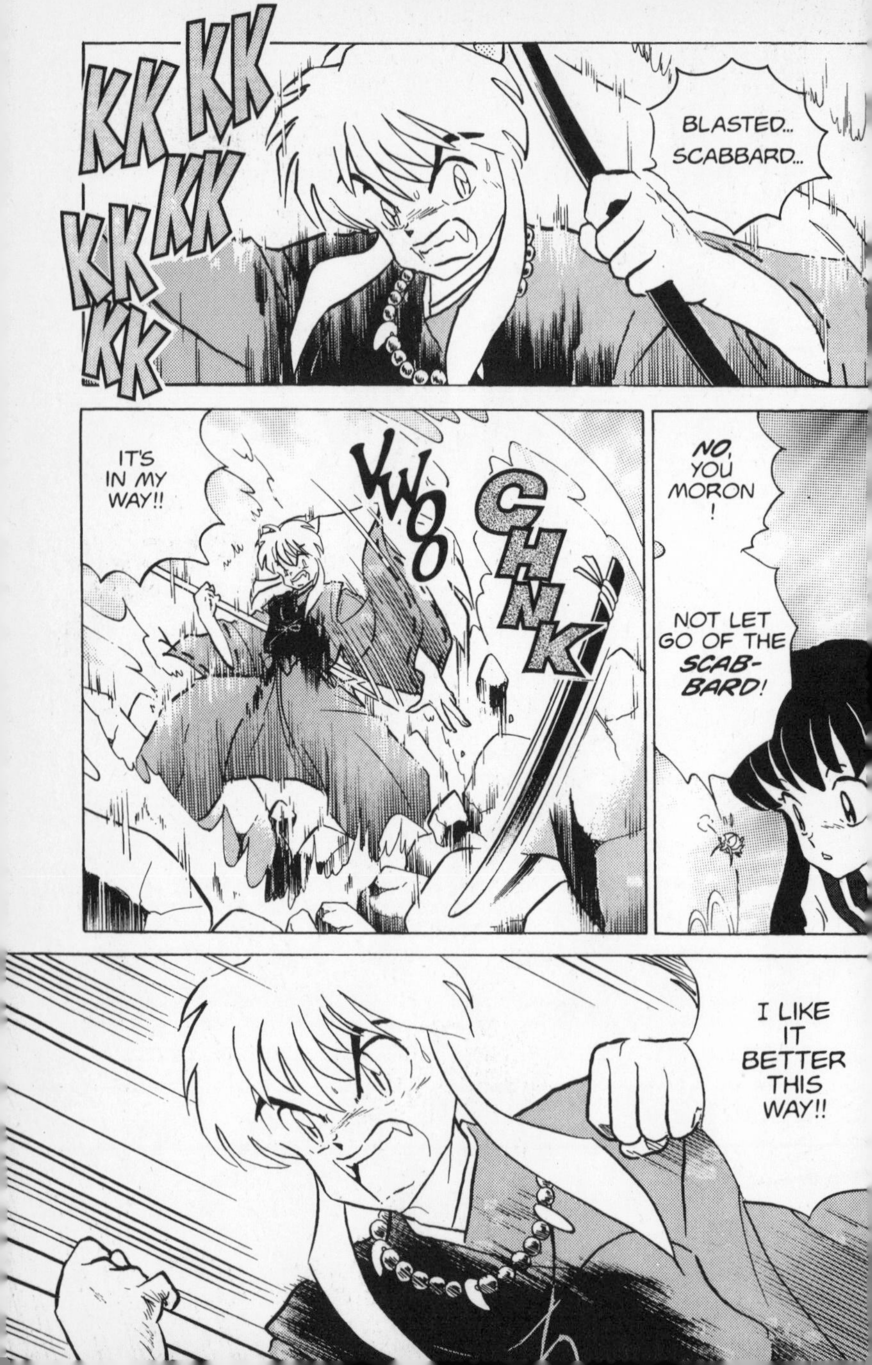
KK KK
KK KK
KK KK
BLASTED... SCABBARD...
IT'S IN MY WAY!!
VWOO
CHNK
NO, YOU MORON!
NOT LET GO OF THE SCABBARD!
I LIKE IT BETTER THIS WAY!!

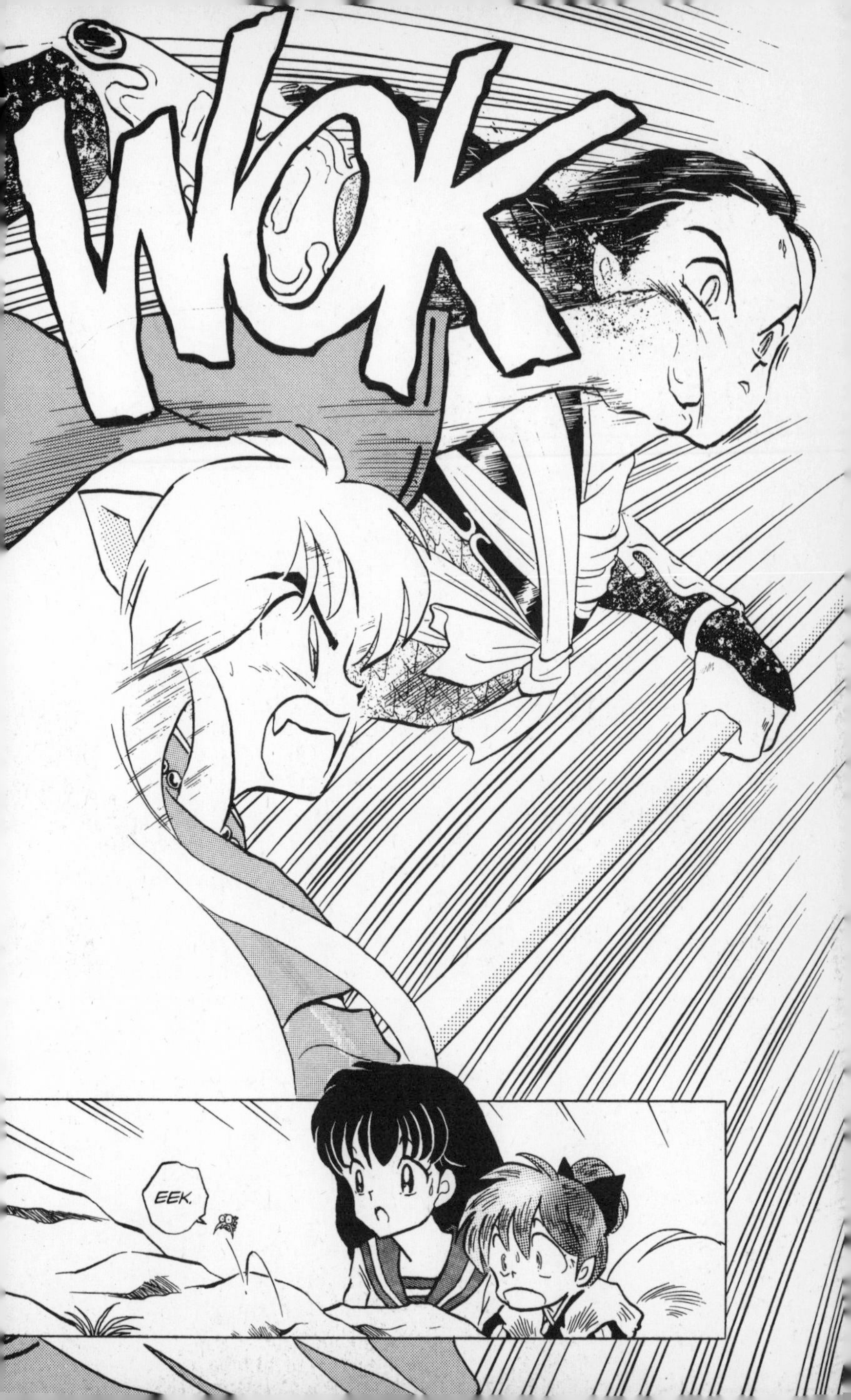
WOK
EEK.

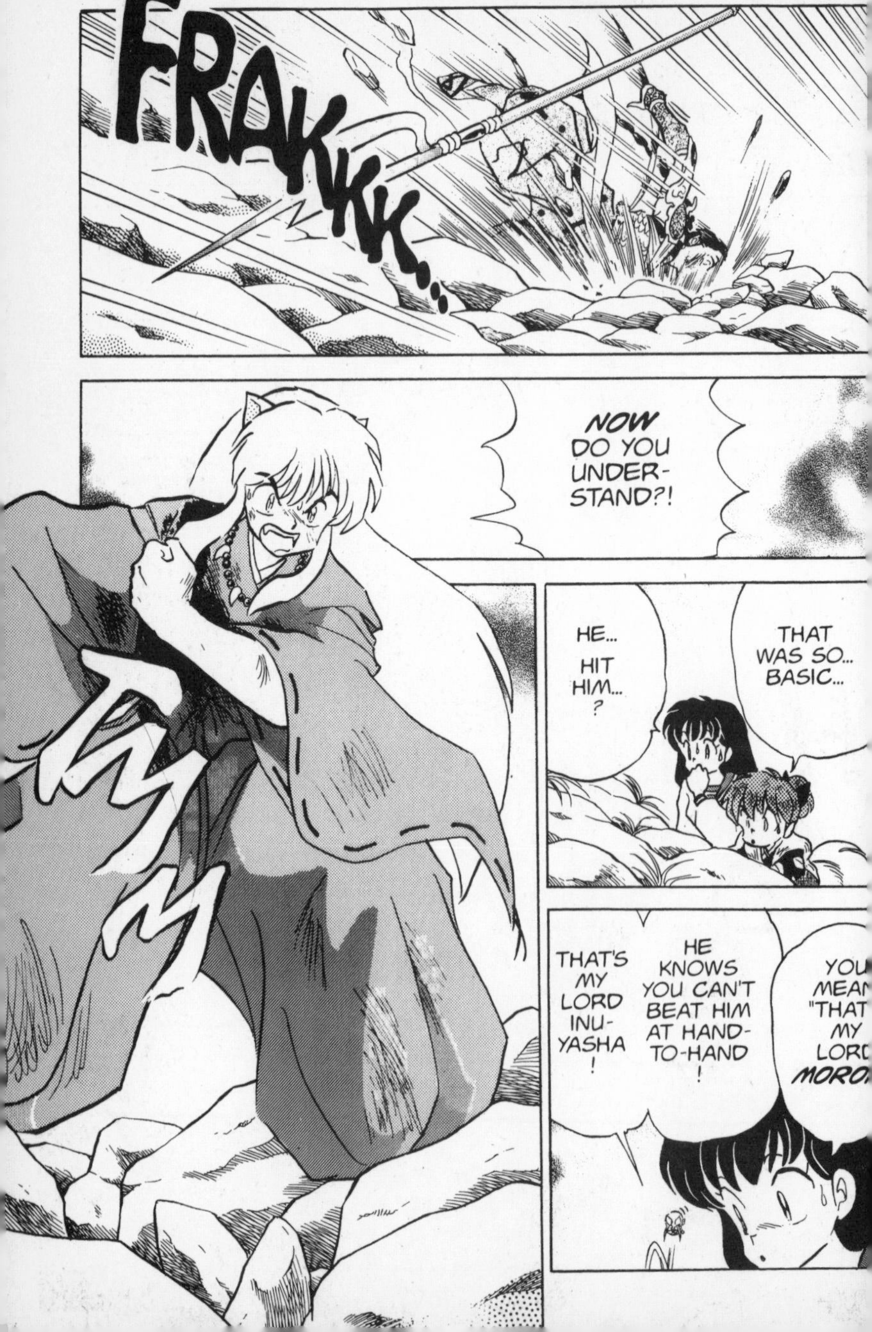
FRAKKKK...
NOW DO YOU UNDER-STAND?!
HE... HIT HIM...?
THAT WAS SO... BASIC...
THAT'S MY LORD INU-YASHA!
HE KNOWS YOU CAN'T BEAT HIM AT HAND-TO-HAND!

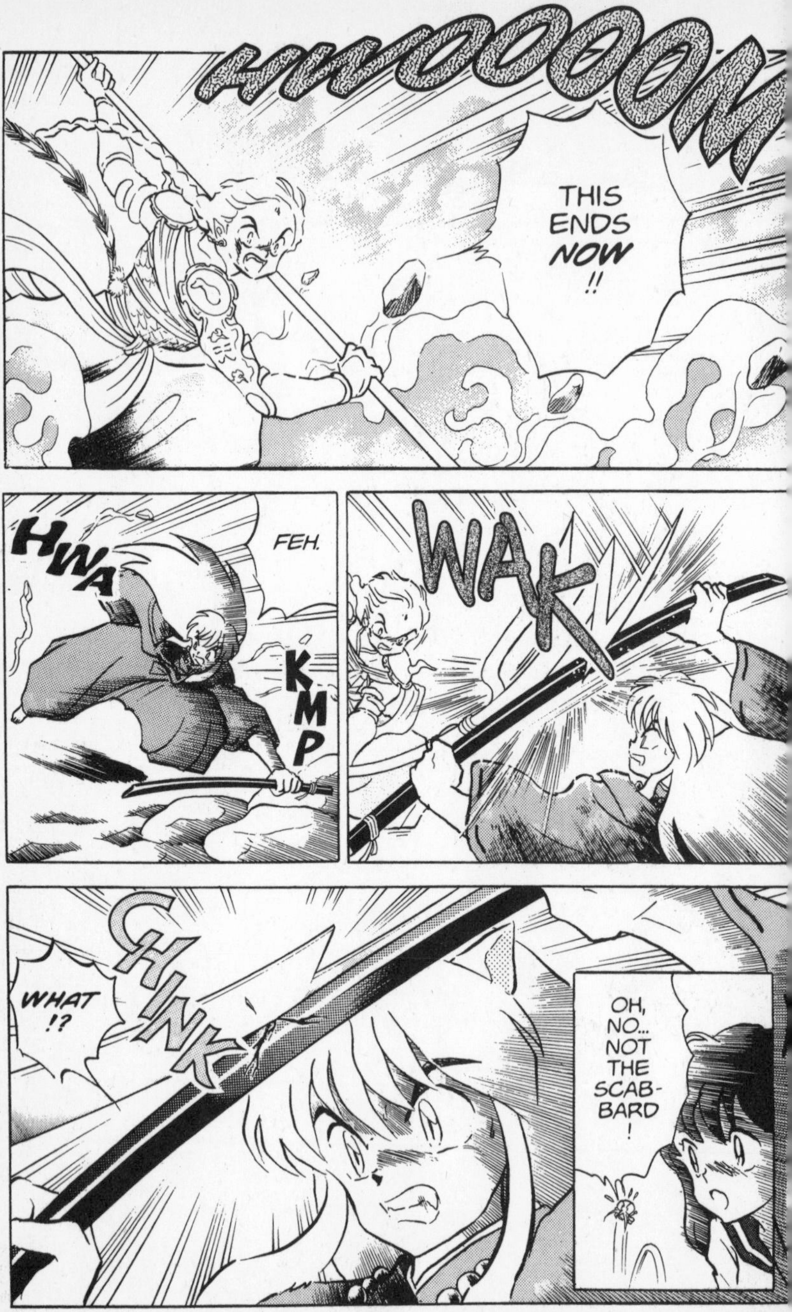
HWOOOOOM
THIS ENDS NOW !!
HWA
FEH.
KMP
WAK
CHINK
WHAT !?
OH, NO... NOT THE SCAB- BARD !

SCROLL SIX

THE CRY

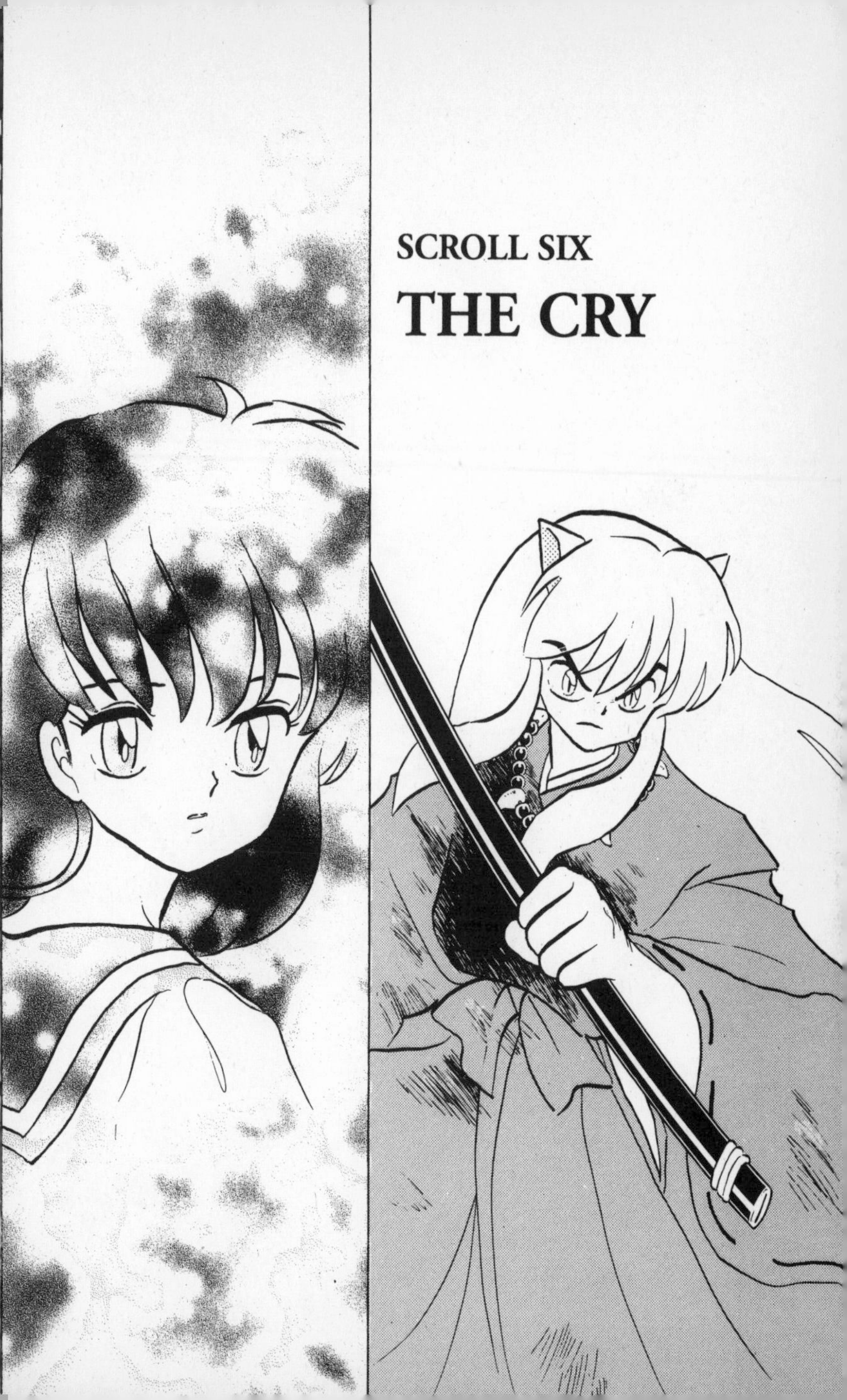

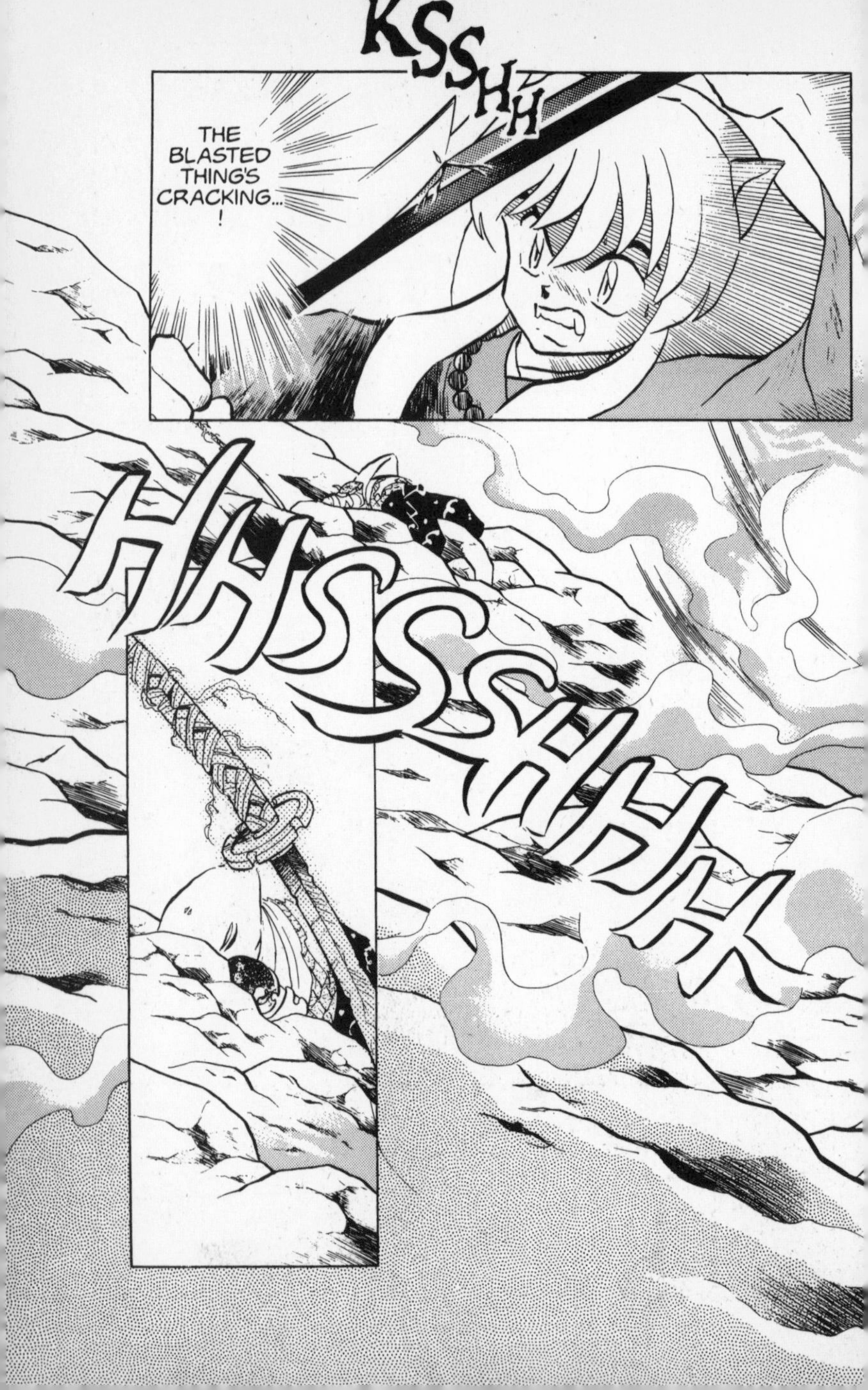
KSSHH
THE BLASTED THING'S CRACKING... !
HHSSSHHH

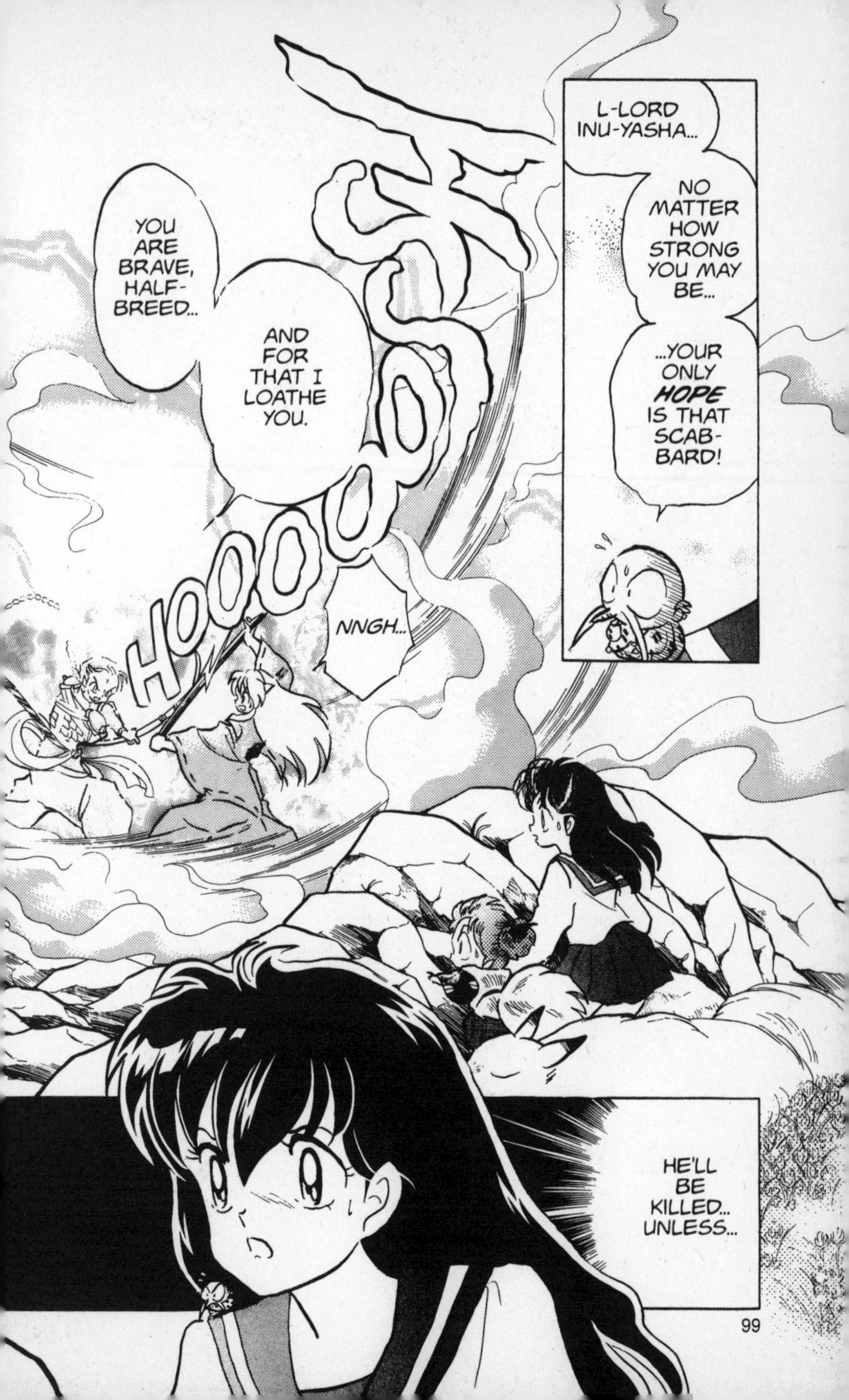
YOU ARE BRAVE, HALF-BREED...
AND FOR THAT I LOATHE YOU.
HOOOOOOSH
NNGH...
L-LORD INU-YASHA...
NO MATTER HOW STRONG YOU MAY BE...
...YOUR ONLY *HOPE* IS THAT SCAB-BARD!
HE'LL BE KILLED... UNLESS...

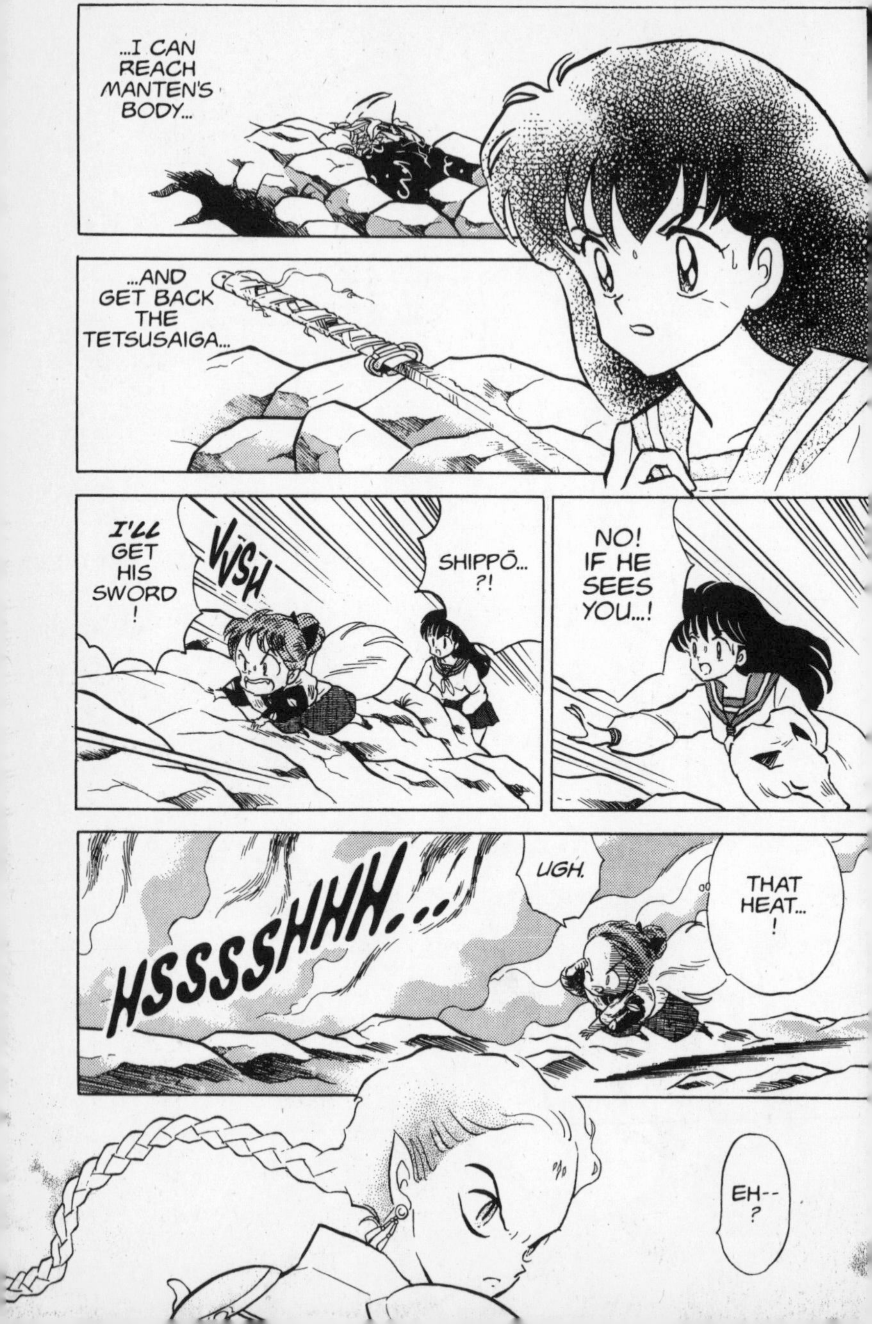
...I CAN REACH MANTEN'S BODY...
...AND GET BACK THE TETSUSAIGA...
I'LL GET HIS SWORD!
VVSH
SHIPPŌ... ?!
NO! IF HE SEES YOU...!
HSSSSHHH...
UGH.
THAT HEAT...!
EH--?

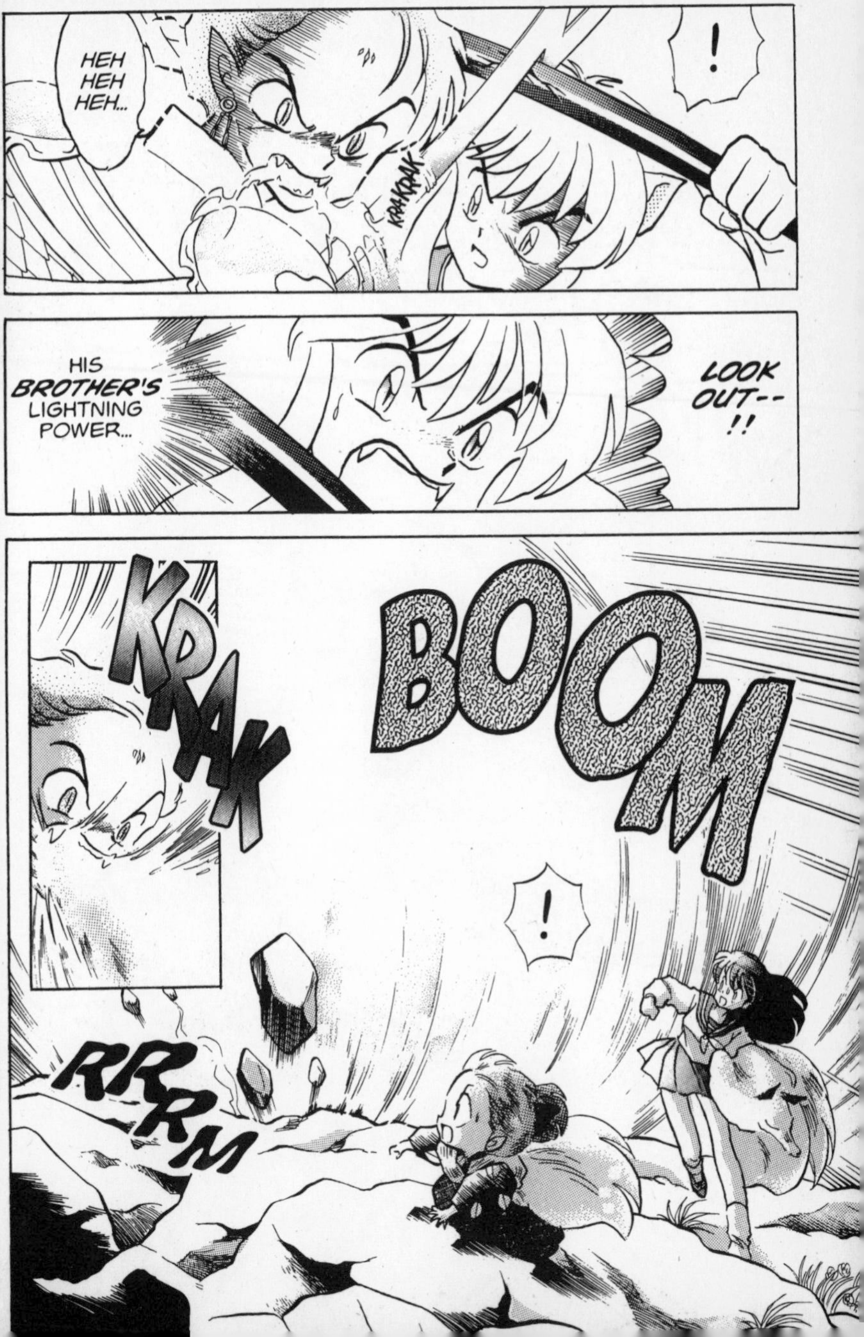
HEH HEH HEH...
KRAKRAK
!
HIS BROTHER'S LIGHTNING POWER...
LOOK OUT-- !!
KRAK
BOOM
!
RRRM

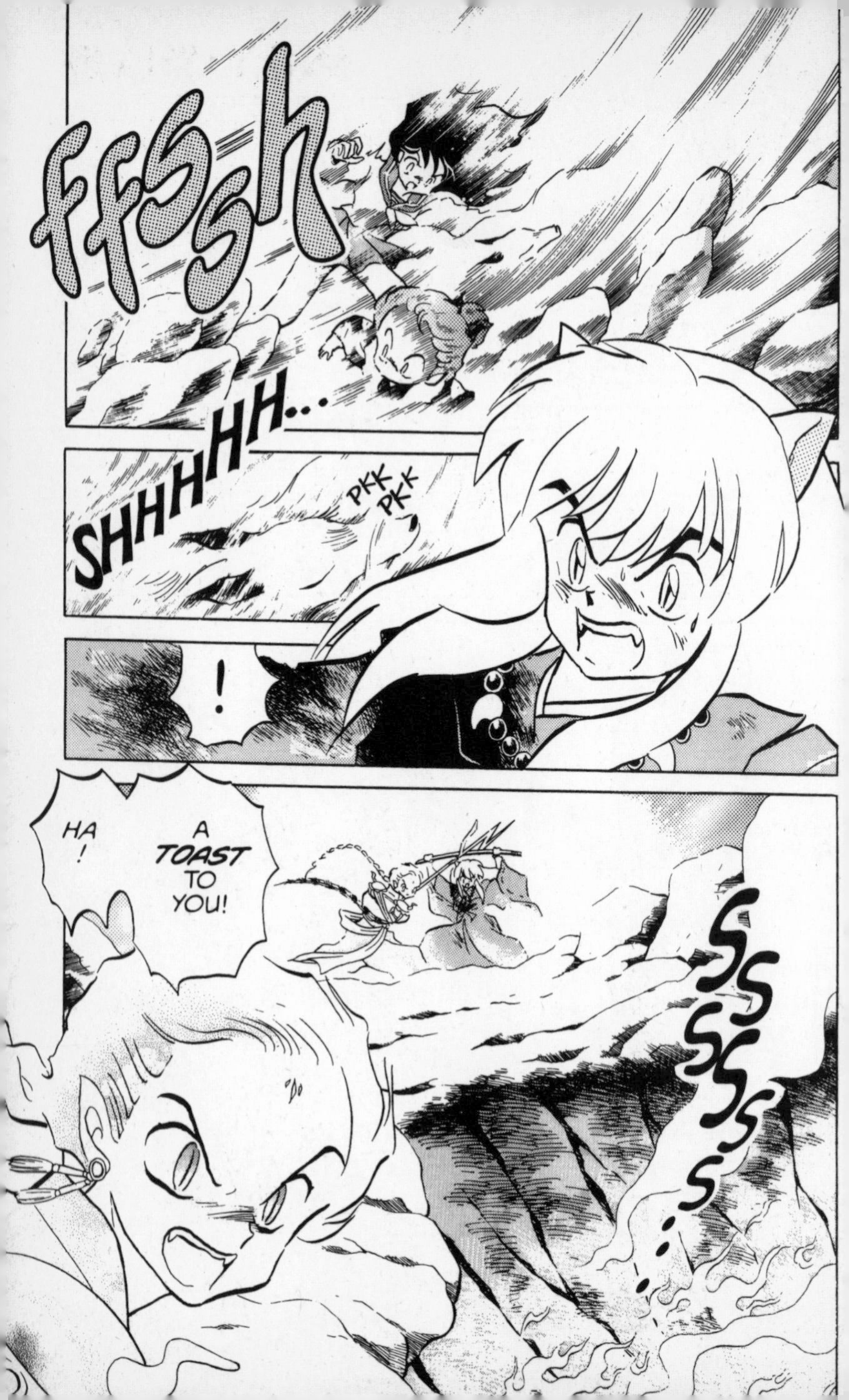
ffssh
SHHHHH...
PKK PKK
!
HA!
A TOAST TO YOU!
SSSSSS...

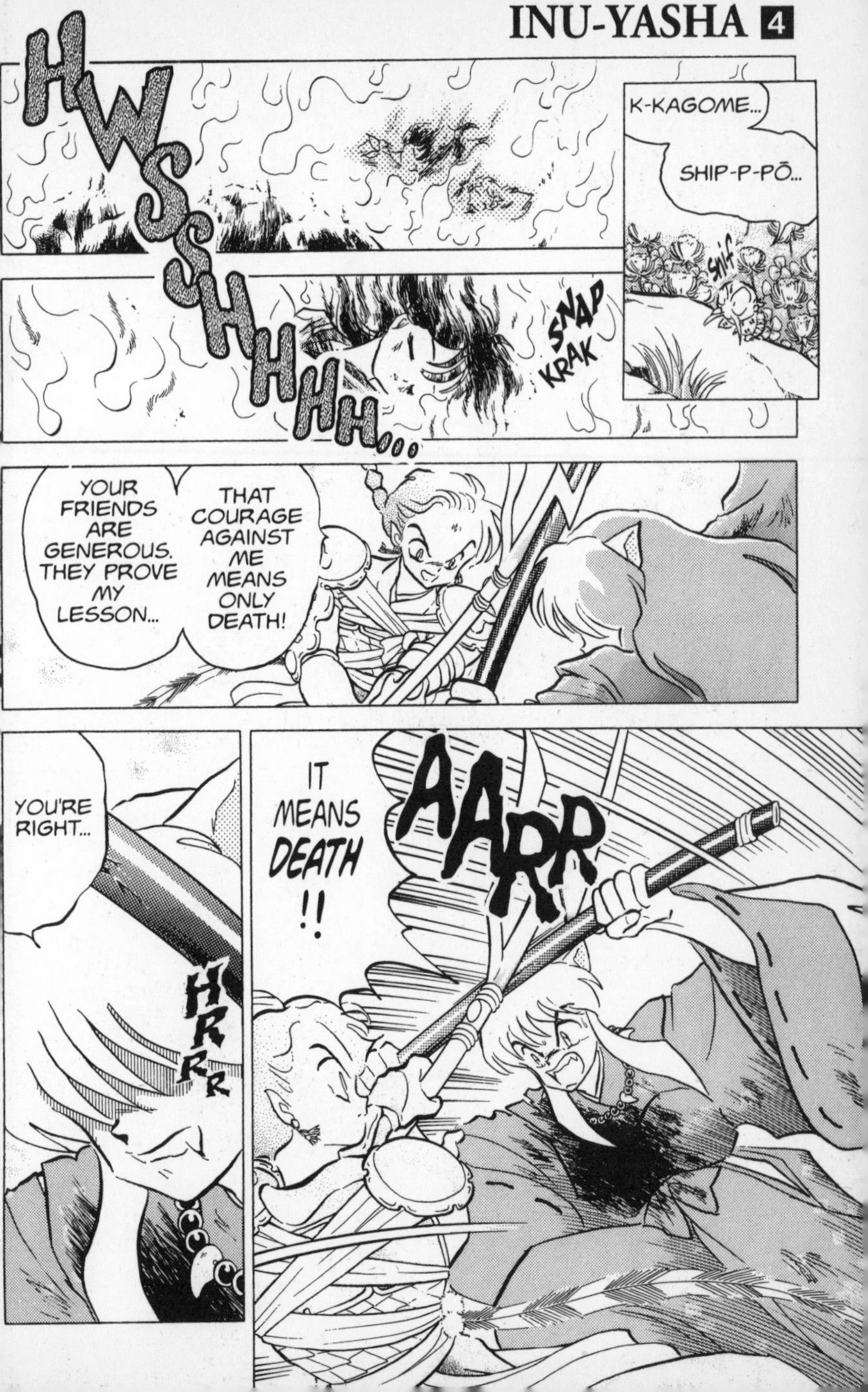
HWSSHHHH...
SNAP
KRAK
K-KAGOME...
SHIP-P-PŌ...
SNIF
YOUR FRIENDS ARE GENEROUS. THEY PROVE MY LESSON...
THAT COURAGE AGAINST ME MEANS ONLY DEATH!
YOU'RE RIGHT...
HRRRR
IT MEANS DEATH!!
AARR

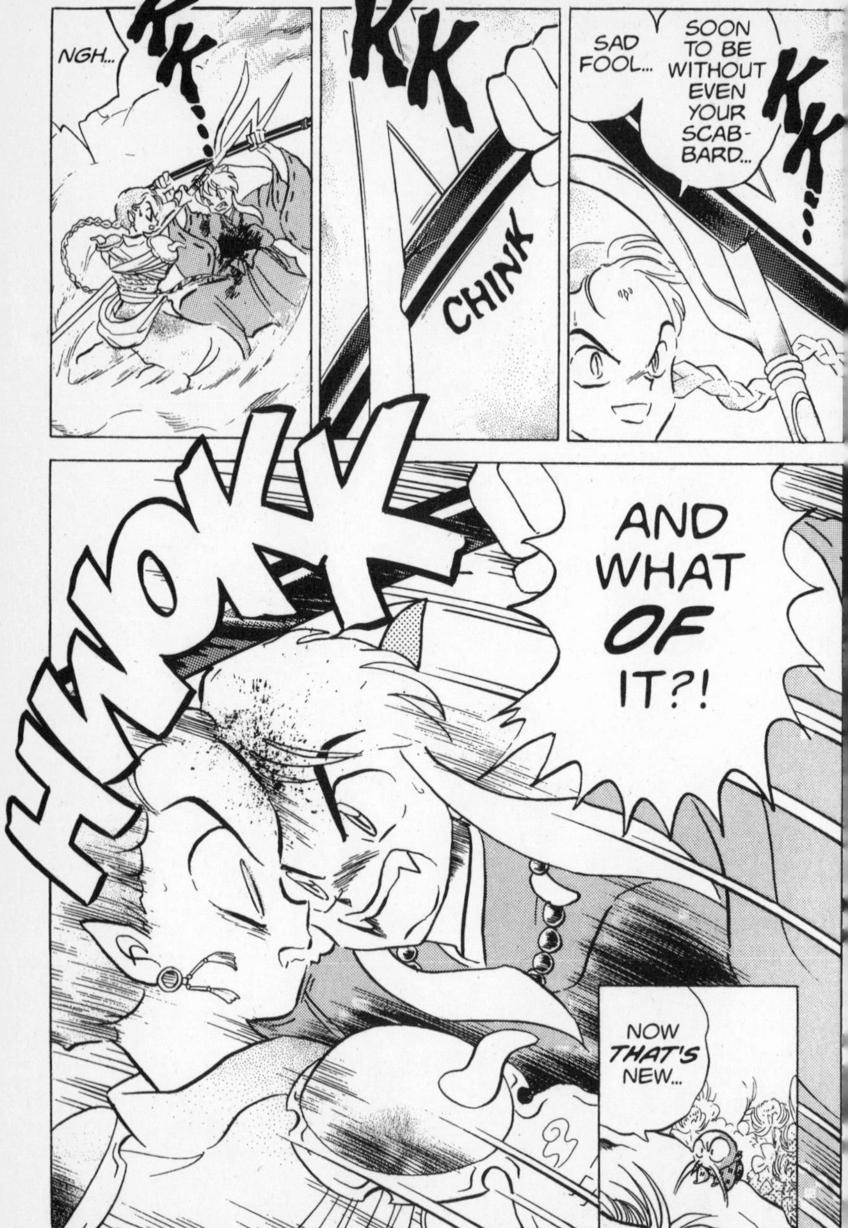
NGH...
KK...
KK
CHINK
SAD FOOL...
SOON TO BE WITHOUT EVEN YOUR SCAB-BARD...
KK...
WHOK
AND WHAT *OF* IT?!
NOW *THAT'S* NEW...

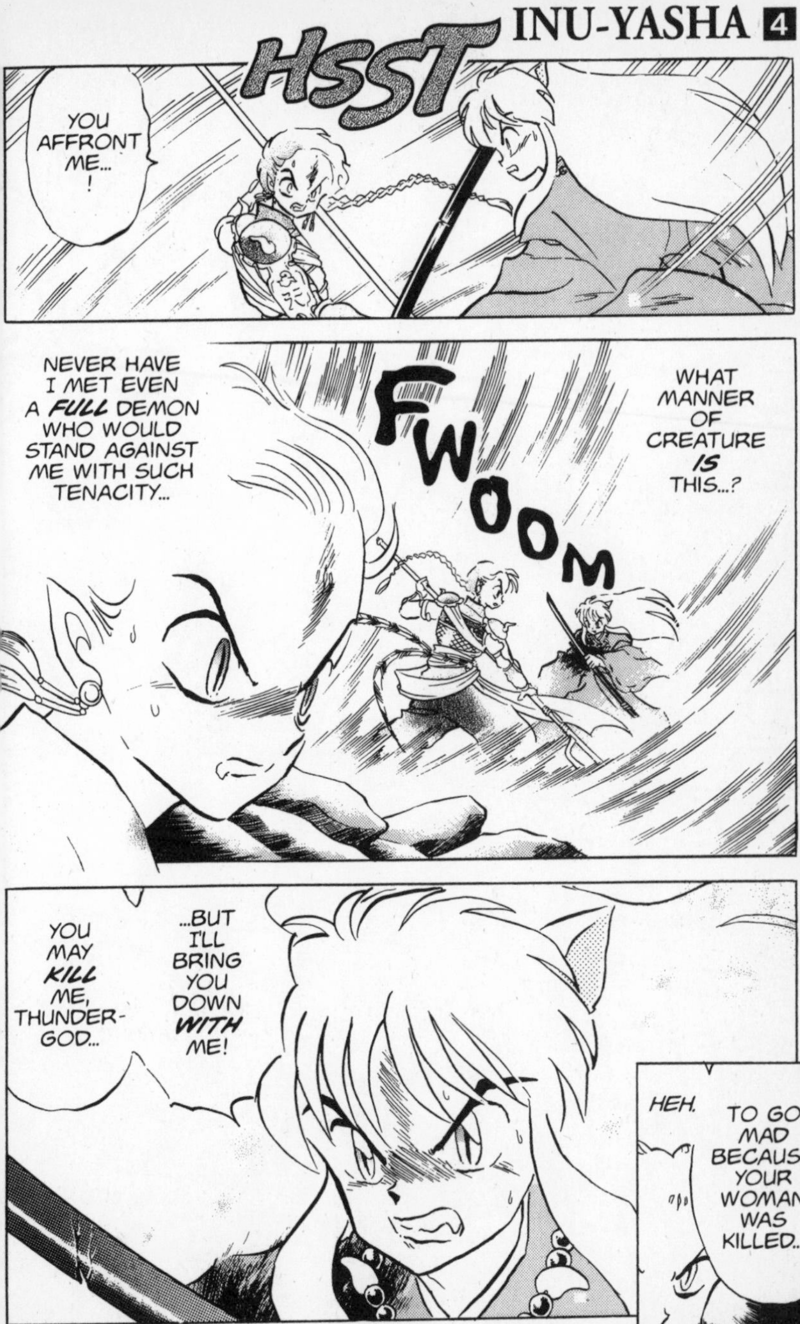
HSST
YOU AFFRONT ME... !
NEVER HAVE I MET EVEN A FULL DEMON WHO WOULD STAND AGAINST ME WITH SUCH TENACITY...
FWOOM
WHAT MANNER OF CREATURE IS THIS...?
YOU MAY KILL ME, THUNDER-GOD...
...BUT I'LL BRING YOU DOWN WITH ME!
HEH.
TO GO MAD BECAUSE YOUR WOMAN WAS KILLED...

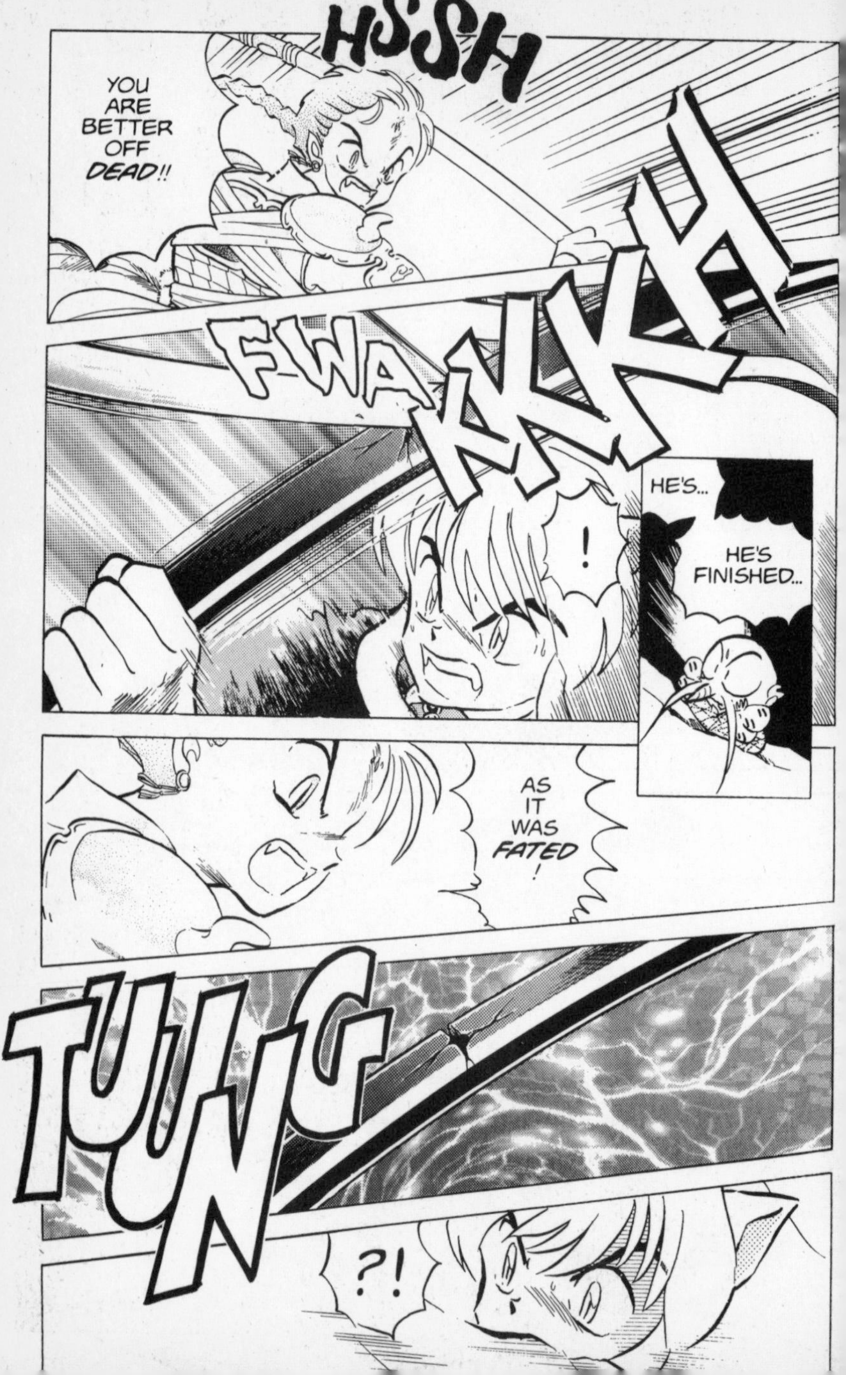
HSSH
YOU ARE BETTER OFF *DEAD*!!
FWAKKKH
!
HE'S...
HE'S FINISHED...
AS IT WAS *FATED*!
TUNG
?!

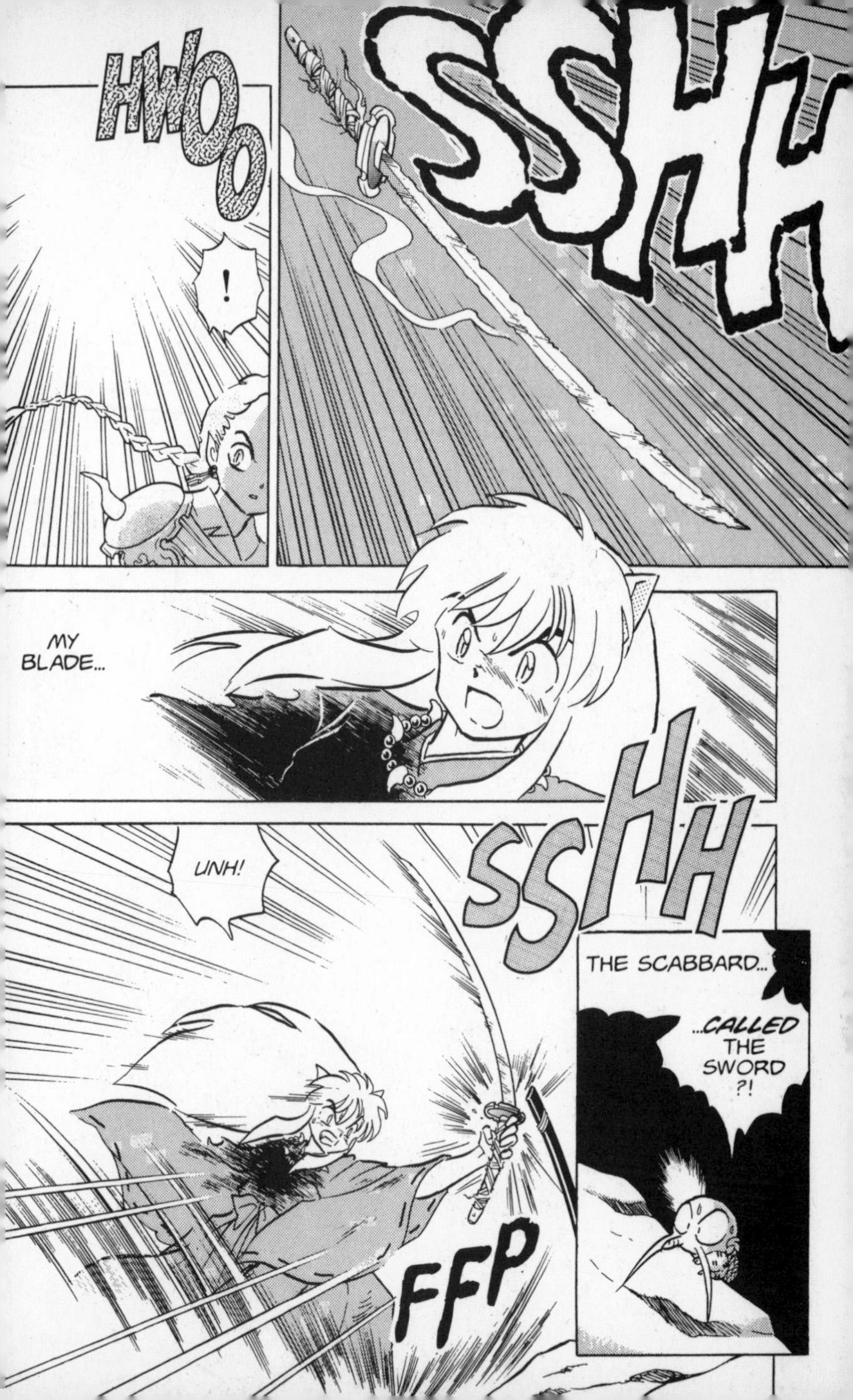
HWOO
!
SSHH
MY BLADE...
UNH!
SSHH
FFP
THE SCABBARD...
...CALLED THE SWORD ?!

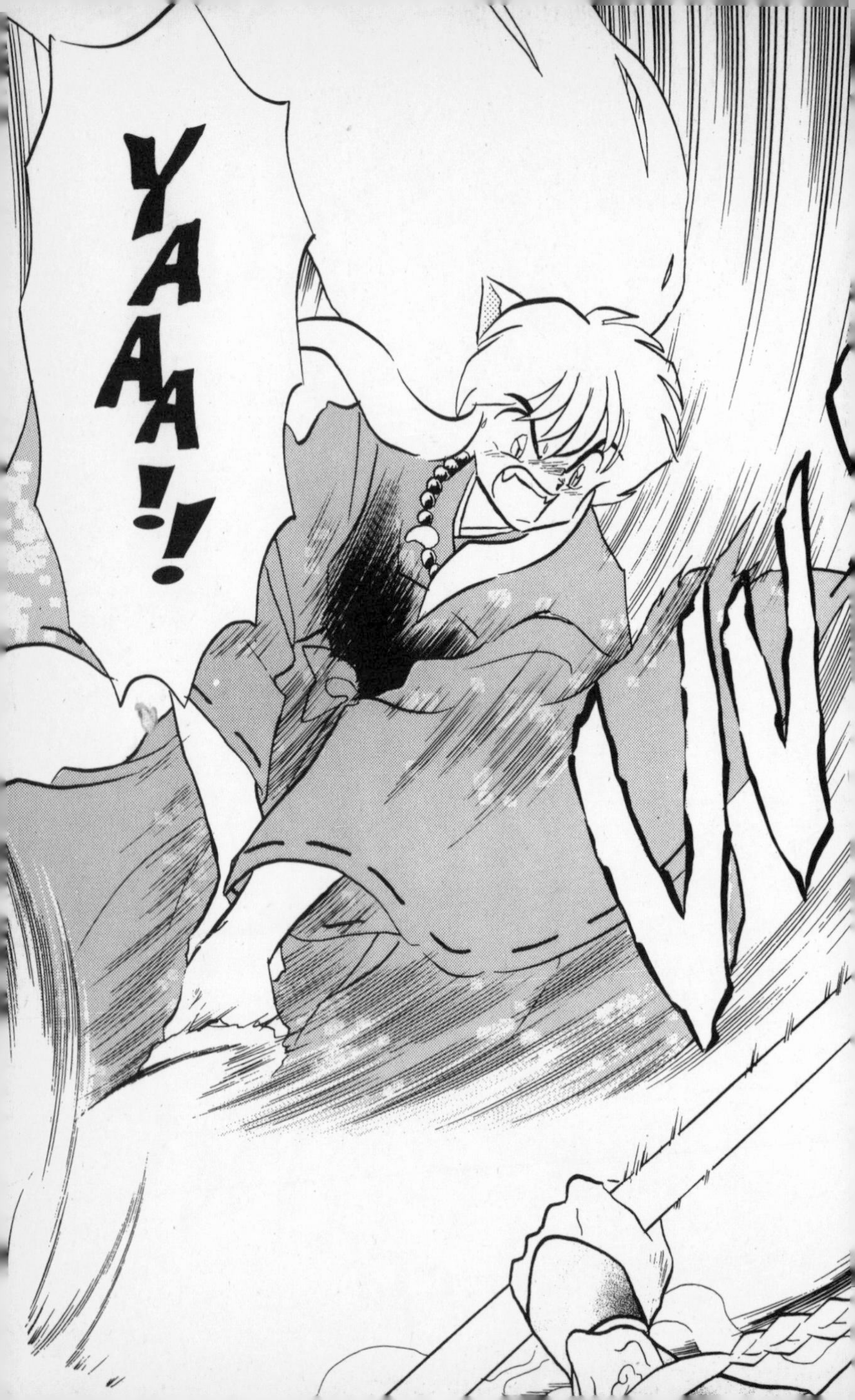
YAAA!!

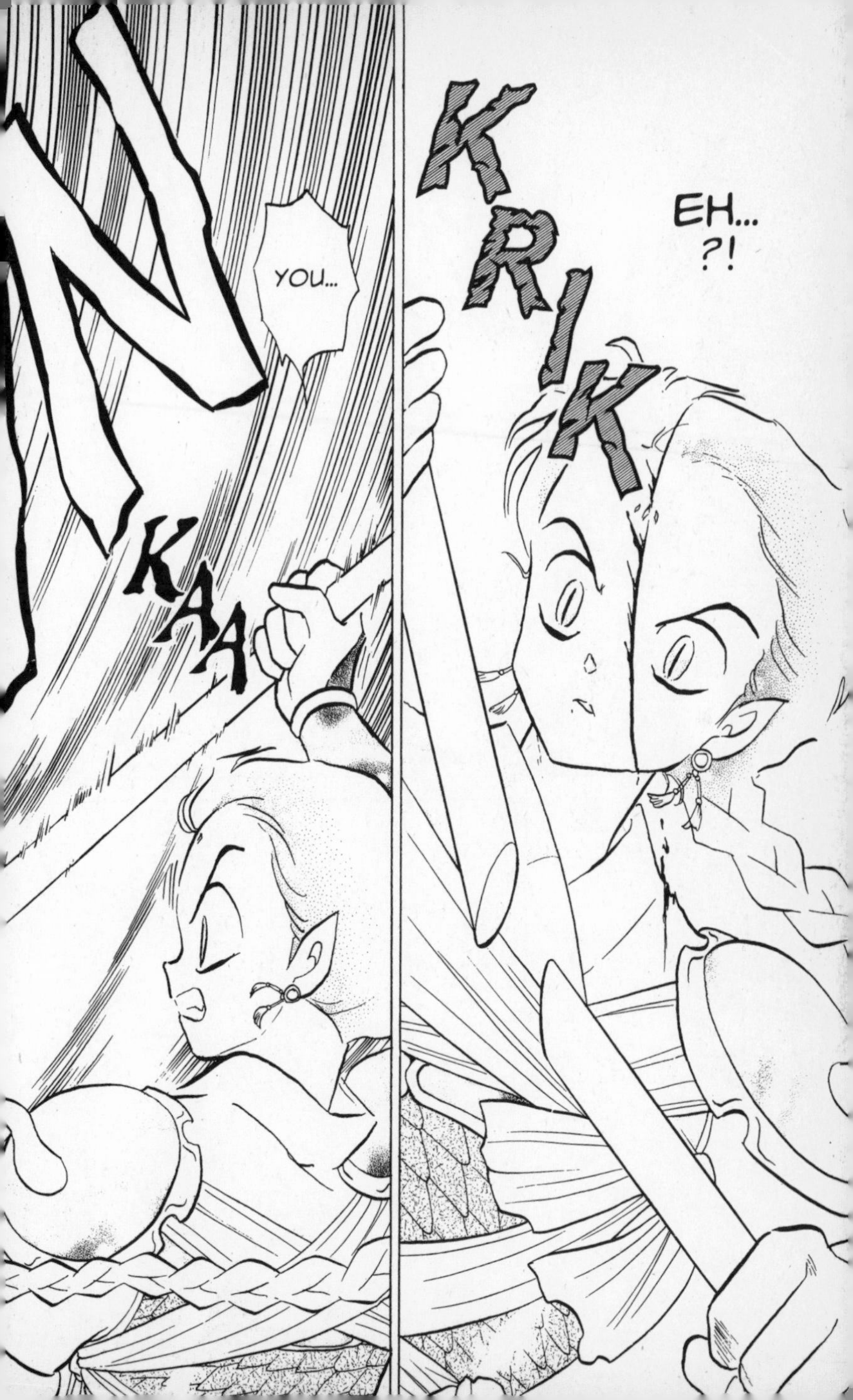
YOU...
KAA
KRIK
EH... ?!

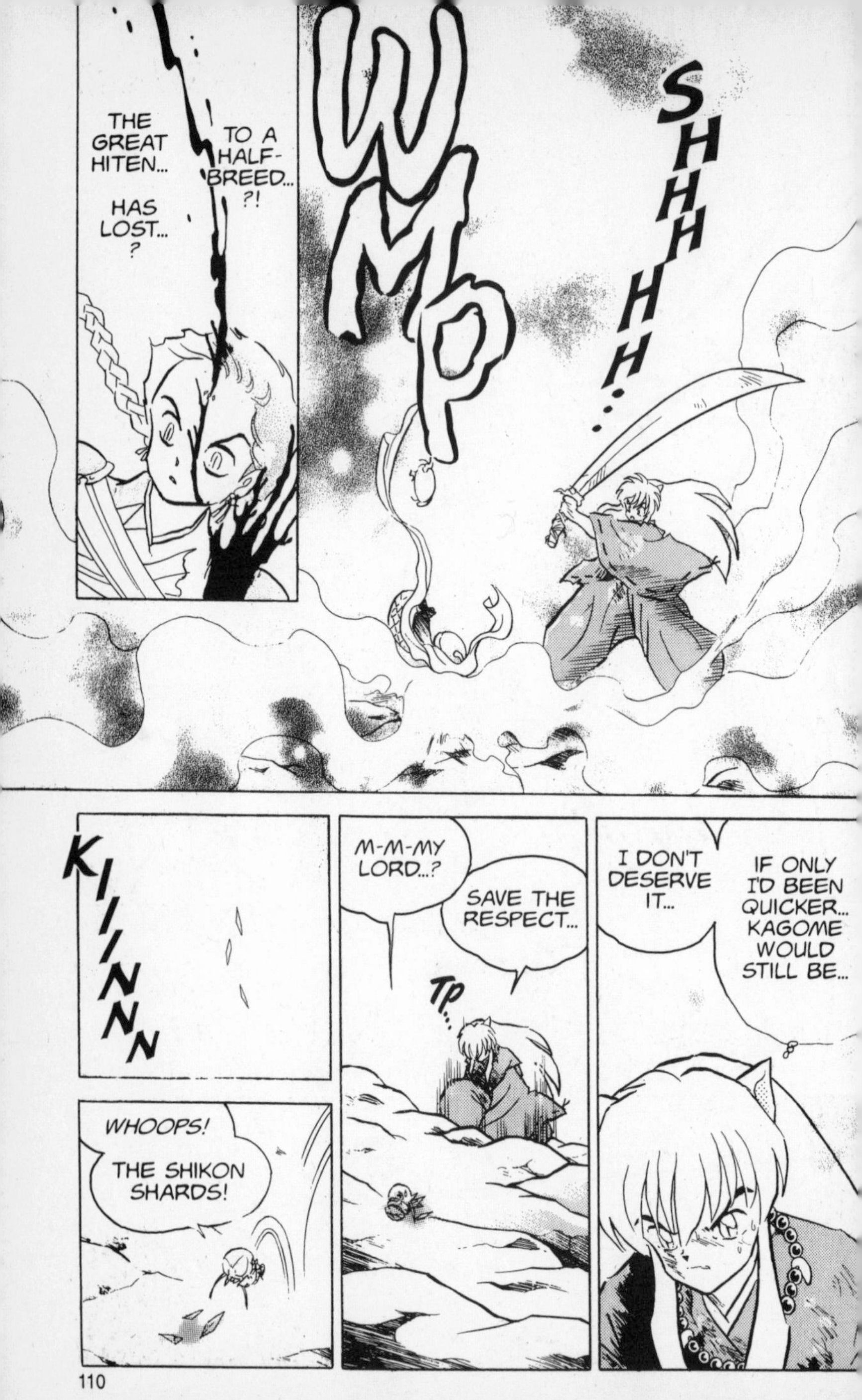
THE GREAT HITEN... HAS LOST...?
TO A HALF-BREED...?!
WUMP
SHHHHHH...
KIIINNN
WHOOPS! THE SHIKON SHARDS!
M-M-MY LORD...?
SAVE THE RESPECT...
TP...
I DON'T DESERVE IT...
IF ONLY I'D BEEN QUICKER... KAGOME WOULD STILL BE...

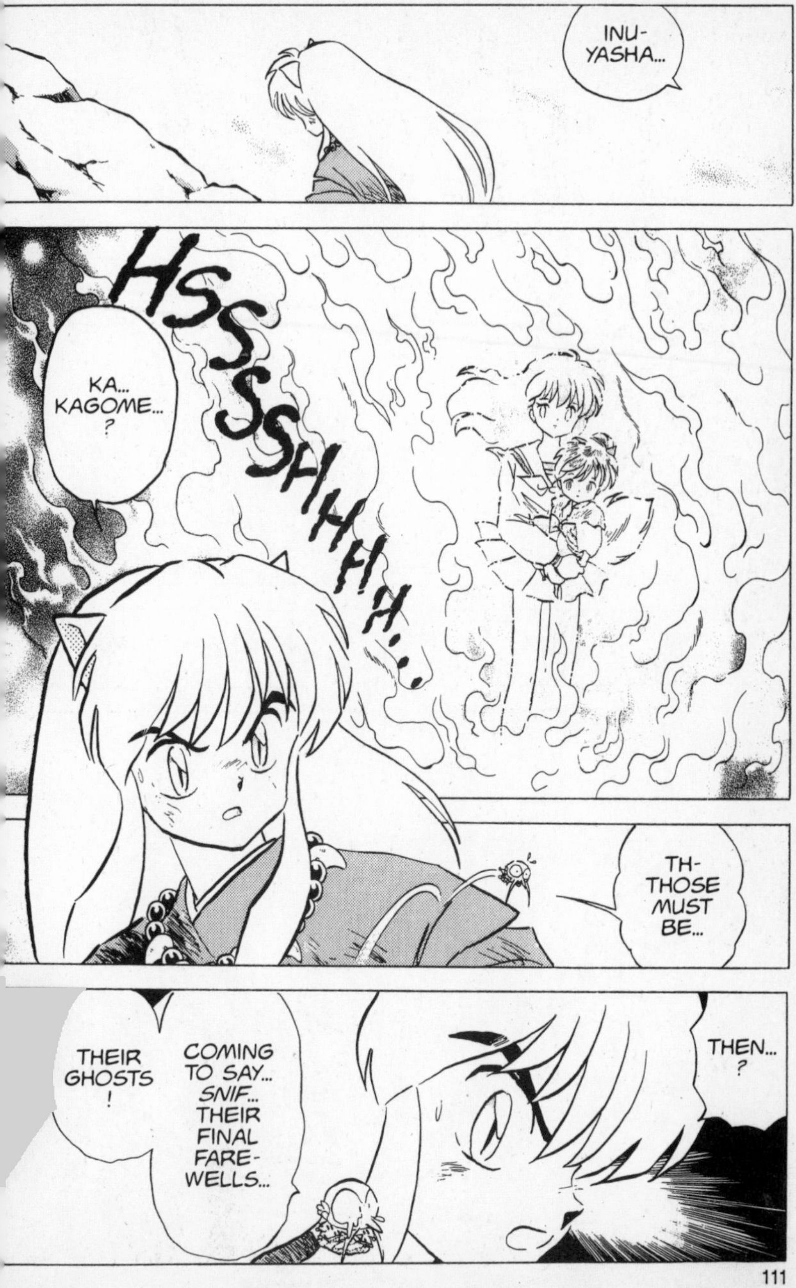
INU-
YASHA...
KA...
KAGOME...
?
HSSSSHHHH...
TH-
THOSE
MUST
BE...
THEIR
GHOSTS
!
COMING
TO SAY...
SNIF...
THEIR
FINAL
FARE-
WELLS...
THEN...
?

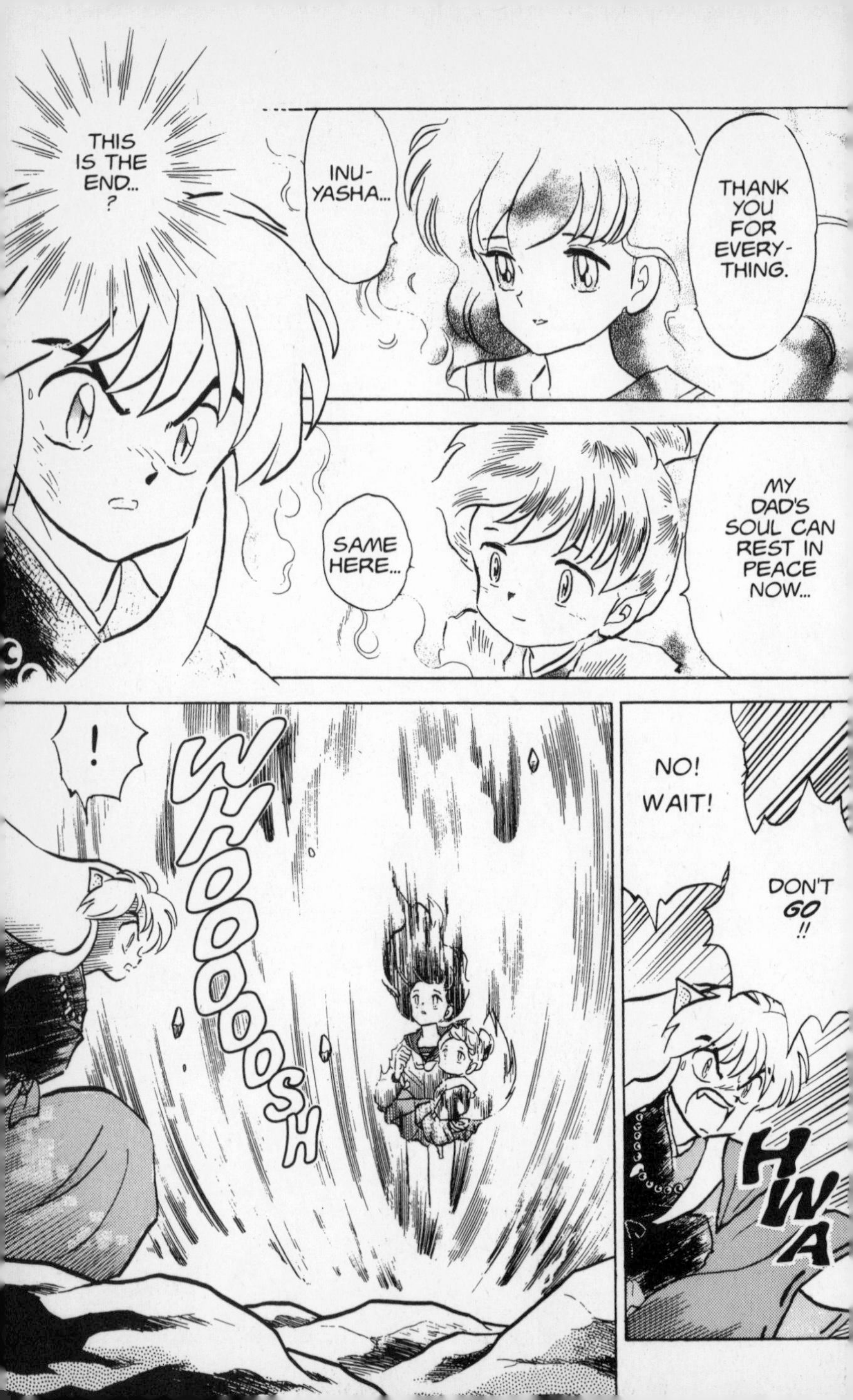
THIS IS THE END... ?
INU-YASHA...
THANK YOU FOR EVERY-THING.
SAME HERE...
MY DAD'S SOUL CAN REST IN PEACE NOW...
!
WHOOOOOSH
NO! WAIT!
DON'T GO !!
HWA

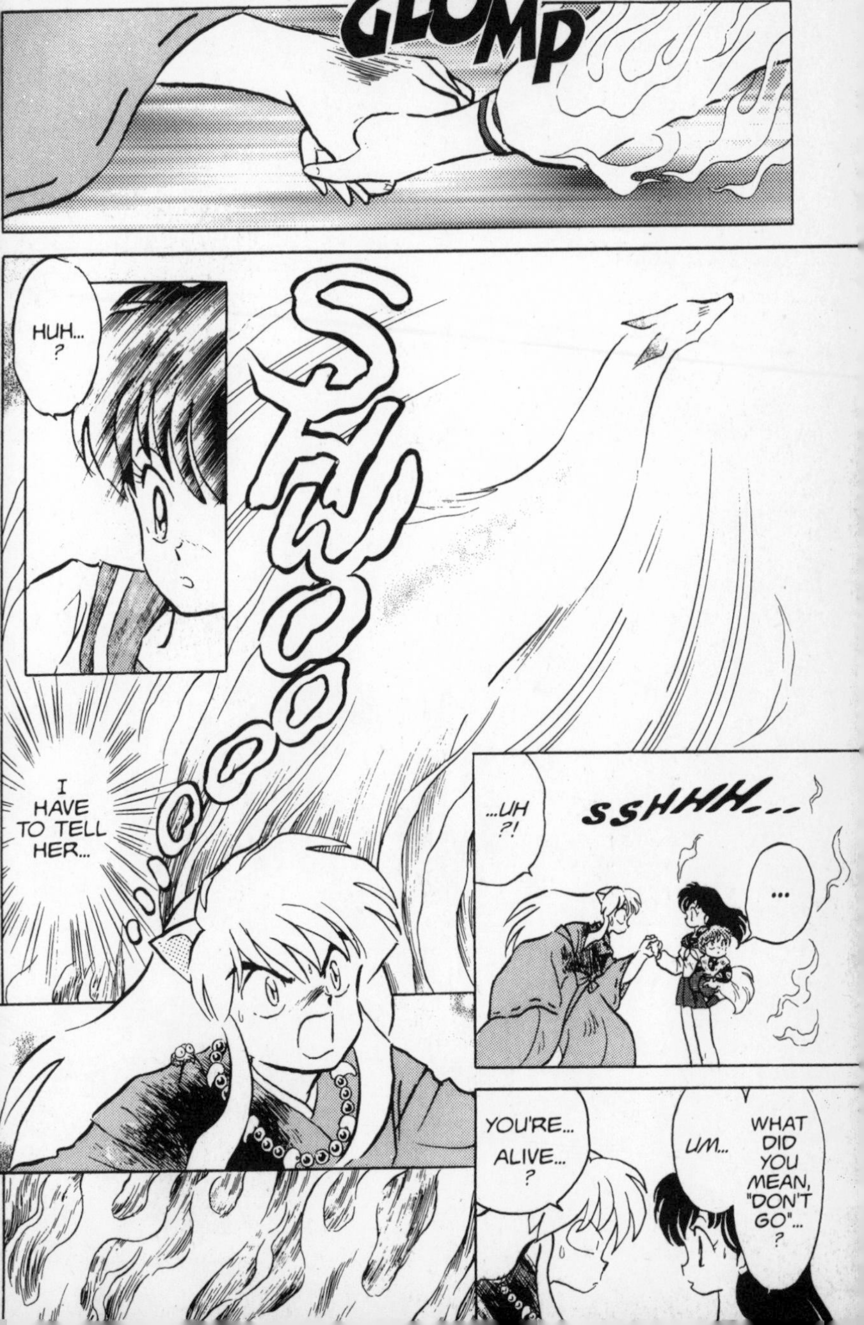
GLOMP
HUH... ?
SHWOOOOOO
I HAVE TO TELL HER...
...UH ?!
SSHHH...
...
YOU'RE... ALIVE... ?
UM...
WHAT DID YOU MEAN, "DON'T GO"... ?

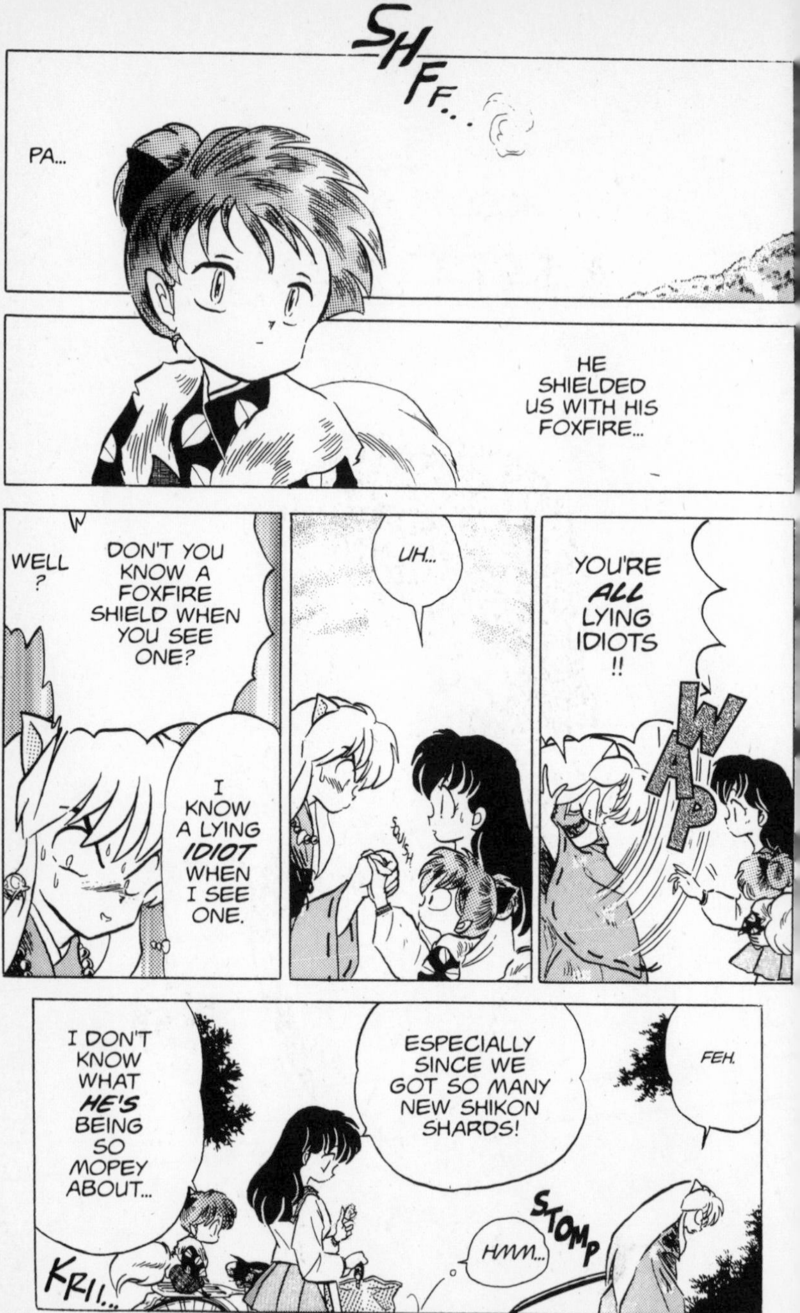
SHFF...
PA...
HE SHIELDED US WITH HIS FOXFIRE...
WELL?
DON'T YOU KNOW A FOXFIRE SHIELD WHEN YOU SEE ONE?
I KNOW A LYING IDIOT WHEN I SEE ONE.
UH...
SQUISH
YOU'RE ALL LYING IDIOTS!!
WAP
I DON'T KNOW WHAT HE'S BEING SO MOPEY ABOUT...
KRII...
ESPECIALLY SINCE WE GOT SO MANY NEW SHIKON SHARDS!
HMM...
STOMP
FEH.

SCROLL SEVEN
A LITTLE IMP

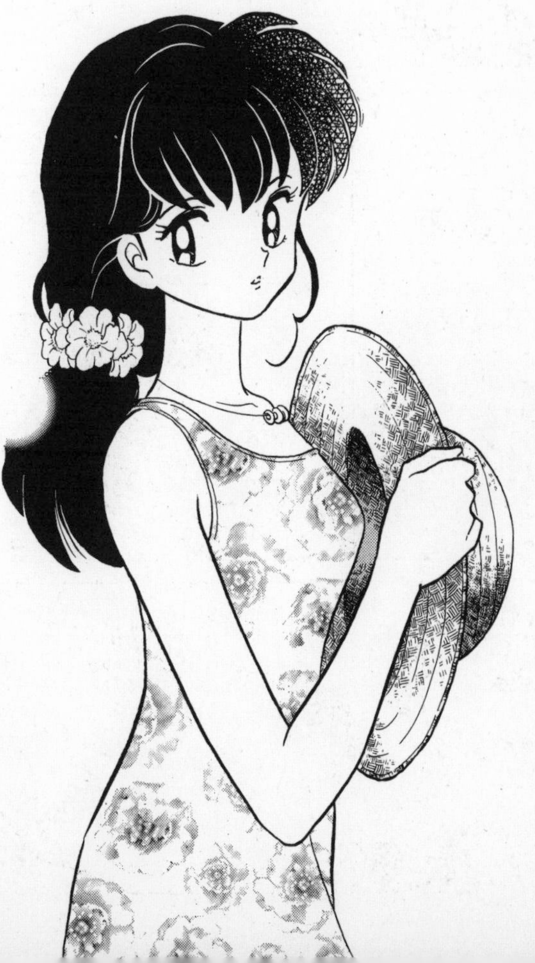

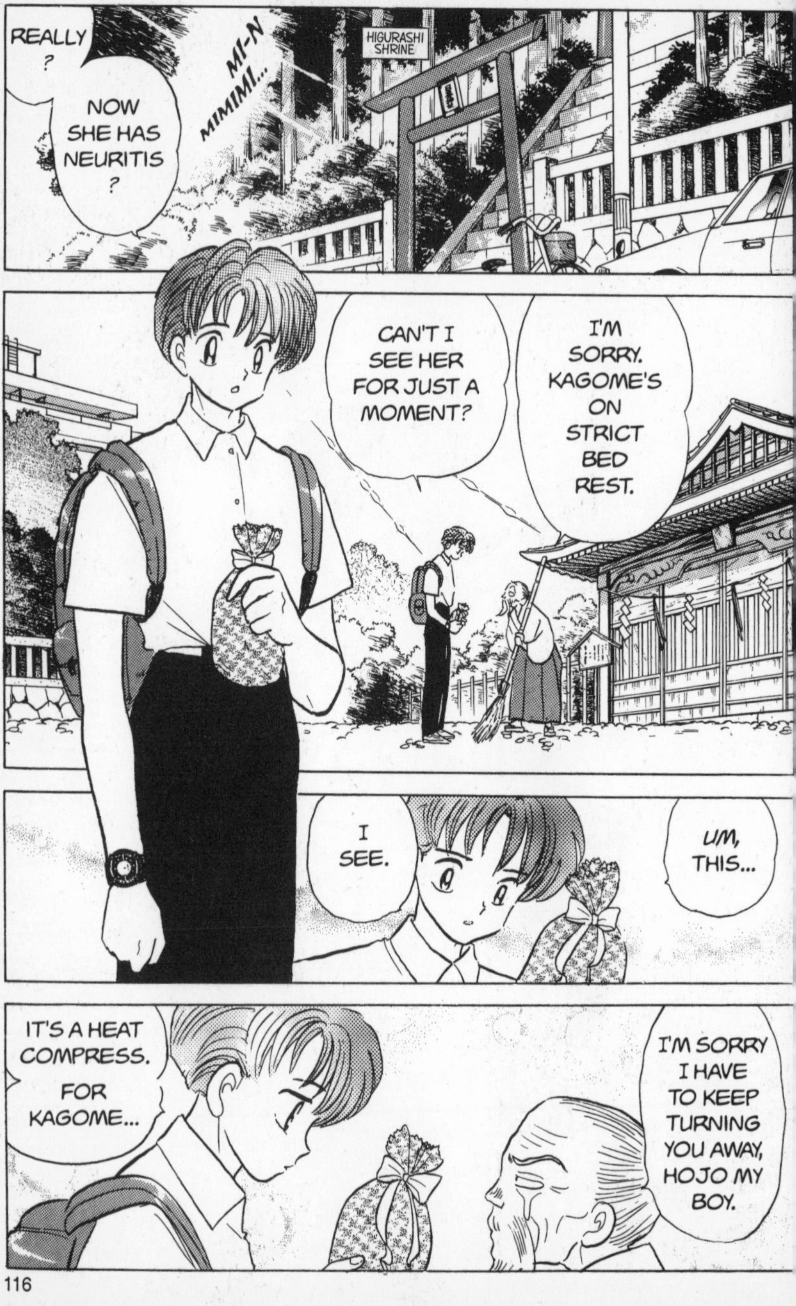
REALLY?
NOW SHE HAS NEURITIS?
MI-N MIMIMI...
HIGURASHI SHRINE
CAN'T I SEE HER FOR JUST A MOMENT?
I'M SORRY. KAGOME'S ON STRICT BED REST.
I SEE.
UM, THIS...
IT'S A HEAT COMPRESS.
FOR KAGOME...
I'M SORRY I HAVE TO KEEP TURNING YOU AWAY, HOJO MY BOY.

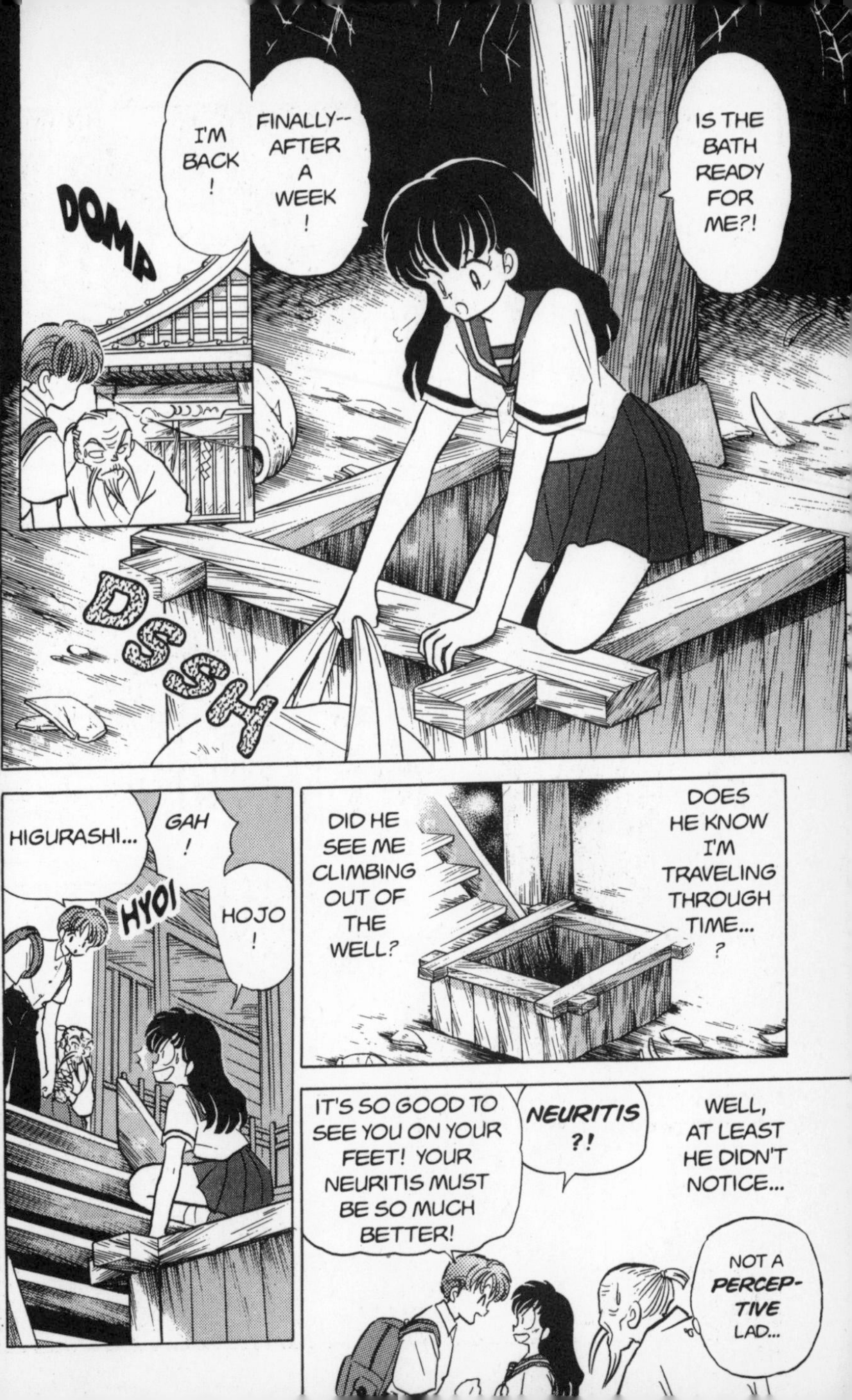
I'M BACK!
FINALLY-- AFTER A WEEK!
DOMP
IS THE BATH READY FOR ME?!
DSSH
HIGURASHI...
GAH!
HYOI
HOJO!
DID HE SEE ME CLIMBING OUT OF THE WELL?
DOES HE KNOW I'M TRAVELING THROUGH TIME...?
IT'S SO GOOD TO SEE YOU ON YOUR FEET! YOUR NEURITIS MUST BE SO MUCH BETTER!
NEURITIS?!
WELL, AT LEAST HE DIDN'T NOTICE...
NOT A PERCEPTIVE LAD...

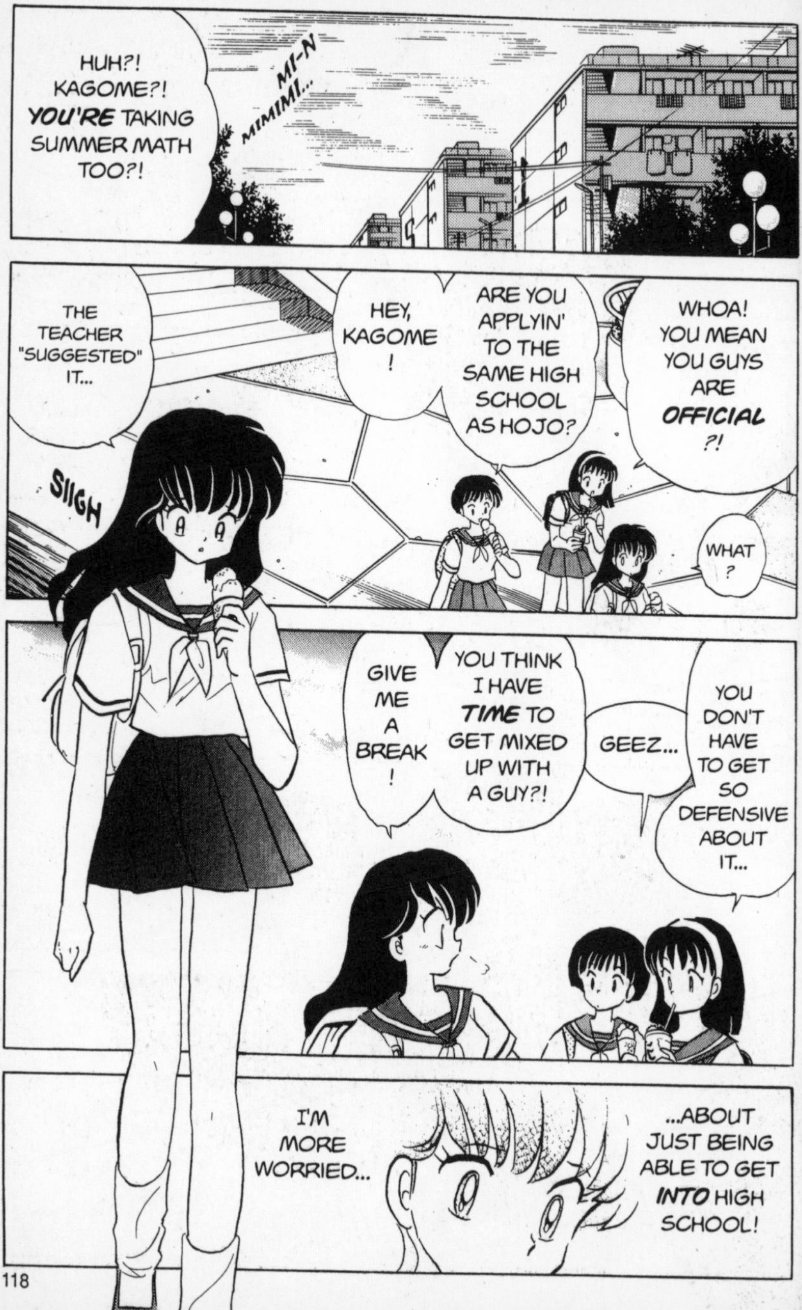
HUH?! KAGOME?! YOU'RE TAKING SUMMER MATH TOO?!
MI-N MIMIMI...
THE TEACHER "SUGGESTED" IT...
SIIGH
HEY, KAGOME!
ARE YOU APPLYIN' TO THE SAME HIGH SCHOOL AS HOJO?
WHOA! YOU MEAN YOU GUYS ARE OFFICIAL?!
WHAT?
GIVE ME A BREAK!
YOU THINK I HAVE TIME TO GET MIXED UP WITH A GUY?!
GEEZ...
YOU DON'T HAVE TO GET SO DEFENSIVE ABOUT IT...
I'M MORE WORRIED...
...ABOUT JUST BEING ABLE TO GET INTO HIGH SCHOOL!

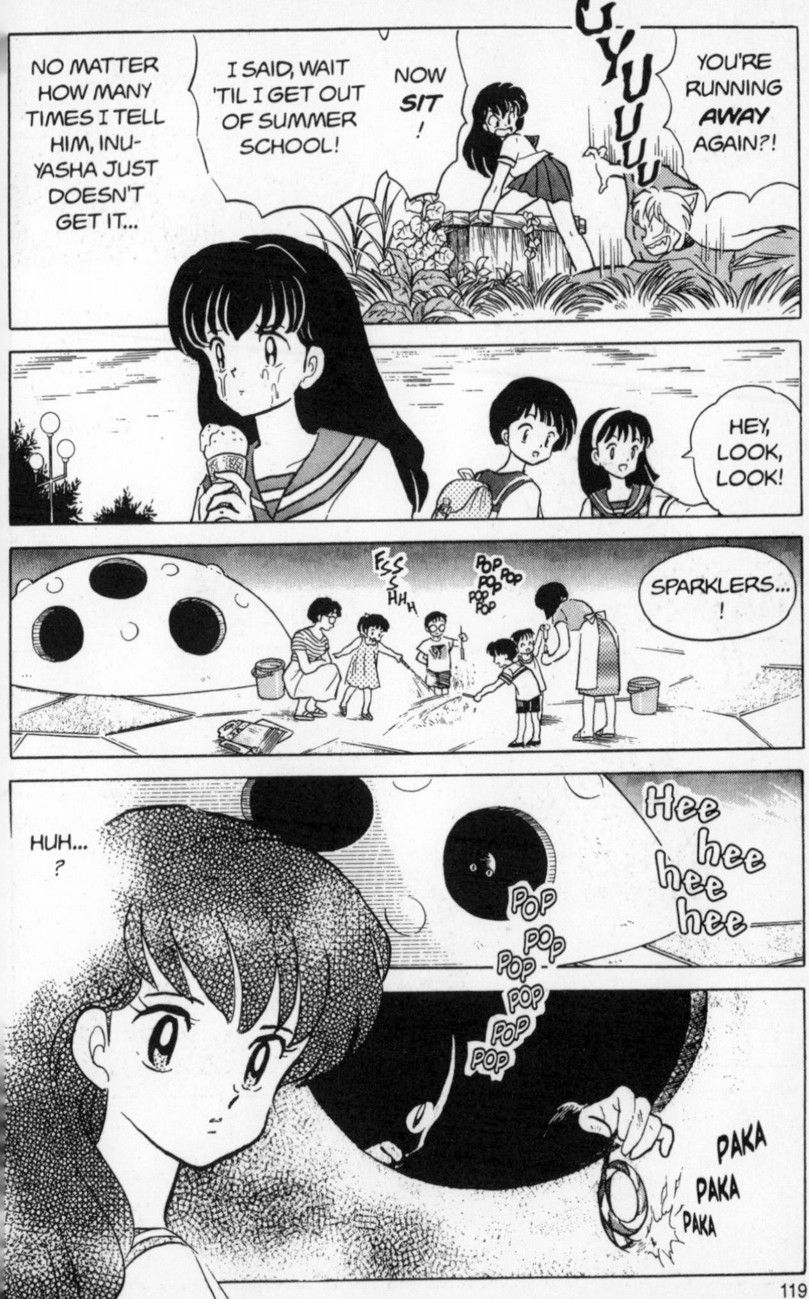

NO MATTER HOW MANY TIMES I TELL HIM, INU-YASHA JUST DOESN'T GET IT...
I SAID, WAIT 'TIL I GET OUT OF SUMMER SCHOOL!
NOW SIT!
GYUUUU
YOU'RE RUNNING AWAY AGAIN?!
HEY, LOOK, LOOK!
FSSSHHH
POP POP POP POP POP POP
SPARKLERS...!
HUH...?
Hee hee hee hee
POP POP POP POP POP POP
PAKA PAKA PAKA

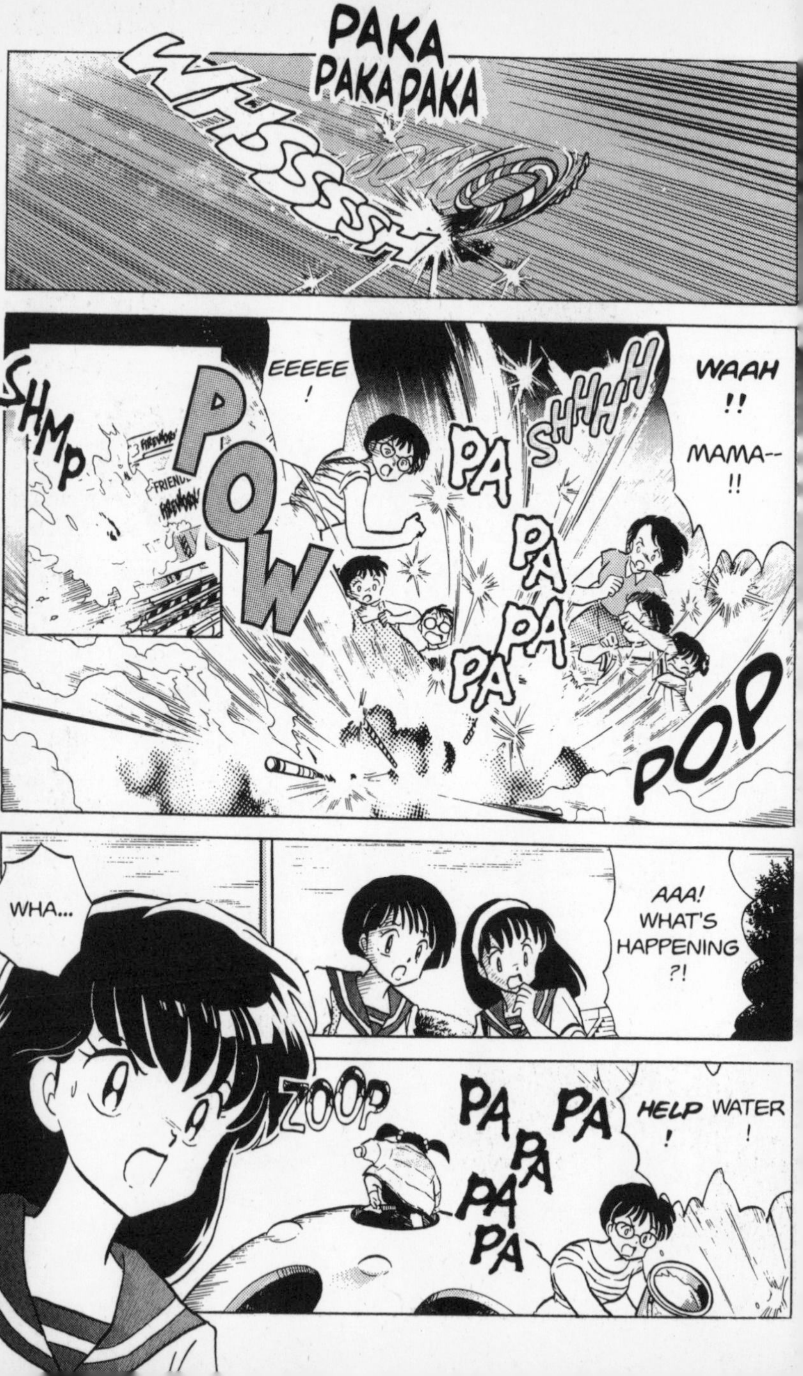
PAKA
PAKA PAKA
WHSSSSH
SHMP
POW
EEEEE!
PA
SHHHH
PA
PA
PA
PA
WAAH!!
MAMA--!!
POP
WHA...
AAA! WHAT'S HAPPENING?!
ZOOP
PA
PA
PA
PA
PA
PA
HELP!
WATER!

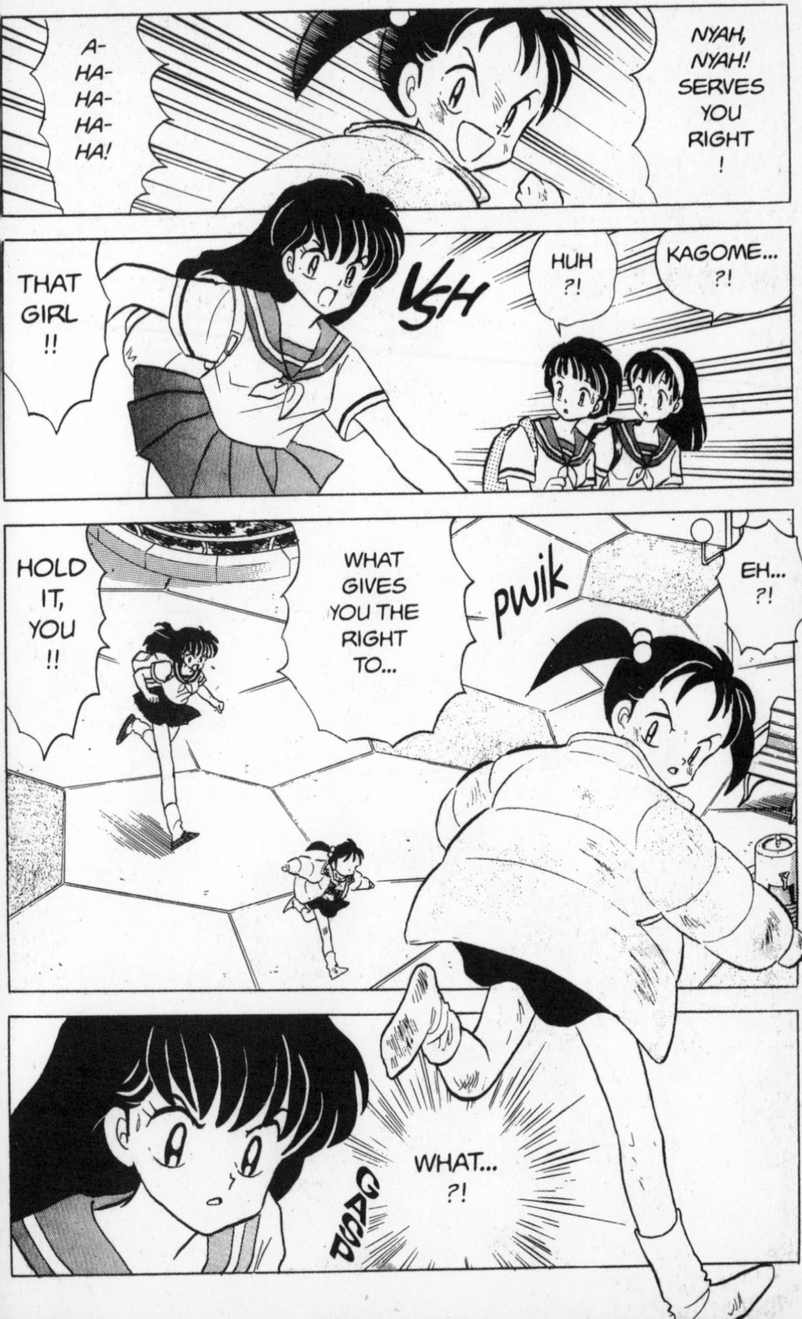
A-HA-HA-HA-HA!
NYAH, NYAH! SERVES YOU RIGHT!
THAT GIRL!!
VSH
HUH?!
KAGOME...?!
HOLD IT, YOU!!
WHAT GIVES YOU THE RIGHT TO...
PWIK
EH...?!
WHAT...?!
GASP

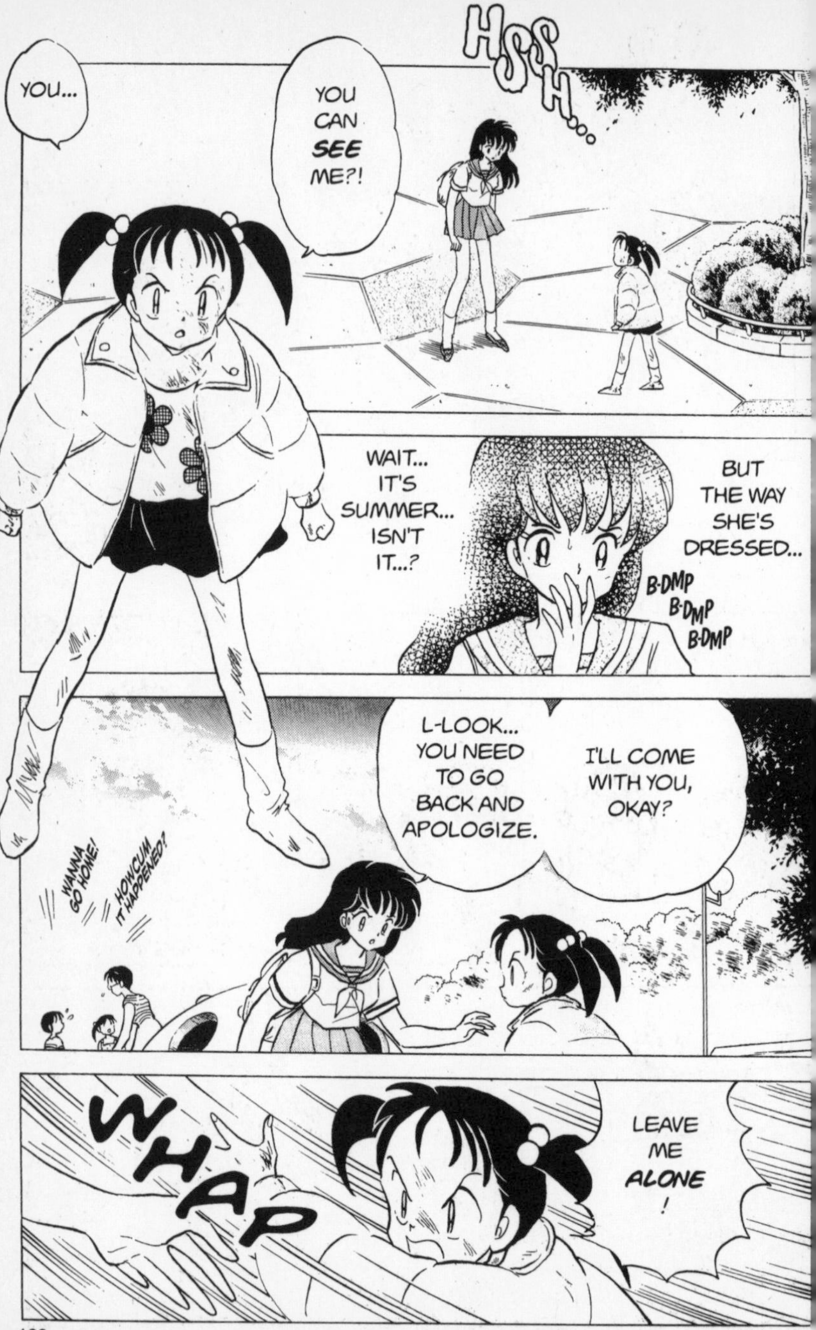
YOU...
YOU CAN SEE ME?!
HSSH...
WAIT... IT'S SUMMER... ISN'T IT...?
BUT THE WAY SHE'S DRESSED...
B-DMP B-DMP B-DMP
WANNA GO HOME!
HOWCUM IT HAPPENED?
L-LOOK... YOU NEED TO GO BACK AND APOLOGIZE.
I'LL COME WITH YOU, OKAY?
WHAP
LEAVE ME ALONE!

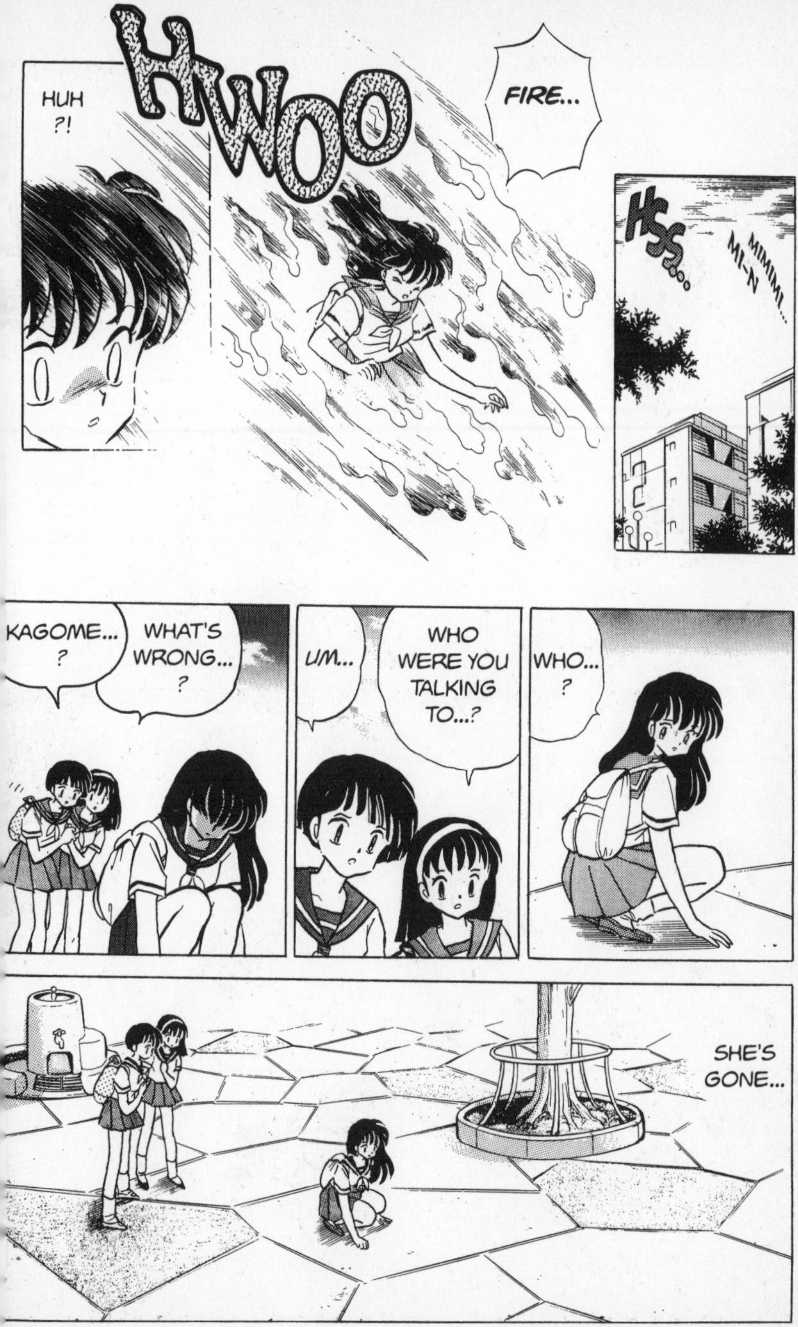
HWOO
HUH ?!
FIRE...
HSS...
MIMIMI MI-N...
KAGOME... ?
WHAT'S WRONG... ?
UM...
WHO WERE YOU TALKING TO...?
WHO... ?
SHE'S GONE...

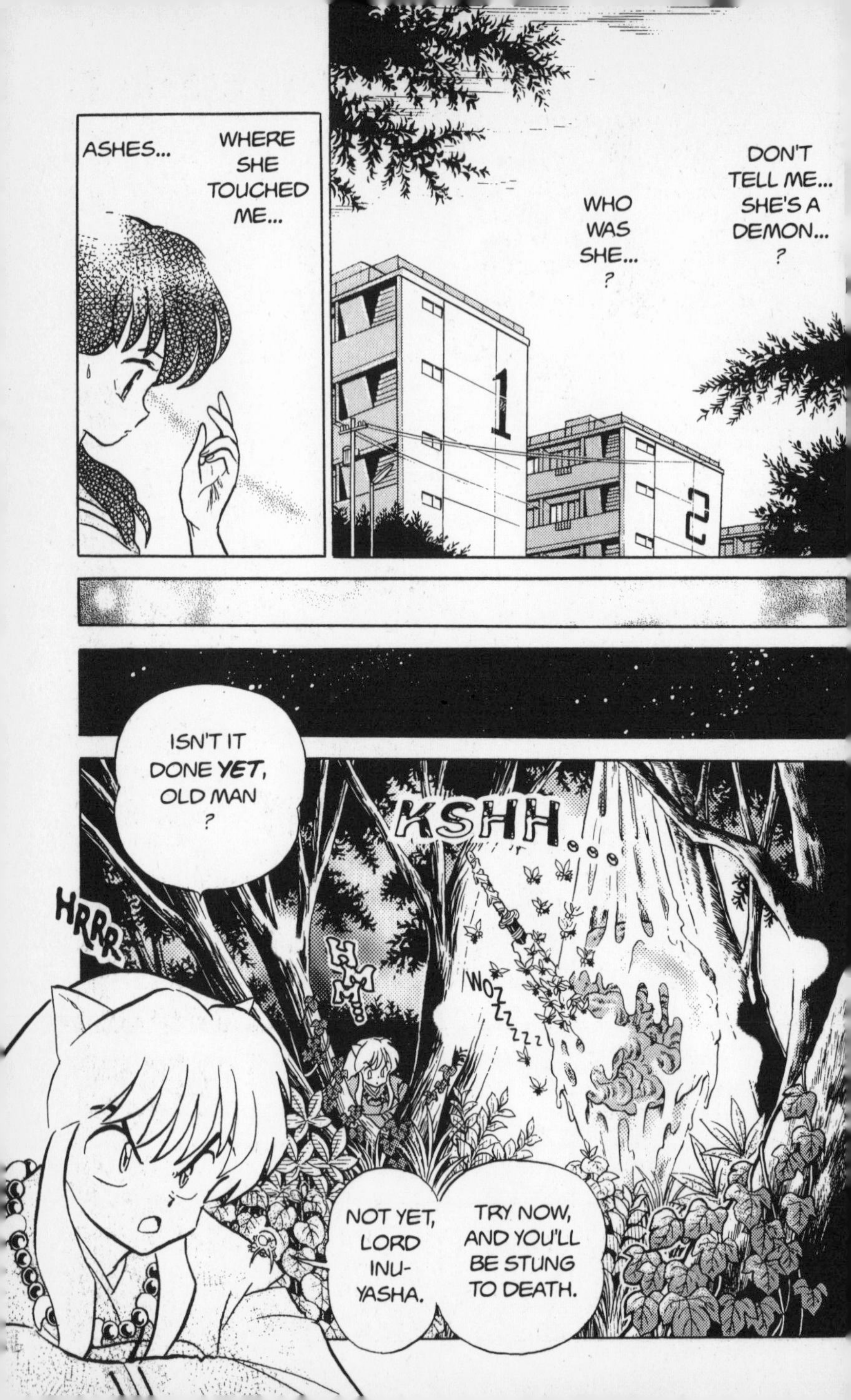
ASHES...
WHERE SHE TOUCHED ME...
WHO WAS SHE... ?
DON'T TELL ME... SHE'S A DEMON... ?
ISN'T IT DONE YET, OLD MAN ?
KSHH...
HRRR
HMM..
WOZZZZZZ
NOT YET, LORD INU-YASHA.
TRY NOW, AND YOU'LL BE STUNG TO DEATH.

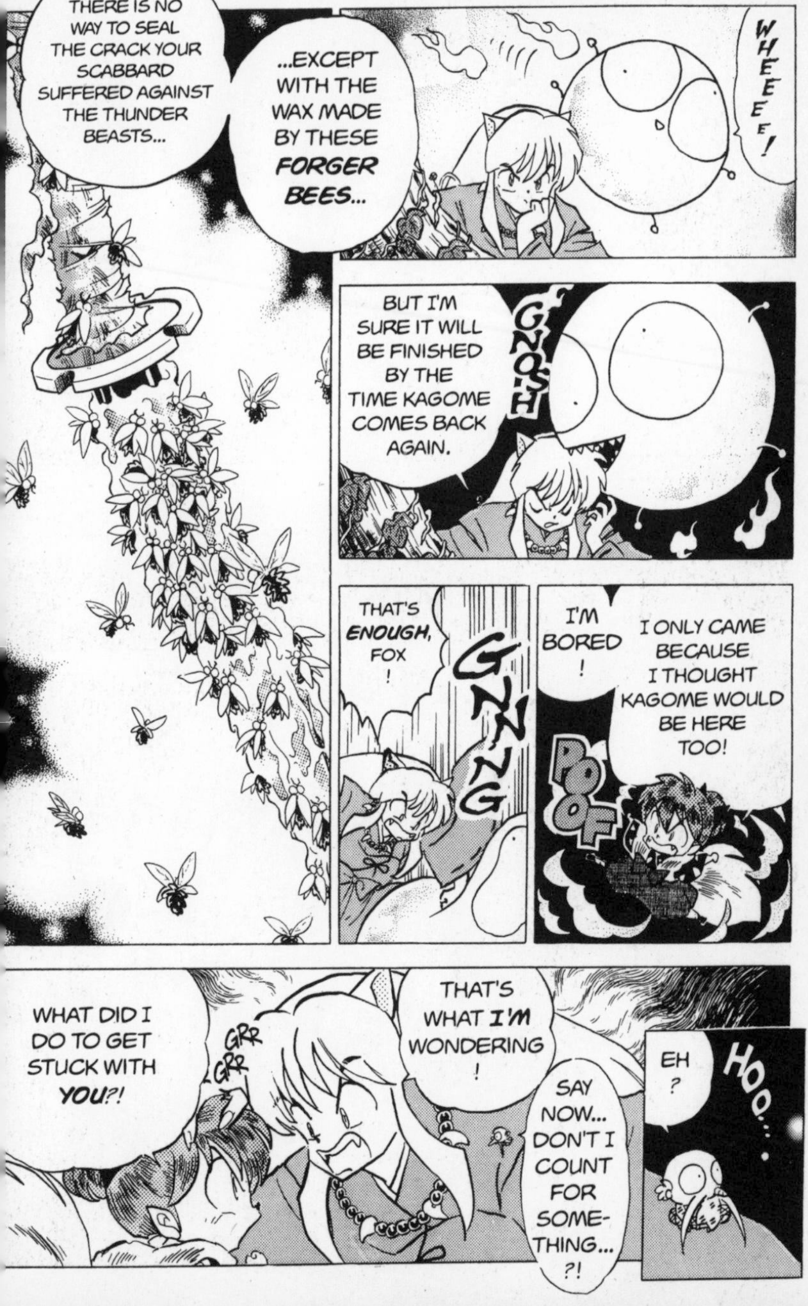
THERE IS NO WAY TO SEAL THE CRACK YOUR SCABBARD SUFFERED AGAINST THE THUNDER BEASTS...
...EXCEPT WITH THE WAX MADE BY THESE FORGER BEES...
WHEEEEE!
BUT I'M SURE IT WILL BE FINISHED BY THE TIME KAGOME COMES BACK AGAIN.
GNOSH
THAT'S ENOUGH, FOX!
GNNNG
I'M BORED!
I ONLY CAME BECAUSE I THOUGHT KAGOME WOULD BE HERE TOO!
POOF
WHAT DID I DO TO GET STUCK WITH YOU?!
GRR GRR
THAT'S WHAT I'M WONDERING!
SAY NOW... DON'T I COUNT FOR SOME-THING...?!
EH?
HOO...

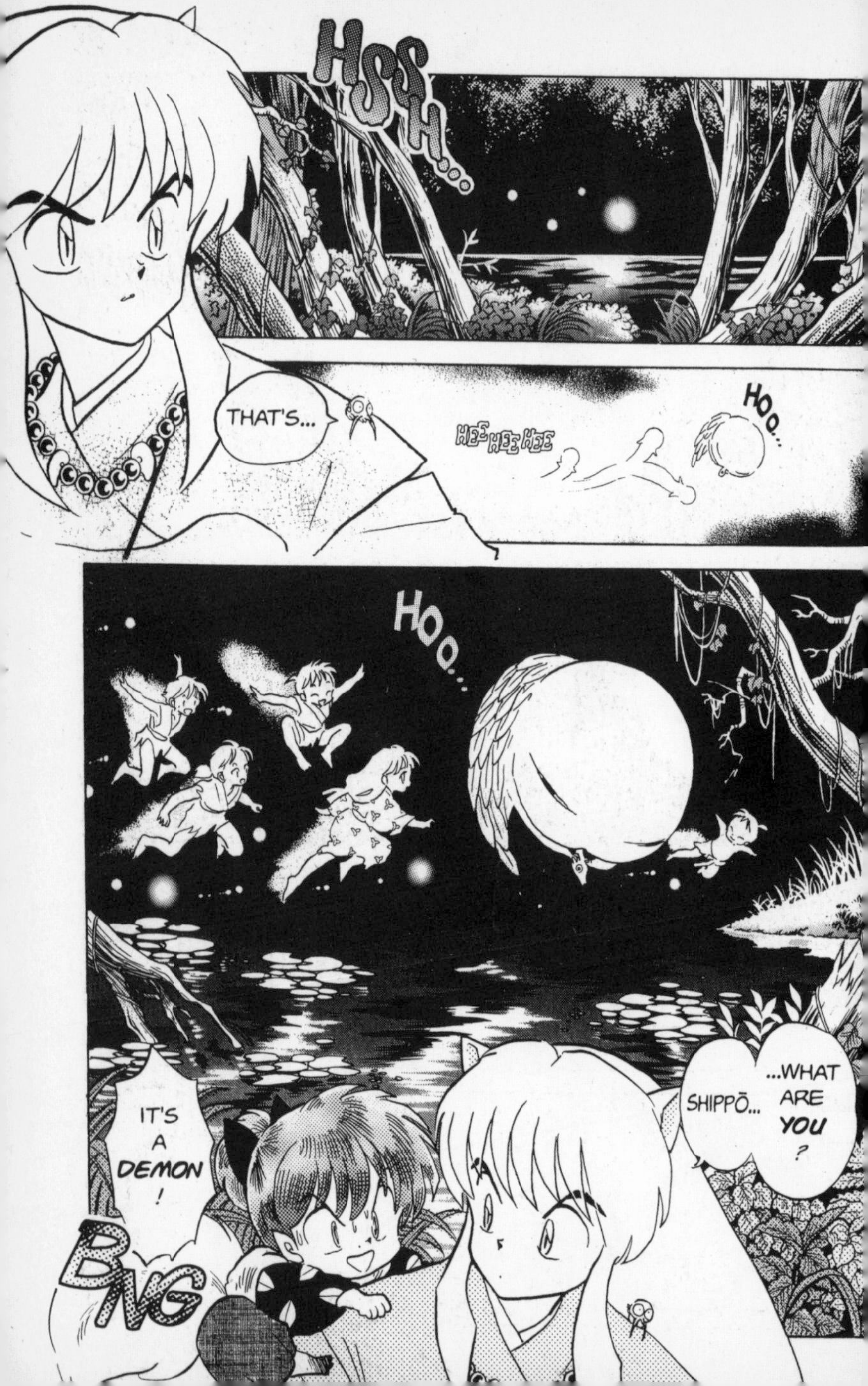
HSSH!...
THAT'S...
HEE HEE HEE
HOO...
HOO...
IT'S A DEMON!
BNG
SHIPPŌ...
...WHAT ARE YOU?

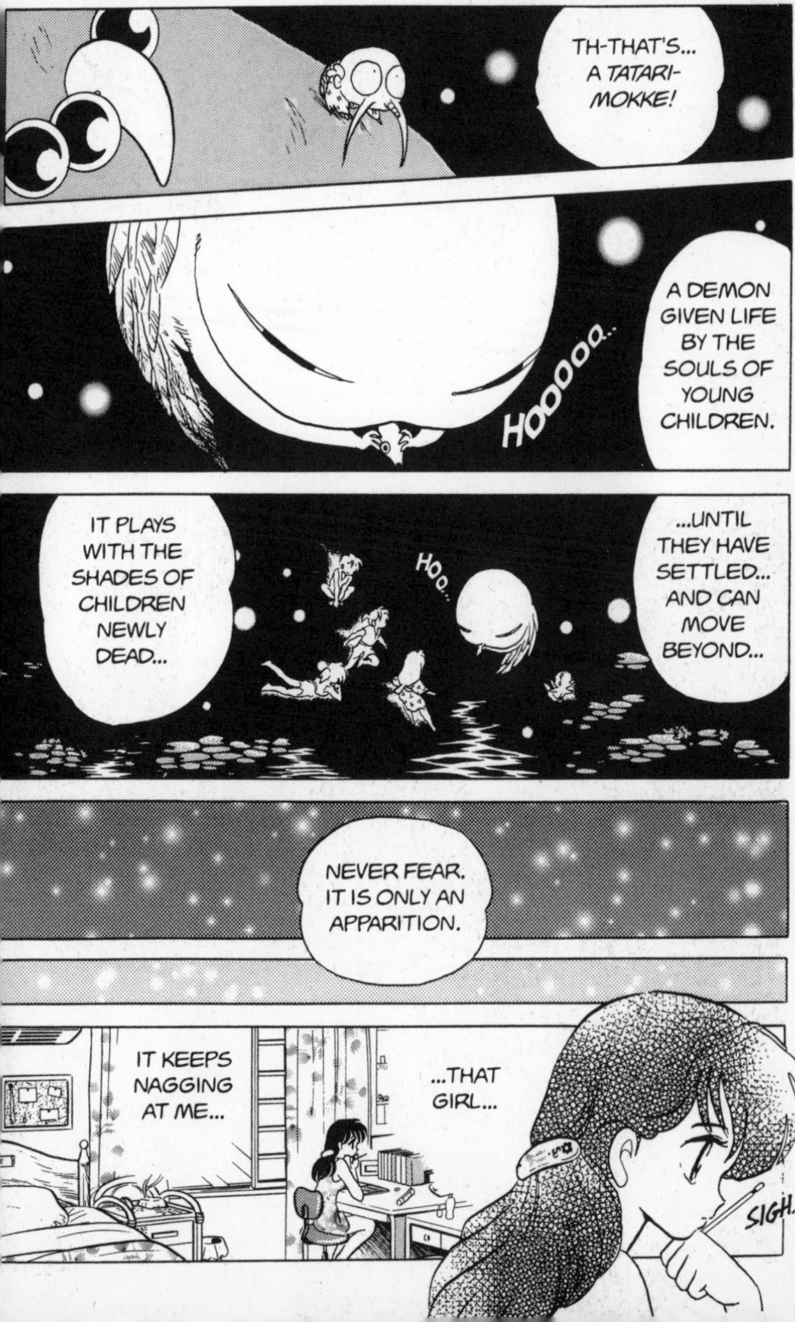
TH-THAT'S... A TATARI-MOKKE!
HOOOOO...
A DEMON GIVEN LIFE BY THE SOULS OF YOUNG CHILDREN.
IT PLAYS WITH THE SHADES OF CHILDREN NEWLY DEAD...
HOO...
...UNTIL THEY HAVE SETTLED... AND CAN MOVE BEYOND...
NEVER FEAR. IT IS ONLY AN APPARITION.
IT KEEPS NAGGING AT ME...
...THAT GIRL...
SIGH...

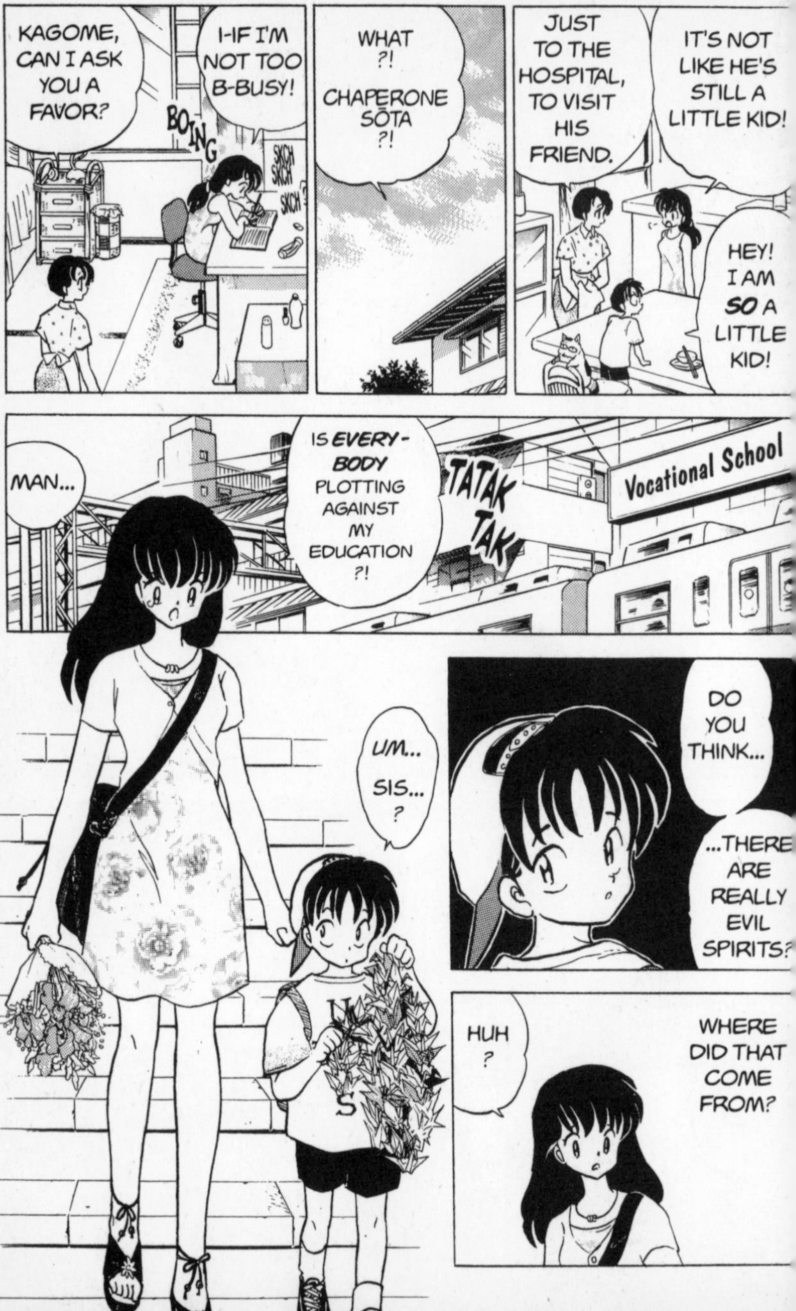
KAGOME, CAN I ASK YOU A FAVOR?
I-IF I'M NOT TOO B-BUSY!
BOING
SKCH SKCH SKCH
WHAT ?! CHAPERONE SŌTA ?!
JUST TO THE HOSPITAL, TO VISIT HIS FRIEND.
IT'S NOT LIKE HE'S STILL A LITTLE KID!
HEY! I AM *SO* A LITTLE KID!
MAN...
IS *EVERYBODY* PLOTTING AGAINST MY EDUCATION ?!
TATAK TAK
Vocational School
UM... SIS... ?
DO YOU THINK...
...THERE ARE REALLY EVIL SPIRITS?
HUH ?
WHERE DID THAT COME FROM?

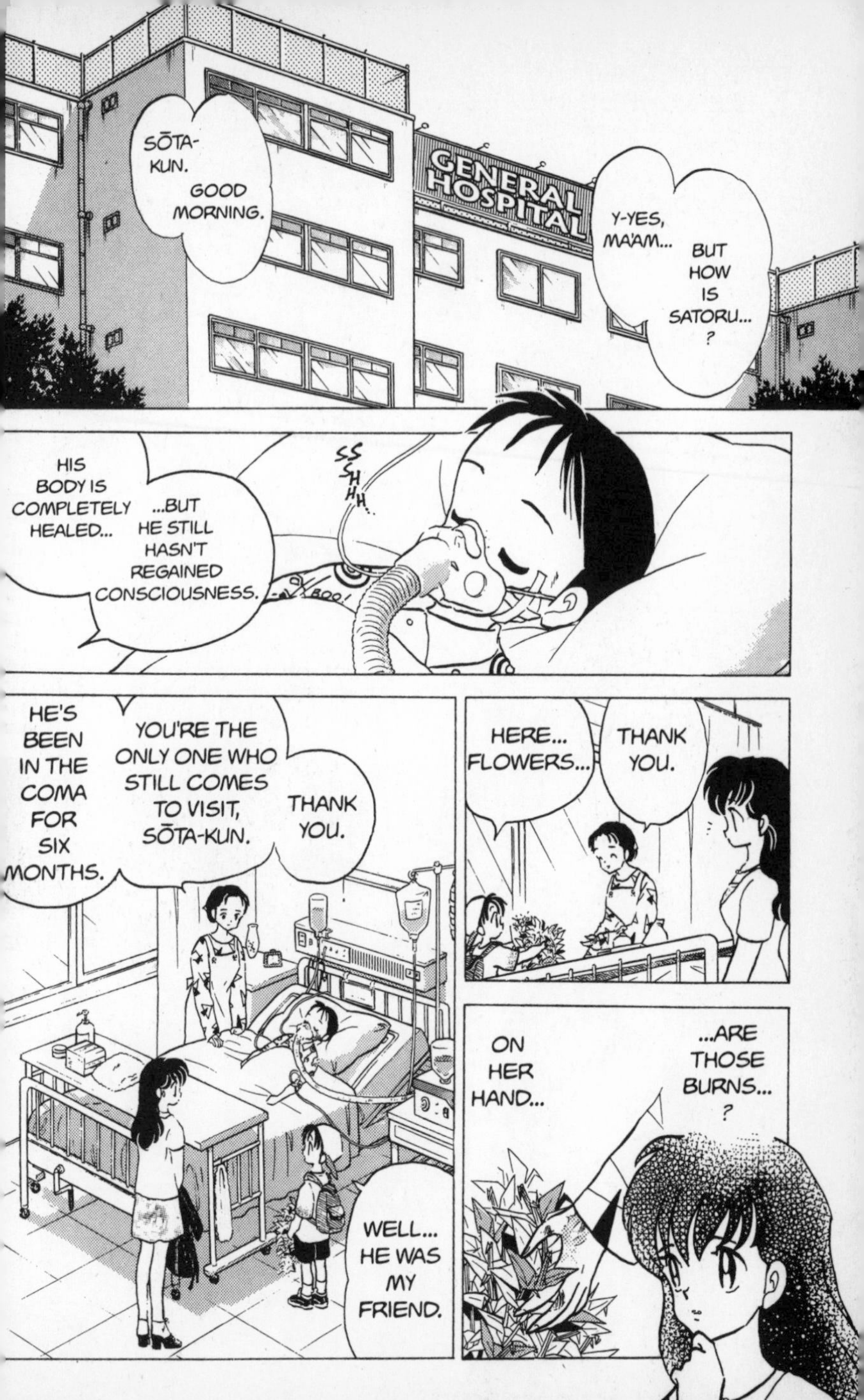
GENERAL HOSPITAL
SŌTA-KUN. GOOD MORNING.
Y-YES, MA'AM... BUT HOW IS SATORU...?
HIS BODY IS COMPLETELY HEALED...
...BUT HE STILL HASN'T REGAINED CONSCIOUSNESS.
SSSHHH..
BOO!
HE'S BEEN IN THE COMA FOR SIX MONTHS.
YOU'RE THE ONLY ONE WHO STILL COMES TO VISIT, SŌTA-KUN.
THANK YOU.
WELL... HE WAS MY FRIEND.
HERE... FLOWERS...
THANK YOU.
ON HER HAND...
...ARE THOSE BURNS...?

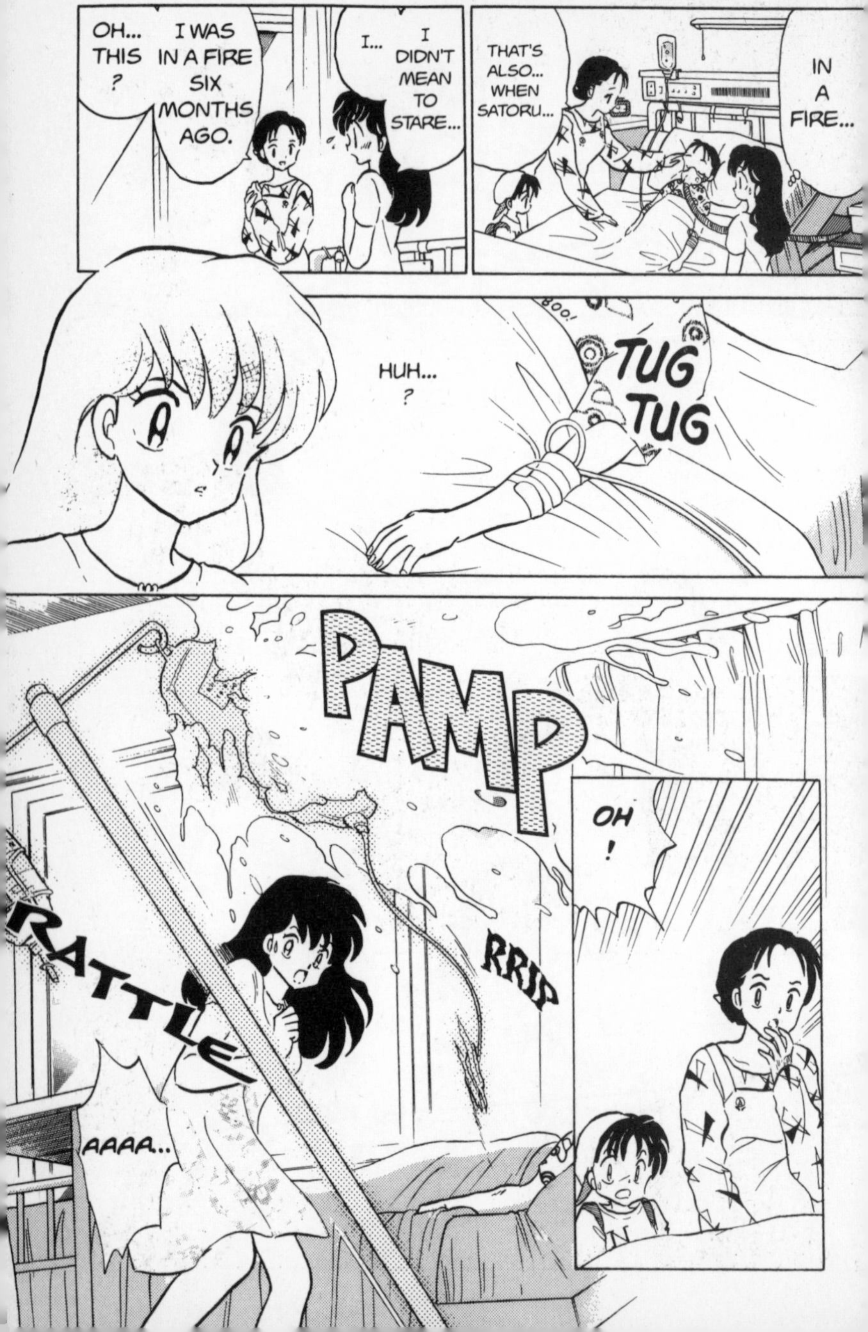

OH... THIS ?
I WAS IN A FIRE SIX MONTHS AGO.
I... I DIDN'T MEAN TO STARE...
THAT'S ALSO... WHEN SATORU...
IN A FIRE...
HUH... ?
TUG TUG
PAMP
RATTLE
RRIP
AAAA...
OH !

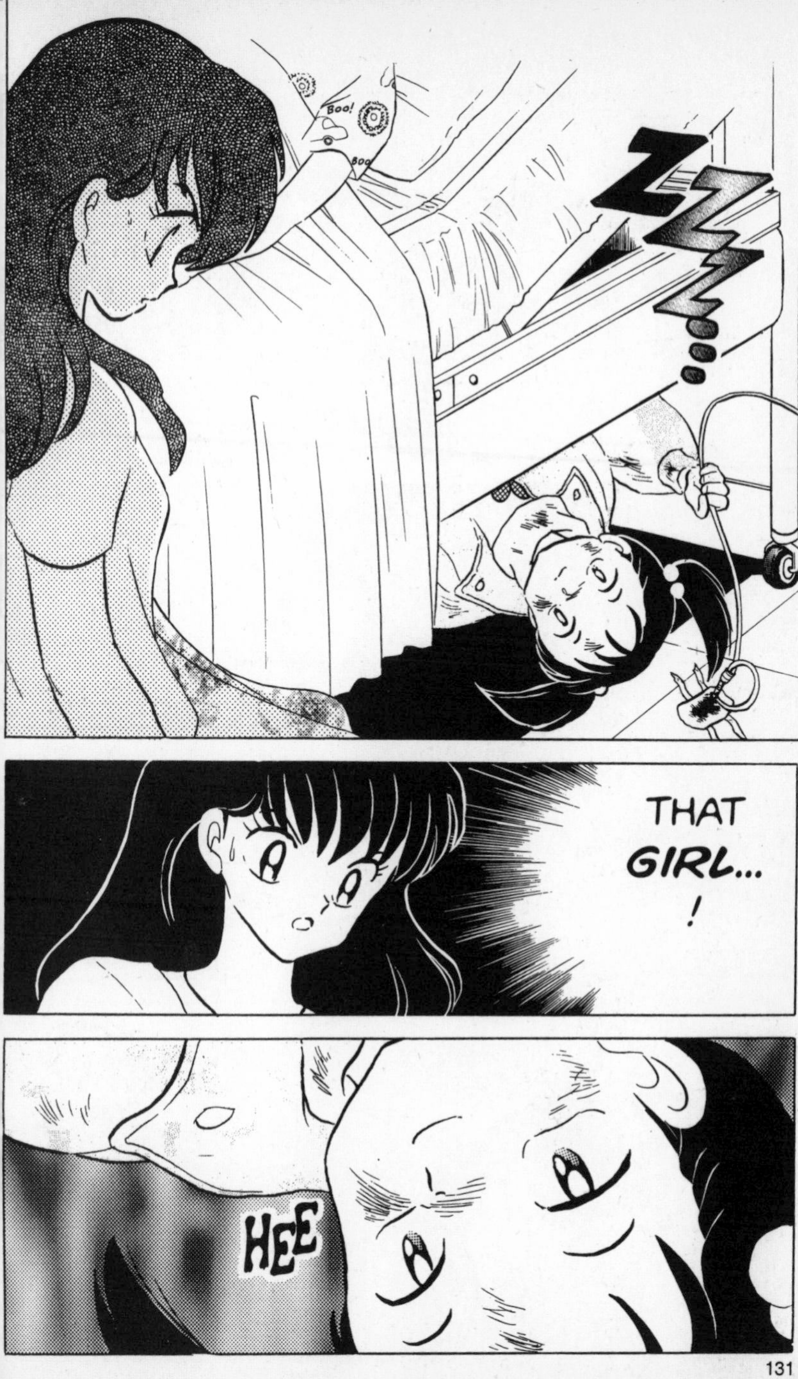
Boo!
ZZZ...
THAT GIRL...
!
HEE

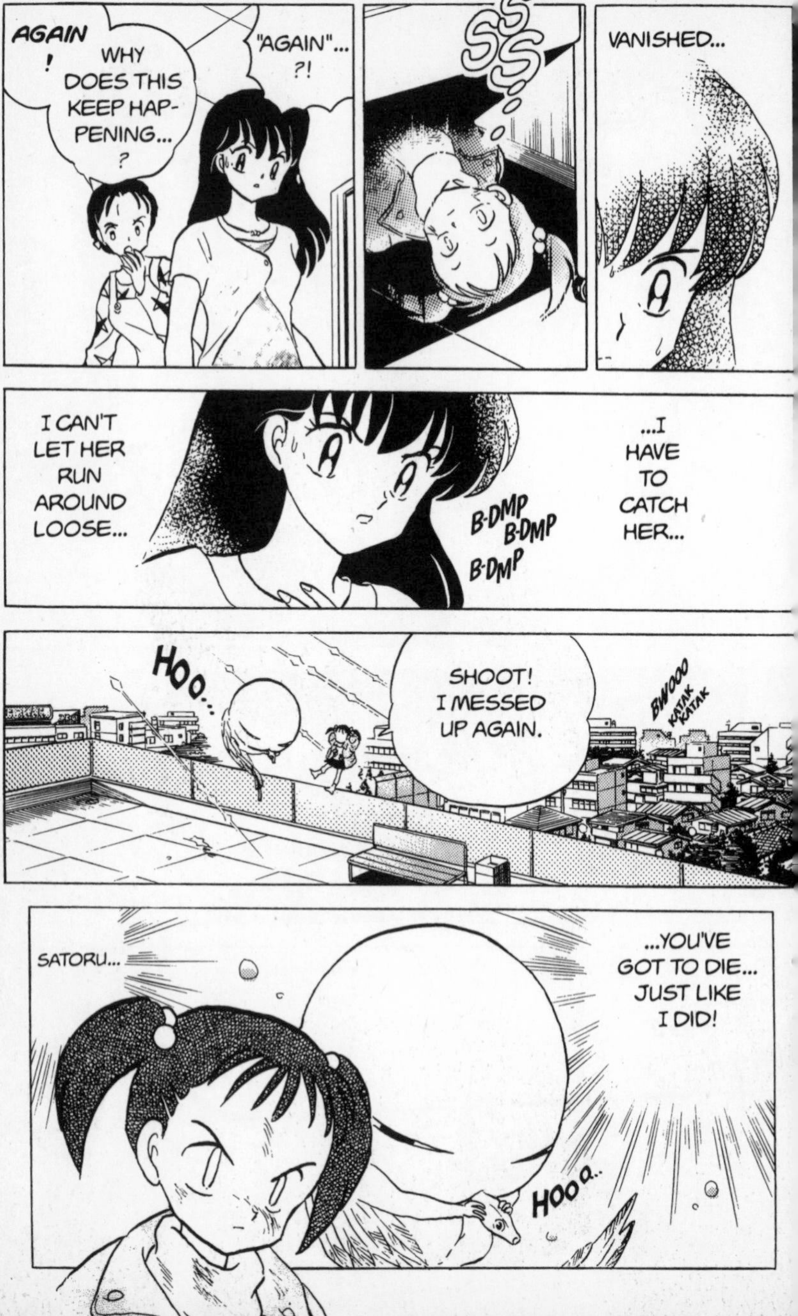
AGAIN!
WHY DOES THIS KEEP HAPPENING...?
"AGAIN"...?!
SSS
VANISHED...
I CAN'T LET HER RUN AROUND LOOSE...
B-DMP B-DMP B-DMP
...I HAVE TO CATCH HER...
HOO...
SHOOT! I MESSED UP AGAIN.
BWOOO
KATAK KATAK
SATORU...
...YOU'VE GOT TO DIE... JUST LIKE I DID!
HOOO..

SCROLL EIGHT

UNTIL MY EYES OPEN

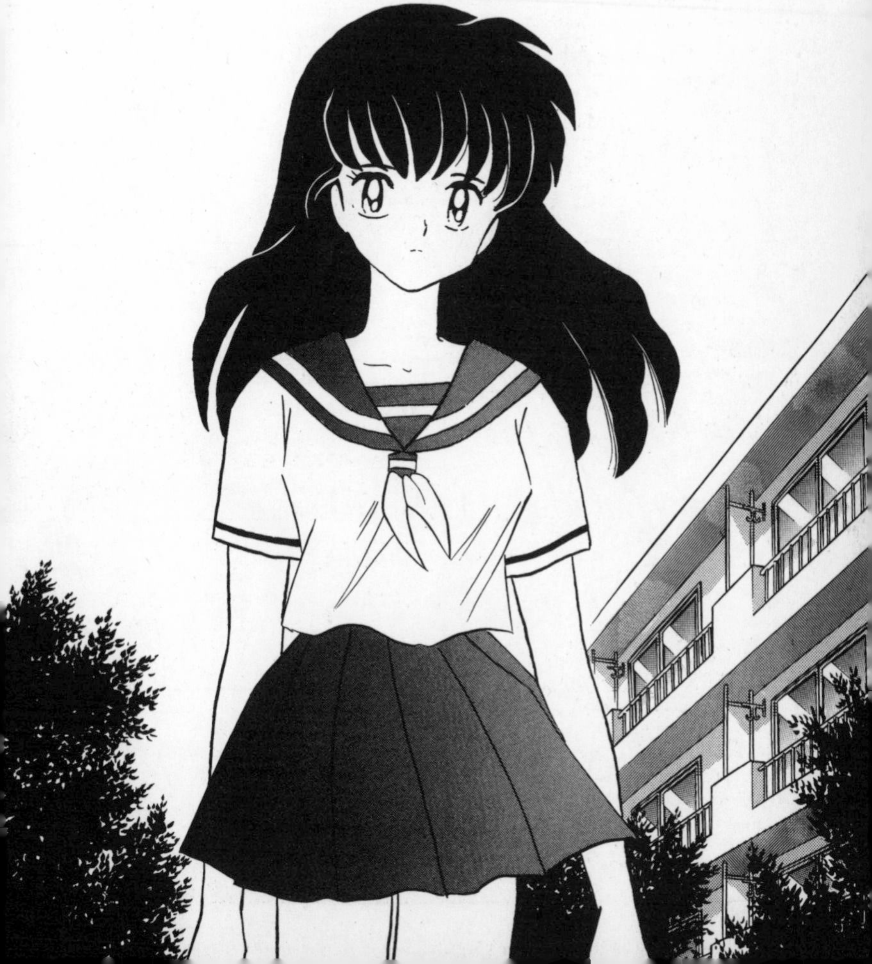

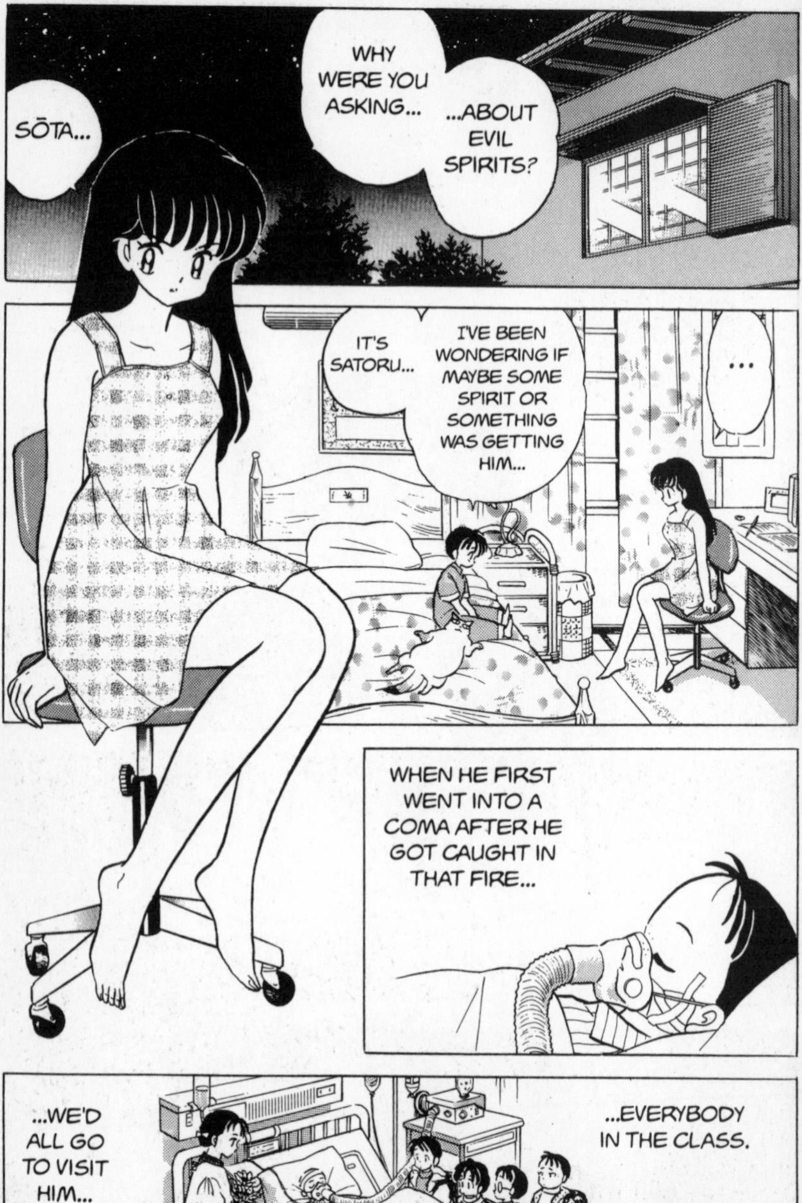
SŌTA...
WHY WERE YOU ASKING...
...ABOUT EVIL SPIRITS?
IT'S SATORU...
I'VE BEEN WONDERING IF MAYBE SOME SPIRIT OR SOMETHING WAS GETTING HIM...
...
WHEN HE FIRST WENT INTO A COMA AFTER HE GOT CAUGHT IN THAT FIRE...
...WE'D ALL GO TO VISIT HIM...
...EVERYBODY IN THE CLASS.
BUT...

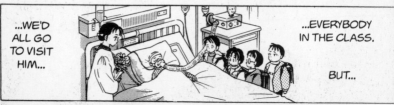

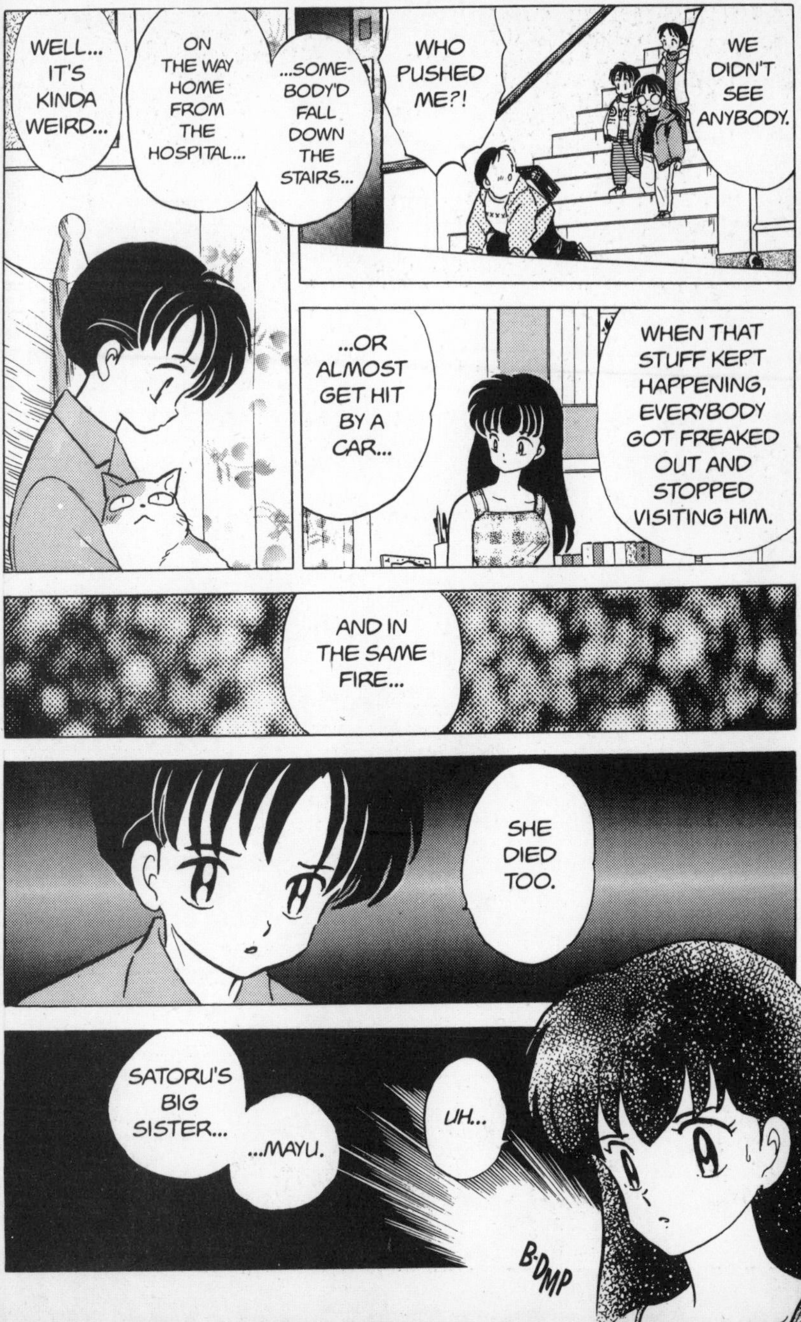
WELL... IT'S KINDA WEIRD...
ON THE WAY HOME FROM THE HOSPITAL...
...SOME-BODY'D FALL DOWN THE STAIRS...
WHO PUSHED ME?!
WE DIDN'T SEE ANYBODY.
...OR ALMOST GET HIT BY A CAR...
WHEN THAT STUFF KEPT HAPPENING, EVERYBODY GOT FREAKED OUT AND STOPPED VISITING HIM.
AND IN THE SAME FIRE...
SHE DIED TOO.
SATORU'S BIG SISTER...
...MAYU.
UH...
B-DMP

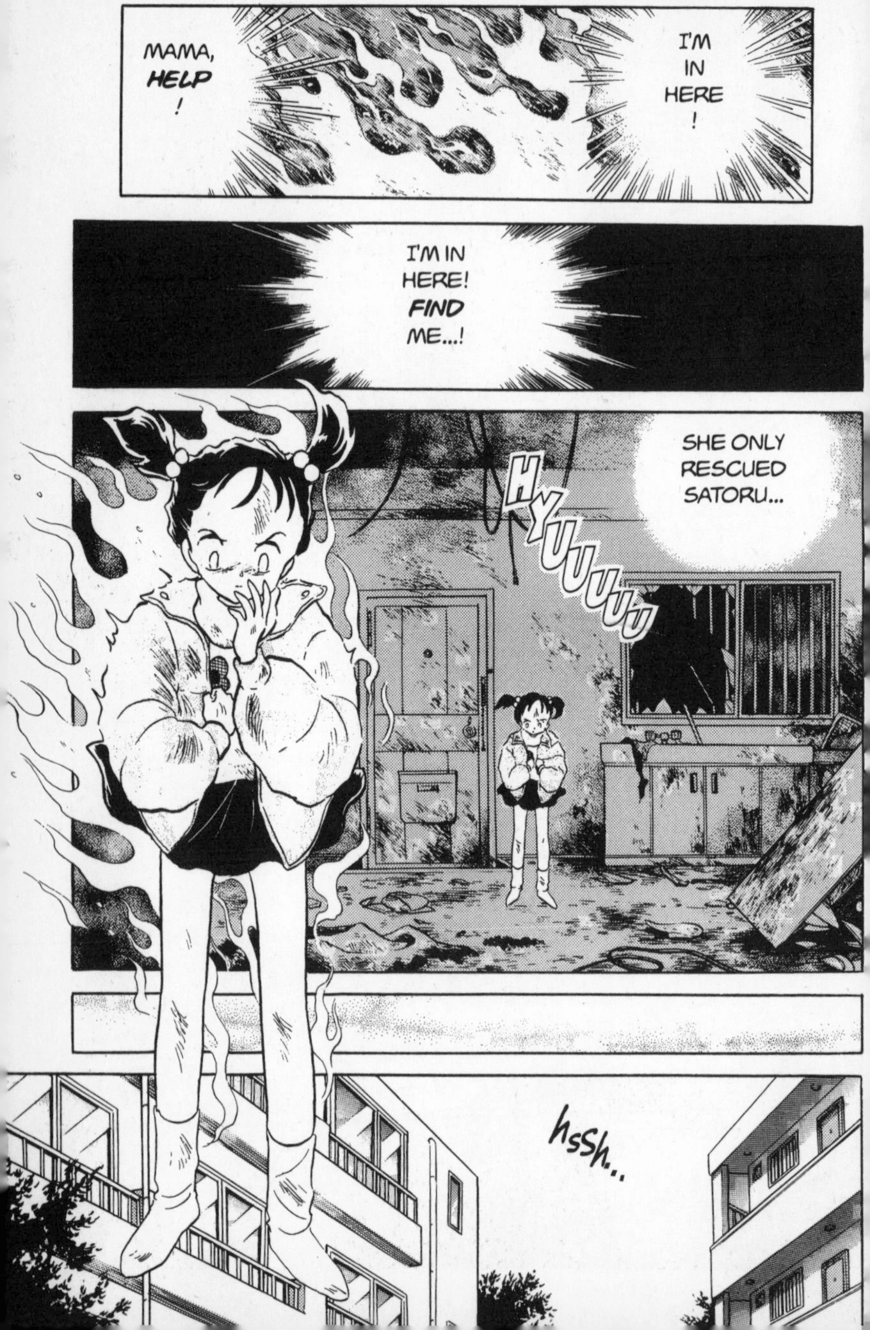
MAMA, HELP!
I'M IN HERE!
I'M IN HERE! FIND ME...!
HYUUUUU
SHE ONLY RESCUED SATORU...
hsSh...

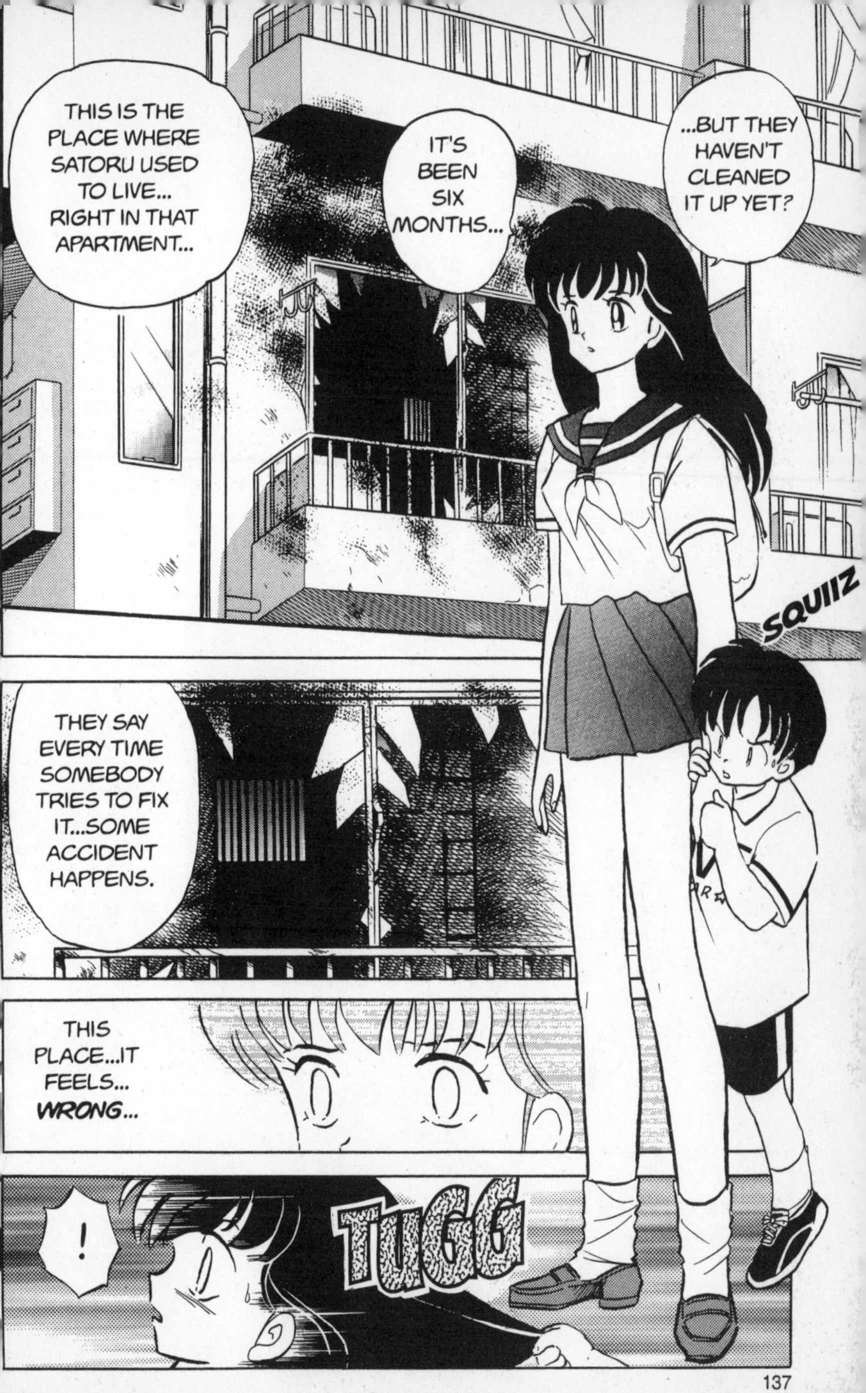
THIS IS THE PLACE WHERE SATORU USED TO LIVE... RIGHT IN THAT APARTMENT...
IT'S BEEN SIX MONTHS...
...BUT THEY HAVEN'T CLEANED IT UP YET?
SQUIIZ
THEY SAY EVERY TIME SOMEBODY TRIES TO FIX IT...SOME ACCIDENT HAPPENS.
THIS PLACE...IT FEELS... WRONG...
!
TUGG

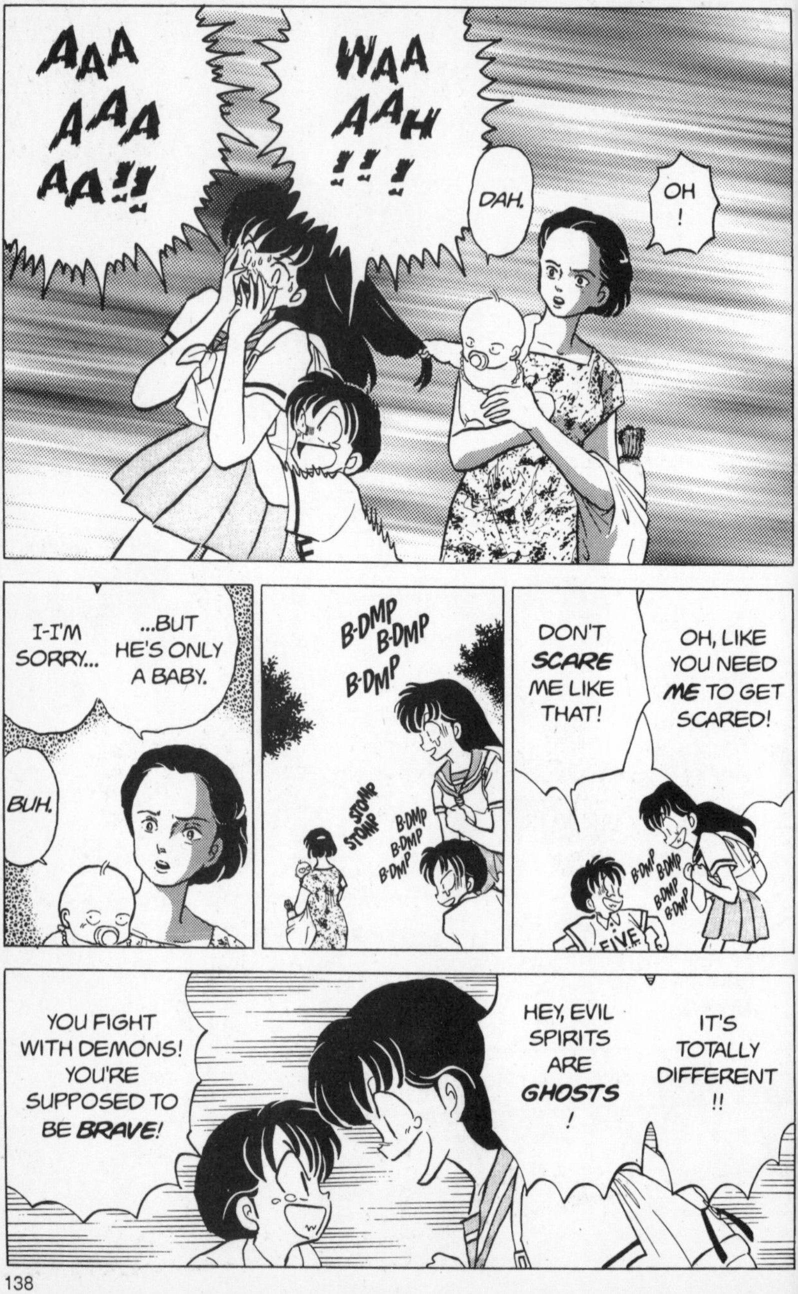
AAA AAAA AA!!
WAA AAH!!!
DAH.
OH!
I-I'M SORRY...
...BUT HE'S ONLY A BABY.
BUH.
B-DMP B-DMP B-DMP
STOMP STOMP
B-DMP B-DMP B-DMP
DON'T SCARE ME LIKE THAT!
OH, LIKE YOU NEED ME TO GET SCARED!
B-DMP B-DMP B-DMP B-DMP
FIVE
YOU FIGHT WITH DEMONS! YOU'RE SUPPOSED TO BE BRAVE!
HEY, EVIL SPIRITS ARE GHOSTS!
IT'S TOTALLY DIFFERENT!!

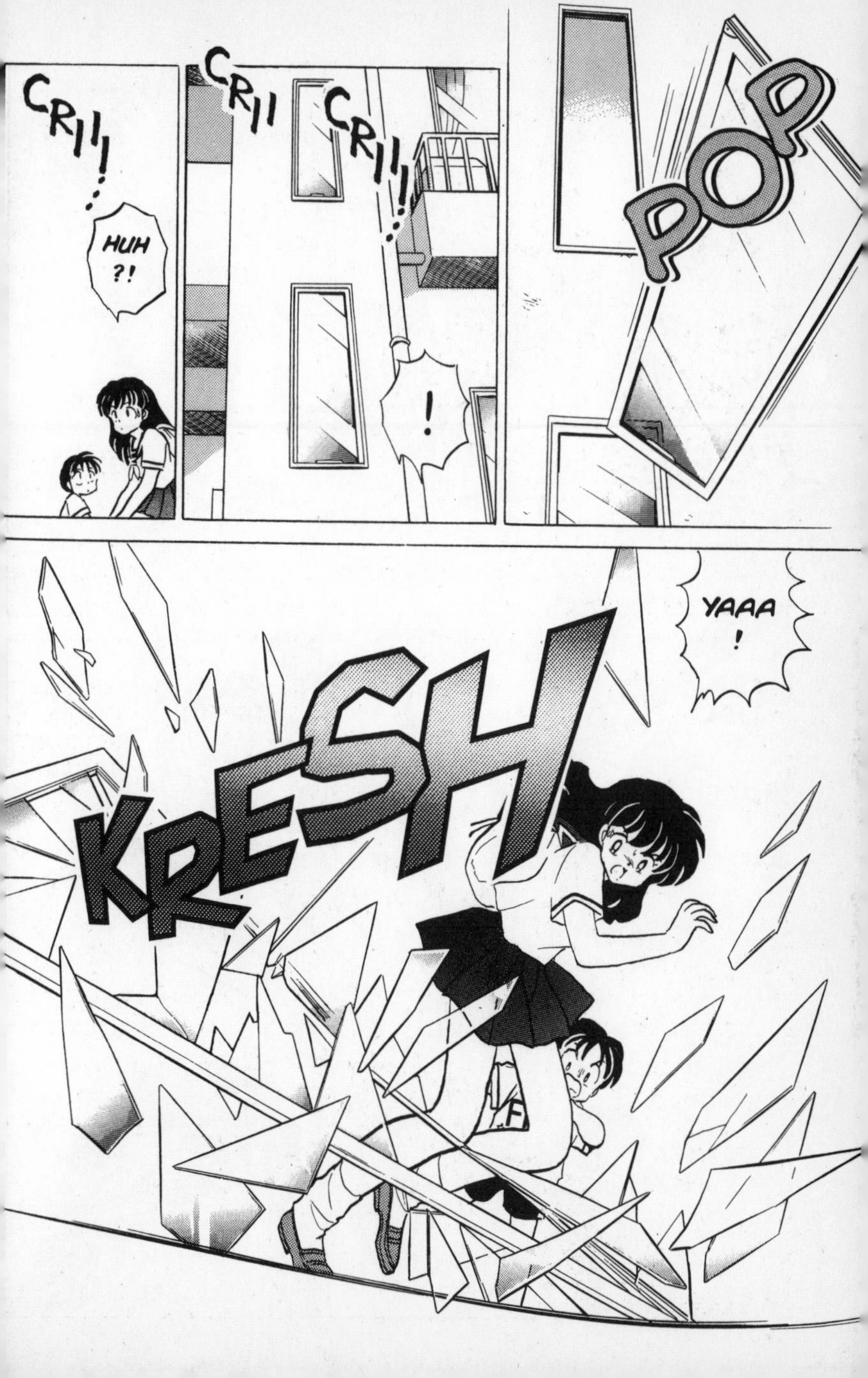
CRI!
HUH ?!
CRI
CRI!
!
POP
KRESH
YAAA !

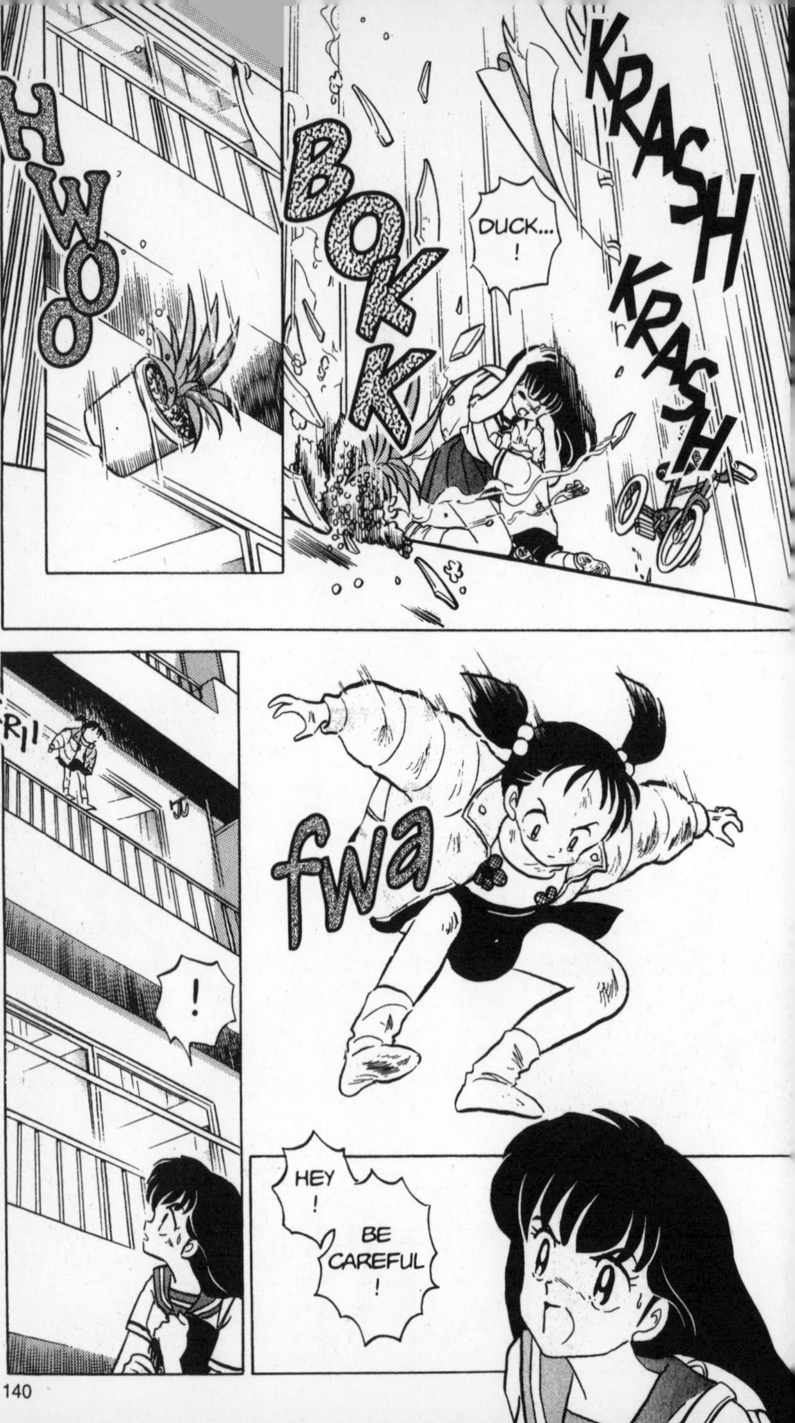

HWOO
BOKK
DUCK... !
KRASH
KRASH
CRI
!
fwa
HEY !
BE CAREFUL !

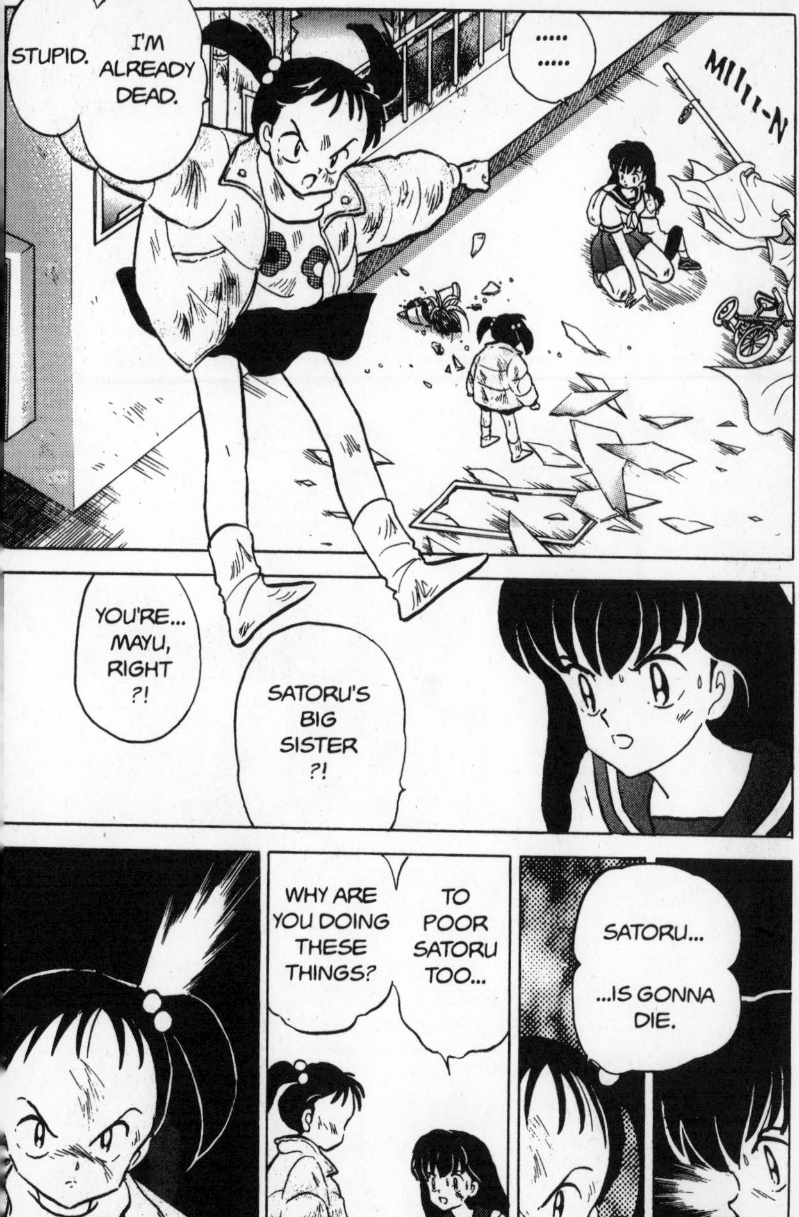
STUPID.
I'M ALREADY DEAD.
.....
.....
MIIII-N
YOU'RE... MAYU, RIGHT ?!
SATORU'S BIG SISTER ?!
WHY ARE YOU DOING THESE THINGS?
TO POOR SATORU TOO...
SATORU...
...IS GONNA DIE.

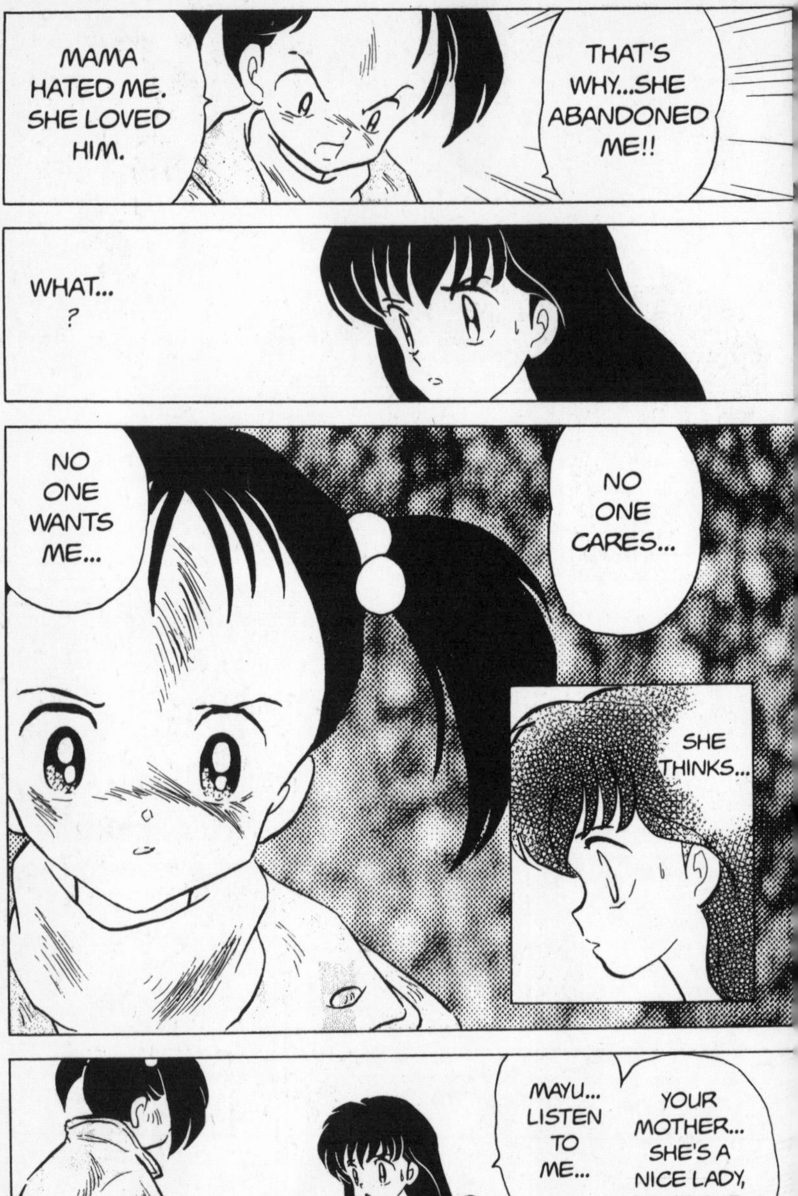
MAMA HATED ME. SHE LOVED HIM.
THAT'S WHY...SHE ABANDONED ME!!
WHAT... ?
NO ONE WANTS ME...
NO ONE CARES...
SHE THINKS...
MAYU... LISTEN TO ME...
YOUR MOTHER... SHE'S A NICE LADY, ISN'T SHE ?

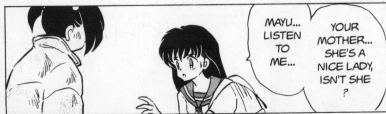

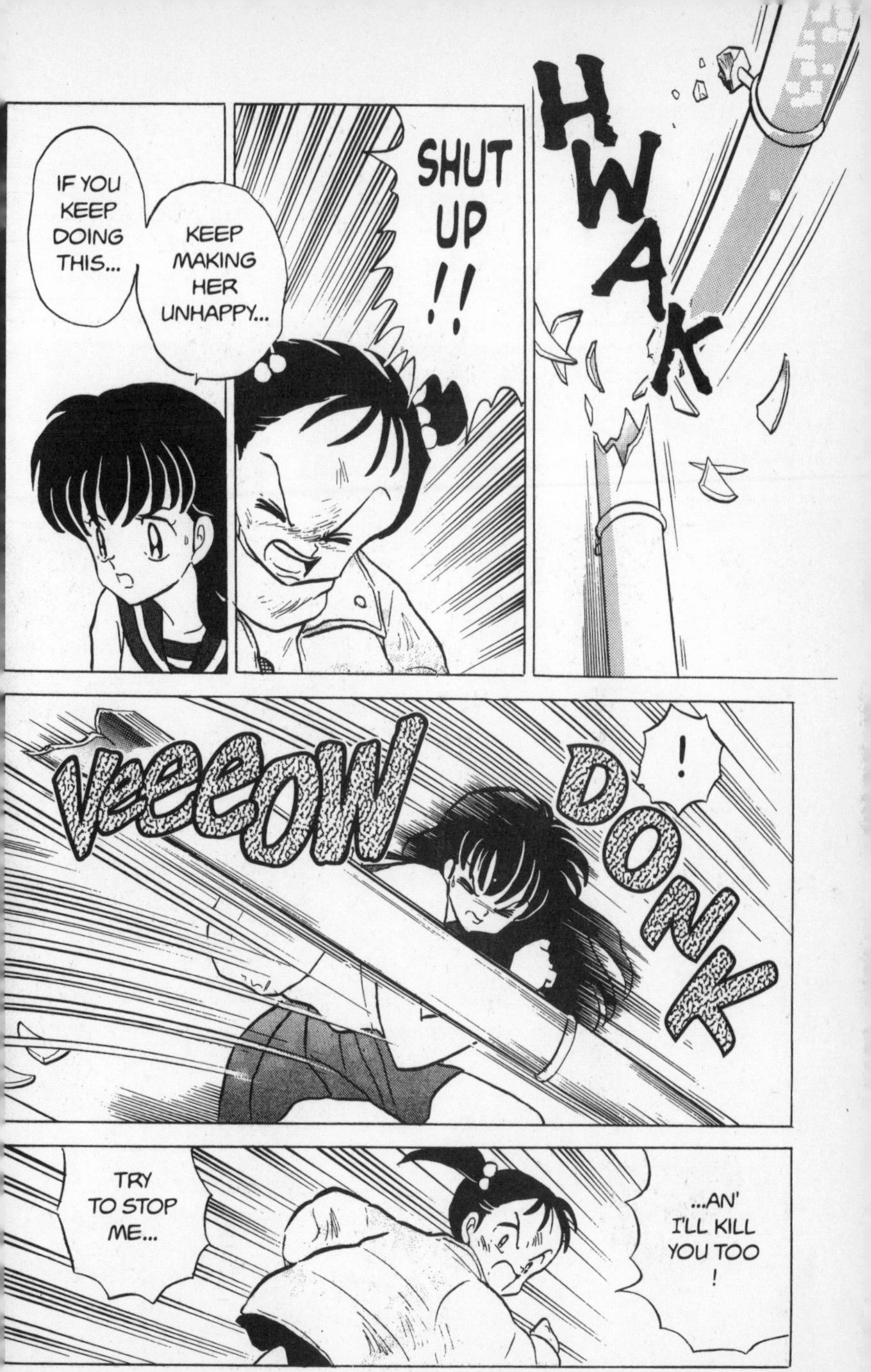
IF YOU KEEP DOING THIS...
KEEP MAKING HER UNHAPPY...
SHUT UP !!
HWAK
VEEEOW
DONK
!
TRY TO STOP ME...
...AN' I'LL KILL YOU TOO !

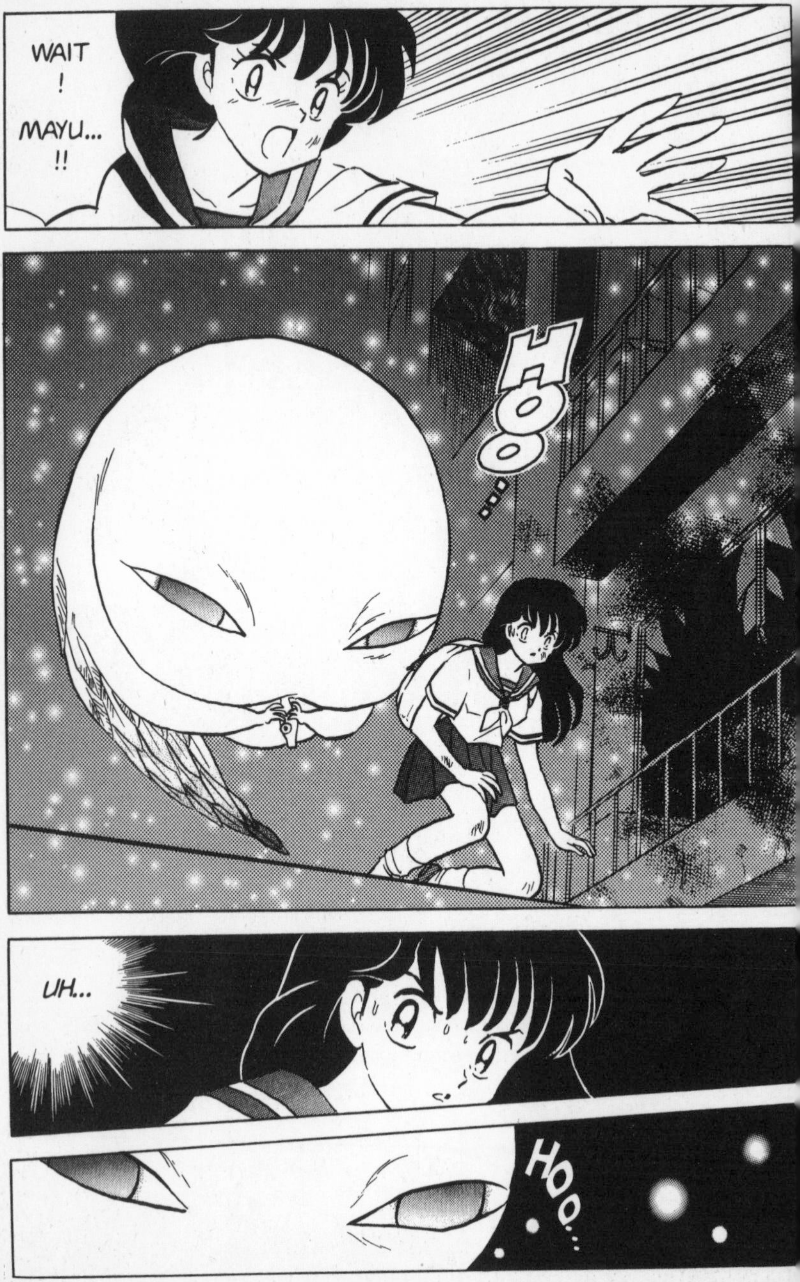
WAIT ! MAYU... !!
HOO...
UH...
HOO...

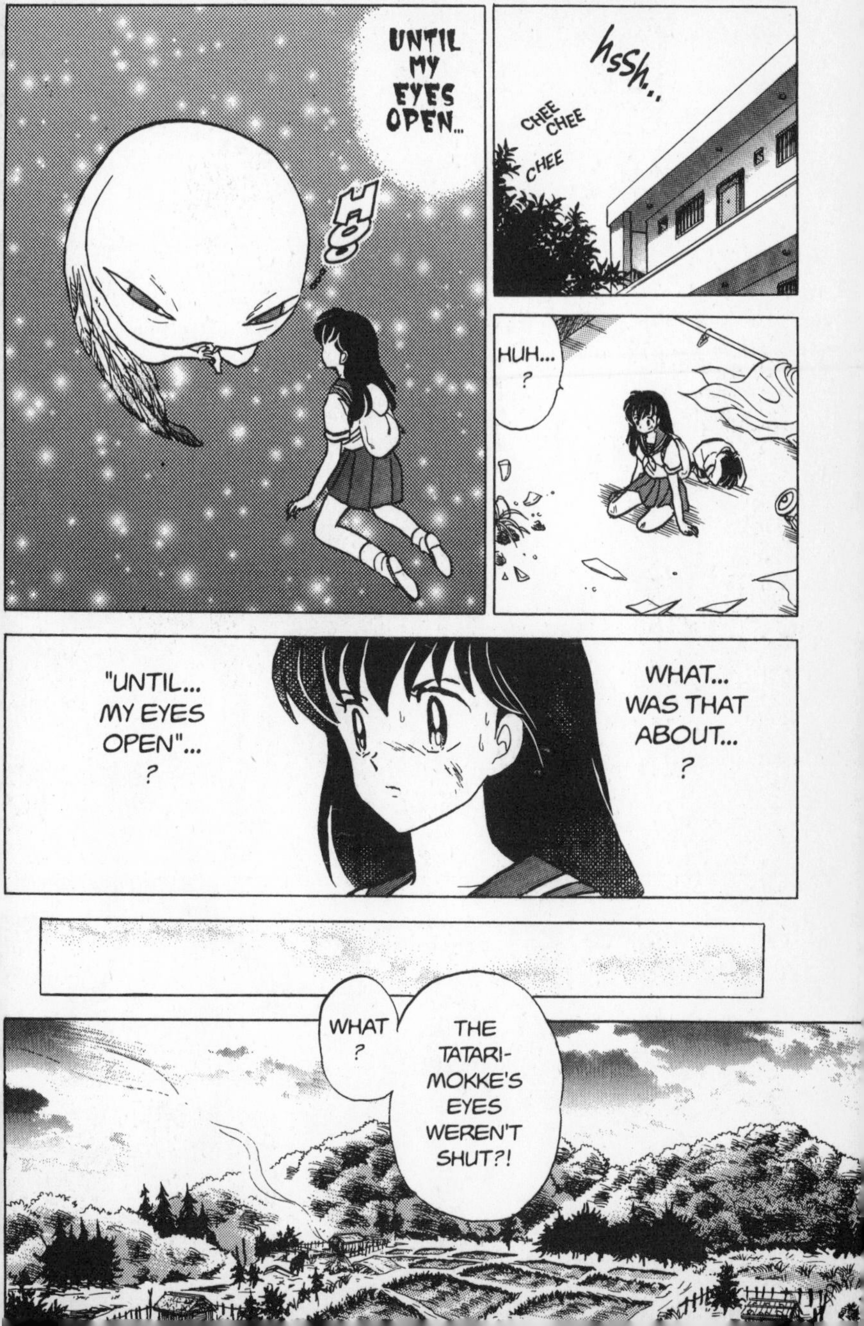
UNTIL MY EYES OPEN...
HOO
hsSh...
CHEE CHEE
CHEE
HUH... ?
"UNTIL... MY EYES OPEN"... ?
WHAT... WAS THAT ABOUT... ?
WHAT ?
THE TATARI-MOKKE'S EYES WEREN'T SHUT?!

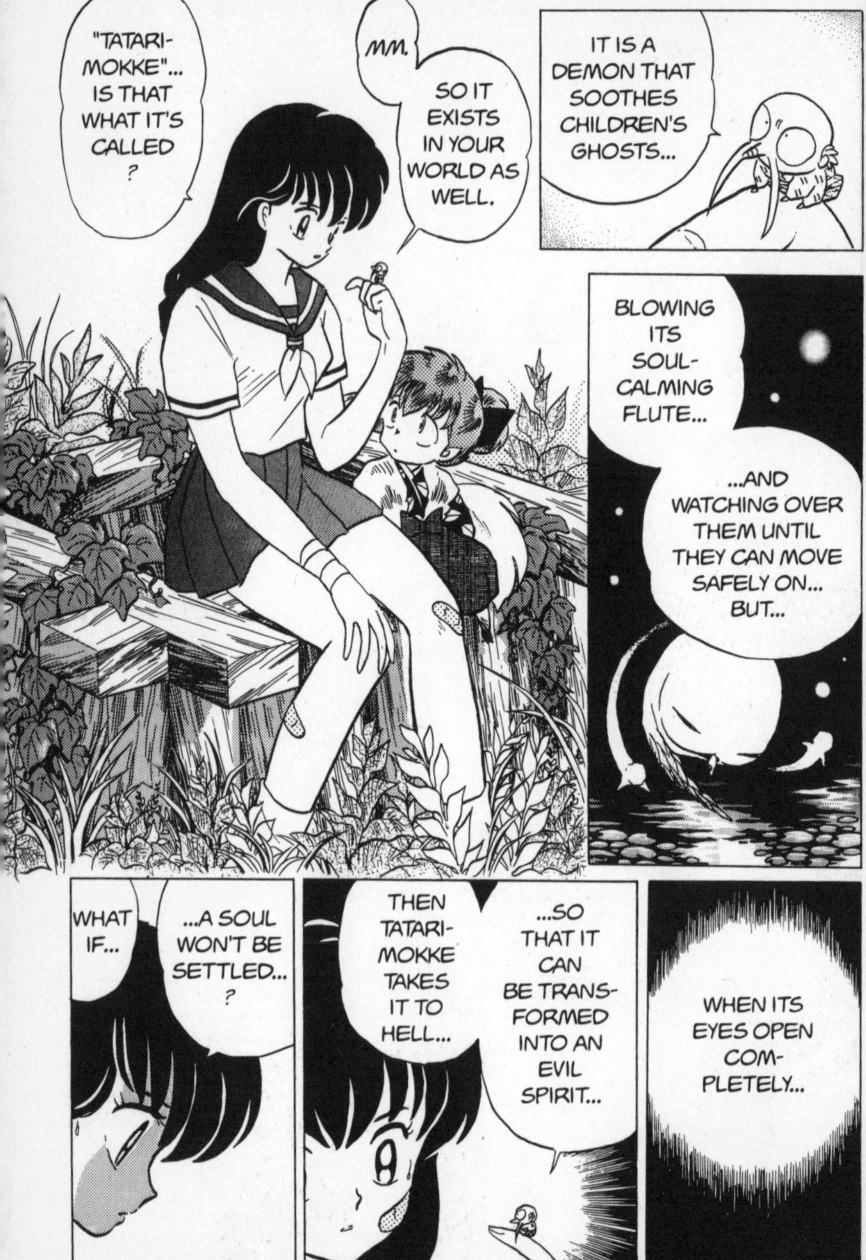
"TATARI-MOKKE"... IS THAT WHAT IT'S CALLED?
MM.
SO IT EXISTS IN YOUR WORLD AS WELL.
IT IS A DEMON THAT SOOTHES CHILDREN'S GHOSTS...
BLOWING ITS SOUL-CALMING FLUTE...
...AND WATCHING OVER THEM UNTIL THEY CAN MOVE SAFELY ON... BUT...
WHAT IF...
...A SOUL WON'T BE SETTLED...?
THEN TATARI-MOKKE TAKES IT TO HELL...
...SO THAT IT CAN BE TRANS-FORMED INTO AN EVIL SPIRIT...
WHEN ITS EYES OPEN COM-PLETELY...

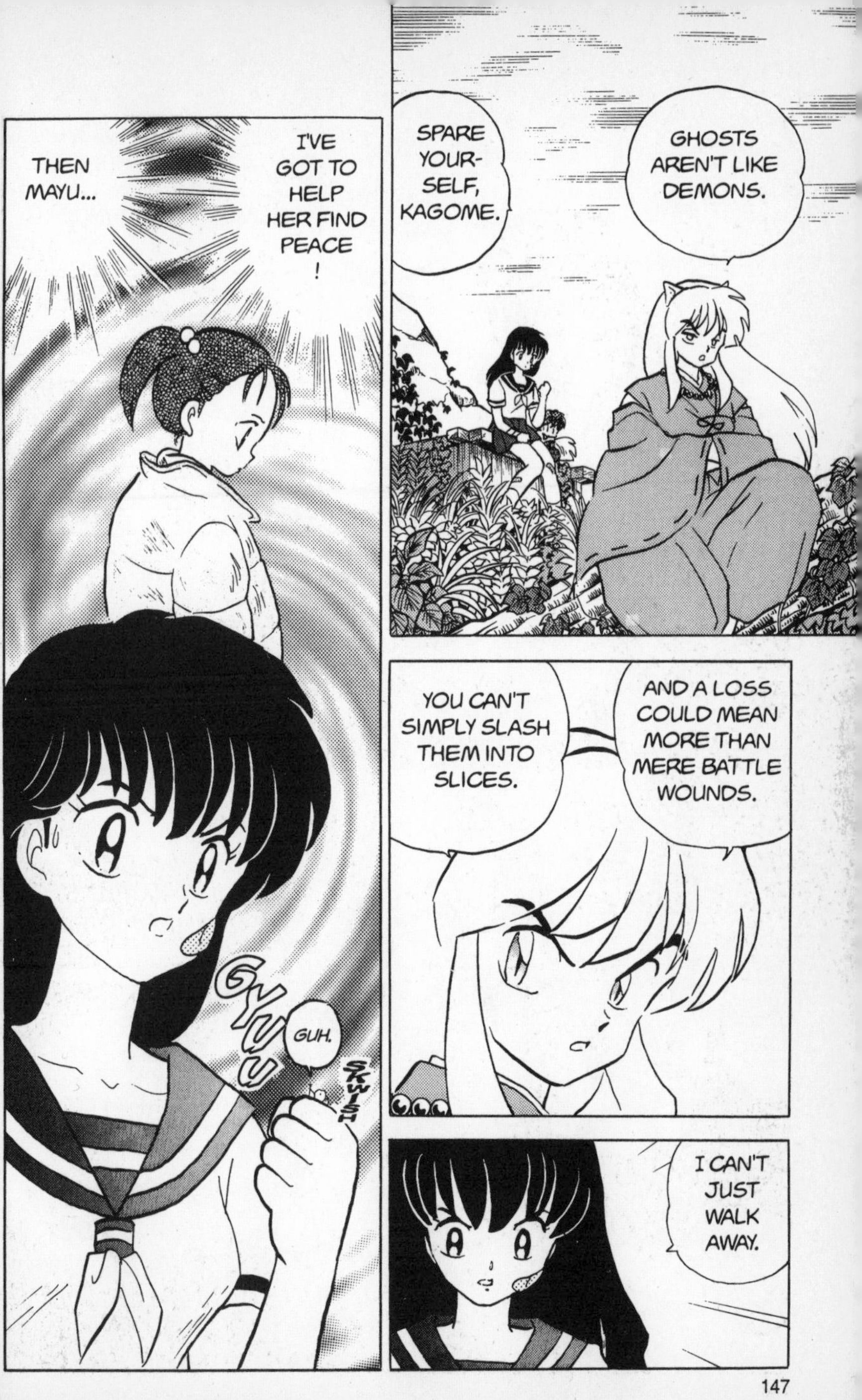
THEN MAYU...
I'VE GOT TO HELP HER FIND PEACE!
GYUU
GUH.
SKWISH
SPARE YOUR-SELF, KAGOME.
GHOSTS AREN'T LIKE DEMONS.
YOU CAN'T SIMPLY SLASH THEM INTO SLICES.
AND A LOSS COULD MEAN MORE THAN MERE BATTLE WOUNDS.
I CAN'T JUST WALK AWAY.

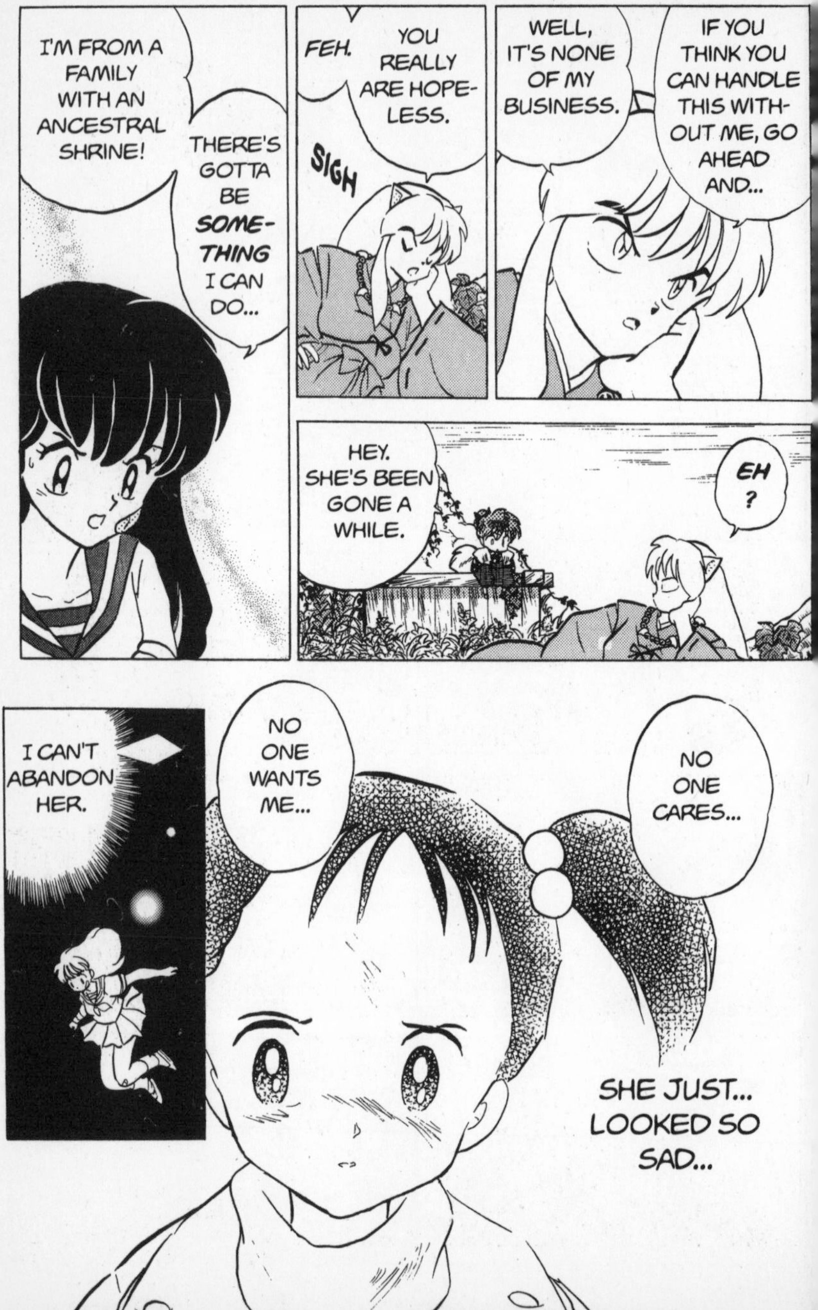
I'M FROM A FAMILY WITH AN ANCESTRAL SHRINE!
THERE'S GOTTA BE *SOME-THING* I CAN DO...
FEH.
YOU REALLY ARE HOPE-LESS.
SIGH
WELL, IT'S NONE OF MY BUSINESS.
IF YOU THINK YOU CAN HANDLE THIS WITH-OUT ME, GO AHEAD AND...
HEY. SHE'S BEEN GONE A WHILE.
EH?
I CAN'T ABANDON HER.
NO ONE WANTS ME...
NO ONE CARES...
SHE JUST... LOOKED SO SAD...

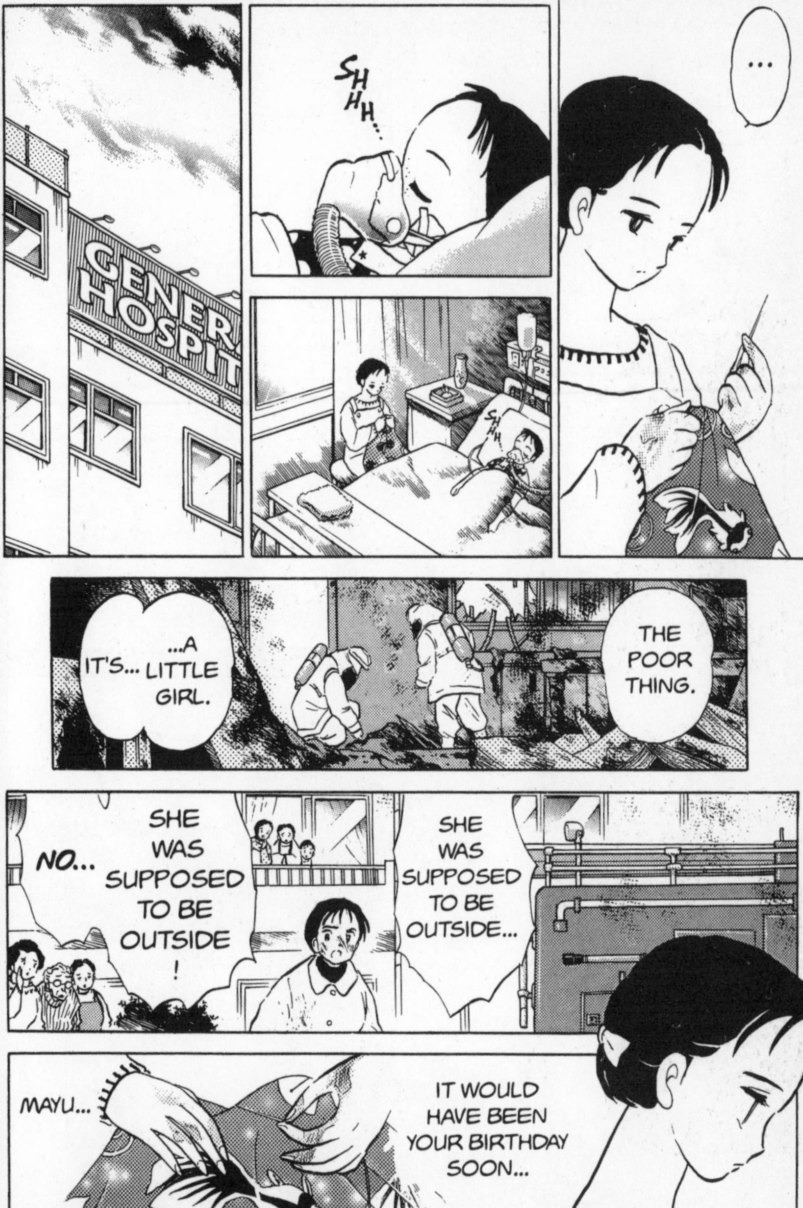
GENER
HOSPIT
SHHH...
SHHH
...
IT'S...
...A LITTLE GIRL.
THE POOR THING.
NO...
SHE WAS SUPPOSED TO BE OUTSIDE!
SHE WAS SUPPOSED TO BE OUTSIDE...
MAYU...
IT WOULD HAVE BEEN YOUR BIRTHDAY SOON...

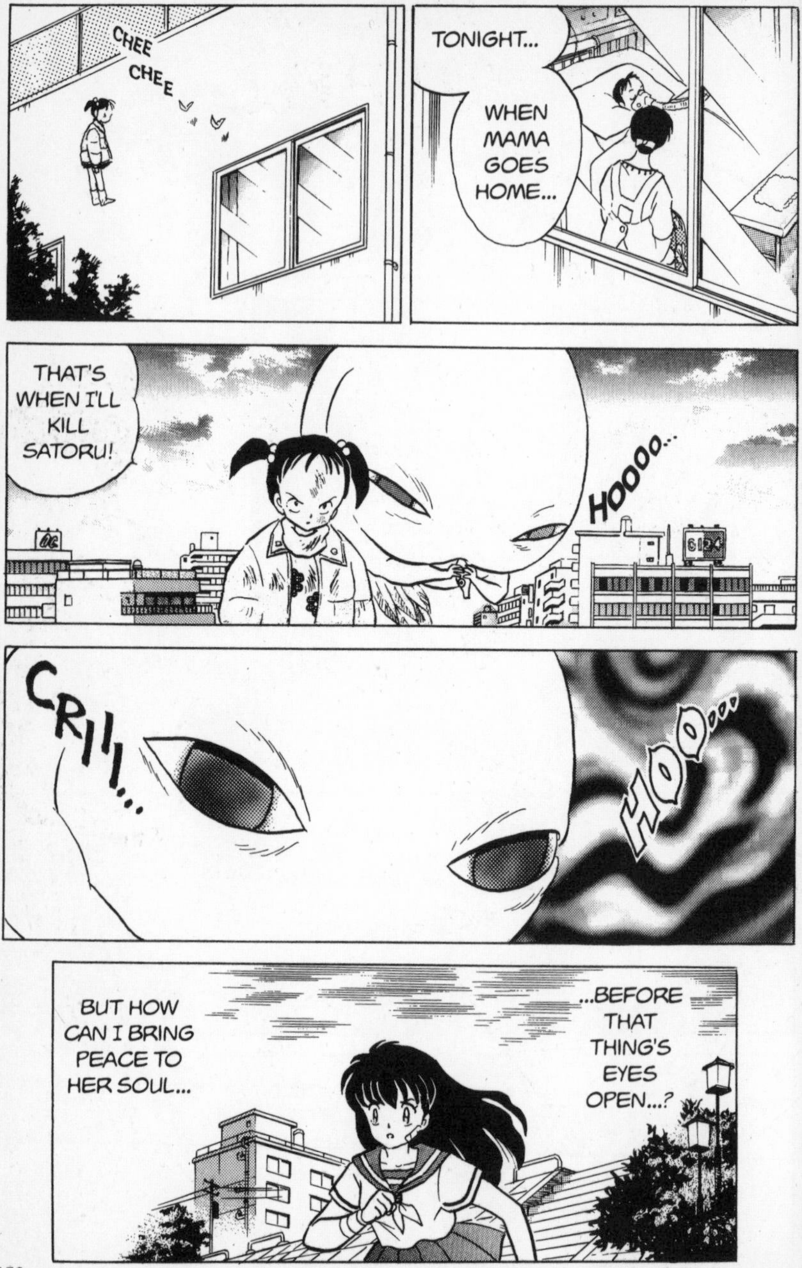
CHEE CHEE
TONIGHT...
WHEN MAMA GOES HOME...
THAT'S WHEN I'LL KILL SATORU!
HOOOO...
CRIIII...
HOO...
BUT HOW CAN I BRING PEACE TO HER SOUL...
...BEFORE THAT THING'S EYES OPEN...?

SCROLL NINE
TO HELL

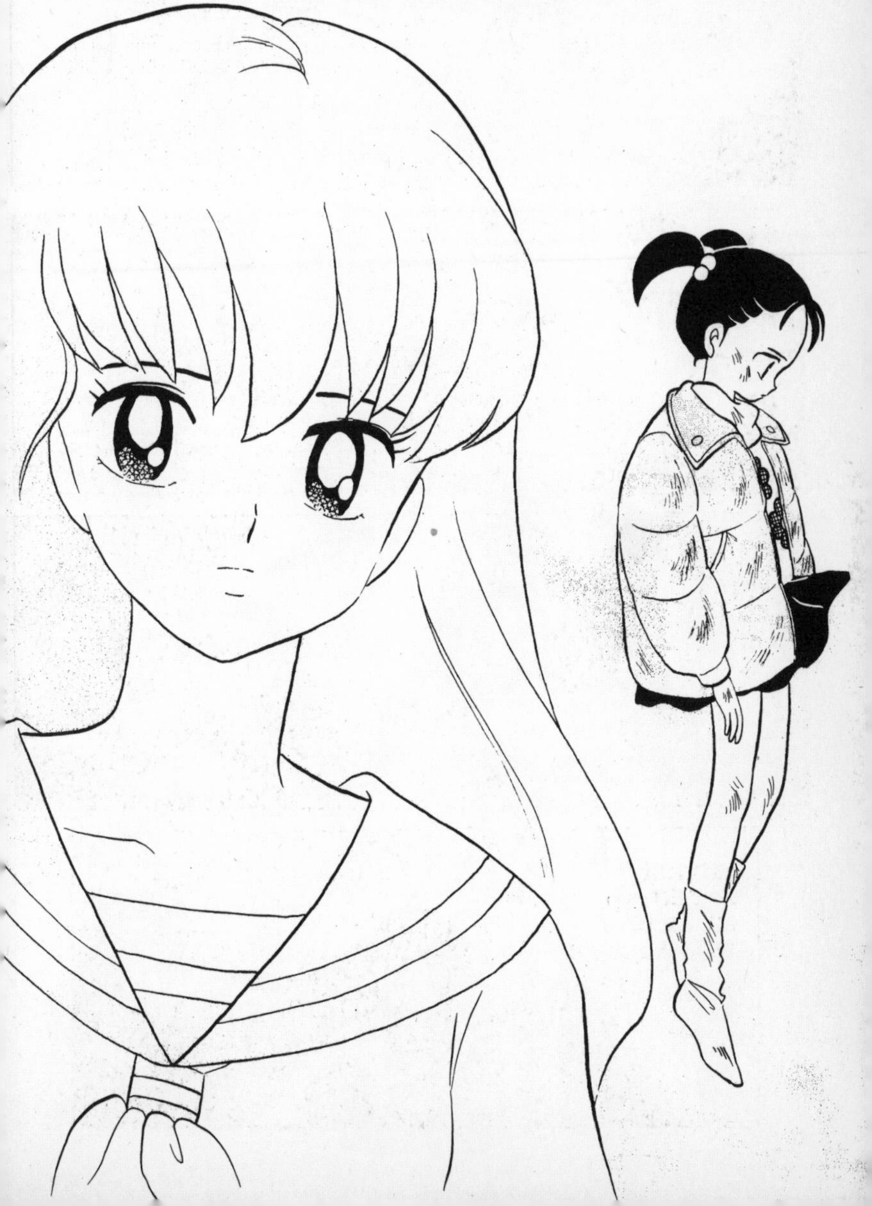

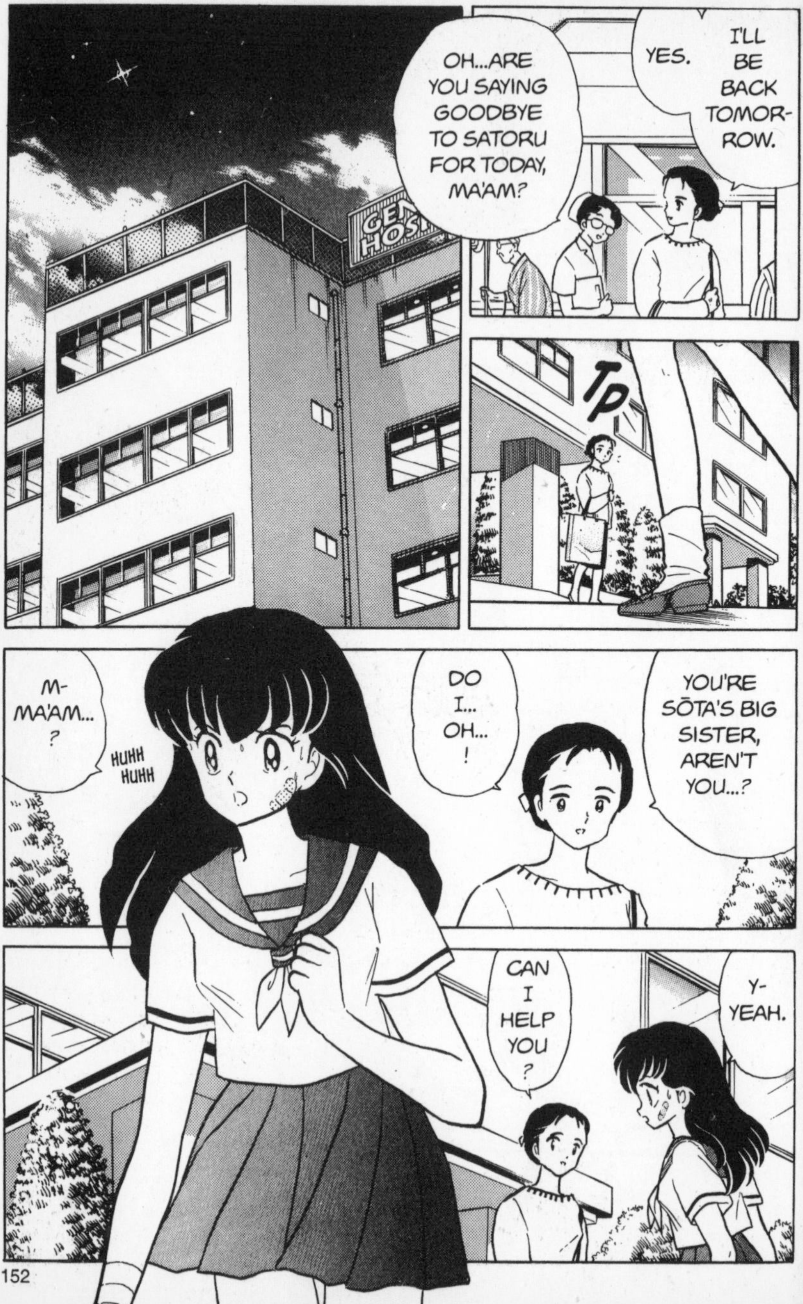
GEN HOS
OH...ARE YOU SAYING GOODBYE TO SATORU FOR TODAY, MA'AM?
YES.
I'LL BE BACK TOMORROW.
TP
M-MA'AM...?
HUHH HUHH
DO I... OH...!
YOU'RE SŌTA'S BIG SISTER, AREN'T YOU...?
CAN I HELP YOU?
Y-YEAH.

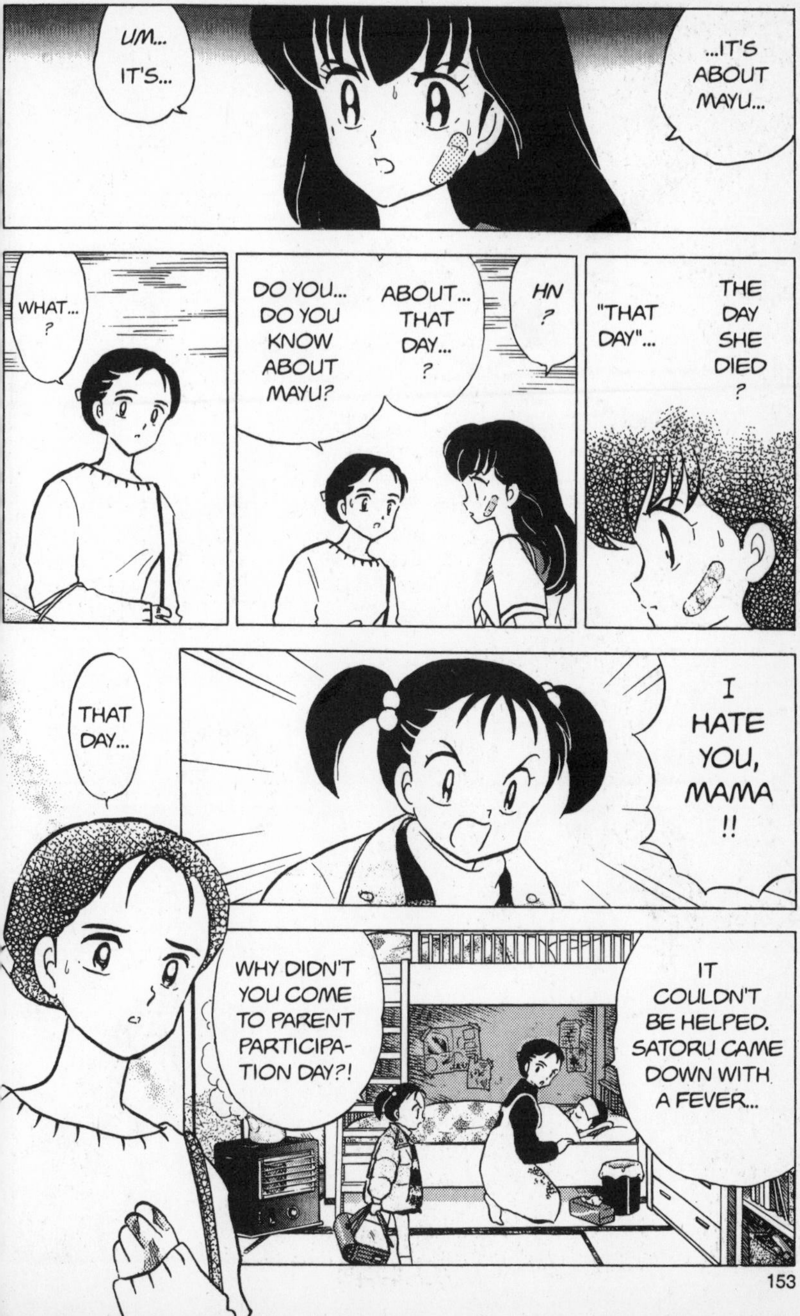
UM... IT'S...
...IT'S ABOUT MAYU...
WHAT...?
DO YOU... DO YOU KNOW ABOUT MAYU?
ABOUT... THAT DAY...?
HN?
"THAT DAY"...
THE DAY SHE DIED?
THAT DAY...
I HATE YOU, MAMA!!
WHY DIDN'T YOU COME TO PARENT PARTICIPATION DAY?!
IT COULDN'T BE HELPED. SATORU CAME DOWN WITH A FEVER...

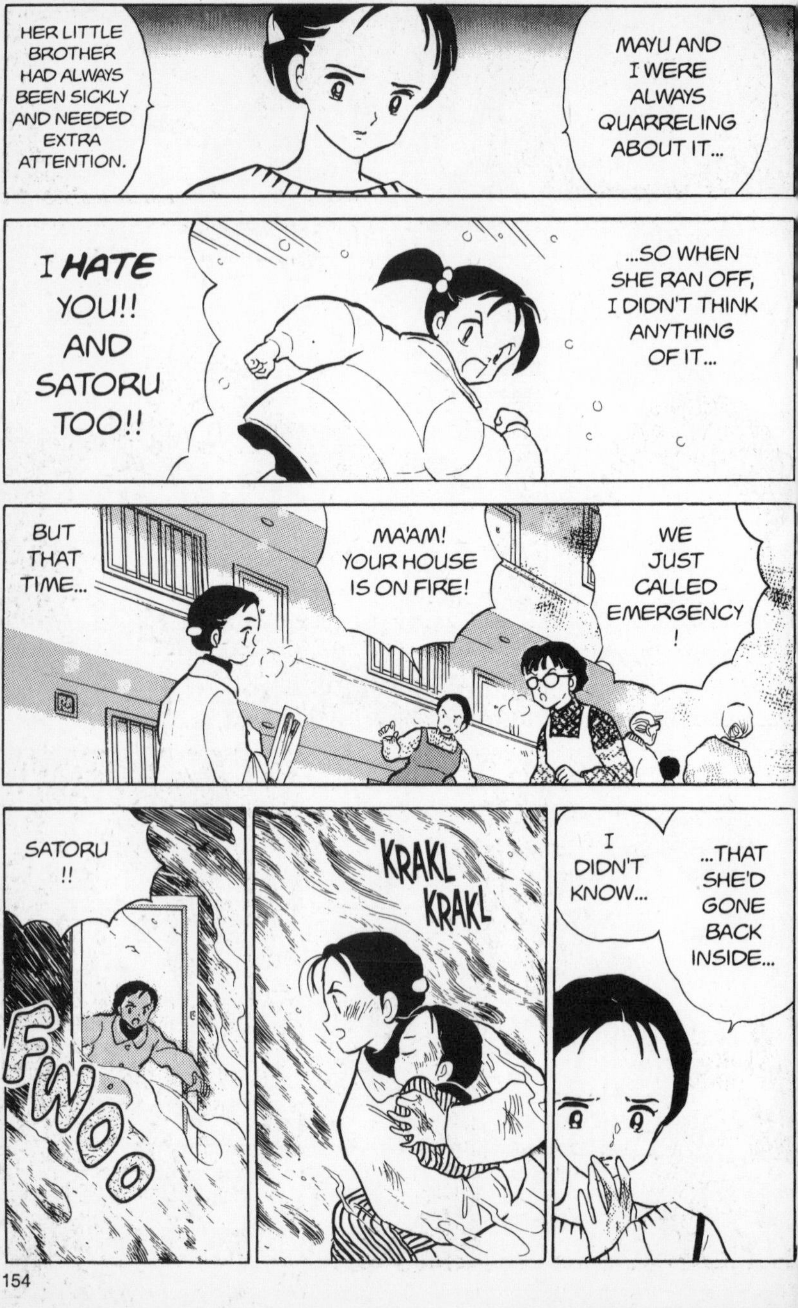
HER LITTLE BROTHER HAD ALWAYS BEEN SICKLY AND NEEDED EXTRA ATTENTION.
MAYU AND I WERE ALWAYS QUARRELING ABOUT IT...
I HATE YOU!! AND SATORU TOO!!
...SO WHEN SHE RAN OFF, I DIDN'T THINK ANYTHING OF IT...
BUT THAT TIME...
MA'AM! YOUR HOUSE IS ON FIRE!
WE JUST CALLED EMERGENCY!
SATORU!!
FWOOO
KRAKL KRAKL
I DIDN'T KNOW...
...THAT SHE'D GONE BACK INSIDE...

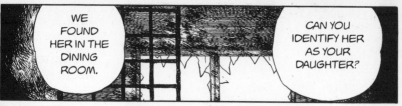

WE FOUND HER IN THE DINING ROOM.

CAN YOU IDENTIFY HER AS YOUR DAUGHTER?

IF I'D ONLY KNOWN...

I'D HAVE SAVED HER...

MII-NN
CHWII
CHWII
CHWII

IT'S THE TRUTH... I CAN TELL...

MAMA HATED ME!!

THAT'S WHY SHE ABANDONED ME!!

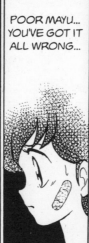

POOR MAYU... YOU'VE GOT IT ALL WRONG...

KRASHHH

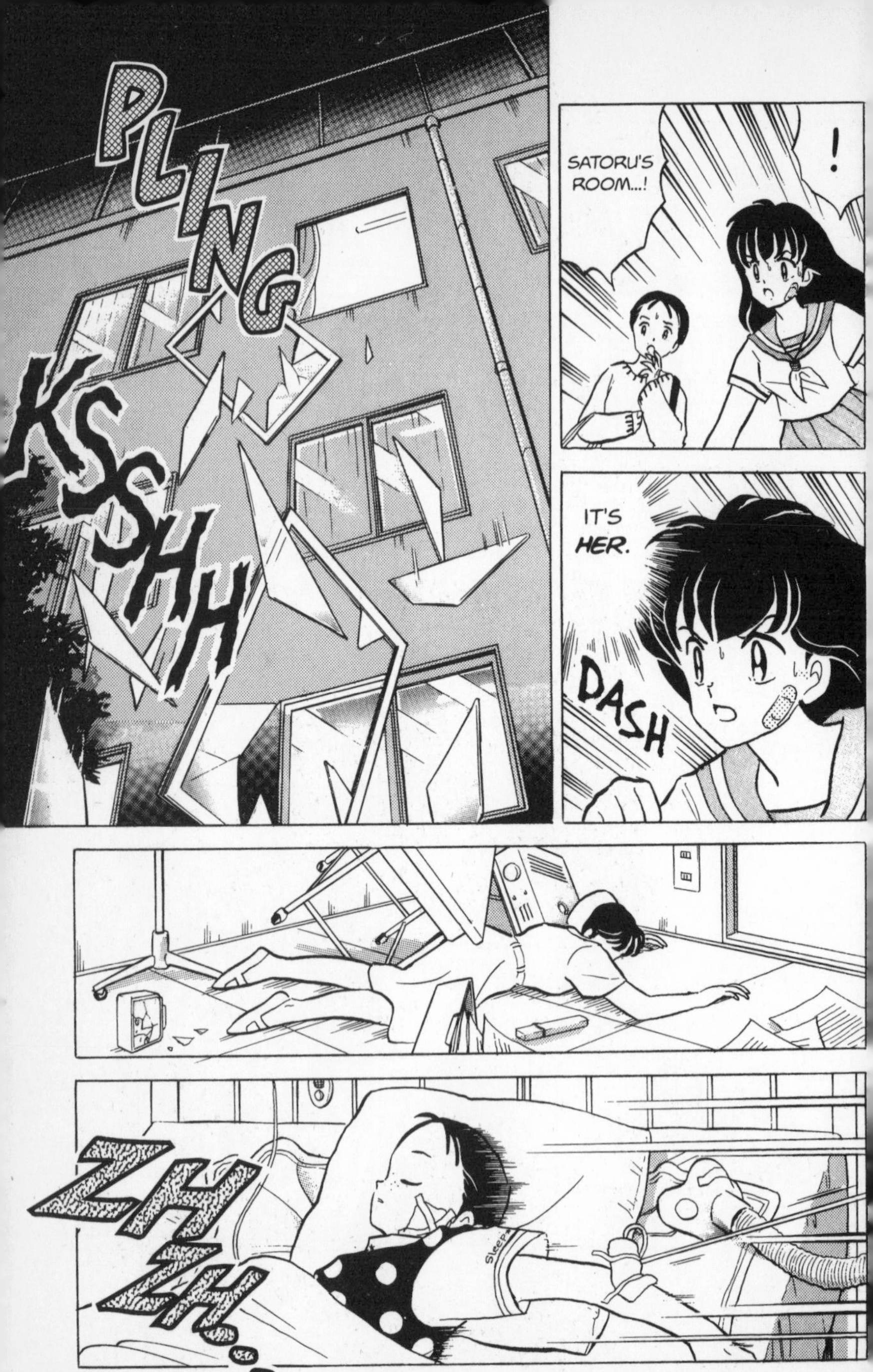
PLING
KSSHH
!
SATORU'S ROOM...!
IT'S HER.
DASH
ZHHH...

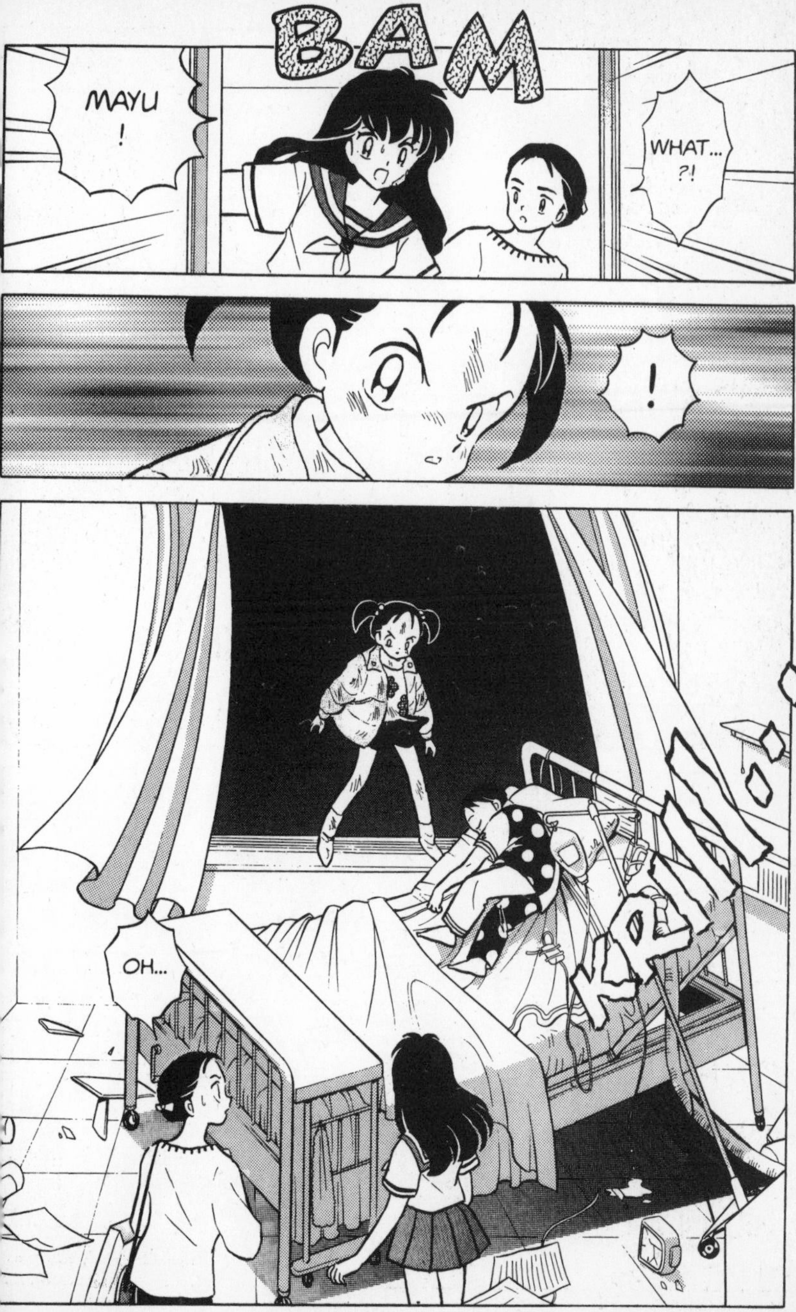
BAM
MAYU
!
WHAT...
?!
!
OH...
KR

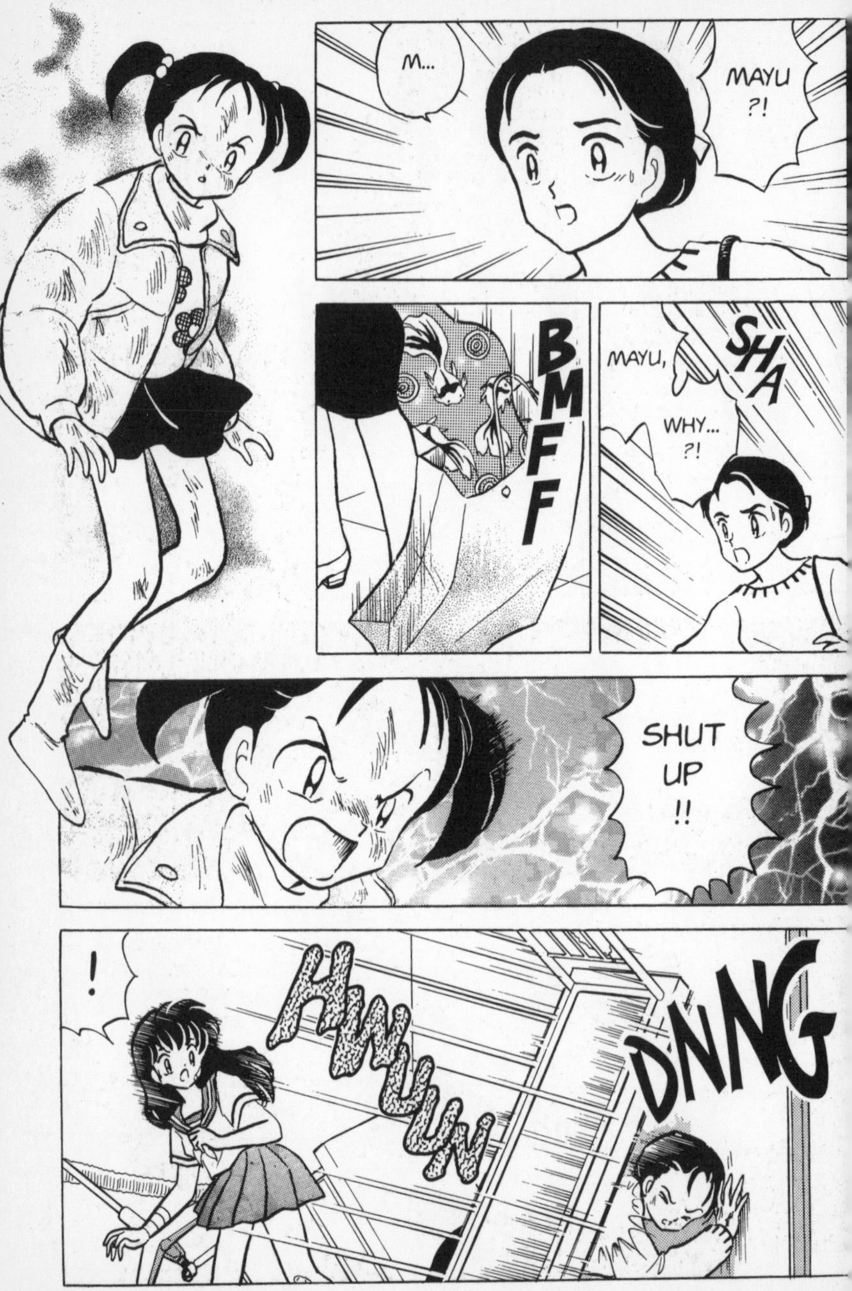
M...
MAYU ?!
BMFF
MAYU,
WHY... ?!
SHA
SHUT UP !!
!
HWUUN
DNNG

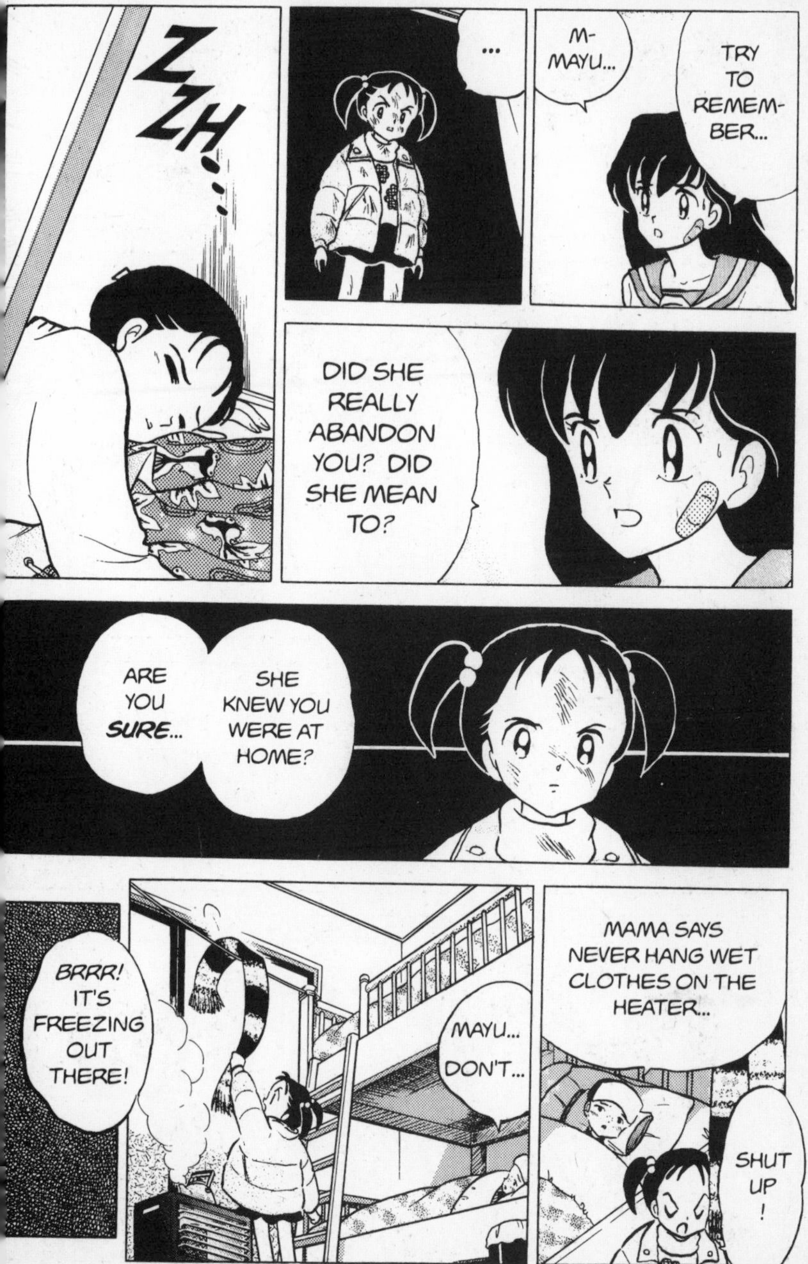
ZZZH...
...
M-
MAYU...
TRY TO REMEMBER...
DID SHE REALLY ABANDON YOU? DID SHE MEAN TO?
ARE YOU SURE...
SHE KNEW YOU WERE AT HOME?
BRRR! IT'S FREEZING OUT THERE!
MAYU... DON'T...
MAMA SAYS NEVER HANG WET CLOTHES ON THE HEATER...
SHUT UP!

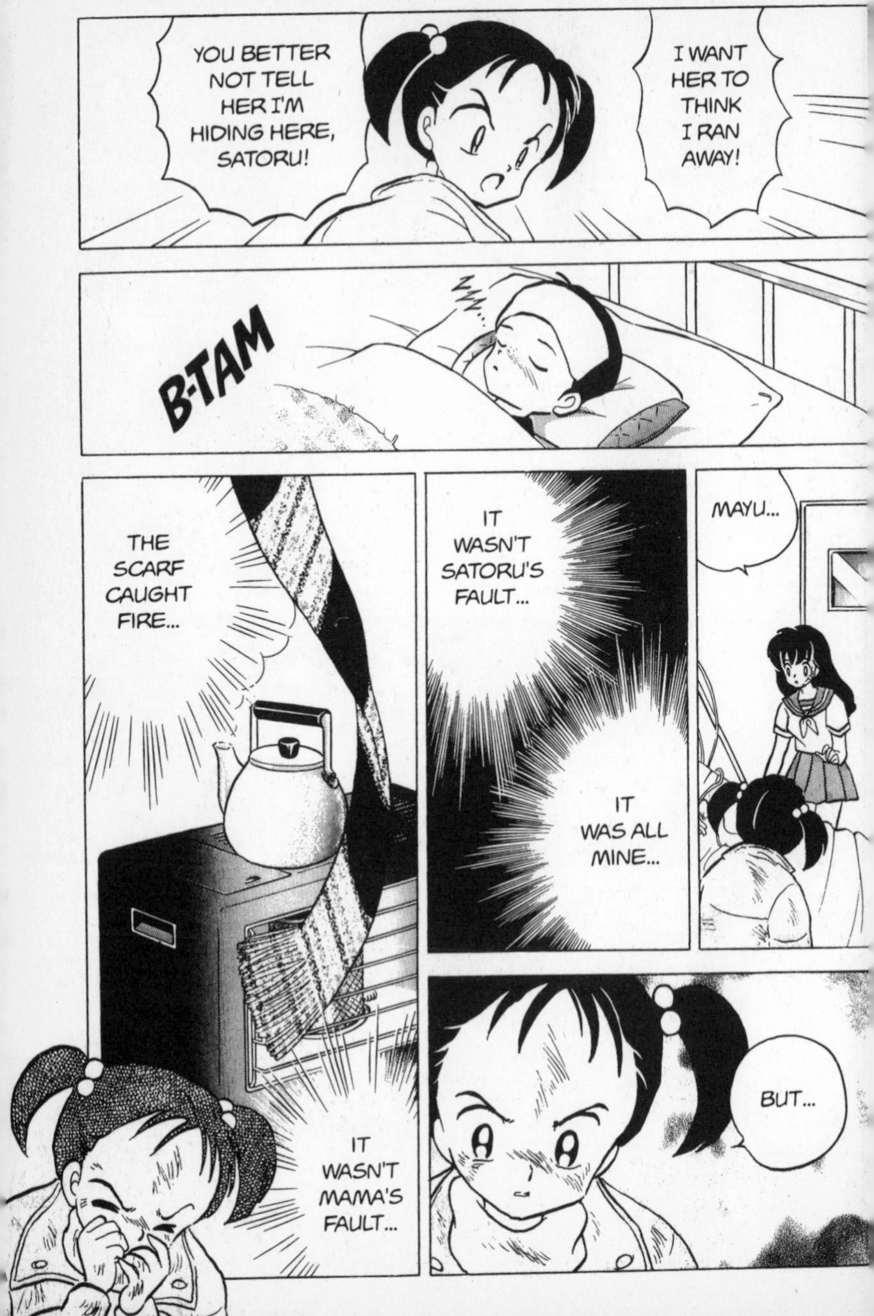
YOU BETTER NOT TELL HER I'M HIDING HERE, SATORU!
I WANT HER TO THINK I RAN AWAY!
B-TAM
THE SCARF CAUGHT FIRE...
IT WASN'T MAMA'S FAULT...
IT WASN'T SATORU'S FAULT...
IT WAS ALL MINE...
MAYU...
BUT...

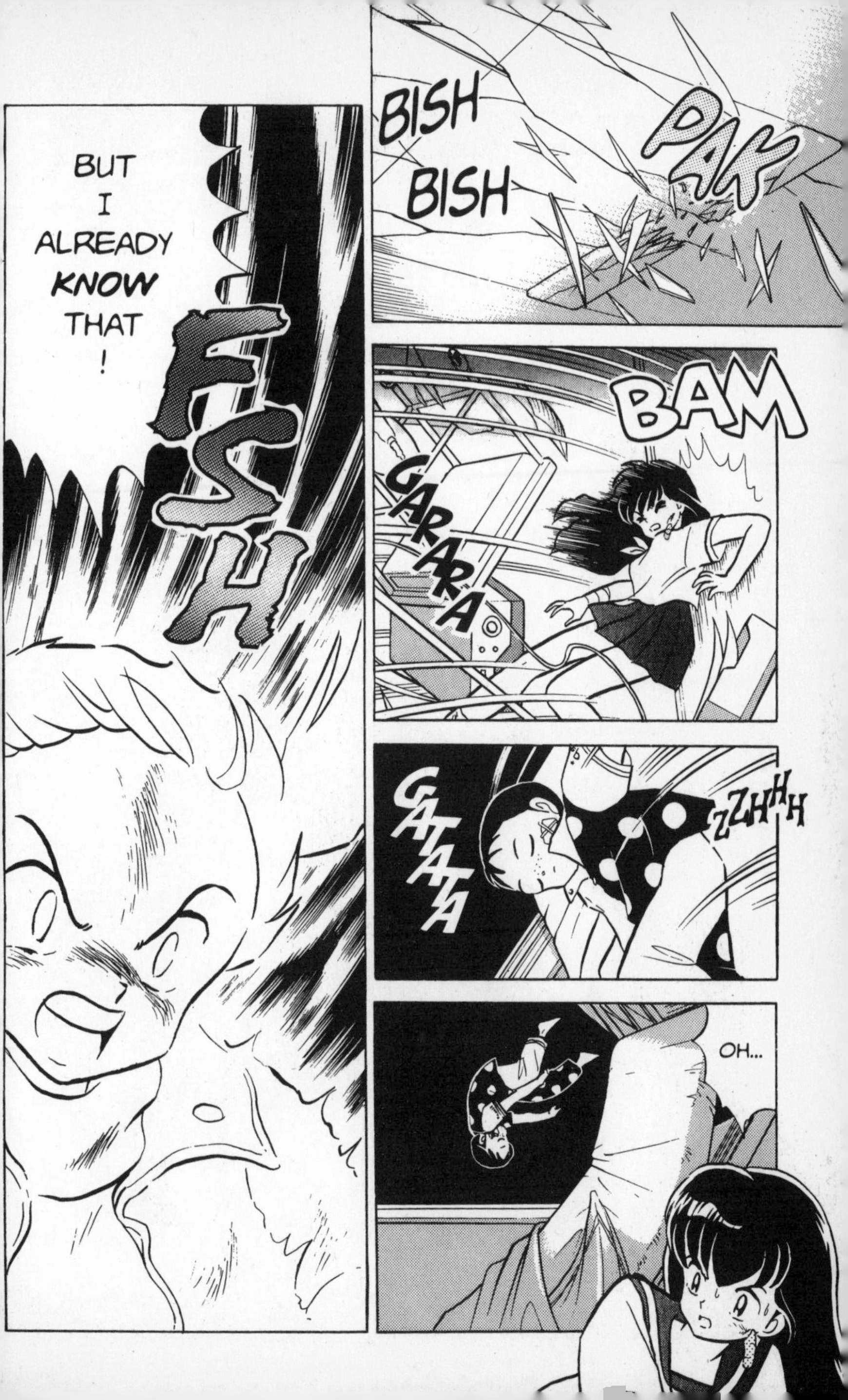
BUT I ALREADY KNOW THAT!
FSH
BISH
BISH
PAK
BAM
GARARA
GATATA
ZZHHH
OH...

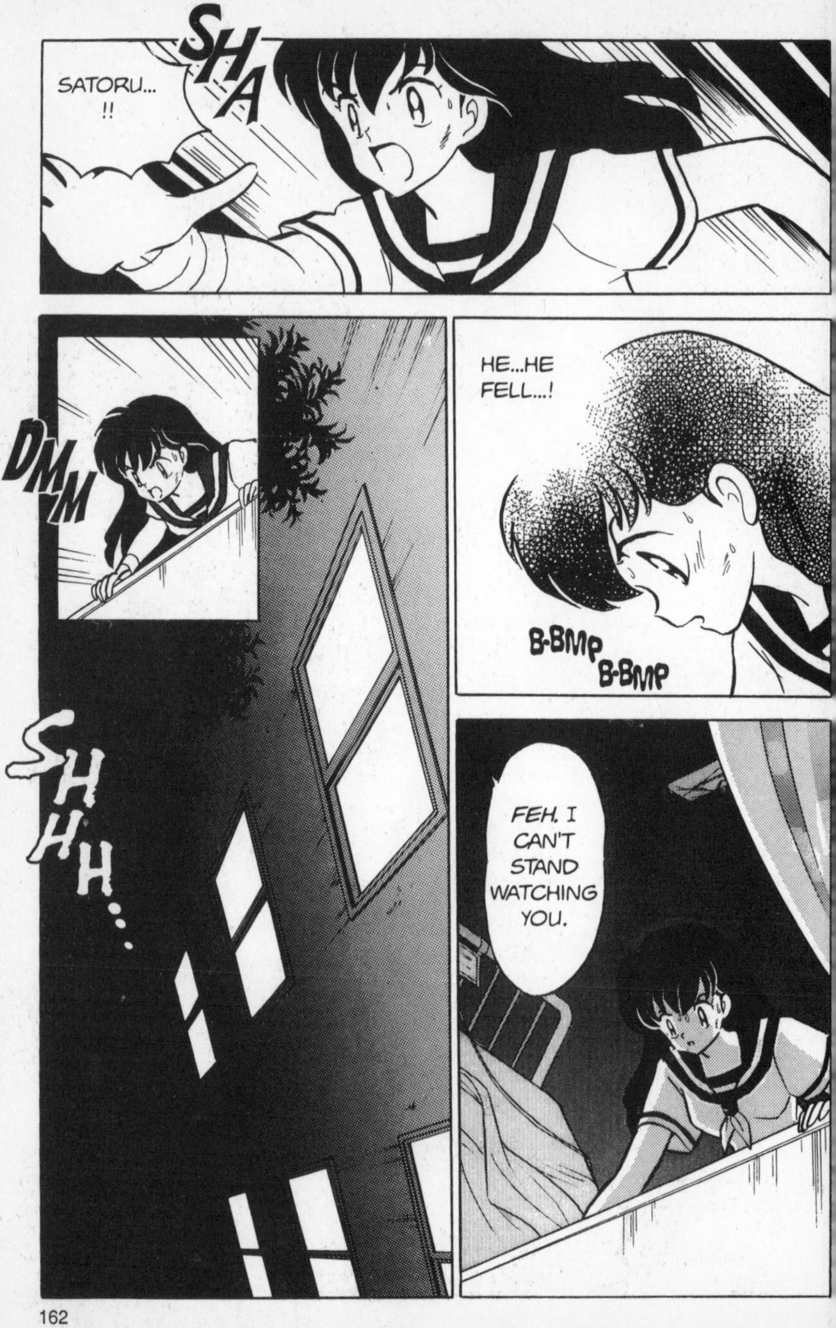
SHA
SATORU... !!
HE...HE FELL...!
B-BMP B-BMP
DMM
SHHH...
FEH. I CAN'T STAND WATCHING YOU.

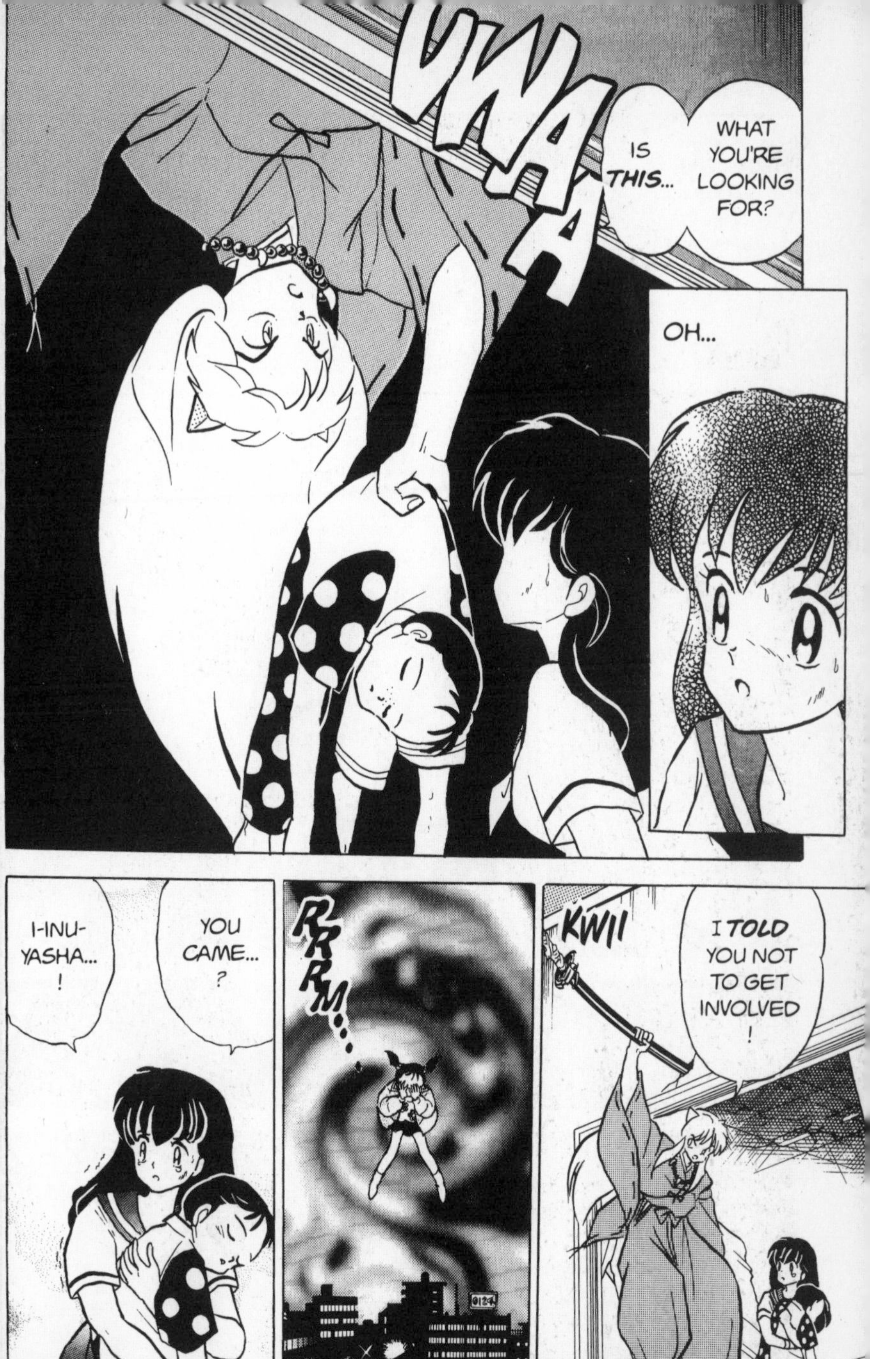
VWAA
IS THIS...
WHAT YOU'RE LOOKING FOR?
OH...
I-INU-YASHA... !
YOU CAME... ?
RRRM...
KWII
I TOLD YOU NOT TO GET INVOLVED !

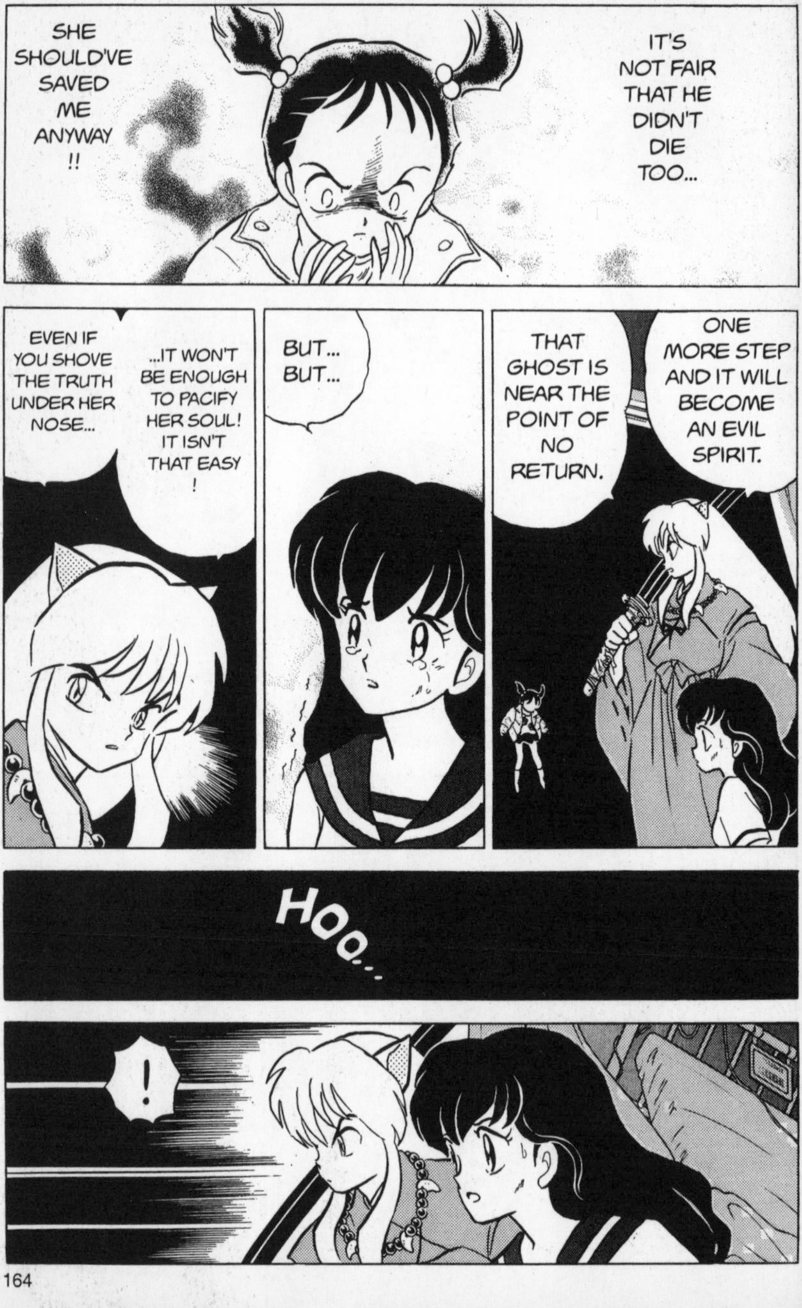
SHE SHOULD'VE SAVED ME ANYWAY !!
IT'S NOT FAIR THAT HE DIDN'T DIE TOO...
EVEN IF YOU SHOVE THE TRUTH UNDER HER NOSE...
...IT WON'T BE ENOUGH TO PACIFY HER SOUL! IT ISN'T THAT EASY !
BUT... BUT...
THAT GHOST IS NEAR THE POINT OF NO RETURN.
ONE MORE STEP AND IT WILL BECOME AN EVIL SPIRIT.
HOO...
!

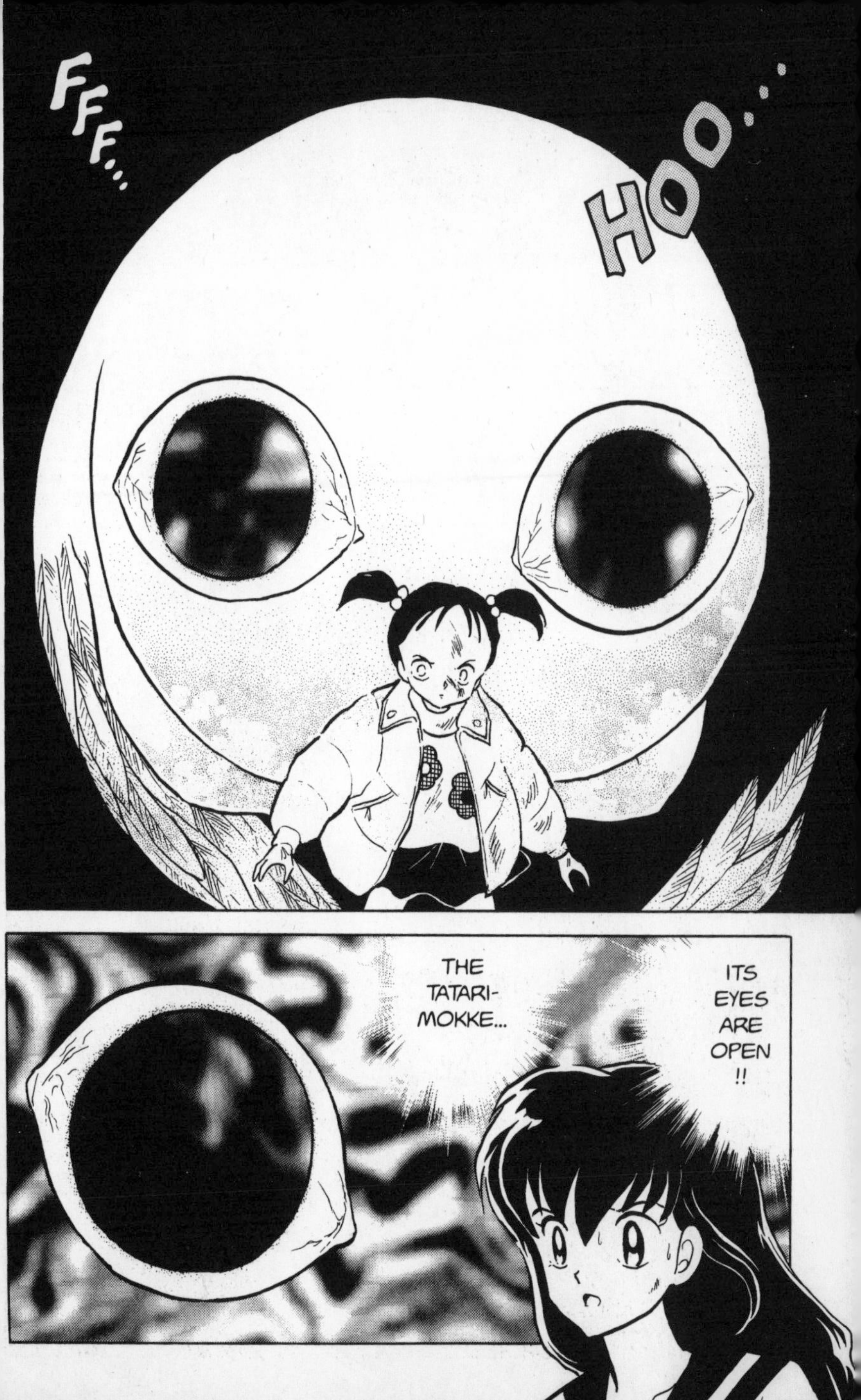
FFF...
HOO...
THE TATARI-MOKKE...
ITS EYES ARE OPEN!!

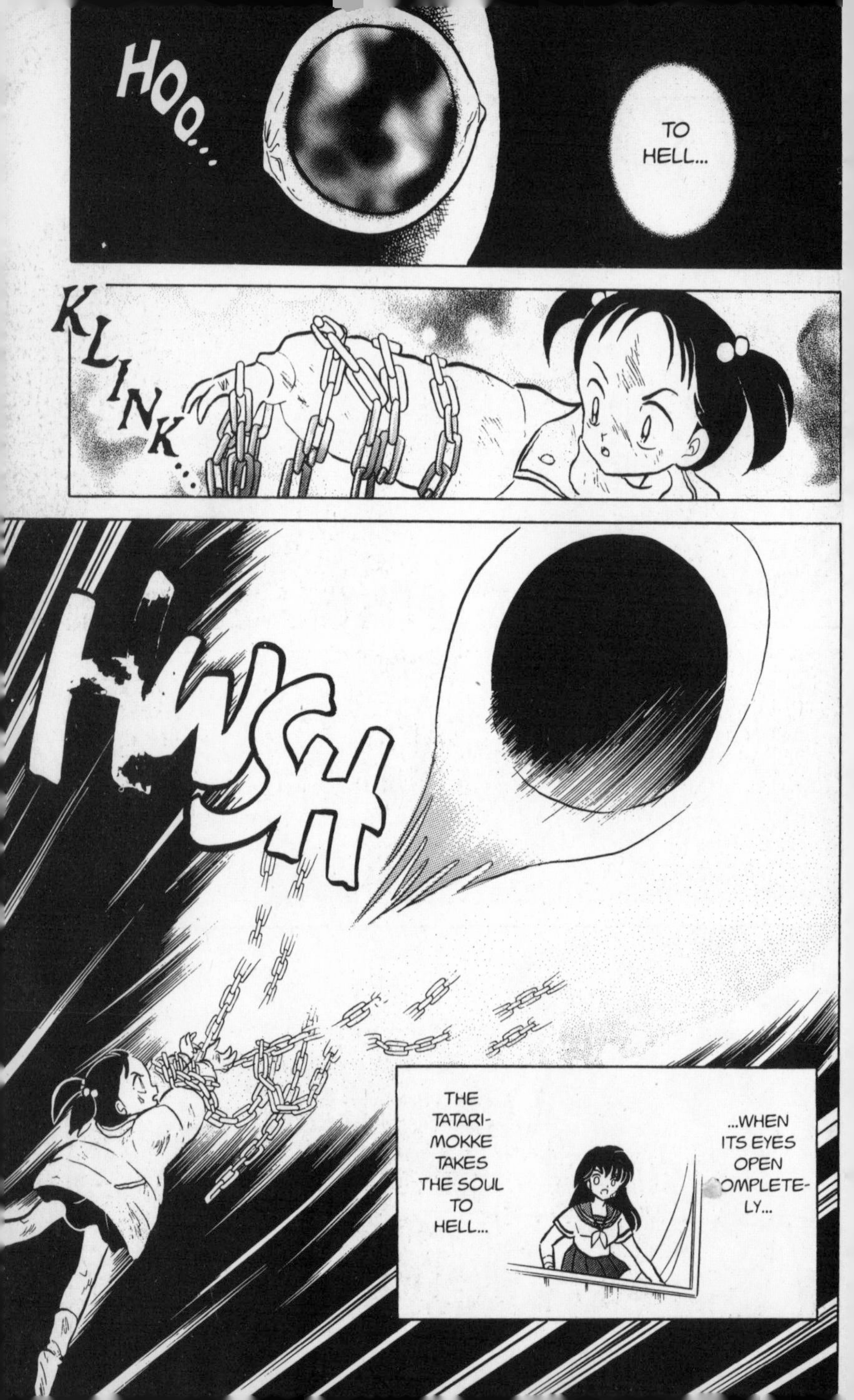
HOO...
TO HELL...
KLINK...
HWSH
THE TATARI-MOKKE TAKES THE SOUL TO HELL...
...WHEN ITS EYES OPEN COMPLETE-LY...

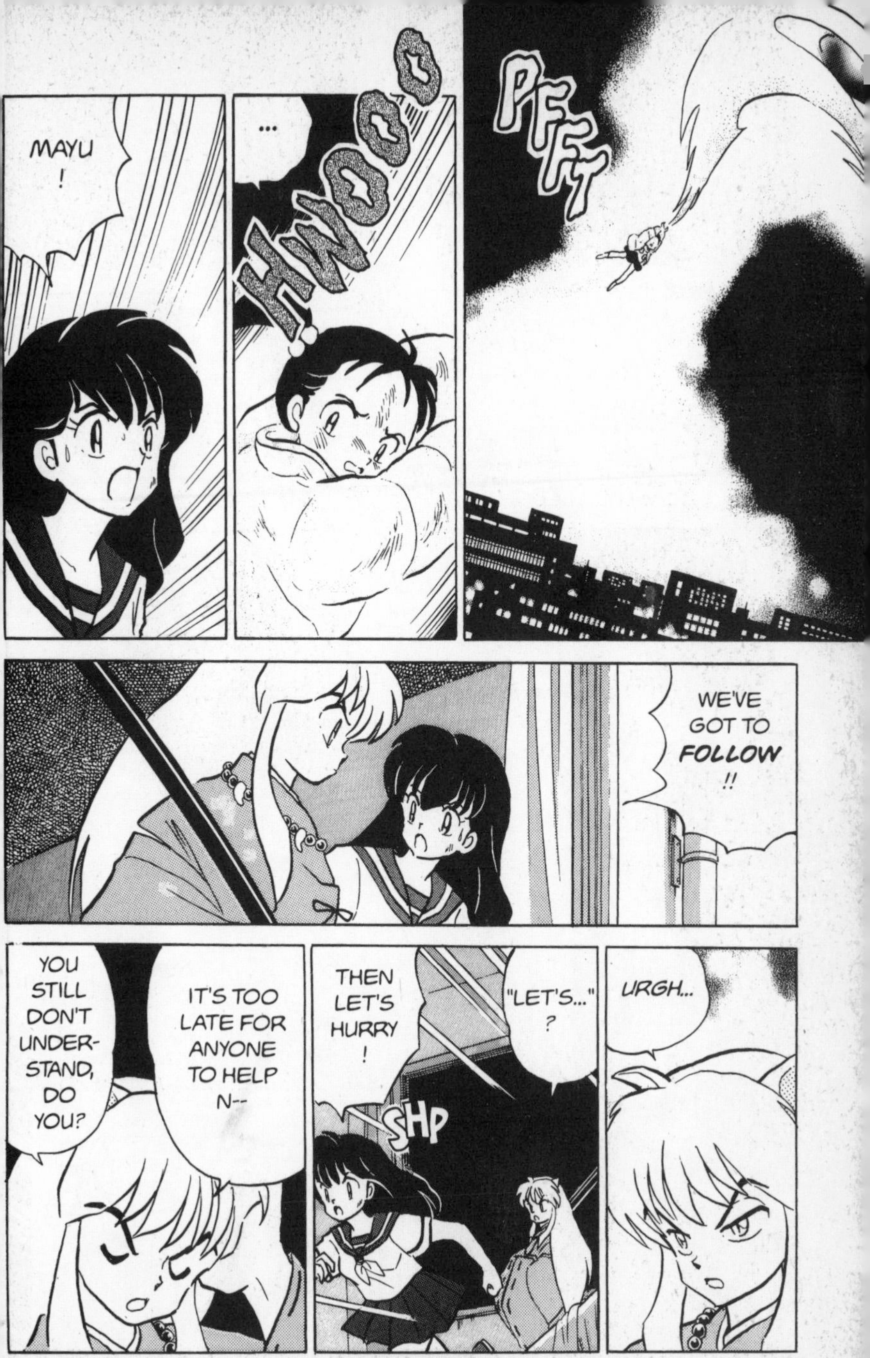
MAYU !
...
HWOOO
PFFT
WE'VE GOT TO FOLLOW !!
YOU STILL DON'T UNDER-STAND, DO YOU?
IT'S TOO LATE FOR ANYONE TO HELP N--
THEN LET'S HURRY !
SHP
"LET'S..." ?
URGH...

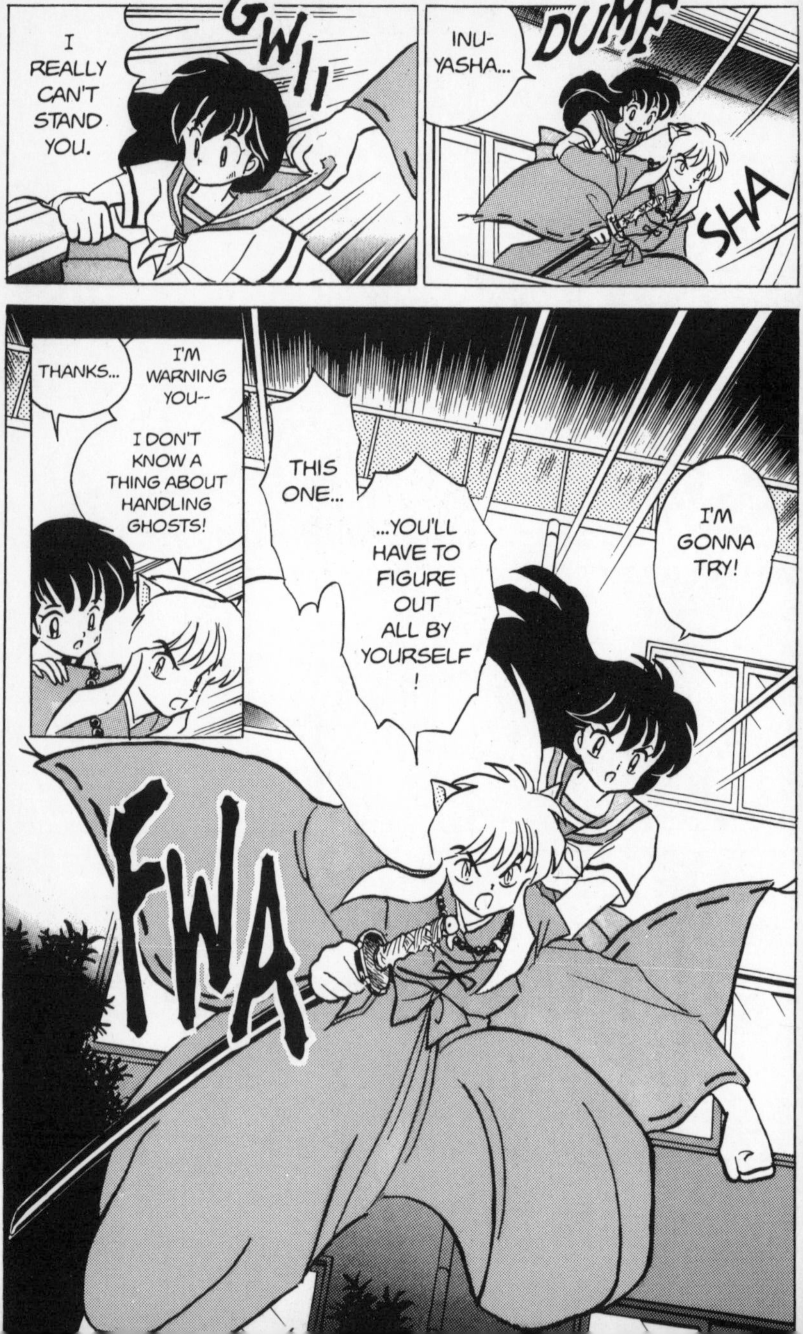

GWII
I REALLY CAN'T STAND YOU.
DUMF
INU-YASHA...
SHA
THANKS...
I'M WARNING YOU--
I DON'T KNOW A THING ABOUT HANDLING GHOSTS!
THIS ONE...
...YOU'LL HAVE TO FIGURE OUT ALL BY YOURSELF!
I'M GONNA TRY!
FWA

SCROLL TEN
TO REST

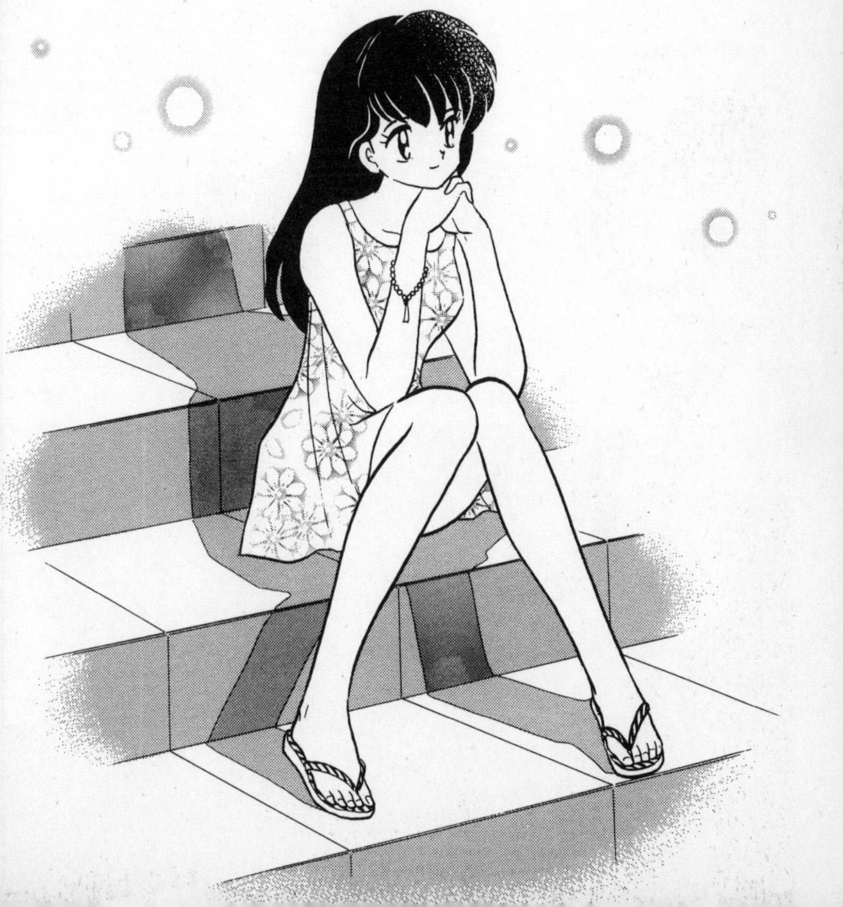

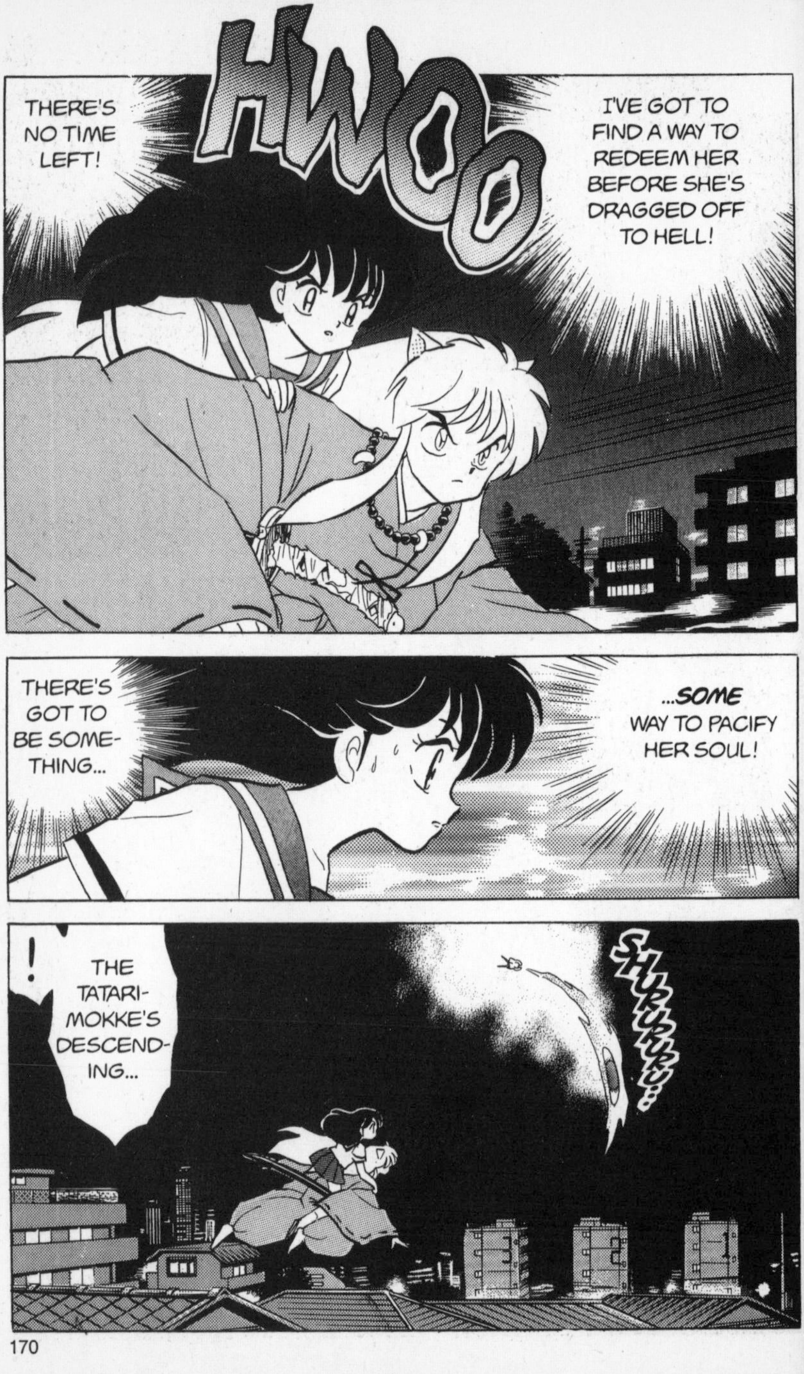
HWOO
THERE'S NO TIME LEFT!
I'VE GOT TO FIND A WAY TO REDEEM HER BEFORE SHE'S DRAGGED OFF TO HELL!
THERE'S GOT TO BE SOME-THING...
...SOME WAY TO PACIFY HER SOUL!
!
THE TATARI-MOKKE'S DESCEND-ING...
SHURURURU...

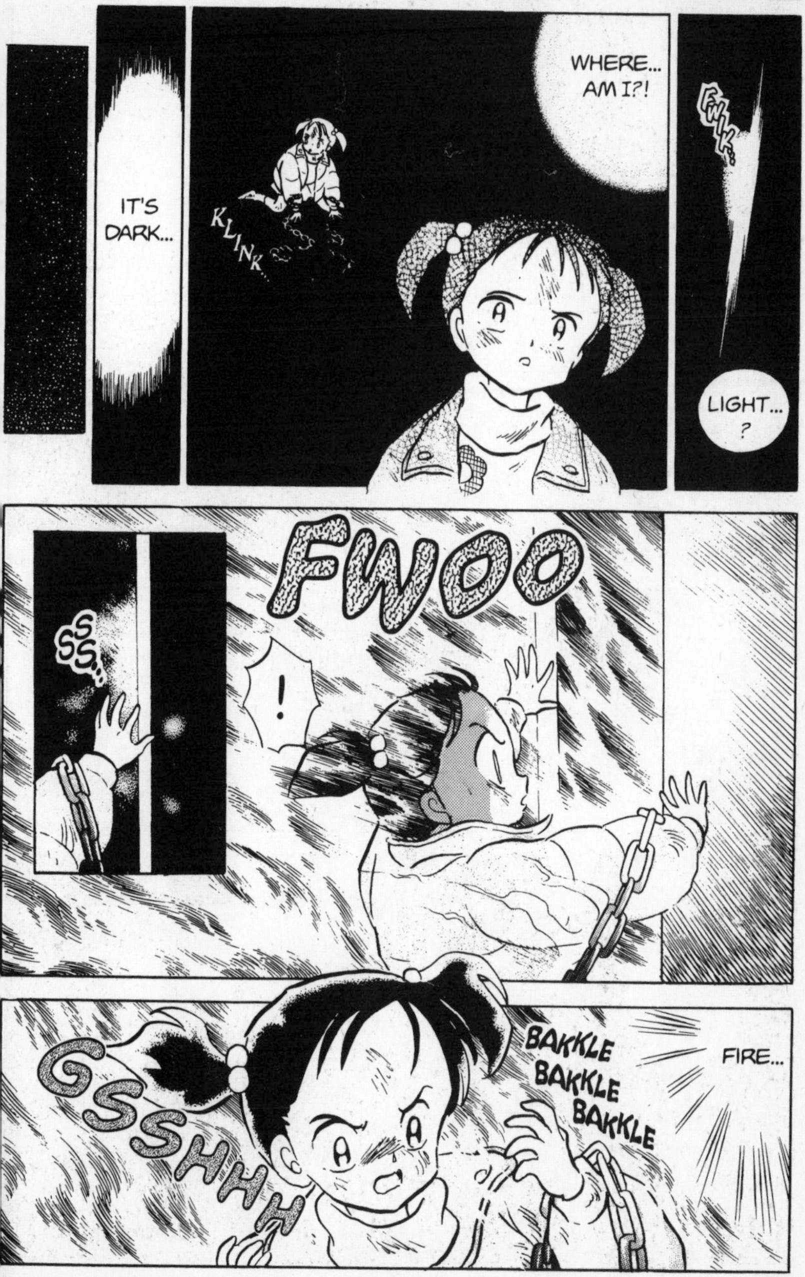
IT'S DARK...
KLINK...
WHERE... AM I?!
FWIK...
LIGHT... ?
SSS...
FWOO
!
GSSHHH
BAKKLE BAKKLE BAKKLE
FIRE...

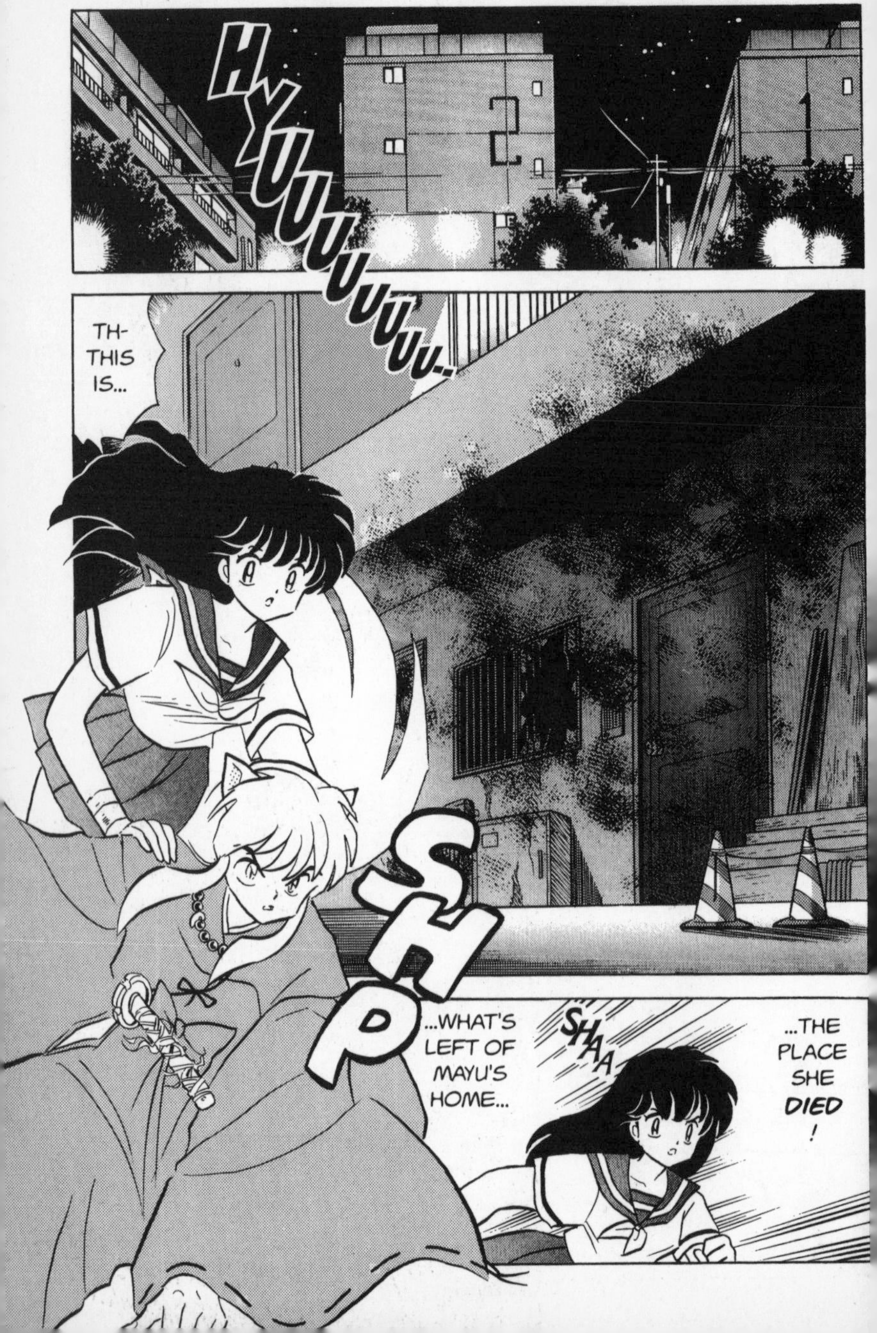
HYUUUUUUUUU..
TH- THIS IS...
SHP
...WHAT'S LEFT OF MAYU'S HOME...
SHAA
...THE PLACE SHE **DIED**!

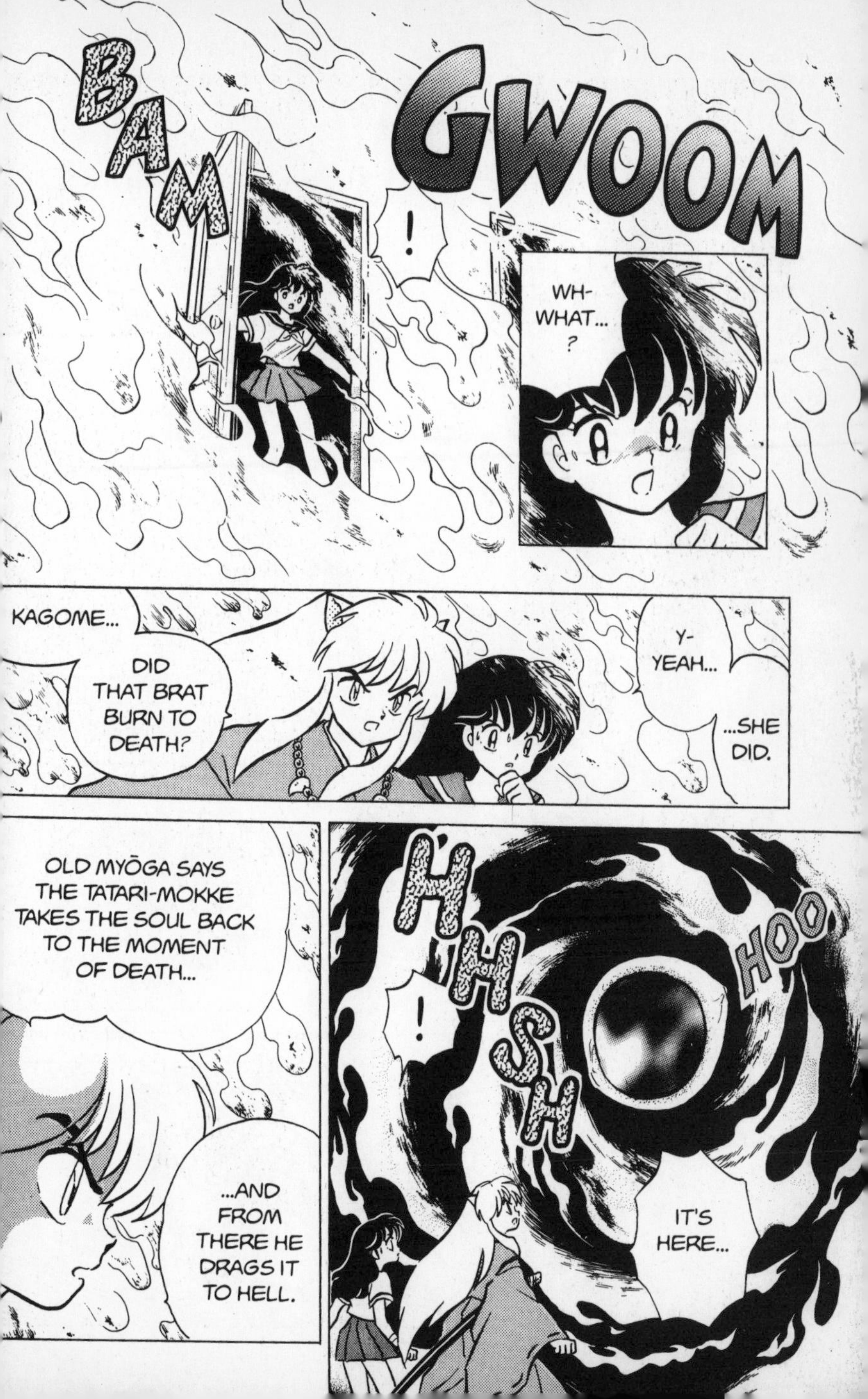
BAM
GWOOM
!
WH-WHAT...?
KAGOME...
DID THAT BRAT BURN TO DEATH?
Y-YEAH...
...SHE DID.
OLD MYŌGA SAYS THE TATARI-MOKKE TAKES THE SOUL BACK TO THE MOMENT OF DEATH...
...AND FROM THERE HE DRAGS IT TO HELL.
HHSH
HOO
!
IT'S HERE...

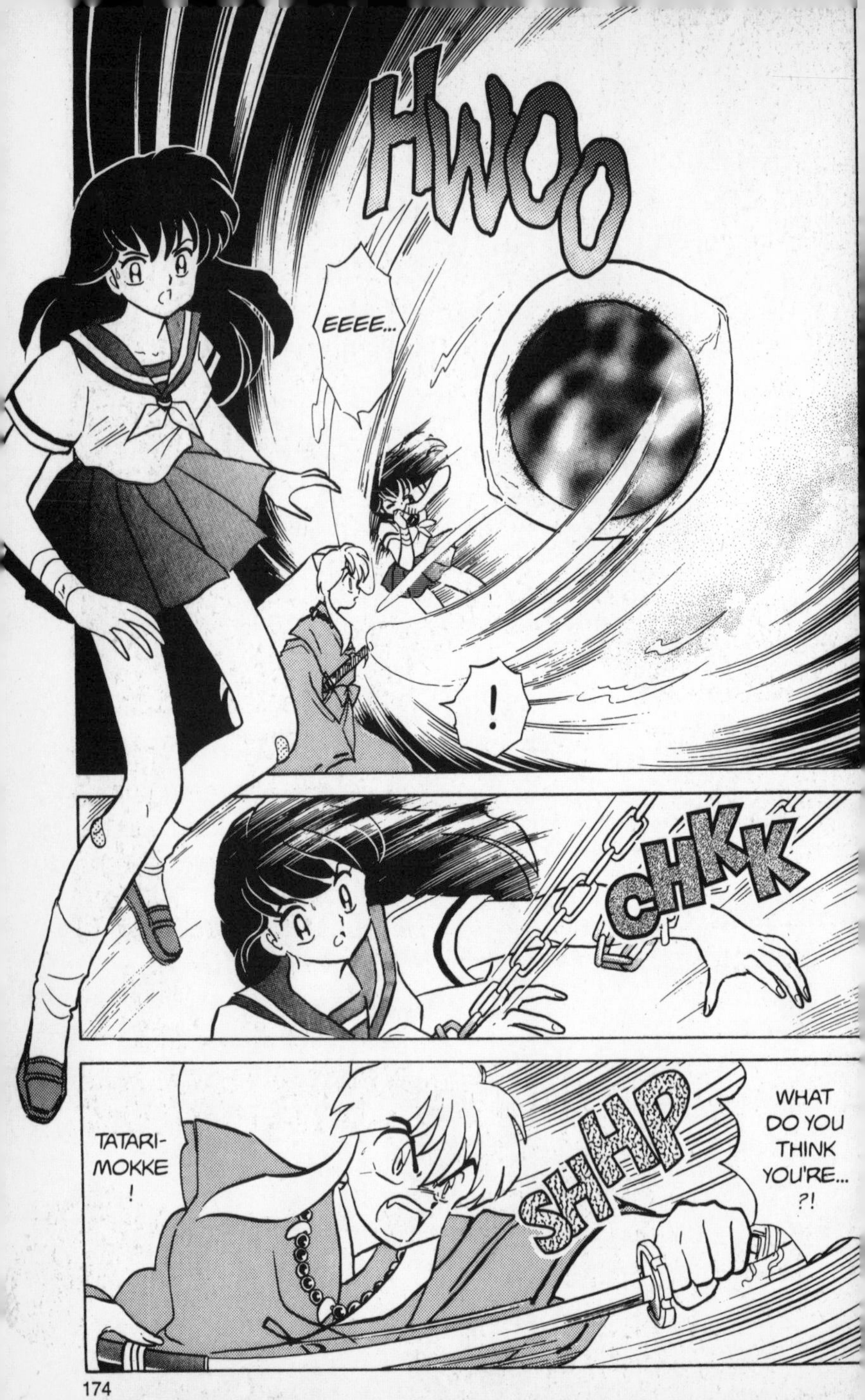
HWOO
EEEE...
!
CHKK
TATARI-MOKKE!
SHHP
WHAT DO YOU THINK YOU'RE...?!

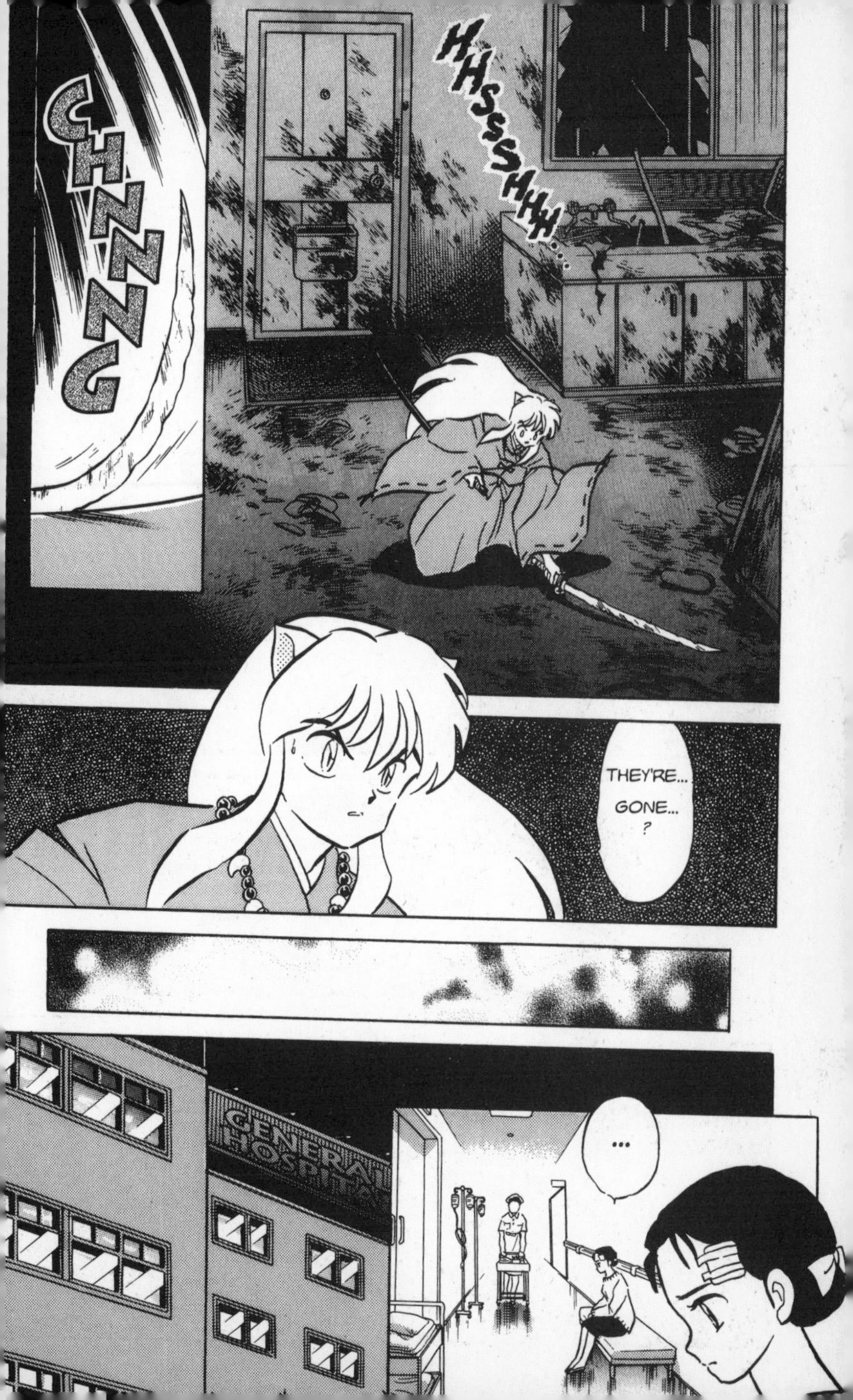
CHNNNG
HHSSSHHH...
THEY'RE... GONE... ?
GENERAL HOSPITAL
...

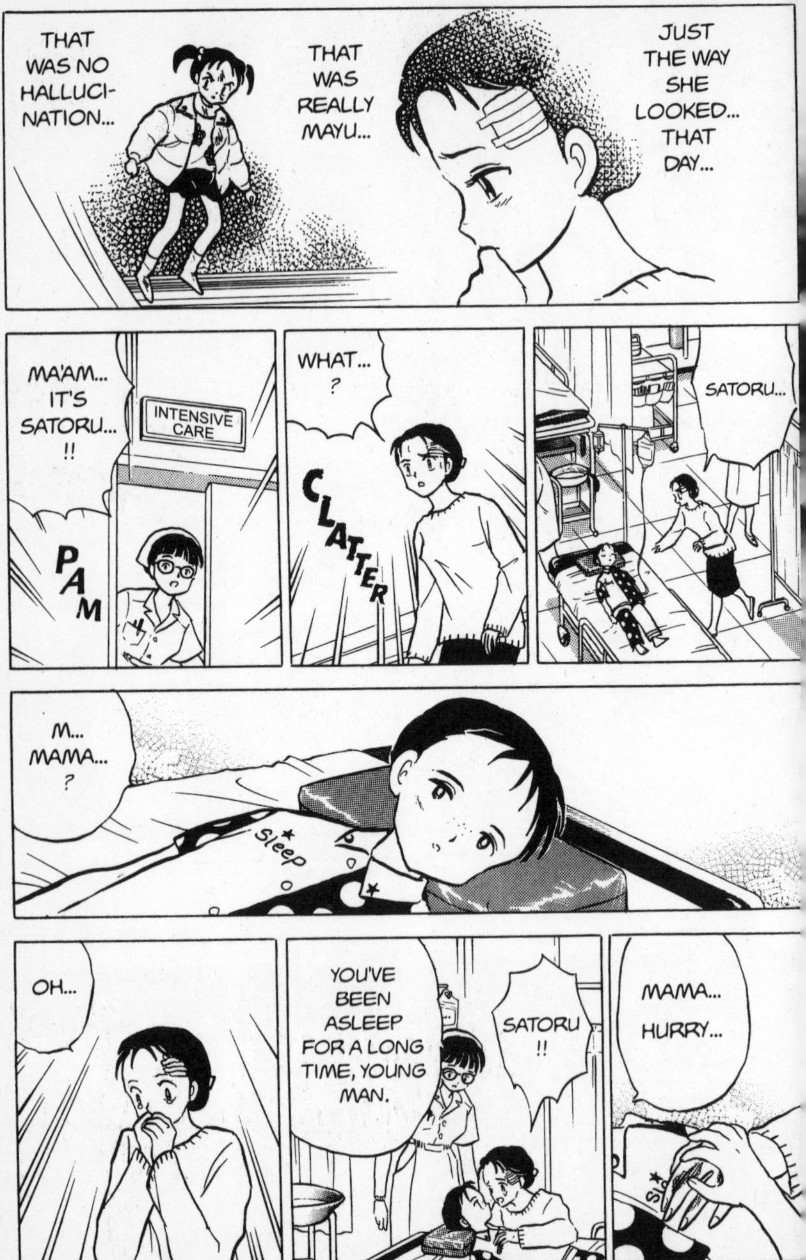
THAT WAS NO HALLUCI-NATION...
THAT WAS REALLY MAYU...
JUST THE WAY SHE LOOKED... THAT DAY...
MA'AM... IT'S SATORU... !!
INTENSIVE CARE
PAM
WHAT... ?
CLATTER
SATORU...
M... MAMA... ?
Sleep
OH...
YOU'VE BEEN ASLEEP FOR A LONG TIME, YOUNG MAN.
SATORU !!
MAMA... HURRY...

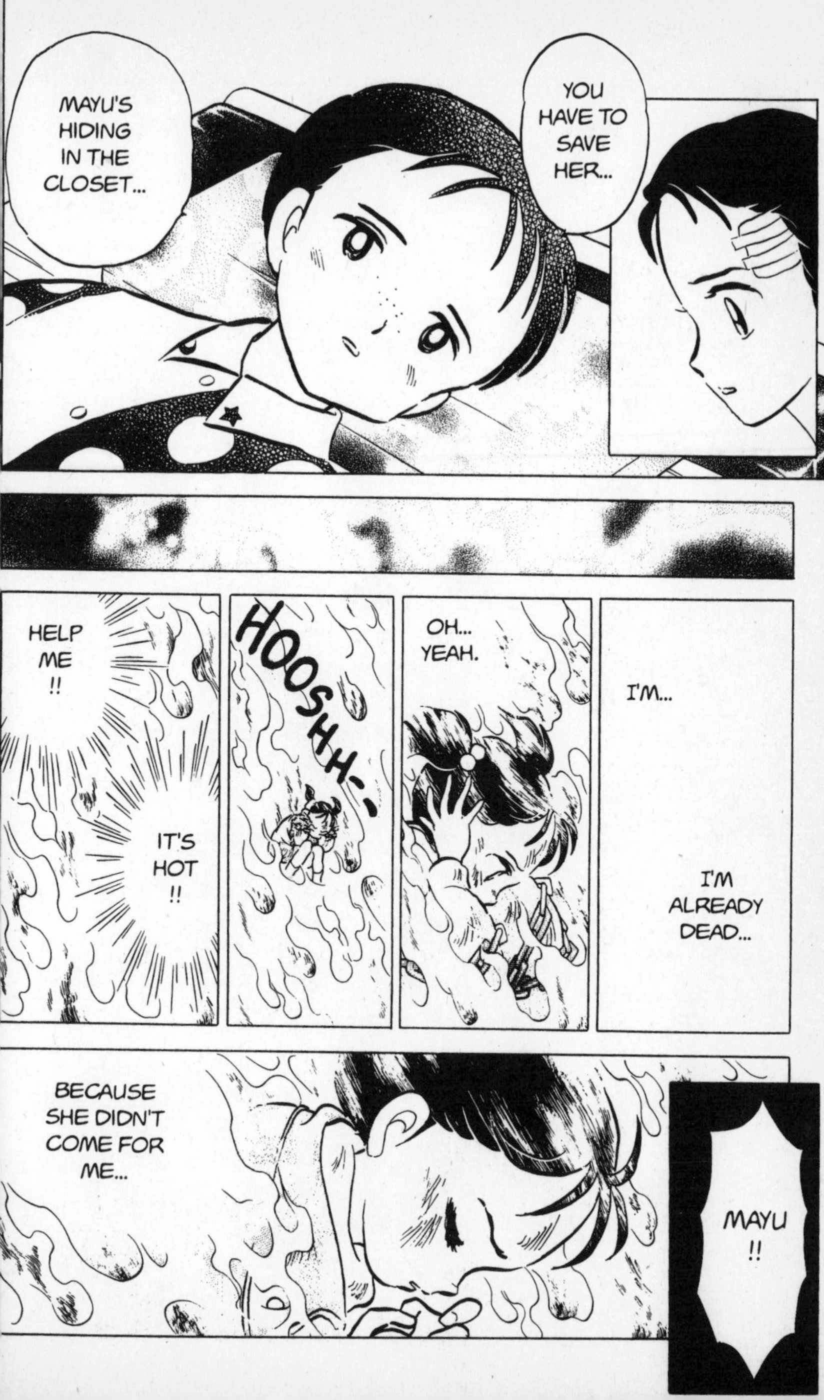
MAYU'S HIDING IN THE CLOSET...
YOU HAVE TO SAVE HER...
HELP ME !!
IT'S HOT !!
HOOSHH--
OH... YEAH.
I'M...
I'M ALREADY DEAD...
BECAUSE SHE DIDN'T COME FOR ME...
MAYU !!

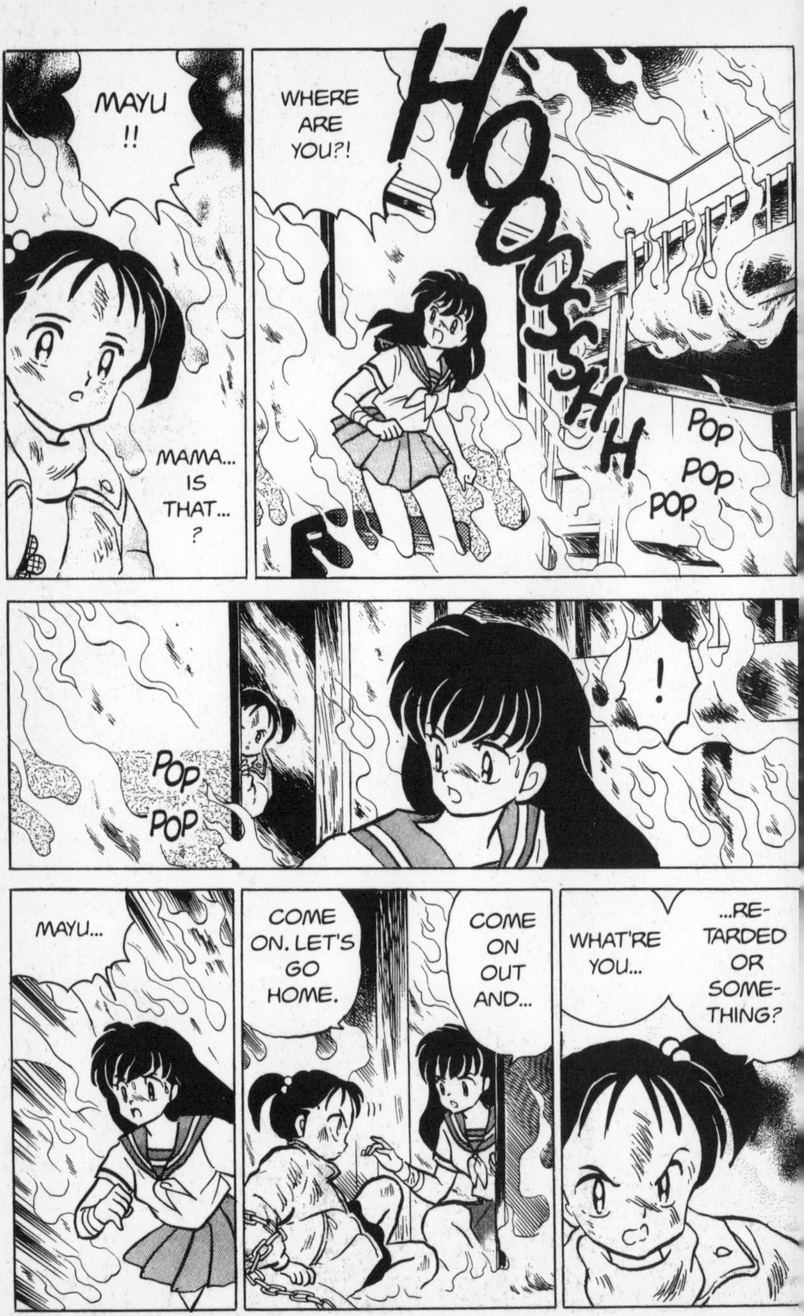
MAYU !!
MAMA... IS THAT... ?
WHERE ARE YOU?!
HOOOSHHH
POP POP POP
POP POP
!
MAYU...
COME ON. LET'S GO HOME.
COME ON OUT AND...
WHAT'RE YOU...
...RE-TARDED OR SOME-THING?

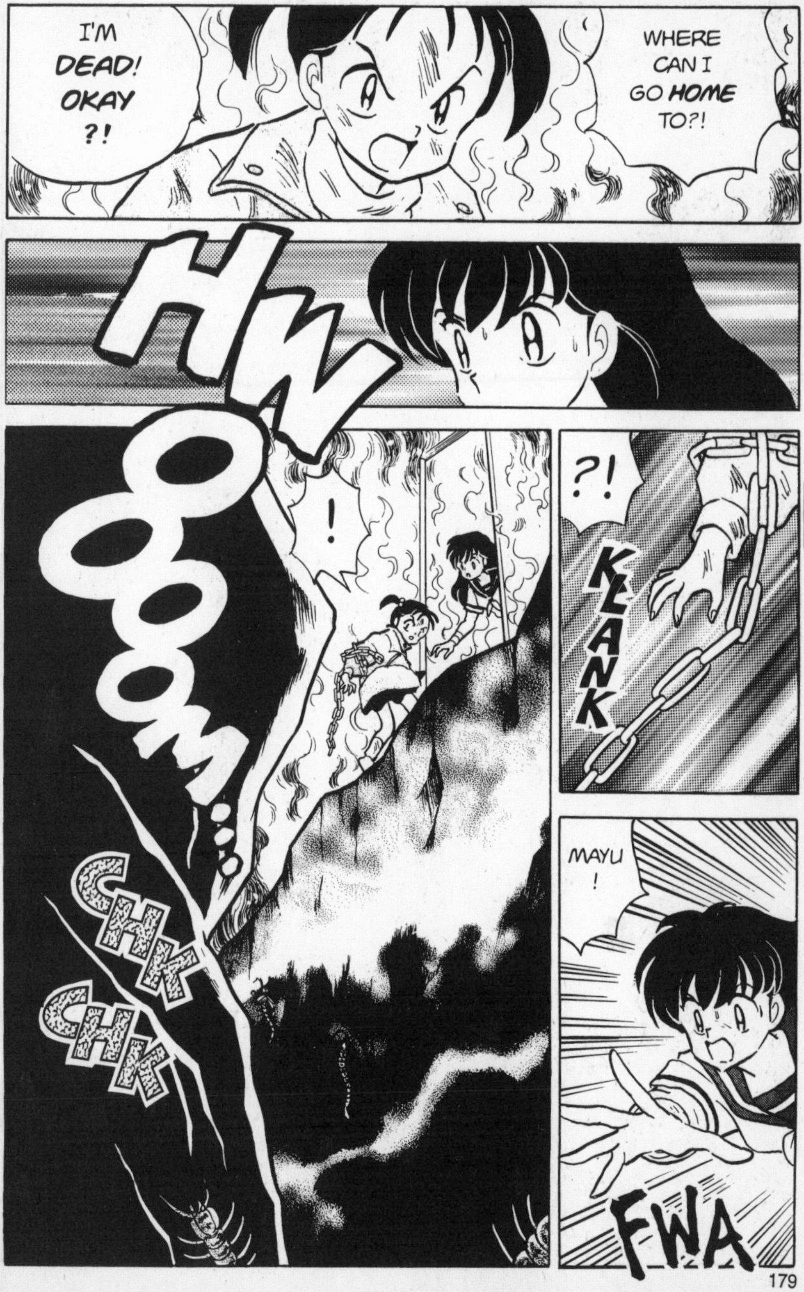
I'M DEAD! OKAY ?!
WHERE CAN I GO HOME TO?!
HWOOOOM...
!
CHK CHK
?!
KLANK
MAYU !
FWA

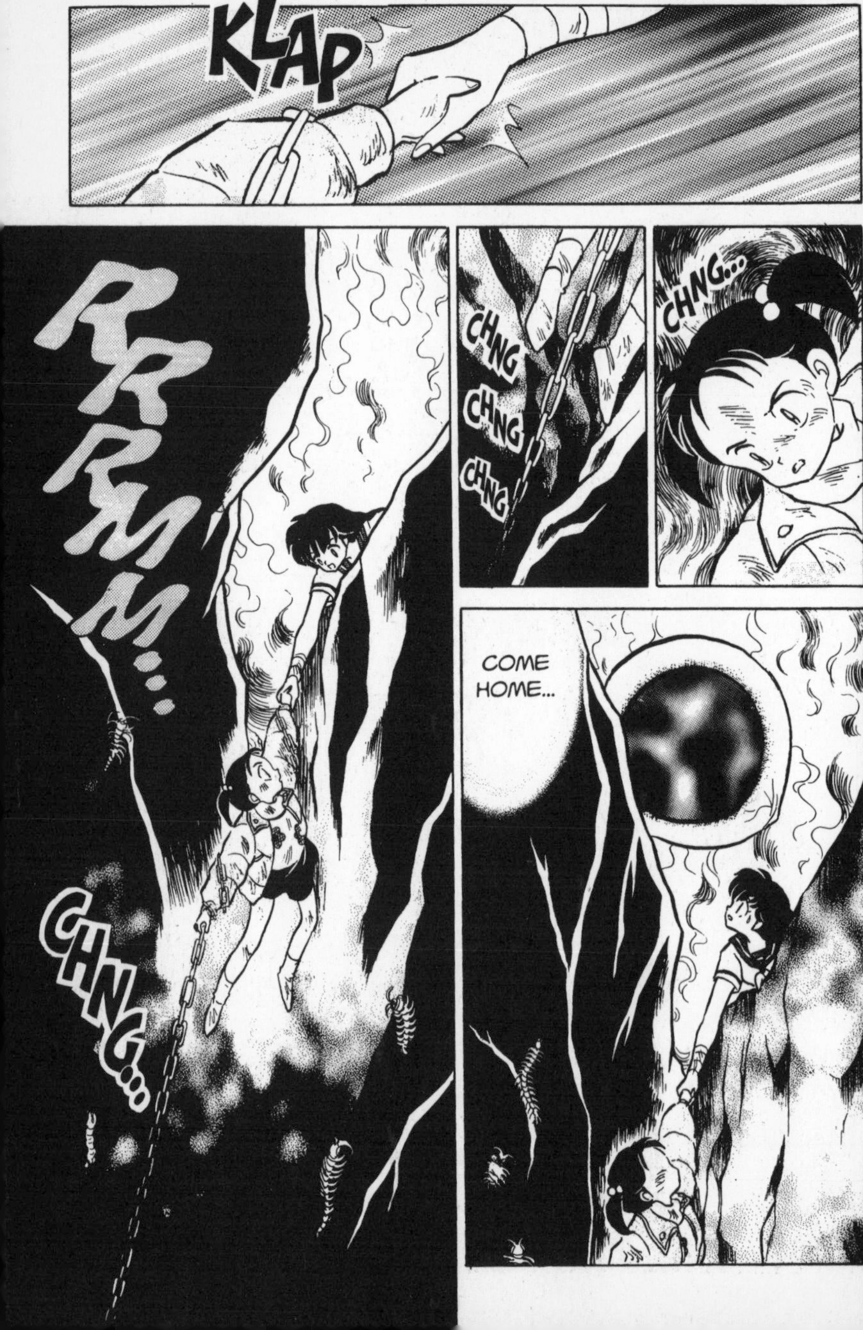
KLAP
RRMM...
CHNG...
CHNG
CHNG
CHNG
CHNG...
COME HOME...

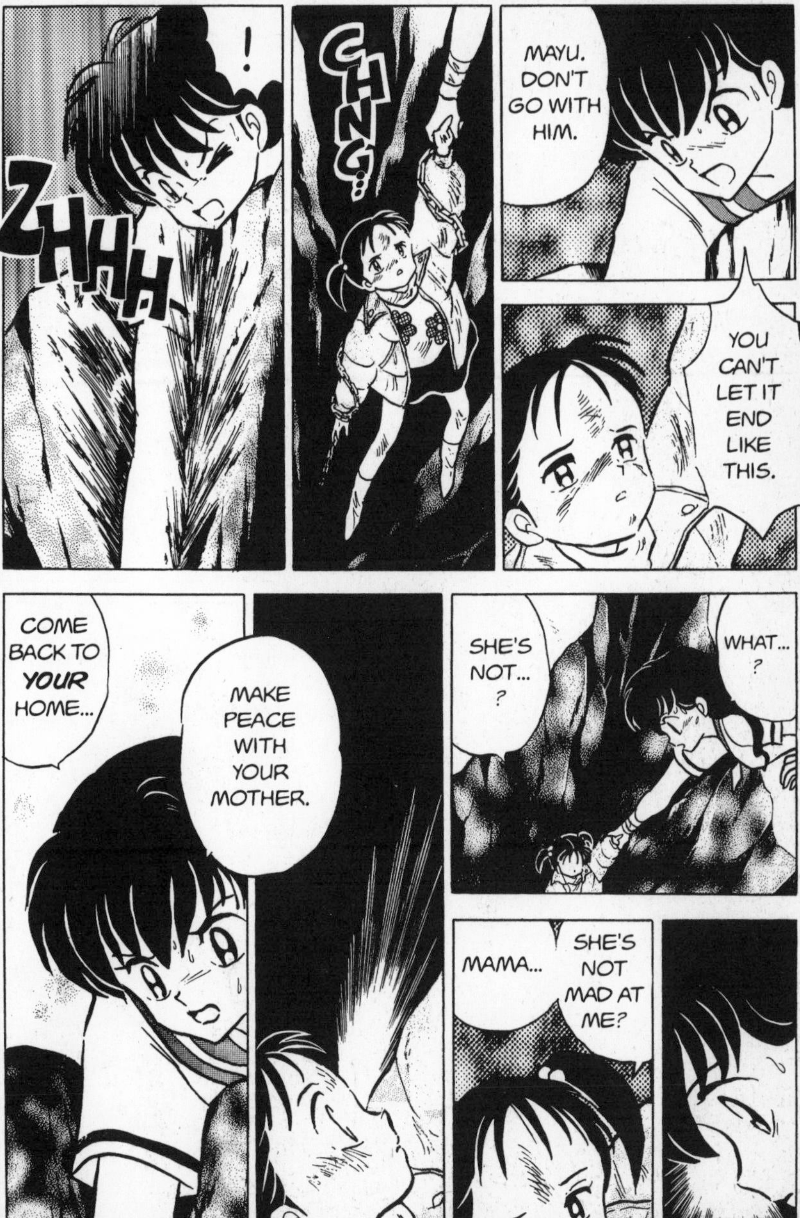
!
ZHHHH
CHNG
MAYU. DON'T GO WITH HIM.
YOU CAN'T LET IT END LIKE THIS.
COME BACK TO YOUR HOME...
MAKE PEACE WITH YOUR MOTHER.
SHE'S NOT...?
WHAT...?
MAMA...
SHE'S NOT MAD AT ME?

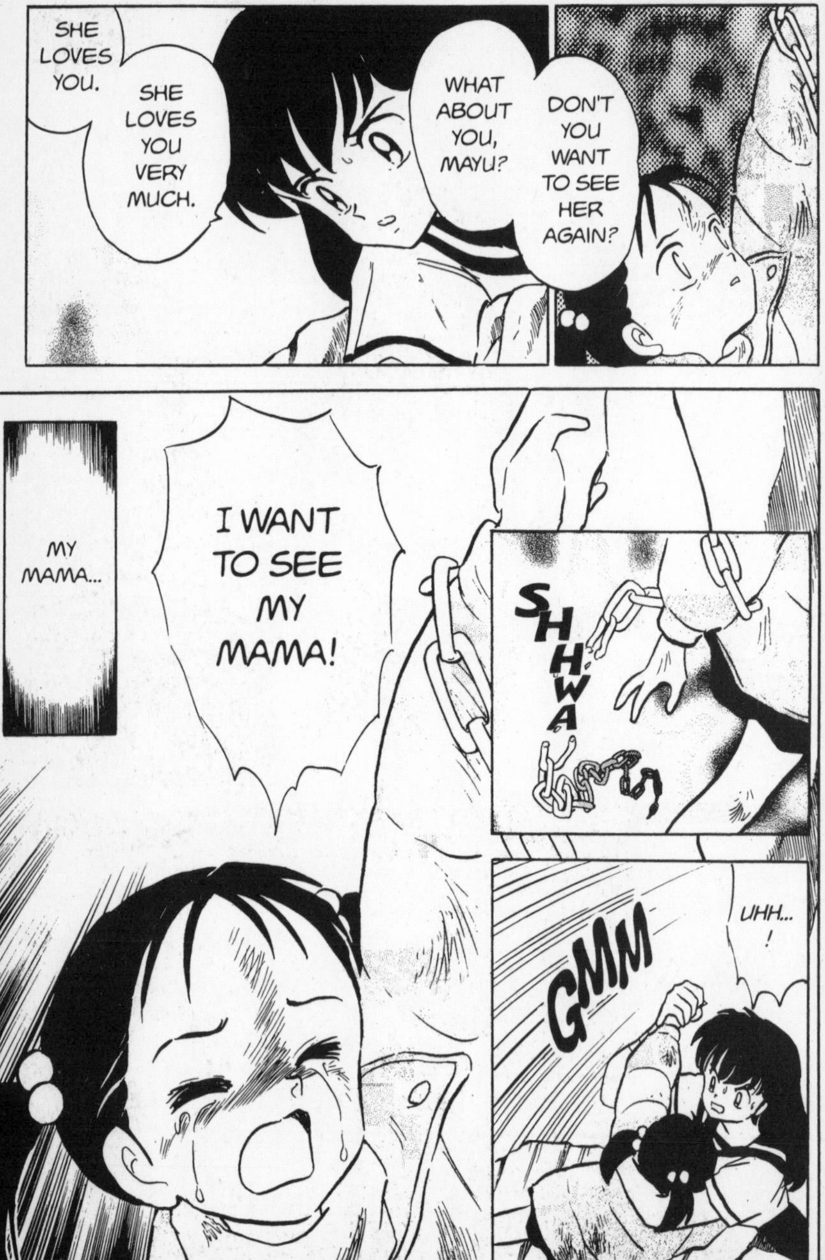
SHE LOVES YOU.
SHE LOVES YOU VERY MUCH.
WHAT ABOUT YOU, MAYU?
DON'T YOU WANT TO SEE HER AGAIN?
MY MAMA...
I WANT TO SEE MY MAMA!
SHHWA
GMM
UHH... !

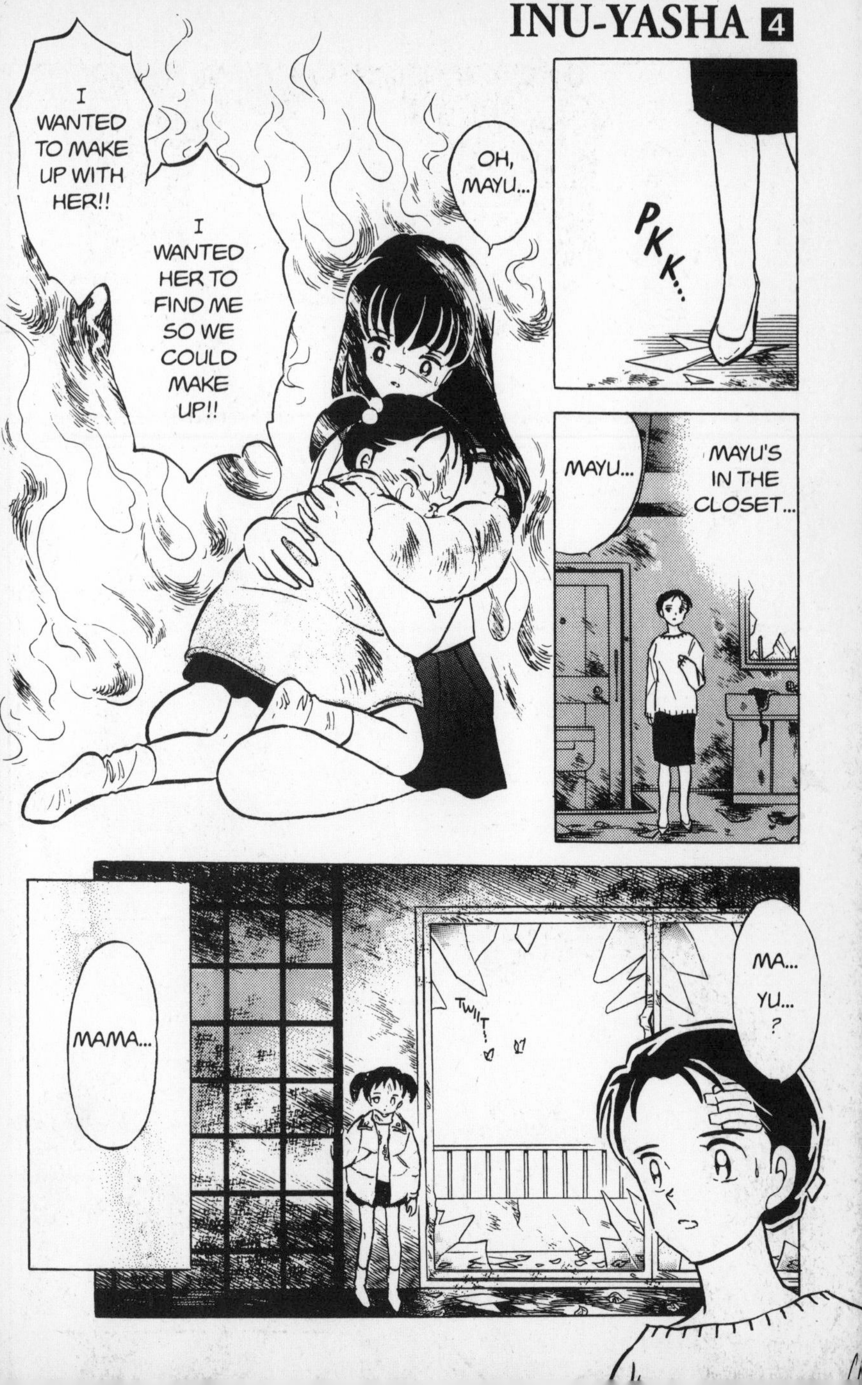
I WANTED TO MAKE UP WITH HER!!
I WANTED HER TO FIND ME SO WE COULD MAKE UP!!
OH, MAYU...
PKK...
MAYU...
MAYU'S IN THE CLOSET...
MAMA...
TWIIT...
MA... YU... ?

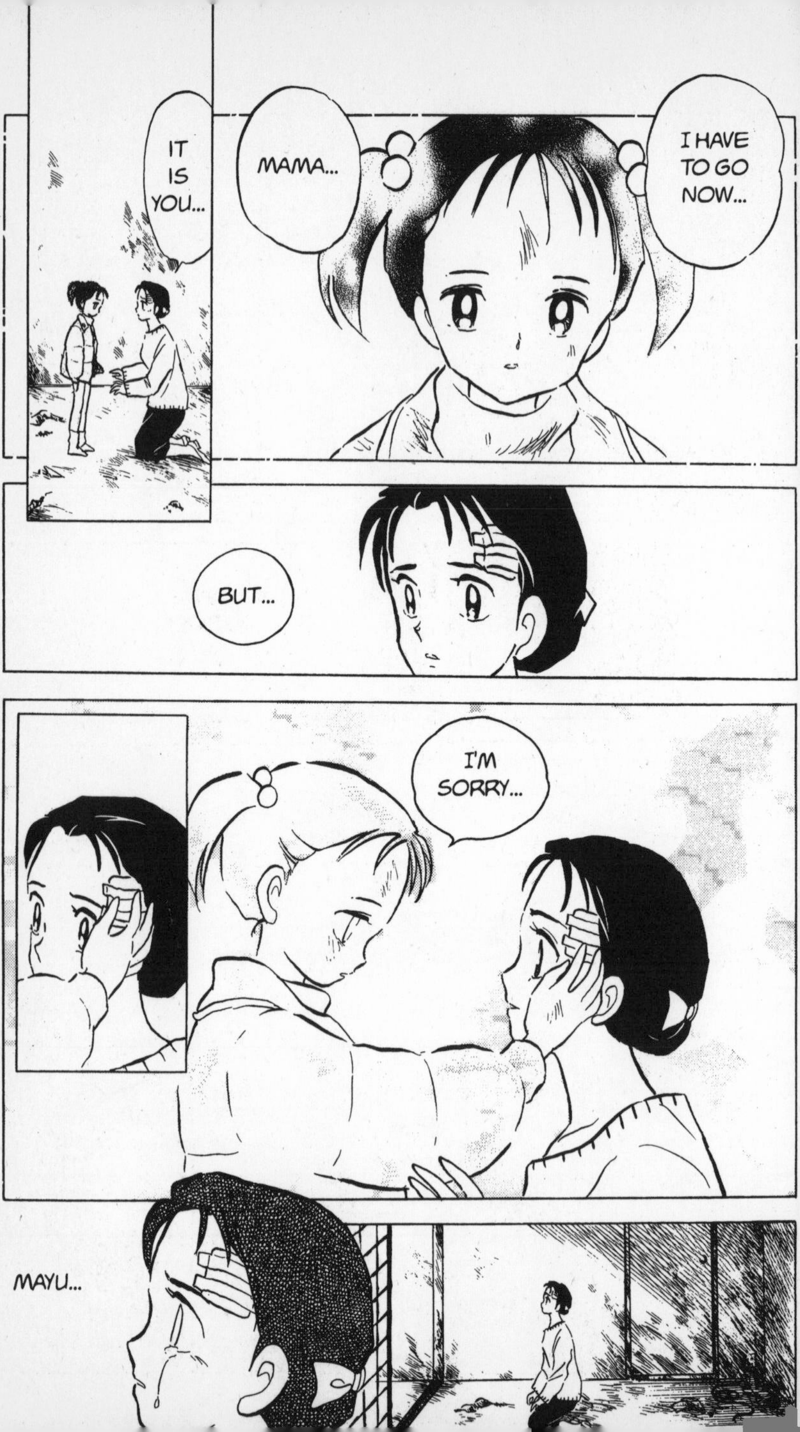
IT IS YOU...
MAMA...
I HAVE TO GO NOW...
BUT...
I'M SORRY...
MAYU...

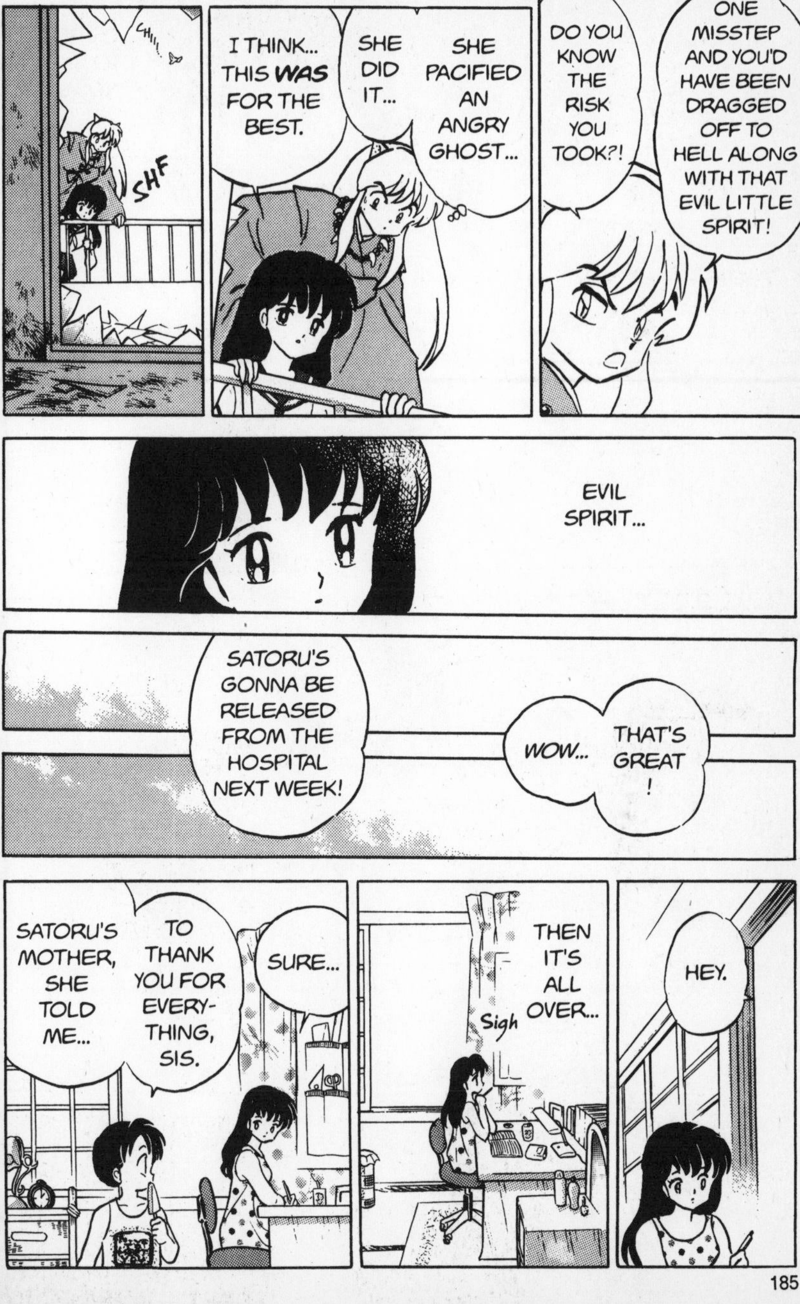
CHIII
SHF
I THINK... THIS **WAS** FOR THE BEST.
SHE DID IT...
SHE PACIFIED AN ANGRY GHOST...
DO YOU KNOW THE RISK YOU TOOK?!
ONE MISSTEP AND YOU'D HAVE BEEN DRAGGED OFF TO HELL ALONG WITH THAT EVIL LITTLE SPIRIT!
EVIL SPIRIT...
SATORU'S GONNA BE RELEASED FROM THE HOSPITAL NEXT WEEK!
WOW...
THAT'S GREAT!
SATORU'S MOTHER, SHE TOLD ME...
TO THANK YOU FOR EVERY-THING, SIS.
SURE...
Sigh
THEN IT'S ALL OVER...
HEY.

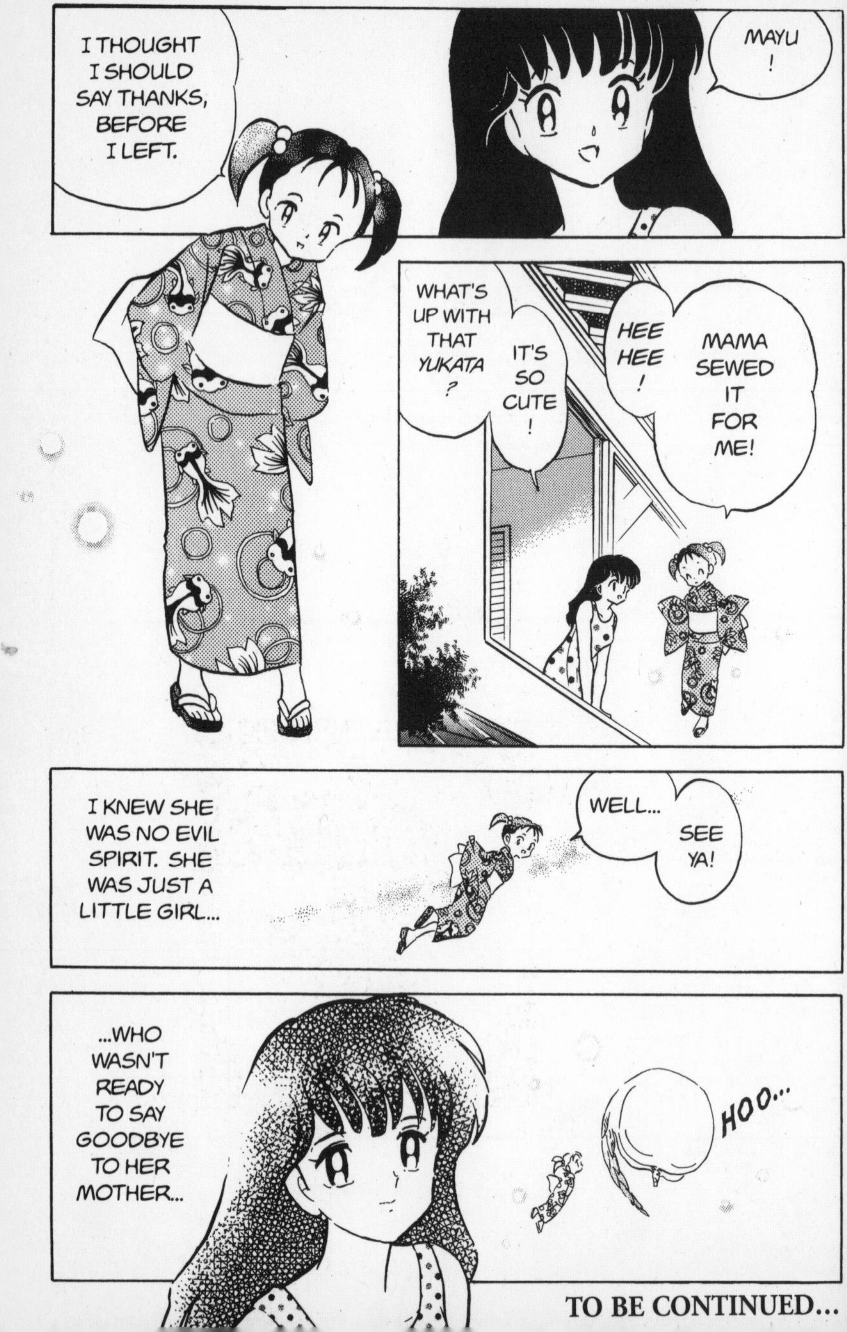
I THOUGHT I SHOULD SAY THANKS, BEFORE I LEFT.
MAYU!
WHAT'S UP WITH THAT *YUKATA*?
IT'S SO CUTE!
HEE HEE!
MAMA SEWED IT FOR ME!
I KNEW SHE WAS NO EVIL SPIRIT. SHE WAS JUST A LITTLE GIRL...
WELL... SEE YA!
...WHO WASN'T READY TO SAY GOODBYE TO HER MOTHER...
HOO...

TO BE CONTINUED...

About Rumiko Takahashi

Born in 1957 in Niigata, Japan, Rumiko Takahashi attended women's college in Tokyo, where she began studying comics with Kazuo Koike, author of CRYING FREEMAN. She later became an assistant to horror-manga artist Kazuo Umezu (OROCHI). In 1978, she won a prize in Shogakukan's annual "New Comic Artist Contest," and in that same year her boy-meets-alien comedy series URUSEI YATSURA began appearing in the weekly manga magazine SHÔNEN SUNDAY. This phenomenally successful series ran for nine years and sold over 22 million copies. Takahashi's later RANMA 1/2 series enjoyed even greater popularity.

Takahashi is considered by many to be one of the world's most popular manga artists. With the publication of Volume 34 of her RANMA 1/2 series in Japan, Takahashi's total sales passed *one hundred million* copies of her compiled works.

Takahashi's serial titles include URUSEI YATSURA, RANMA 1/2, ONE-POUND GOSPEL, MAISON IKKOKU and INUYASHA. Additionally, Takahashi has drawn many short stories which have been published in America under the title "Rumic Theater," and several installments of a saga known as her "Mermaid" series. Most of Takahashi's major stories have also been animated, and are widely available in translation worldwide. INUYASHA is her most recent serial story, first published in SHÔNEN SUNDAY in 1996.

d you like *INUYASHA?* Here's
at we recommend you try next:

RANMA 1/2 is the manga Rumiko
Takahashi was working on previous
to *INUYASHA*. It's more comedic than
INUYASHA—sort of a cross between a
screwball comedy and a martial-arts
action movie—but it's chock full of
unique characters and complicated
romantic entanglements.

© 1988 Rumiko Takahashi/Shogakukan

MAISON IKKOKU is Takahashi's
most romantic series. It's set in
modern-day Japan, and traces the
lives of the residents of a boarding
house. It's intense, it's angsty, and
it's one of the most absorbing
manga romances ever written.

© 1984 Rumiko Takahashi/Shogakukan

CERES: CELESTIAL LEGEND is a
sort of supernatural mystery by
FUSHIGI YÛGI's creator, Yû Watase. It's
about a modern-day 16-year-old girl
whose body houses a legendary
power, and her family is determined
to kill her in order to suppress it.
The story draws heavily on
Japanese legends.

© 1997 Yuu Watase/Shogakukan

COMPLETE OUR SURVEY AND LET US KNOW WHAT YOU THINK!

☐ Please do NOT send me information about VIZ products, news and events, special offers, or other information.

☐ Please do NOT send me information from VIZ's trusted business partners.

Name: _____

Address: _____

City: _____ **State:** _____ **Zip:** _____

E-mail: _____

☐ Male ☐ Female **Date of Birth** (mm/dd/yyyy): ___/___/_____ (Under 13? Parental consent required)

What race/ethnicity do you consider yourself? (please check one)

☐ Asian/Pacific Islander ☐ Black/African American ☐ Hispanic/Latino

☐ Native American/Alaskan Native ☐ White/Caucasian ☐ Other: _____

What VIZ product did you purchase? (check all that apply and indicate title purchased)

☐ DVD/VHS _____

☐ Graphic Novel _____

☐ Magazines _____

☐ Merchandise _____

Reason for purchase: (check all that apply)

☐ Special offer ☐ Favorite title ☐ Gift

☐ Recommendation ☐ Other _____

Where did you make your purchase? (please check one)

☐ Comic store ☐ Bookstore ☐ Mass/Grocery Store

☐ Newsstand ☐ Video/Video Game Store ☐ Other: _____

☐ Online (site: _____)

What other VIZ properties have you purchased/own? _____

_____

How many anime and/or manga titles have you purchased in the last year? How many were VIZ titles? (please check one from each column)

ANIME	MANGA	VIZ
☐ None	☐ None	☐ None
☐ 1-4	☐ 1-4	☐ 1-4
☐ 5-10	☐ 5-10	☐ 5-10
☐ 11+	☐ 11+	☐ 11+

I find the pricing of VIZ products to be: (please check one)

☐ Cheap ☐ Reasonable ☐ Expensive

What genre of manga and anime would you like to see from VIZ? (please check two)

☐ Adventure ☐ Comic Strip ☐ Science Fiction ☐ Fighting

☐ Horror ☐ Romance ☐ Fantasy ☐ Sports

What do you think of VIZ's new look?

☐ Love It ☐ It's OK ☐ Hate It ☐ Didn't Notice ☐ No Opinion

Which do you prefer? (please check one)

☐ Reading right-to-left

☐ Reading left-to-right

Which do you prefer? (please check one)

☐ Sound effects in English

☐ Sound effects in Japanese with English captions

☐ Sound effects in Japanese only with a glossary at the back

THANK YOU! Please send the completed form to:

NJW Research
42 Catharine St.
Poughkeepsie, NY 12601

All information provided will be used for internal purposes only. We promise not to sell or otherwise divulge your information.